The
Explorations
of
Edmund
Snow
Carpenter

The Explorations of Edmund Snow Carpenter

Anthropology Upside Down

Richard Cavell

McGill-Queen's University Press
Montreal & Kingston • London • Chicago

ISBN 978-0-2280-2271-8 (cloth)
ISBN 978-0-2280-2272-5 (paper)
ISBN 978-0-2280-2308-1 (ePDF)
ISBN 978-0-2280-2309-8 (ePUB)

Legal deposit fourth quarter 2024
Bibliothèque nationale du Québec

Printed in Canada on acid-free paper that is 100% ancient forest free
(100% post-consumer recycled), processed chlorine free

This book has been published with the help of a grant from the Canadian
Federation for the Humanities and Social Sciences, through the Awards to
Scholarly Publications Program, using funds provided by the Social Sciences
and Humanities Research Council of Canada.

Funded by the Government of Canada | Financé par le gouvernement du Canada | Canada | Canada Council for the Arts | Conseil des arts du Canada

We acknowledge the support of the Canada Council for the Arts.
Nous remercions le Conseil des arts du Canada de son soutien.

McGill-Queen's University Press in Montreal is on land which long served
as a site of meeting and exchange amongst Indigenous Peoples, including the
Haudenosaunee and Anishinabeg nations. In Kingston it is situated on the
territory of the Haudenosaunee and Anishinaabek. We acknowledge and thank
the diverse Indigenous Peoples whose footsteps have marked these territories
on which peoples of the world now gather.

LIBRARY AND ARCHIVES CANADA CATALOGUING IN PUBLICATION

Title: The explorations of Edmund Snow Carpenter : anthropology upside down /
    Richard Cavell.
Names: Cavell, Richard, 1949– author.
Description: Includes bibliographical references and index.
Identifiers: Canadiana (print) 20240402022 | Canadiana (ebook) 20240402073 |
    ISBN 9780228022718 (cloth) | ISBN 9780228022725 (paper) |
    ISBN 9780228023081 (ePDF) | ISBN 9780228023098 (ePUB)
Subjects: LCSH: Carpenter, Edmund, 1922-2011. | LCSH: Anthropologists—
    United States—Biography. | LCGFT: Biographies.
Classification: LCC GN21.C37 C38 2024 | DDC 301.092—dc23

This book was designed and typeset by Lara Minja in Minion Pro 11 pt.
Copyediting by Jared Toney.

for Raviv Ganchrow

I accept the old fashioned notion that the ethnologist is the twice-born spiritual adventurer whose fieldwork is nothing less than the spirit quest; that he exposes his dearest beliefs & habits to doubt & diversity, and returns changed by this intellectual ordeal. If he tells the truth about these experiences, he writes what is ultimately an autobiography: the metaphysics of me. If he carefully conceals what really happened to him, those experiences – inward & outward – he actually underwent or failed to undergo, then he writes the sort of intellectual foolishness currently popular in academic anthropology.

EDMUND SNOW CARPENTER

Contents

Acknowledgments

NO ONE WRITES A BOOK ALONE; the sea of research is not silent, as Carpenter was wont to remind us. Jonathan Crago, associate director and editor in chief of McGill-Queen's University Press, was immediately receptive to the idea of a book about Carpenter, and the three anonymous readers of the manuscript for the press were generous with their comments; one reader in particular held my feet to the anthropological flames. The MQUP production team was stellar. Sean Mooney, director of the Rock Foundation, has been supportive since that long conversation about Carpenter we had in 2016. I am grateful to the foundation for the permission given to quote from Carpenter's writings, published and unpublished. Robert Bringhurst provided crucial information about the relationship between Bill Reid and Carpenter. Katharine Hall, Special Collections, UBC Library, led me to the Hawthorn archives, and Alissa Cherry, research manager, Audrey and Harry Hawthorn Library and Archives, Museum of Anthropology, University of British Columbia, provided me with copies of their holdings on Carpenter and his correspondence with Marjorie Halpin. Danille Davis, reference archivist, National Anthropological Archives, Smithsonian Institution, Suitland, Maryland, assisted me in navigating the Carpenter Papers in their holdings. Lisa Barkley, Menil Archives, the Menil Collection, Houston, Texas, directed me to their material on Carpenter. Teresa Wong, digital archivist, John M. Kelly Library, University of St Michael's College at the University of Toronto, made rare material in the library available to me, as did Liz Rodolfo with material in the Fisher Library at the University of Toronto. Lonny Schiller, proprietor of Superbbooks, San Francisco, helped me obtain a scarce copy of Frits Staal's *Agni*. From William Matthews, proprietor of the Haunted Bookshop (Sidney, British Columbia), I was able to obtain a complete run of the first editions (all eight of them) of *Explorations*. Solange Adum Abdala brought her exceptional skills to the processing of the artwork. Peter Dickinson – *primus inter pares* – constantly reminded me not to put everything into footnotes. And I have known Raviv Ganchrow, professor in the Institute of Sonology, The Hague, for a decade and a half, but only when I began work on this book did he make me aware that he was deeply involved with Carpenter's ethnographic studies. Raviv was characteristically generous with his thoughts about Carpenter, a number of which I have incorporated into the book, and it is with gratitude that I dedicate it to him.

Vancouver-Washington-Houston-Amsterdam

Note on References

IN REFERENCE NOTES I have abbreviated the title of *Explorations*, issues 1 to 8, as follows: References from the original eight volumes are given in **boldface** (e.g., **E4, 12**) and then, immediately following, from Michael Darroch and Janine Marchessault, eds., *Explorations: Studies in Culture and Communication* (8 vols., Eugene, Oregon: Wipf and Stock, 2016) in *italic* type, with the page number only (e.g., *12*). It should be noted that this reissue does not conform to the pagination of the original and that in some cases it changes or adds to the text. References to the *Varsity Graduate* "Explorations" supplements are abbreviated as "E."

Harald E.L. Prins and John Bishop, "Edmund Carpenter: Explorations in Media and Anthropology," *Visual Anthropology Review* 17.2 (2001) 110–40, is "the first publication to deal extensively with his oeuvre" (110). I refer to it herein as Prins and Bishop, VAR, with the page number. An edited version of this text appears as "Edmund Carpenter: A Trickster's Explorations of Culture and Media," in Beate Engelbrecht, ed., *Memories of the Origins of Ethnographic Film* (Frankfurt: Peter Lang, 2007) 207–45. I refer to this version as Prins and Bishop, "Trickster," with the page number.

Unpublished material by Edmund Carpenter is held at the National Anthropological Archives, Smithsonian Institution, Suitland, Maryland. Citations are to NAA.2017-27 and the relevant box number.

The
Explorations
of
Edmund
Snow
Carpenter

Introduction

Spirit Quest

THIS BOOK TRACES the intellectual odyssey of Edmund Snow Carpenter. Hailed as a "groundbreaking" anthropologist, Carpenter did not leave a consolidated body of work through which his achievements could be assessed within a disciplinary context, and thus he has tended to disappear from the anthropological record. Although he began an academic career at the University of Toronto in 1948, his subsequent affiliations (after he left Toronto) were itinerant, and the years after the 1970s were spent as an independent scholar. This term, however, does not do full justice to him, since his early work in the Canadian North had established him as a major ethnographical voice, and he carried that status with him in the subsequent *Wanderjahre* that led him away from academia and into editing, publishing, collecting, curation, and public service. Carpenter worked throughout his career within the framework established by the legendary journal *Explorations*, and the present study traces the connections and interstices of that journal's overarching importance in Carpenter's career. After his marriage to Schlumberger heiress Adelaide de Menil, Carpenter was able to follow his own trajectory without heeding the financial (or academic) constraints of a university appointment. With research projects funded by the Rock Foundation that Adelaide de Menil founded, Carpenter (as vice-president of the foundation) had access to funds allowing him to pursue projects that would otherwise have been inconceivable. It is in this context that he produced publications such as the twelve-volume *Materials for the Study of Social Symbolism* and the exhibitions in Paris and Houston, *Upside Down*, while also supporting documentary film production and scholarly publications produced by colleagues.

The Explorations of Edmund Snow Carpenter began as an inquiry into the relationship between Carpenter and his quondam University of Toronto confrère, Marshall McLuhan, with whom Carpenter produced *Explorations*. While that relationship never completely soured, Carpenter became increasingly critical of what he believed to be McLuhan's unbridled acceptance of new media, while at the same time claiming that he had made major, unacknowledged contributions to McLuhan's *Understanding Media*. I have sought to clarify the complex relationship between Carpenter and McLuhan, but in doing so I have discovered greater complexities in Carpenter's convoluted career and character. He was at once austere, generous, and unpredictable. He claimed at various points in his career to have been a metallurgist who fell into anthropology; he claimed to have written books that he didn't write; he claimed to have taught at major research universities over an academic career spanning forty years. None of these statements is true in and of itself, but, taken together, they constitute the truth of a highly complex individual.

Part of the ambiguity characterizing Carpenter's career as an anthropologist derived from his ambiguous relationship with the discipline of anthropology itself. Deeply critical of what he called "misanthropology," Carpenter believed fervently that much of anthropology had served to deprive Indigenous cultures of their artistic legacies, either by appropriating Indigenous artifacts or by failing to understand these objects in terms of the contexts that produced them. These concerns came together when he served on the board of the Museum of the American Indian (MAI) in New York, which he discovered was illegally deaccessioning artifacts to remain financially afloat. Carpenter sought to end this process by sponsoring several lawsuits and by engaging the attorney general of the state of New York in an investigation of the MAI. At the same time, Carpenter was buying and selling such artifacts himself. The travails of the MAI were taking place as anthropology was becoming increasingly political in conjunction with the concomitant politicization of Indigenous peoples. As a result, questions of provenance and restitution began to emerge that caused Carpenter considerable discomfiture. As a result, he was at times precipitated into highly controversial disputes from which he did not always emerge unscathed.

Although associated with "visual anthropology," Carpenter spent his career critiquing visual culture and exploring the implications of acoustic space and its implications for a holistically sensorial approach to anthropology. He sought to complexify anthropology by inserting its specifically local context, which was in any case irrecuperable, into a broader context that was global without being universal (a pitfall he did not always avoid), dynamic rather than static, configurational rather than teleological. His pioneering work in media and in anthropology was increasingly conjoined in his career, and while he is now considered a founder of the redundantly named "visual anthropology," this categorization fails to capture the intellectual convolutions of his career. It is this intellectual achievement that is the subject of the following pages. This is a critical study that argues the importance of *Explorations* to Carpenter's career as an anthropologist, especially the concept of "acoustic space" that emerged from the Explorations seminars. The anthropological impetus for media studies has largely been forgotten, and this study seeks to restore that memory. It also seeks to restore Carpenter to himself. He had complained in 1982, two years after McLuhan's death, that he often felt his own work to be shadowed by McLuhan's. My research confirms this assessment: I was astounded by the extent, the richness, and the variety of his published work (largely my focus here), his radio, TV, and film work, together with his collecting, his public service, and his museum curatorship.

When I wrote my first book, on McLuhan, I had several biographies and studies to consult and guide me through McLuhan's work. With Carpenter, there was much less. The primary source for the study of Carpenter's work has been an article (republished as a book chapter) by Harald E. Prins and John Bishop, plus their documentary film on Carpenter. All of these seek to place Carpenter in the context of visual anthropology and thus they leave much out (which was, in fact, a critique of the documentary).[1] I have tried to fill in the blanks, though I must stress that this is not a biography, and I am not an anthropologist. A biography would have been beyond the scope of my interest in Carpenter, which was piqued by his connection to McLuhan, but in writing this book I have discovered that Carpenter was not (nor did he seek to be) a McLuhan manqué. After he left Toronto, he moved increasingly back to anthropology; as he himself noted in 1982, "I returned to traditional culture."[2] My entry into anthropological discourse has been via critical theory, which, after Lévi-Strauss and the advent of structuralism, followed an increasingly anthropological trajectory, from structuralism to deconstruction, until these methodologies gave way to the media theory of the Kittlerians and their repudiation of "man." What anthropology can teach media theory, however, is precisely the role of the *anthropos* in our current understanding of media. Carpenter's focus on media had, as its ultimate trajectory, the articulation of anthropology not as an investigation of the "other," but of the subject engaged in that study – the "metaphysics of me," as he put it. "Anthropology," in other words, was mediated, and mediation in the digital era was by definition recursive. This insight, in effect, turned anthropology upside down. The "other" was simply a binary of the same; what Carpenter effected was the extension of "man" beyond that "otherness" to what Michel Serres has called the "third element,"[3] namely, the in-between, or what Aristotle termed *tò metaxú*. That is, Carpenter opened anthropology onto a processual understanding whereby the meaning of "man" is mediated. It was Michel Foucault who had asserted that the traditional focus of anthropology was a discursive construct, but, unlike Carpenter and McLuhan, he failed to understand that humanist discourse was a product of mediation (print, in the case of humanism). Far from disappearing as a discursive construct, as Foucault had suggested, "man" has loomed ever larger, remediated cybernetically as data in the era of global media and the Anthropocene, producing a space that no longer conforms to the linearity of visuality but is configured through its connecting patterns. It was this configurational space that the Explorations seminar dubbed "acoustic," and the articulation of this space was a constant in Carpenter's career, culminating in his masterworks, the exhibitions *Upside Down*.

1

Cold War Explorations

THE FOUNDING of the journal *Explorations* in 1953 was one of the signal events of the post-war cultural landscape,[1] not only in Canada but internationally, through its inauguration of a discourse about media in a broadly anthropological context that would ultimately provoke questions taken up in poststructuralist theory in the 1960s, '70s, and '80s. The journal was born into a decade of social upheaval characterized by the civil rights movement in the United States and by Chairman Mao's Great Leap Forward, as well as by decolonial movements that spanned the globe. A new phase of the Cold War was marked by the 1953 death of Stalin and by the 1956 Hungarian Revolution. Although Joseph McCarthy (referred to on the cover of **E2**) was condemned by the US Senate in 1954, his fearmongering outlasted him, and, as Carpenter was to note, was felt even in the pages of *Explorations*. This was the period when suspected communists and homosexuals were hounded from the civil service, and when the DEW line was built, remediating the Canadian North, where much of Carpenter's anthropological research took place, from the margins to the centre of geopolitical tensions. Culturally, the period was marked by the 1952 performance of John Cage's *4' 33"*, which proclaimed the profound shift from visual to acoustic space, the central theme of *Explorations* and of Carpenter's own career as an anthropologist. The era of print culture was under threat from electronic media; the death of Dylan Thomas in 1953 was memorialized in *Explorations* 4 in terms of the remediation of the bardic era through phonograph recordings. Pop art and the Beat movement were on the rise. The emergence of the "organization man," as theorized by William H. Whyte, Jr (discussed in **E8**), proposed that individual ideals were being replaced by the groupthink that was exacerbated by mass media. Technologically, the launch of Sputnik in 1957 inaugurated not only the era of space travel but also of global communication and surveillance technologies facilitated by satellites. In 1958, the *Harvard Business Review* declared that we had entered into the age of information, and Watson and Crick's 1953 proposal of the double helix model for DNA inaugurated the era of the "inforg" – the information organism. The Canadian Broadcasting Corporation, where Carpenter worked both in radio and on TV, began transmitting television shows in 1952, and IBM produced its first computer in 1953. The decade ended with the 1959 patenting of the microchip, inaugurating the era of the personal computer. And the hydrogen bomb, as the cover of *Explorations* 2 noted, was in the process of development, the US testing a prototype in March of 1954; the test was filmed, and televised nationally on 1 April of that year.[2]

Describing the inception of *Explorations* forty years later, Carpenter wrote that it was "a journal I founded, named, edited, marketed, mailed, partly financed, then tried (unsuccessfully) to bury."[3] The story of *Explorations* was much more complicated than this, however. The founding of the journal was at Marshall McLuhan's initiative; Carpenter was sole editor for only part of its run, and, far from trying to bury it after McLuhan began editing it as an adjunct to University of Toronto's *Varsity Graduate* magazine, Carpenter published signally important essays in it. It is true that the name *Explorations* derived from the eponymous program that Carpenter had been producing for the CBC,[4] and that its look was Carpenter's doing. As Philip Marchand notes, the "key element in starting the magazine ... was ... the talent and energy of Ted Carpenter. 'He was a brilliant editor,' one of the graduate students attached to the [Explorations seminar] group recalls. 'Everything about the magazine that eventually came out was impeccable – the copy, layout, design. It would have been a mediocre production without Ted.'"[5] From the outset, Carpenter envisioned an international cadre of contributors for the journal. "I asked [T.S.] Eliot, [Wyndham] Lewis, [e.e.] cummings, and others" to contribute, he wrote. Carpenter was curious about how the typewriter had influenced these writers' styles. "I was particularly interested in what [Ezra] Pound might say, for his typed correspondence was like no one else's. His response [Pound demurred], from St. Elizabeth's Hospital, killed that article" (237). Carpenter also wrote "to Russian linguists, asking for articles on the effect of electronic media, especially TV, on Marxist theory and practice ... I wanted to know if, or how, anyone thought Marxism, so clearly a product of print, could possibly survive an electronic storm. So I wrote and wrote, suffered Soviet and RCMP visitors, and in the end only got the party line" (237–8). While Carpenter admits that he was not always pleased with the articles he received, he also notes that "something must have got through. Readers who 'found' the journal included Eric Havelock, Edmund Leach, Susan Sontag, Jacques Derrida, Claude Lévi-Strauss, [and] Roland Barthes" (238), a list that comprises major figures in classical studies, anthropology, postmodernism, deconstruction, structural anthropology, and poststructuralism, fields which largely divide twentieth-century cultural theory among them.

Carpenter had an affinity with Ezra Pound, in that Pound was not only a poet but also an editor, although that doesn't do justice to Pound's wholesale interventions in T.S. Eliot's *The Waste Land*, or to Carpenter's editing career, which extended from *Explorations* to the anthropologist Carl Schuster's study of intercultural symbolic structures which became, under Carpenter's editing, the massive twelve-volume *Materials for the Study of Social Symbolism*. The editing work placed Carpenter in the – at times conflicted – position of seeing himself as both author and editor, a conflation that extended to his relationship with Marshall McLuhan. McLuhan is most often cited as Carpenter's chief associate in the production of *Explorations*, but as Carpenter sought to make clear in his retrospective account of the journal, it was the product of many minds. What united these thinkers were the connections they made between "language, value, and perception" (239). Dorothy Lee, for example, with a doctorate in anthropology (like Carpenter), wrote a series of articles on "languages that lacked or minimized temporal tenses, adjectives, metaphors, first-person singular, as well as all equivalents to our verbs *to be* and *to become*; languages that blurred the distinction between nouns and verbs, that conjugated and declined from plural to singular, but also possessed forms alien to Standard Indo-European languages" (240). This passage not only summarizes Lee's work, which Carpenter describes as "*Explorations*' most influential force" (240), but also provides an example of Carpenter's acuity of analysis.

That Carpenter should become an "unconventional" (his word) anthropologist whose career would become inextricably connected with the shift to electronic media in post-war culture was not immediately foreseeable based on his upbringing and education. Born in Rochester, New York, in 1922, he preferred going on digs to using a Kodak, and this led him to the study of anthropology with Frank Speck at the University of Pennsylvania in 1940. Carpenter took a leave of absence two years later to enter military service with the US Marine Corps, seeing action in New Guinea (to which he would return as an anthropologist in 1968), the Solomon Islands, the Marianas, and Iwo Jima. After the war, he commanded a large group of Japanese prisoners in Guam, engaging them in an archaeological dig. Returning to U Penn after the war, Carpenter earned his doctorate in anthropology in 1950 with a dissertation on the archaeology of Indigenous people in the northeastern US. He had already been appointed an assistant professor at the University of Toronto in 1948, and by 1950 was also working a side gig as a radio programmer for the Canadian Broadcasting Corporation, where he produced a program called "Explorations." That same year, he made his first foray into the Canadian Arctic, returning there in 1951–52 and 1955. By 1952, he had migrated from CBC radio to the television network, bringing the "Explorations" program with him. Having met Marshall McLuhan at the University of Toronto, the two began a collaboration that obtained a Ford Foundation grant allowing them to convene a seminar on culture and communication that led to the founding of the journal *Explorations* (1953–59).[6]

By 1959, Carpenter had left the University of Toronto and joined San Fernando Valley State College (the future Northridge campus of the University of California) where he took the department of anthropology in an interdisciplinary direction, making film and art part of the academic program. He became chair of the program in 1961, producing films in addition to teaching, but by 1967 the program was closed. That same year, Carpenter joined Marshall McLuhan at Fordham University (New York) as part of a research team funded by a large grant McLuhan had received. At the end of the academic year, Carpenter moved to UC Santa Cruz, where he remained for a year before accepting a position at the University of Papua New Guinea. There he conducted his anthropological research in conjunction with ethnographical photographer Adelaide de Menil (subsequently his partner). Carpenter and de Menil used film, photography, and sound recording not only to produce anthropological documentation, but to actively intervene in the culture they were studying, resulting in a degree of disciplinary self-reflection that became the subject of the book *Oh, What a Blow That Phantom Gave Me!* (1972). That book had been preceded by *They Became What They Beheld* (1970), which reflected Carpenter's increasingly critical assessment of anthropological practices, and of academia generally.

Returning to the United States in 1970, Carpenter began an itinerant career as a lecturer in anthropology at Adelphi University, Harvard, the New School, and New York University. He also began editing the massive archive of anthropological material left by the researcher Carl Schuster, resulting in the multi-volume *Materials for the Study of Social Symbolism* (1986). During this period, Carpenter published an extensive roster of journal articles, as well as serving on the increasingly contentious board of the Museum of the American Indian. With Adelaide de Menil, he was also involved in the preservation and restoration of historic buildings in East Hampton, where he and de Menil maintained an estate. Increasingly involved in collecting and museology through his association with the Menil Collection in Houston, Texas, Carpenter produced a career-capping exhibition in 2008 at the Musée Branly, Paris, titled *Upside Down: Les Arctiques*, which featured a number of the small Inuit carvings he had collected over his career, as well as Yup'ik masks. His interest in the circumpolar North unabated into his eighties, Carpenter's last archaeological dig was in Siberia. He died in 2011, his contributions to media studies and anthropology deemed "groundbreaking" in his *New York Times* obituary.[7]

Writing for and editing *Explorations* was without doubt a turning point in Carpenter's career, his approach to anthropology swerving drastically when he began his involvement with the journal. His first publications were formal and scientific in tone, and focused on minute studies of individual artifacts, more ethnographical (in being comparative) than anthropological. A 1942 article in *American Antiquity* on Iroquoian figurines testifies to Carpenter's lifelong interest in Indigenous artforms; some of the figurines the article examines were located in the Municipal Museum of Rochester, New York, the city where Carpenter was born. Also found in New York, southern Ontario, and Pennsylvania, the figurines "are strikingly similar. In general, they are delicately carved of bone or antler to represent a nude female figure with the hands covering the sex organs. They average four inches in length, and are usually found in the graves of children and infants."[8] The small number of male figurines "show the phallus" (110). Carpenter notes the difficulty he had in obtaining data for his study, especially from Canada, given the war; he also registers the facts that some of the tribes he was studying were "removed from their original territory" (108) and that others, in Ontario, were "exterminated" (109). Carpenter concludes his study with the theory that the figurines represent a confluence of Indigenous and settler culture: "it would seem highly probable that the human figurine of the characteristic nude female figure came as a result of influence from the whites, the position of the hands suggesting Jesuit missionaries" (112). Other early career articles include a series on the tumuli of Pennsylvania and artifacts associated with them.[9]

"An Unusual Pottery Jar from East Milton," published in the *Bulletin of the Massachusetts Archaeological Society*[10] in 1943, is a short account of a bowl owned by Carpenter's father, Fletcher H. Carpenter, an artist and educator. What interested Carpenter (and this is consistent with his writing about Aivilik artifacts) are the signs of the bowl's "coming into being" as a human artifact. "Unquestionably, the pot was shaped by holding a single piece of red clay in one hand and molding and shaping the bowl with the thumb and index finger of the opposite hand. Next, the soft clay was probably rolled on an old, worn down witch-hazel or corn-husk mat, producing a rough and uneven surface" (38). In another early article, written under the aegis of Carpenter's dissertation supervisor, Frank Speck (its co-author, along with Royal B. Hassrick), Carpenter et al. write about "Rappahannock Taking Devices: Traps, Hunting and Fishing."[11] The publication is largely descriptive of various "taking" devices used by Indigenous people in Virginia. There is a discussion of "weather-lore" (7), including the "classification of snow," and "practices of signalling," whereby, for example, "boys communicated their intentions ... by 'whooping' back and forth between their farms" (8). There is concern that some traditional "taking" devices have degenerated into toys, such as the bow and arrow. Carpenter would largely abandon minute analysis in the 1950s, turning towards the grand and sweeping theories associated with Carl Schuster, only returning to minute ethnographic analysis towards the end of his career, as exemplified by the case studies in *Chief and Greed* (2005). As Carpenter wrote half a century after the "Taking Devices" article, "I have never said goodbye to Frank. He remains my guide, my fond companion, my guardian spirit."[12]

AN UNUSUAL POTTERY JAR FROM EAST MILTON

Edmund S. Carpenter

A unique earthenware, cup-like container (Fig.10), discovered in 1892 in the Blue Hills of Milton, seems to possess sufficient interest to warrant comment in these pages. The discovery was made by a lad named Michael Murray near some Quincy granite outcroppings and quarries across from the Murray home on Gun Hill Road, East Milton. Shortly after it was unearthed, the cup came into the possession of my father, Fletcher H. Carpenter. Nothing more is known of its background.

While further evidence of the bowl's origin is lacking, this subtracts little from its unusual character. It is brick to brown in color and small, measuring 3.6 cm. high, 6.8 cm. in outer diameter, 4.6 cm. in inner diameter and 5.7 cm. in diameter at the bottom. Tempering, if any, consists of fine sand. Firing was slight, and hardness is only 2 to 2.5. Unquestionably, the pot was shaped by holding a single piece of red clay in one hand and molding and shaping the bowl with the thumb and index finger of the opposite hand. Next, the soft clay was probably rolled on an old, worn down witch-hazel or cornhusk mat, producing a rough and uneven surface. (1)

In casting about for a possible prototype in nature, the jar could theoretically be duplicated in essential form and size by a robin's nest.

Flat-bottomed vessels, though rare, were not unknown to the prehistoric groups living along the Atlantic littoral. Streaks of red ochre in the niches of the outer surface suggest that this specimen might once have served as a paint pot.

University of Pennsylvania
Philadelphia
December, 1942

Fig.10

(1) Experiments conducted by the late Dr. V.J. Fewkes failed to disclose the technique employed in decorating this bowl. It was suggested by Dr. Frank G. Speck that the vessel was rolled on a mat.

Figure 1.1 Carpenter, "An Unusual Pottery Jar from East Milton," *Bulletin of the Massachusetts Archaeological Society*, 1943.

The approach to anthropology in *Explorations* derived largely from its broadly interdisciplinary set of contributors. In addition to Dorothy Lee, the *Explorations* group included the economist Tom Easterbrook, town planner Jaqueline Tyrwhitt,[13] and psychologist Carl Williams. Tyrwhitt played a strong role in applying for the Ford Foundation grant that would fund the seminar (in the amount of US$375,000 in today's currency), and in keeping peace among its participants:

McLuhan had initially informed Tyrwhitt that the Rockefeller Foundation wanted to fund a research center at the University of Toronto in commemoration of the communications scholar Harold Innis (1894–1952), who had died in November 1952. The way McLuhan talked about the proposed center to support the sorts of inter-disciplinary studies Innis had done sounded a lot to Tyrwhitt like [Sigfried] Giedion's ideas for a Faculty of Inter-relations; she got McLuhan excited about the idea of inviting Giedion to be part of it. McLuhan then involved Tyrwhitt in the separate but related proposal to the Ford Foundation, to support an inter-disciplinary study of communications and culture inspired by both Innis and Giedion. Tyrwhitt was one of five faculty sponsors of the proposal, along with McLuhan (English), Edmund Carpenter (Anthropology), and others from Political Economy and Psychology.[14]

The application, which sought to put distance between the research project it was proposing and the "information engineering"[15] approach taken by MIT, did not include a funding request for a journal, however. As William J. Buxton notes, that request came indirectly, through a letter that McLuhan had written to a colleague at Cornell, W.R. Keast, seeking guidance as to how a request to fund a journal would be received after the fact. The Cornell colleague contacted an associate of the Ford Foundation, Bernard Berelson, saying that "McLuhan would like to know if the Foundation 'would be receptive to an application for a small addition to their grant – $2500 a year for the two years'" (3). Berelson stated that the foundation was not in favour of supporting publications. At this point, Claude Bissell, vice-president of the University of Toronto, stepped in, informing Berelson that it would be possible to carve the money for a journal out of the grant if the university were to cover some of the expenses proposed in the grant. Berelson wished to know what sort of a journal was being suggested, and Bissell sent a description, emphasizing that the journal would not publish over the long term, but only during the grant period. The Ford Foundation replied that they would leave the decision to the university, and with that, *Explorations* came into being. McLuhan, who wrote the annual reports to the foundation about the project, noted in one of these that "the project fuelled intense 'inter-faculty gossip,' which in turn increased demand for *Explorations* to the point at which no copies were available to the public" (8). McLuhan's reports on the seminars tended to summarize "his own opinions, which he himself had broached and canvassed, without providing an account of how they had been received by the other project members" (9). At the end of the project, McLuhan reported that the seminar was the site of considerable tensions, especially between Carleton Williams and Carpenter, although the success of the journal tended to be a point of collective pride.

While the group experienced conflicts based on their disciplinary differences and biases,[16] they were highly intrigued, as Carpenter notes, by Williams's notion of auditory space, which McLuhan renamed "acoustic space." Writing in **E4**, Williams asserts some of the major insights of the Explorations seminar: that "the binding power of oral tradition is so strong that the eye is subservient to the ear" (**15**; *10*); that, "whereas the eyes are bounded … the ears are all encompassing" (**19**; *14*); and that "pure visual space is flat … while pure acoustic space is spherical" (**20**; *15*). The concept of acoustic space took hold immediately, writes Carpenter:[17] "Marshall … quoted Symbolist poetry. Jackie mentioned the Indian city of Fatehpur Sikri. Tom saw parallels in Mediaeval Europe. I talked about Eskimos [*sic*]" ("Sea," 241).[18] As Carpenter's comment suggests, what they had discovered was more than a media concept; they had discovered a methodology that would allow them to interrelate their various interests, and thus to "proceed without reference to boundaries" (**97**; *92*), as David Riesman puts it in **E2**. The key question emerging from this intellectual confluence was articulated by Carpenter: "were the senses themselves primary media?" ("Sea," 241). Did hearing mediate the world around us in a way that differed from visual mediation? The question would become foundational to the work of Carpenter and of McLuhan, albeit differently articulated and diversely pursued. As Carpenter put it, "No medium is wholly neutral. Certain ideas lend themselves kindly to specific media, others do not. If all media were alike, we would need only one" (241). This was the defining concept that motivated the most lasting insights emerging from *Explorations*.

Carpenter's retrospective account of *Explorations* had been written in response to an article in *Canadian Notes and Queries* by Toronto's resident pundit Robert Fulford, in which he asserted that there had been tension between Carpenter and McLuhan during the *Explorations* years, while alluding to Carpenter's "editorial blunders."[19] Carpenter replied that "in thirty-two years of friendship" (242), he and McLuhan had only two disagreements. One of those disagreements had to do with funding, Carpenter stating that *Explorations* 8, edited by McLuhan and his "first involvement" in the journal, didn't move, McLuhan stashing the issue at home, its costly printing leaving no funds for *Explorations* 9 (to be edited by Carpenter).

This was the gist of an undated letter Carpenter wrote to McLuhan that complained of "one helluva shortage that can only be explained in terms of copies given away, cash receipts not banked, and possibly, though unlikely, one University Bookstore bill of $140. unpaid."[20] Carpenter states that the financial shortfall "increases the problem of getting out #9," suggesting that either they cancel it and return subscribers' money or ask John Bassett (the Toronto newspaper publisher who had already contributed to the publication of the journal) to fund it. "We've been in financial straits regularly with Explorations, each time first denying the problem, then blaming this person or that for mismanagement, finally facing up to the problem and getting on with the job of raising funds. This time, however, we can't delay." Carpenter's account of McLuhan's acerbic reply seriously misquotes it, however, and leaves most of it out, with the result that McLuhan appears to ignore Carpenter's concerns about the fiscal status of the journal. This was not the case; McLuhan's handwritten letter, included in the Carpenter papers, states that issue 7 had not moved at all – "none of those nos[.] left my hands for months and months except for fully paid subscriptions ... I may owe nearly a 100 bucks. Probably 25 less ... But 40 copies of 7 will not alter your budget. Nor 400 of no. 8. Now, what's all the hurry about no. 9? ... Why must no. 9 come out right away? Please explain ... Nobody is going to be any the worse if no. 9 is later than now. How many are complaining? Contributors? [Carpenter was the sole author of no. 9, published as *Eskimo*] ... [John] Bassett was the <u>only</u> guy I ever asked for a buck for Explorations. I'm sure I can raise more if needed. But damn it, you are the boy who moves with the dough-boys ... I can't believe, Ted, that <u>you</u> couldn't raise 10,000 for Explorations any day you <u>decided</u> to do so. I just couldn't take the money side as the serious side of that great mag. And I <u>mean</u> it, it <u>is a</u> great mag."[21]

Carpenter also suggests in "That Not-So-Silent Sea" that McLuhan's characterization of the *Explorations* years with the Coleridge quote (from that threnody on the oral tradition, *The Rime of the Ancient Mariner*), "We were the first that ever burst / Into that silent sea," mischaracterized the project, which built on the research of numerous scholars who had preceded himself and McLuhan (and hence the "sea" of incipient media studies was not as "silent" as McLuhan had suggested).[22] Carpenter believed that the journal had achieved what it had set out to do by the time it reached issue number nine, but that McLuhan wanted it to go on, with the result that the journal "became an unread supplement in an alumni quarterly" (243). This quarterly was the University of Toronto alumni magazine *The Varsity Graduate*, with the new "Explorations" printed as an insert from 1964 to 1972, McLuhan its sole editor. Despite Carpenter's comments to the contrary, however, he regularly published articles in the supplement throughout almost its entire lifetime, articulating ideas in its pages which subsequently became full-fledged books.[23]

In looking back over the trajectory of *Explorations*, Carpenter expressed particular concern that McLuhan's fame had been earned at the expense of other thinkers, particularly Dorothy Lee.[24] Lee's 1950 article "Lineal and Nonlineal Codifications of Reality,"[25] Carpenter asserted, became McLuhan's "Typographic Man" (244), the subtitle of McLuhan's 1962 masterwork *The Gutenberg Galaxy*.[26] The reference to Lee as having inspired McLuhan's media theory, however, reveals an intellectual difference between Carpenter's notion of media studies and McLuhan's. McLuhan did not cite Dorothy Lee in his work because he sought to hide his sources, as Carpenter suggests, but because he had already rejected the linguistic approach to the study of cultural production, realizing that language itself required a medium, the *sine qua non* of communication that McLuhan had learned from Innis. As David Riesman compellingly puts it in "The Oral and Written Traditions" (E6), "the late Harold A. Innis took a rather crabbed, Spenglerian pleasure in showing that the materials on which words were written have often counted for more than the words themselves" (**24**; *19*). Lee's scholarship, however, was produced within the ambit of the Sapir-Whorf hypothesis, which argued that language constitutes an individual's and a culture's worldview. Thus, in "Lineal and Nonlineal Codifications of Reality," she writes:

The following study is concerned with the codification of reality, and more particularly, with the nonlineal apprehension of reality among the people of the Trobriand Islands, in contrast to our own lineal phrasing. Basic to my investigation is the assumption that a member of a given society not only codifies experienced reality through the use of the specific language and other patterned behavior characteristic of his culture, but that *he actually grasps reality only as it is presented to him in this code* [emphasis added]. The assumption is not that reality itself is relative; rather, that it is differently punctuated and categorized, or that different aspects of it are noticed by, or presented to the participants of different cultures. (89)

The reference to "our own lineal phrasing" fails to take into account that phrasing is not lineal at all: the idea that speech is spherical (as Carleton Williams proposed) is present throughout *Explorations*. Speech is an oral medium, and as such is different from the medium of print, which is indubitably lineal. The difference Lee observes, thus, is not between lineal and nonlineal "languages," but between orality and literacy, as McLuhan was fully aware.[27] Hence his focus on "typographic man" was not a result of "his unfailing genius for coining phrases" (6) in an attempt to hide his debt to Lee (whose work he did not cite), but a complete reformulation of the structuralist bias towards language (a bias which Carpenter would likewise reject in his articulation of a sensorial approach to anthropological research). As McLuhan put it in "The Agenbite of Outwit," "literacy stresses *lineality*, a one-thing-at-a-time awareness and mode of procedure," as opposed to "that sphere of simultaneous relations created by the act of hearing," experienced as "*auditory space*" in which "the components co-exist without direct lineal hook-up or connection," as on a newspaper page.[28] It was precisely this notion of simultaneous relations that powered the mosaic approach of the journal, as well as of the Explorations seminar and its research initiatives.

Anthropologica Torontonensis

Explorations was ineluctably connected to Toronto, but negatively: it was designed to challenge its somnolent conservatism.[29] As Carpenter put it, "Even into the 1950s, the city remained a depressing place: its architecture, food, meanness ... Not a joyous place at all. Leopold Infeld described it as perhaps the finest city in which to die, especially on Sunday afternoon when 'the transition between life and death would be continuous, painless and scarcely noticeable'" (250).[30] McLuhan's disdain extended to Canada itself, which he dubbed a "mental vacuum" (Marchand, 73). When the Massey Report was published in 1951, with its deeply conservative take on the prospects of Canadian culture, McLuhan erupted, corralling Carpenter into producing a response. Carpenter recalled "an afternoon when Marshall flipped through Vincent Massey's 1951 call for High Kulcha in Canada. He laughed & laughed, then scribbled a response modeled after Wyndham Lewis, BLAST, 1914. I immediately set it in type on a museum labeling machine. COUNTERBLAST, 1954, privately printed, appeared a few days later" ("Sea," 245). While the work might appear to be a piece of ephemera, it is in fact highly significant, because it scores its points via typographical manipulation, rather than by text alone. This use of the medium as the message would come to characterize *Explorations*, especially through the typographical experiments of Harley Parker.

By 1970, Carpenter was asserting that "most so-called communication media are grossly mislabeled."[31] Rather than organizing his book, *They Became What They Beheld*, according to the parameters of print, Carpenter was interested in highlighting the implications of "postliterate" culture; as he states, "large areas of meaning are now ruled by nonverbal languages such as mathematics or symbolic logic or film" (n.p.). The shift away from print as the dominant form of communication was signalled by the paradoxical materialization of the alphabet in the tendency toward concrete poetry that otherwise appears anomalous in *Counterblast*, which was typeset by Carpenter, a tendency extending into issue 5 of *Explorations*, featuring Harley Parker's use of Flexitype for the excerpt from James Joyce's *Anna Livia Plurabelle*, and issue 8, on the interfaces of the verbal, the vocal, and the visual. The boldfacing, capitalization, and flexing of words orients them away from linear signification towards simultaneity. The dematerialization of the alphabet as a linear, sequential, connected process is thus accompanied by its rematerialization as icon,[32] a notion that would become the *cri de coeur* of conceptualist art in the 1960s, and that characterizes the "staccato"[33] mode of expression adopted by Carpenter in *They Became What They Beheld*. The alphabetic medium had suddenly become visible, but as a result, it no longer communicated in the way that the alphabet had done. The concretization of the alphabet meant that meaning was now perceived iconically, an aspect emphasized by the use of Chinese characters (E4)[34] and Mayan glyphs (E5) as section markers in two issues of *Explorations*. Icons and logographs heralded acoustic space because they produced meaning holistically and configurationally, rather than in a linear, segmented, sequential, and teleological way.

B L E S S

BLESS the sports page, upholder of

HOMERIC CULTURE

the comic strips, pantheon of

PICKLED GODS and

ARCHETYPES

advertising art, for its pictorial

VITALITY

and verbal CREATIVITY

BLESS the locomotives WHISTLING

on the prairies proclaiming

the SEPARATENESS

Of Man

BLESS FOTOPRINT able to modulate

the printed visual image to the

full range of acoustic space.

Figure 1.2 McLuhan, *Counterblast*, 1954.

The 1954 *Counterblast*[35] was published just after *Explorations* had gotten underway in 1953, and the connections are strong: not only did the journal republish items from *Counterblast*, such as "Five Sovereign Fingers Taxed the Breath" and "Media Log" in issue 4,[36] but a number of journal articles satirized[37] the intellectual and cultural conservatism alluded to in the masthead note that "Explorations is [not] designed ... as a permanent reference journal that embalms the truth for posterity" (issue 1, Dec. 1953). Embalming is, in fact, the focus of an anonymous satirical piece in issue 3, "Meat Packing and Processing." Taking Sigfried Giedion's notion of "anonymous history" (**152**; *147*) as its point of departure, it examines an ad for the journal *Casket and Sunnyside* (which was the trade journal for morticians from 1932 to 1988)[38] in a manner reminiscent of McLuhan's procedure in *The Mechanical Bride* (1951). The object of the satire is not the funeral trade, however, but the tendency of academics who study literature to set up canons that encourage them to ignore writing outside the mainstream. "Academics generally limit their reading to scholarly books and thus ignore the bulk of printed material. Magazines, mail-order catalogues, trade journals, university presidents' reports, *Who's Who* – what Sigfried Giedion calls 'anonymous history' – are never reviewed, presumably because they are regarded as neither literary nor scholarly" (**152**; *147*). The tendency of electronic media, however, is to break down such canons, "flattening" high culture in anticipation of postmodernism. "Nowadays there's much talk about the threat of the new media to print, upon whose monopoly of knowledge the health of Western letters is alleged to depend" (**152**; *147*). However, the effect of print, this item suggests, is not healthy at all; it seeks to embalm the new media culture that is now replacing it.

This was precisely the program put forward by the Massey Report that occasioned Carpenter's and McLuhan's satirical ire in *Counterblast*. What was particularly ironic is that the literate bias that the report counselled the Canadian Broadcasting Corporation to adopt, in order to counter the "mere" entertainment of US broadcasting, produced unremitting blandness – statist ideology masquerading as broadcasting. An anonymous entry in **E4** addresses this under the title "Our Enchanted Lives" (which does not appear in the index). Referencing this entry in the "Note on Contributors," the editor writes that "recently we obtained a number of directives circulated inside various mass-media organizations and decided to reprint two" (**155**; *150*).

Both of these appear to have been doctored for effect before they were printed in *Explorations*. The one pertaining to television directs its producers to ensure that "the moral code of the characters in our dramas will be that of the bulk of the Canadian middle class ... The usual middle-class taboos on sex subjects will be observed. Material dealing with sex perversion, miscegenation, and rape is banned ... Scripts should be checked to ensure that lines with conscious or unconscious ambiguities are eliminated ... Intoxicants will not be mentioned ... We will avoid any reference to the past conflicts between the French and English Canadians ... If a businessman is cast in the role of a villain, it must be made clear that he is not typical" (**63–4**; *58–9*). In clear violation of the spirit of these norms, the editor remarks that "we did not have room for [a directive] written by a well-known psychoanalyst for a home permanent company and sent to their ad writers. It explained why a neutralizer should be sold with each home permanent kit. Tight curls, it said, are symbolic of pubic hair and might prove embarrassing if a woman weren't prepared to see the thing through" (**155**; *150*).

The other anonymous satirical piece, "The Party Line" (likewise unindexed), claims to be a directive from the editors of *Time* magazine[39] to its various bureaus; the focus is on the art world[40] and the art that is seeking to "shake loose from the grip of Picasso and other early modern leaders and to face up to reality in this chaotic period" (**91**; *86*). *Time* magazine had, in fact, written about New York's 1913 Armory show that introduced Marcel Duchamp's *Nude Descending a Staircase* to the world, that it was "part of the general movement, discernible all over the world, to disrupt and degrade, if not to destroy, not only art, but literature and society too."[41] The irony of the *Explorations* piece is astutely well focused, given the role that art and critique played in the Cold War, both knowingly and unknowingly. This "Battle for Art," the directive notes, has an "area of combat [that] is quite broad, ranging from the public itself to directors of museums, critics, collectors, artists and so on" (**92**; *87*). The directive notes that the "war profoundly inspired many young painters to shift toward reality," citing as an example "Edward Melcarth ... [who] has refused to retreat again into what he calls 'a technical world of matiere [*sic*], mathematics and mysticism,' and has turned out some powerfully realistic scenes of the effects of war" (**93**; *88*). The reference to Melcarth (1914–1973)[42] is doubly ironic, given that he was sympathetic to communism and lived openly as a homosexual, painting a number of homoerotic works – precisely the sort of "reality" that *Time* magazine sought to eliminate through its promulgation of the containment culture that characterized post-war America.[43]

The sort of art valorized by the *Time* directive would be redolent of the "peaceful grandeur of the Hudson River" school of painting (**94**; *89*), a recourse to blandness that is satirized by e. e. cummings in his "Poem, or Beauty Hurts Mr. Vinal" (**E4**). The poem had originally been published in 1923 by the little magazine *S 4 N* ("Space for Name," the journal's title never having been decided on), devoted to "the conviction that opposing points of view would by an alchemy of the spirit produce a cultural unity."[44] This *modus operandi* was shared to a certain extent by *Explorations*, and that journal, like *S 4 N*, came to the realization that "where views differ, personalities might also clash" (Hoffman et al., 108). Cummings's poem, with its critique of advertising and the cultural banality it produced, is very much in the spirit of *Explorations*. The "Mr Vinal" of its title was Harold Vinal, the founder of *Voices: A Journal of Verse*, that professed itself to be "alarmed" over "the 'surrender' of some modern poetry to the harsh realities of 'the modern distemper,'" and *Voices* sought to "preserve poetry or to rescue it from the danger of modern attacks upon its sensibilities" (Hoffman et al., 264). Cummings links this conservatism to advertising culture, the proliferation of ads appealing to the lowest common denominator. As Lewis H. Miller writes:

> In "Poem, or Beauty Hurts Mr Vinal" [cummings writes] that America's bad, anaemic poetry had much in common with the cloying appeals of America's advertising. Both sprang from and contributed to a sterile, mechanized world which, as Cummings saw it, feeds on predictable, stock attitudes and responses. As an indictment of a consumer-oriented society and of the verbal and visual clichés which accompanied and promoted that society, "Poem, or Beauty Hurts Mr Vinal" provides a unique antidote to the optimism of its time and to the consumer fetishism which continues to shape our individual and collective desires and goals … Cummings' underlying comparison of bad poetry with the tired commercial phrases of his time is mischievously introduced by his selection of Mr Harold Vinal as a representative contemporary poet. Vinal, a New Englander like Cummings,

had moved from his bucolic family compound in Maine to take up residency in New York City where he quickly became secretary of the Poetry Society of America and where he published his own poetry journal, *Voices*, a short-lived periodical to which Cummings applies the paradoxical, uncomplimentary modifiers, "radically defunct."[45]

Cummings, after ironically praising America as the "land of the Cluett / Shirt Boston Garter and Spearmint / Girl With the Wrigley Eyes," and "above all of Just Add Hot Water and Serve," states that "i do however protest, anent the un /-spontaneous and otherwise scented merde which / greets one (Everywhere Why) as divine poesy" in Vinal's journal (22–3; 17–18). This tone is consistent not only with the specifically parodic pieces in *Explorations* but with the journal as a whole, although the nature of the parody there is of academic disciplinarianism and the banalities that it produces.

This element of parody as characteristic of *Explorations* was highlighted in a page-length note appended by Lachlan MacDonald to Carpenter and McLuhan's article "The New Languages," published in the Spring 1956 issue of *Chicago Review*. (An article of that title was published under Carpenter's name in *Explorations* 7 [1957], and was reprinted under his name in the anthology of journal articles, *Explorations in Communication* [1960], although all three versions of the article are different.)[46] What is significant about MacDonald's note is that by 1956, *Explorations* had not only been recognized by William Arthur Deacon, then the dean of Canadian critics, as "a coming of age in Canada,"[47] but had achieved similar recognition internationally by critics such as Lachlan MacDonald.[48] MacDonald's "note" observes that

> To reach beyond their own classroom walls the members of this Toronto seminar decided to publish a journal, *Explorations*, devoted to a study of media biases ... The first numbers of the magazine have already become collector's items ... Faced with a shortage of relevant material the editors were required to pad with extraneous but often stimulating articles. Such items as "Letter File" and "Idea File" are penetrating comments on popular culture that merit reprinting. A gem of parody is "Meat Packing and Processing" which exhumes some quirks of the embalming profession.[49]

MacDonald goes on to comment on the covers of issues 2 ("Feenicht's Playhouse") and 5 (the newspaper page with the Mother Goddess super-imposed), stating that "a major result of the publication venture is that the seminar has gained acceptance at Toronto as an apparent result of the praise directed toward the University and *Explorations* from elsewhere." MacDonald concludes by referring to "the encouraging possibility that the Toronto group will launch another series within the next two years" and that "perhaps they will thus begin to answer their own question: 'What can print do better than any other medium and is that worth doing?'"

That question is posed in the last sentence of the article as published in **E7**, which argues that languages are mass media, and that the new media – "film, radio, TV" (4; 1) – are likewise mass media, each of them codifying reality differently. This assertion demonstrates that Carpenter was very much under the influence of the Sapir-Whorf hypothesis when he was con-tributing to this article. He had published an article on Whorf in the April 1953 issue of *Canadian Forum*[50] (at a time when Whorf's theories of the relationship between language and cultural expression were coming under attack), whom he terms "an anthropologist's anthropologist," his articles on metalinguistics changing "the entire course of much anthropological research" in their quest to "understand the true, covert relations among language, mind, and reality" (9). Whorf's major insight, writes Carpenter, is that "each language ... conceals a unique metaphysics. There is no reason for assuming that a native who knows only his own language and the cul-tural ideas of his own society has the same notions, often supposed to be intuitions, of time and space that we have and that are generally assumed to be universal" (9). This is Boasian cultural diversity transformed into a linguistic model; what cannot be expressed linguistically would be "liter-ally unthinkable" (10). Carpenter suggests that Whorf's theories can be applied to the domains of art, perception, and philosophy to ask questions about space orientations such as "three dimensional perspective," which, as he notes, "is only about five centuries old" (10).[51] How was space per-ceived before that, and why did that perception change? This is an area of research to which Carpenter would make a major contribution with his study of space concepts among the Inuit, a study that he elaborated with his 2008 and 2011 exhibitions *Upside Down: Les Arctiques / Upside Down: Arctic Realities.*[52]

By the time he wrote "That Not-So-Silent Sea," Carpenter acknowl-edged the criticism that Whorf's readers had visited upon "his determin-istic view of the relationship between language and culture" (284 n.2), and distances himself from that view.[53] When writing his E7 article, however, Whorf's theories led Carpenter to define media themselves as languages: "Writing, for example, didn't record oral language; it was a new language" (1). Writing wasn't a new language, however; it was a new medium, and the encoding was at the level of the medium, not of the language. Thus, it was the medium of script that "encouraged an analytical mode of thinking with emphasis upon lineality," not the language that was written. Similarly, it was orality that "tended to be polysynthetic, composed of great, tight conglomerates" (4; 1), not the languages that were spoken. The rigidity of approach leads here to generic readings; poetry and drama retain their "multi-perspective" when printed, but "histories, autobiographies, [and] novels" (6; 3) do not. Similarly, TV is said to be a dramatic medium, rather than an electronic one. Certain ideas are said to belong to one medium, and can best be communicated through that medium. "TV is a tiny box into which people are crowded and must live; film gives us the wide world" (9; 6). These comments provide a glimpse of the "rearview mirrorism" of early media studies. What is far more significant in this article is its documen-tation of an experiment staged at the University of Toronto to determine the *effects* of media, expressed in terms of retention of meaning. A lecture delivered in a TV studio, heard on screen, heard on the radio, and read in manuscript were compared, both in terms of what aspects of content were dictated by the specific medium, and in terms of the effectiveness of the given medium. To the surprise of many, "TV won" (18; 15).[54] Carpenter, who had worked for the CBC in both its radio and TV divisions in the late 1940s and the early 1950s, writes with particular animus about the reaction to this experiment by CBC executives, who were "furious, not because TV won, but because print lost ... At heart they hate radio and TV, which they employ merely to disseminate the value of book culture. They feel they should dedicate themselves to *serious* culture. This is why they can't use radio and TV with conviction and are afraid to use it comically, and so they end up with wishy-washy" (21; 18).[55] This is a classic example of how "official culture still strives to force the new languages to do the work of the old"

(**21**; *18*). But Carpenter issues a resounding "no" to the question "can books' monopoly of knowledge survive the challenge of the new languages?" (**21**; *18*). This meant that intellectual inquiry would have to engage with new media, which would inevitably raise new questions.

A Little Magazine

Like the *Chicago Review* in which "The New Languages" was published, *Explorations* was one of the "little magazines" that had their heyday in the 1950s, although it differs from most of these through the high production values that Carpenter brought to the journal. Each of the covers of the eight uniform issues was different; all eight had sewn bindings. Issue 2's fake front page is continued on the inside cover, and on the inside and outside of the back covers. Issue 7 has a tipped-in portion of a "front page" from *The New York Times*, printed on newspaper stock, and the article "eternal ones of the dream" (**77–84**) has its opening and closing pages printed in silver type on black card stock, with its central pages on glossy stock that includes a colour photo reproducing the images of Indigenous masks from issue 1. Issue 8 uses rubricated type throughout, and the section on manifestos is printed on yellow stock with gold typography.

Explorations has been excluded from consideration in the major studies of the little magazine phenomenon,[56] largely because little magazines tended to have a literary focus. The literary dimension is present in *Explorations*, though within a mediatic context. The issue (**E4**) partly devoted to the poetry of Dylan Thomas, for instance, focuses on how the oral dimension of his poetry is remediated by the recordings of Thomas reciting his verse. This is not to say that *Explorations* was alone in considering new media within the context of literary publication. *The Black Mountain College Review*,[57] for example, contained an article on "High Speed Computing Machines"[58] in its first (and only) issue (1951), written by Natasha Goldowski, who in 1948 had taught a course at Black Mountain College on cybernetics, based on galley proofs from Norbert Wiener's eponymous book.[59] The article itself cites from Wiener's *The Human Use of Human Beings*, and cybernetics would have direct and indirect connections to Carpenter's "little magazine," as would the college via Harley Parker, who took a course there from Josef

Albers on colour theory,[60] about which he wrote in **E6** ("Colour as Symbol," unindexed, **56–7**; *55–6*). Most immediately, *Explorations* was inspired by *trans/formation*, a little magazine published out of New York, that sought to be a "world review" that would produce a "unity of knowledge."[61] McLuhan is on record as having emailed Jaqueline Tyrwhitt wondering if material contributed to the journal might be used in *Explorations* after *trans/formation* had abruptly ceased publication with its third issue.[62]

The focus on communications and media in *Explorations*, rather than on literature, has led to its categorization as an academic journal, but its intentions were decidedly anti-academic. Philip Marchand has described Carpenter and McLuhan as "fellow outcasts in league against the rest of the university," and notes that "Carpenter almost courted notoriety" (116). *Explorations*, like *The Black Mountain College Review*, was linked to an educational institution (although Black Mountain was infinitely more radical than the University of Toronto), but it differed from *The Black Mountain Review* (successor to the *College* review, publishing from 1954–57) itself since its focus was not exclusively poetics. McLuhan had been publishing in little magazines such as *Sewanee Review, Kenyon Review, The Shenandoah* (which reprinted "Five Fingers" from issue 4), and *Poetry*, the classic of literary modernism,[63] since the 1940s and continued to do so throughout the *Explorations* years, but his topics were exclusively literary, with a New Criticism orientation and a whiff of Agrarianism.[64] The exceptions were the *Hudson Review*, for which McLuhan reviewed László Moholy-Nagy and Sigfried Giedion in 1949, and *Neurotica*, edited by Gershon Legman (published in **E1** and 7), a magazine whose orientation was psychosexual, its influence felt most acutely by the Beats, its consistent message being that popular culture was a legitimate expression of cultural production. What distinguished *Explorations* from these little magazines, however, was its juxtapositional nature, essays on poetics followed by ones on urban design, acoustic space, nursery rhymes, and so on, complemented by its brilliant covers and experiments in typography and page design. It is this multidisciplinary approach that links the magazine to one of the most important post-war seminars, the Macy Conferences on cybernetics. Reading through the contributions to the Macy Conferences made by Margaret Mead and Lawrence K. Frank, both of whom were directly or indirectly connected to the Explorations group, however, reveals much tension and little accord that largely derives from thwarted attempts to speak across disciplines.[65] While these tensions were present in the Explorations seminar, the magazine's adoption of the "open field" approach (cognate with what Walter Ong calls "field physics" [**99**; *94*] in **E4**) meant that the tensions were not foregrounded in the magazine itself.

To publish in little magazines during the Cold War was to engage with a cultural atmosphere of "conformity and repression" occasioned by "advancing consumerism and corporate power. This was the era when the terms 'affluent society' and the 'military-industrial complex' were first coined. Dissent was a cause for suspicion and the Left was hounded, most conspicuously in the paranoid campaign against communism led by Senator Joe McCarthy."[66] One offshoot of this repressive atmosphere was the creation of countercultural movements, such as that of the Beats, which extended far beyond the borders of Greenwich Village to places such as Black Mountain, North Carolina, where Charles Olson became rector in 1951, and where *The Black Mountain Review* was influential in establishing a poetics of "the oral and the performative" (Brooker 963) that had a similarly powerful role in *Explorations*, but as the more theoretical notion of "acoustic space." As Carpenter noted in "That Not-So-Silent Sea," McCarthy was as much a presence in Canada as he was in the US, and the anti-communist madness of that era extended to the little magazines themselves through funding supplied to them through the Congress for Cultural Freedom, which was supported by the CIA.[67] *Explorations* was not one of those journals. What is extraordinary about its contributors, however, is that many were victims of the anti-communist politics of the period, leading to the conclusion that Carpenter actively sought to engage these contributors as a counterstatement to McCarthyism. The Cold War theme was introduced in issue 1 by McLuhan, who suggests in "Culture Without Literacy" that the most significant aspect of the McCarthy hearings was that they were being televised (**123**; *118*), thereby connecting politics with media. This theme was further developed by the cover of issue 5 (1955), with its newspaper headlines about the H-bomb, about war in Indochina, about Dulles warning the Reds, and so on. Stanley Edgar Hyman, published in **E2**, was the subject of an FBI investigation in the early 1950s for possible communist leanings; the suspicious circumstance was his large collection of books.[68] Issue 6 published an article by Paddy Chayefsky, who had been outspoken in his opposition to

McCarthy. Issue 7 included an unsigned article (by McLuhan?) about Walt Kelly,[69] who satirized McCarthy in his Pogo comics, as well as an article by Fernand Léger, who had joined the Communist Party in 1945. Karl Polanyi, published in issues 7 and 8, had to live in Canada even though a professor at Columbia because his wife was denied a US visa based on her communist activities. Ashley Montagu, published in issue 6, was hounded out of his position at Rutgers after the McCarthy hearings, and Robert Armstrong, whose article appears in issue 4, was forced to leave the US, based on his communist sympathies, and moved to Africa.

The question of politics and media was addressed directly by McLuhan in his article "New Media as Political Forms" (**E3**), where he writes that the sheer complexity and globality of political interactions in the post-war era has forced a new understanding of politics based on "multiple mental focus" (**121**; *116*) that was more akin to the cinematic eye than the one that read books: "After four centuries of uncritical ebullience and commercial log-rolling it would seem to be safe to have a suspicion about the effects of print. Especially now that print has been knocked off its pedestal by other media" (**123**; *118*). While an understanding of print *as a medium* – with its benefits and defects – could be useful in understanding the new mediascape, this understanding had to be coupled with "music and painting as technical forms of managing experience" if the new media are to be fully comprehended. "It is the almost total coverage of the globe in time and space," McLuhan continues, "that has rendered the book an increasingly obsolete form of communication. The slow movement of the eye along lines of type, the slow procession of items organized by the mind to fit into these endless horizontal columns, these procedures can't stand up to the pressures of instantaneous coverage of the earth" (**123–4**; *119*). The effects of the "rise of TV as a political shaper" have been overlooked because TV has been regarded merely as a provider of entertainment and has thus been deemed "non-political" (**124**; *119*). The power of electronic media is vastly superior to that of the tabloid, however; "movie and TV have the almost uncontrollable power of inflating the most casually selected persons into million horse-powered entities" (**125**; *120*). This is not a linear process. "If politics and the citizen are to survive the new media," then it is imperative to understand them in terms of "constellations and clusters" (**126**; *121*). This was the *procédé* of *Explorations*.

Culture and Communication

McLuhan's essay appeared in an issue (**E3**) that included articles based on papers read at a 1954 seminar in Louisville, Kentucky organized by Ray Birdwhistell on culture and communication. Birdwhistell had taught in the anthropology department at the University of Toronto from 1944 to 1946, where he was Carpenter's colleague.[70] During this time he did research on the Kutenai in British Columbia and (a former ballet dancer) became an expert on body language, or kinesics, arguing that only about one-third of verbal meaning is produced by words themselves. Writing in *Explorations* 3, Birdwhistell provides an overview of "Kinesics and Communication," defining kinesics as "the study of the visually sensible aspects of non-verbal, inter-personal communication" (**31**; 26), and "social kinesics" as "body motion units with contextual meaning, the context being provided by the social situation" (**40**; 35). These connections between culture and communications became the focus of Birdwhistell's Louisville seminars, held annually. The seminar attended by Carpenter et al. in 1954 was one of the two "Cold War salons"[71] (the other being the Macy Conferences) that are contextual to the Explorations seminar. The Louisville conference subsequently became a photographic "case study" (and the medium is significant) in Margaret Mead's reissue of Darwin's *Expression of the Emotions in Man and Animals*.[72] As Mead writes in her introduction to the book, Darwin's study, and the Louisville seminars, were likewise characteristic of an interest in "the non-verbal aspects of human communication."[73] Mead notes that "one interpretive tool which Darwin lacked and which we have is cybernetics," which would have allowed him to understand individual kinesics as "part of an intra or inter-species system of communication" (vi), that is, in terms of feedback. Mead further notes that "moving pictures and large scale photography" (vi) are allowing the questions raised by Darwin to be posed anew.[74] Such is the *modus operandi* of the photo-essay supplementing the volume, which includes photos of the Culture and Communications conference attended by the Explorations groups (one photo is of McLuhan) "in which the group taking part in the development of the new science of kinesics were also objects of their own research" (vi), insofar as these photos caught the speakers mid-lecture, their body language candidly evident. McLuhan had argued in **E2** that the implications of "feedback" had not been fully explored "thanks to the gratuitous assumption that communication is a matter of transmission of information, message or idea," adding that "the *form* of communication ... is more significant than the information or idea 'transmitted'" (**6**; *1*). Kenneth Boulding (one of the founders of systems theory) makes a similar point in his article "Notes on the Information Concept" (**E5**), stating that "we cannot regard knowledge as simply the accumulation of information" because knowledge "must itself be regarded as a structure" (**103**; *98*). The question is, how does some information become knowledge and other information not. Part of the answer is homeostasis: knowledge structures tend to resist new information in order to maintain their established pattern of meaning. Homeostasis is not absolute, however, and in its partiality it is subject to information that can potentially change the knowledge system itself. Societies can thus be understood in terms of adaptive and revolutionary change. If homeostasis is understood in terms of redundancy, then ritual takes on significant importance in terms of its function as "a kind of 'reserve' to fall back on" (**109**; *104*) with communication and language occupying precisely this role of reserve, as that which preserves the structures of a cultural knowledge system. It was Innis, he notes, who suggested that "the wider dynamic processes of society involved in the rise and fall of nations, empires, religions and civilizations may also be closely related with the dynamic laws of the information and communication process" (**112**; *107*). The application to anthropology would suggest that social structures contextualized information – it was through these structures that information gained meaning, and that one such structure of information was art.

2

Media Anthropology

QUESTIONS OF AN ANTHROPOLOGICAL NATURE were central to *Explorations*,[1] and anthropologists were by far the scholars who were best represented in the journal. In the first issue alone, anthropologists included Lord Raglan (Fitzroy Richard Somerset, fourth Baron Raglan), one of the last representatives of nineteenth-century "primitivist" anthropological research, and Edmund Leach (published in issue 4 as well), who would introduce to the Anglosphere the structural anthropology of Claude Lévi-Strauss (who had produced *Les structures élémentaires de la parenté* in 1949 and whom Leach references in **E1**), as well as the cultural anthropologist Melford Spiro. Robert C. Dailey writes in the "Seminar" section of **E3** about Innis and anthropology, suggesting links between media studies and anthropology via Innis's perception of "a causal factor which, though not 'natural' or 'teleological,' could nevertheless account for both cultural stability and change" (**99**; *94*). Comparative ethnologist Meyer Fortes appears in **E4**, which also includes an article (co-authored with G.L. Trager, who had worked with Ray Birdwhistell) by the anthropologist of space, E.T. Hall. The historian of anthropology, Regna Darnell, appears in **E7**. A number of the anthropologists published in *Explorations* had worked with Margaret Mead (who was married for a time to an anthropologist at the University of Toronto),[2] such as Birdwhistell (a close friend of Mead), Martha Wolfenstein (**E3**), Rhoda Métraux (**E5**; she and Mead lived together from 1955 to 1978), and Claire Holt (**E5**).[3] A. Irving Hallowell (**E2**) and Anthony F.C. Wallace (**E3**) studied with Frank Speck at the University of Pennsylvania, as did Carpenter, and Hallowell also studied with the founder of modern anthropology, Franz Boas, as had Speck (and Margaret Mead). A number of these anthropologists were influenced by the Sapir-Whorf hypothesis, such as Dorothy Lee and Joan Rayfield (**E4** and **5**). Rayfield, who taught at York University (Toronto) and subsequently at Northridge, California (as had Carpenter when it was San Fernando College), wrote in **E5** that literate languages are complicated owing to their remediation of speech, and she augurs the beginning of the post-literate era, a theme also broached by McLuhan in "Culture Without Literacy" (**E1**). Francis L.K. Hsu, one of the founders of psychological anthropology, appears in **E5**'s "Idea File." Ralph Maud (**E6**), an expert on Dylan Thomas, also wrote about Pacific Northwest Coast ethnographers, and Ashley Montagu, likewise published in **E6**, was a student of Bronisław Malinowski (as was Meyer Fortes). Montagu, about whom Carpenter reminisces in "That Not-So-Silent Sea," wrote about race and gender. Carpenter's unsigned article[4] in issue 7, printed with white typography on black pages, alludes in its title, "Eternal Ones of the Dream," to Géza Róheim, another of the founders of psychoanalytic anthropology. Jacquetta Hawkes, the first woman to study anthropology at Cambridge University, appears in **E4**. Robert G. Armstrong writes in that same issue about talking instruments that use tonal qualities of speech (as had John F. Carrington in **E1**, who refers to drumming as a form of "broadcasting"); the article develops one of the major themes of *Explorations*, that of acoustic space, or, more broadly, how oral cultural forms are being remediated in the post-literate culture inaugurated by electronic media.

As David Bidney noted in the first issue of the journal, the research associated with the Explorations seminar derived from a linguistic revolution, although this put it mildly and not completely accurately.[5] Carpenter and McLuhan had made the key point in the *Chicago Review*: electronic media were beginning to assert themselves as the dominant form of communication in the post-war era, hence McLuhan's references to culture without literacy (**E1**) and Joan Rayfield's article about post-literacy (**E5**). What made this argument controversial, but also revolutionary, were the combined notions of acoustic space and the remediation of orality by electronic media. If a form of orality was once again becoming dominant, history could no longer be understood as linear, and "primitivism" resurfaced not as an instance of racialized notions of superiority but of a confluence of the old and the new. Margaret Mead reported that Samoan ways "were not so much primitive and backward as intensely modern."[6] The Italian Futurist

Umberto Boccioni had claimed that we are the "primitives of a new sensi-bility,"[7] and it is significant in this context that Futurism began with the call for the breaking down of linguistic structures in order to give words their liberty – *parole in libertà*. If print had fixed the word in visual space, as Ong suggests in "Space and Intellect in Renaissance Symbolism" (**E4, 95–100**; *90–95*), electronic media would liberate it, breaking that space into a mosaic of glowing pieces.

One member of the Explorations seminar, Endel Tulving, referred to the "mosaic" approach Innis took in his last two books (*Empire and Communications* [1950] and *The Bias of Communication* [1951]) as Innis's way of "avoiding lineality" in order to discuss "multiple relationships" (**E3, 101**; *96*), and this mosaic approach was adopted by the journal. As a result, considerable breadth was granted to what was meant by "communication." In the longest contribution to issue 1 (extending to issue 2), for example, David Riesman writes about consumerism as a form of communication. Riesman had published *The Lonely Crowd* at the beginning of the 1950s to considerable acclaim, its thesis that Americans were moving away from inner-directedness to other-directedness meshing with concerns that a culture of mass media would support groupthink and erode traditional values – to know others (including through what they consumed) was to fail to know one's self.[8] The focus of Riesman's two-part article in **E1** and **2** is Thorsten Veblen, whose interdisciplinary analytical practices he praises (**E2, 97**; *92*). This notion of the breaking down of conceptual barriers was of crucial importance to *Explorations*, as Riesman notes, and is articulated compellingly by Stanley Edgar Hyman in "The Pirate's Wardroom" (**E2**). Hyman, a professor at Bennington College, had been deeply influenced by the foundational British anthropologist Jane Ellen Harrison, from whose work he derived an interest in myth and ritual and their origins in oral cul-ture.[9] "The Pirate's Wardroom" is a metaphor deriving from the traditional officers' mess; although the mess of the pirate is well-outfitted with silver and gold, "nothing matches anything else ... for it has all been stolen piece-meal" (**E2, 98**; *93*). The pirate's wardroom in Hyman's account becomes the avatar of André Malraux's "museum without walls," the term Malraux used for the imaginary museum constituted by the artbook, which (writes Hyman) "raises our small acts of cultural piracy to the level of an aes-thetic principle" (**99**; *94*).[10] Reviewing Malraux's *The Voices of Silence* (1951;

English translation 1953), Hyman identifies Malraux's major theme, which is that photography had liberated art from its linearly historical context, the "link between history and art [being] tenuous" (Hyman quoting Malraux, 102; 97). All works of art are co-present in the pages of the art anthology, breaking down hierarchies not only of early or late but also of high and low. (Roland Gelatt makes a similar argument in "The Fabulous Phonograph," quoting Jacques Barzun's comment that "recording has brought back the whole repertory of Western music" [E6, 30 (unindexed); 25].) In this context, Celtic coins are not "clumsy imitations of the work of Macedonian *toreutai*, but a major style of their own ... Similarly, Gothic statues are not botched classical statues, African heads are not failed realistic portrayals" (Hyman, 100; 94–5). Malraux's thesis is dynamic; the breaking down of hierarchies is not merely a reconsideration of aesthetic categories but an active transposition of inside and outside, of container and contained, of "negations" and "affirmations" (101; 96). As such, it meshes closely with the mosaic or open field methodology of the Explorations seminar and its journal, as well as with an understanding of space as the domain of "all-at-onceness," which is the defining element of acoustic space. (In E8, Malraux is termed "an apt instance of the oral or auditory man" [item 6; 12].) As Hyman notes, "all previous hierarchies of culture have been foolishly based on literacy alone" (99). Hyman links "cultural pluralism" (102; 97) to the founder of modern anthropology, Franz Boas (to whom Carpenter could also claim a connection via his mentor Frank Speck), and his theories of "diffusion and acculturation, rather than polygenesis and evolution" (103; 98), while arguing that, for Malraux, "man is a continuity, culture an evolution, and art an absolute" (103; 98), suggesting thereby a tension in Malraux's book between its methodology and its thesis, making it, in Hyman's view, "a tissue of contradictions" (103; 98). Malraux's argument can be redeemed, however, if we understand art as ritual, whereby it is "functional in a context it carries along with it, out of place and time" (105; 100). As Northrop Frye puts it elsewhere in *Explorations*, "ritual, as the content of action ... is something continuously latent in the order of words," and "social and cultural history, which is anthropology in the extended sense, will always be part of the context of criticism" (E4, 88; 83).

Walter Grasskamp has argued that the overlooked protagonist of Malraux's *Voices of Silence* is photography, "which both continues and

Figure 2.1 Maurice Jarnoux, *André Malraux and His Imaginary Museum*, 1953. Reprinted by permission of Getty Images.

invalidates the traditions of the museum collection in that reproductions allow objects to be 'liberated' from their actual locations and combined at will – which was precisely the point of the *musée imaginaire*. It is as though objects enter this imaginary museum by means of technological levitation, which sees stone sculptures –even the weightiest and least mobile that are in reality fixed in position as monuments or architectural ornaments – being transplanted into book illustrations."[11] The actual layout of Malraux's book is further indebted to media through the cinematic montage of its juxtaposed images.[12] The effect of this mediatic "deregulation" (Grasskamp, 105) of the artwork was to remove it from the humanistic discourse that had been made suspect by an imperialism funded by the slave trade and to reposition it within ethnology and anthropology:

> Ethnologists, operating beyond their scientific authority, had ... ennobled the artifacts that were brought back from expeditions and that were now in their collections, well before art historians did the same thing. Ethnologists thus significantly destabilized a concept that had hitherto been under academic protection and beholden to the norms set in museums. Indeed, before the end of the nineteenth century ethnologists had undermined the concept of art more thoroughly than the self-important avant-gardes of the early twentieth century would manage later. (Grasskamp, 105–6)

What enabled this shift was photography, and subsequently film. Anthropology and photography had grown up together, and Carpenter had, in a sense, grown up with photography through his birth in Rochester, NY, home of Kodak. By 1922, the year of Carpenter's birth, Robert Flaherty was filming *Nanook of the North* where Carpenter would later do the research that resonated throughout his career. Beginning as an aid to anthropometry and its racialist biases, photography was increasingly drawn on "as a historical document used to critique received colonial histories or to reclaim indigenous stories and ancestors," as Christopher Morton notes.[13] With the rise of social anthropology in the twentieth century, photography was critiqued as being oriented too much toward the visible, "able to record only cultural appearance rather than social depth and concerned with cultural and physical form rather than social function" (Morton, 2). However, as Malraux's book demonstrated, and as the Explorations seminar reiterated, the deployment of photography in a non-linear fashion constituted an "acoustic" approach that was based less on appearance than on configuration, less on linear meaning than on constellated being. Morton notes, "In recent years there has been a shift in intellectual focus away from anthropology's visual legacy and toward the medium's varied social and cultural lives in non-Western settings. The anthropology of photography therefore straddles established disciplinary boundaries, including approaches from history and the history of science, museum and archival studies, as well as social and visual anthropology and documentary and art practices" (2). One implication of this "deregulation" of art was that it enabled Indigenous artifacts to be considered on a par with European artworks, a confluence that had massive implications within the context of artistic modernity as it was articulated in Europe and America, leading ultimately to the establishment of art institutions such as the Musée Branly, where Carpenter's exhibition of Indigenous artifacts from the Arctic was held in 2008, as well as to Edmund Carpenter and Adelaide de Menil's collections of artifacts that now form part of the Menil Collection in Houston, Texas. But what Carpenter added to this discourse was the deployment of the camera itself. While photography definitively reconfigured the status of "primitive" art, it did so without questioning who was holding the camera. Carpenter addressed this specifically in Papua New Guinea, giving the camera to the native peoples he was researching, another way in which he turned anthropology upside down.

The Cybernetic Challenge

So powerful was the "anthropological turn" in the early years of the twentieth century that it motivated an artist such as Marcel Duchamp to treat "everyday objects of his own industrial culture ... [as] fetishes of art" (Grasskamp, 106). This was the *point de départ* for McLuhan's *Mechanical Bride* (1951), and also for *Understanding Media* (1964), whose anthropological underpinning Carpenter intuited immediately: "By all means call [the new] book 'EXTENSIONS OF MAN' ... UNDERSTANDING MEDIA title classifies it with all the old and current crap."[14] While McLuhan demurred, Carpenter had rightly pinpointed the media-anthropological orientation of the book. The "extensions of man" were thus not (merely) anthropomorphic, as Friedrich Kittler repeatedly suggested,[15] but theoretical: the human could no longer be understood apart from mediation. This connection between anthropology and media emerges powerfully on the cover of **E5**, with the front page of a newspaper in the background and a fetish object superimposed on it. Donald Theall elaborates on this media anthropology in an article published in the second issue of *Explorations* about James Joyce's *Ulysses* and *Finnegans Wake*. "The work of art for Joyce ... plays its role in [the] structuring of knowledge by providing an anthropology – a type of knowledge and insight into man and his cultural artifacts" (**E2, 67;** *62*). In addition, Theall posits a proto-cybernetic element in *Finnegans Wake*:

> Joyce had a high regard for the dialectical, informational element in verbal communication as well as the emotive, participational element. His view of the word was to provide precise information about emotions and the operations of the mind. Modern communication engineers have discovered in the physical sphere that communication of information begins with uncertainty – the maximum uncertainty, the maximum potentiality of communication. Joyce applied this fact to the esthetic sphere. (**68;** *63*)

Joyce thus provides a major paradigm for understanding media in anthropological terms, and he does so by critiquing the "flatland" (cf. **E4, 133;** *128*) of print: "'Sink deep or touch not the Cartesian spring!' for it is depth analysis that the Cartesian world generally lacks, thus failing to achieve a technique of digesting the totality of human experience in art" (Theall, **69;** *64*). This notion of depth was likewise associated with the spherical nature of acoustic space – with ground rather than figure.

Theall's invocation of cybernetics in his discussion of Joyce's total field effect as a form of cultural anthropology is echoed and extended by Victor Papanek, who writes in **E8** (subsequently republished with the Joycean title *Verbi-Voco-Visual Explorations*)[16] about the bridge between anthropology and technology. In the mid-1950s, when he was teaching at the Ontario College of Art, Papanek had yet to achieve the global fame that would come to him with the 1971 publication of *Design for the Real World*, and his appearance in this issue must be considered a publishing coup, along with that of Jorge Luis Borges in **E4**.[17] As Papanek's biographer, Alison J. Clarke notes, "The snow-filled Canadian state [*sic*] of Ontario ... introduc[ed] him to the groundbreaking work of anthropologist Edmund Snow Carpenter and philosopher and media theorist Marshall McLuhan, as well as their emerging intellectual circle theorizing the societal influence of new media technologies."[18] Clarke states that Carpenter was "an abiding influence on Papanek" (296n49), the two of them connected through research they had done among the Inuit. Part of Papanek and Carpenter's rapport emerged from the designer's sensitivity to the local and vernacular, as Clarke puts it:

What began as a critique of the "sexed-up" frivolities of a design culture ramped up to meet the demands of unbridled postwar consumer culture had, by the 1960s, culminated in a full-blown global campaign against a profession that wreaked irreversible ecological damage, endorsed neocolonial development and perpetuated social inequality – with *Design for the Real World* its erstwhile manifesto. Translated into more than twenty languages and taken up by a generation of designers and design students desperately seeking an alternative politics of design, Papanek's work took on a life of its own – its clarion call weaponized in the dismantling of the beaux arts hierarchies and modernist teachings of European design schools, and the opening-out of design beyond the reductionist dualities of Western and non-Western. As a designer and critic of international renown, Papanek consciously pitted himself against the ideologies of his modernist émigré forebears who had viewed mass-produced, standardized industrial design through the lens of Western rationalism. Describing the Bauhaus style, in a piece of his earliest design criticism, as a "fascist negation of living that is now proven a lie," he proposed in its place a humane, indigenized design approach imbued with anthropological sensitivity to the local, the vernacular, and an understanding of the broader cultural nuances of design's power in undermining or solidifying social inclusion ... As an integral part of the social design agenda, he advocated non-Western tropes of design – from material cultures of the Inuit to the Suku Bali, as holistic models of design whereby things are understood as inseparable from the social relations, customs, rituals, and histories in which they are embedded. The politics of design, in other words, relied on understanding the practice as a cultural rather than rational, problem-solving phenomenon. (2–3)

Clarke's contextualization of Papanek's work as anthropological, with the particular reference to Inuit culture, locates his interests within the parameters of Carpenter's own research. As with many other contributors to *Explorations*, Papanek's "A Bridge in Time"[19] stresses the importance of "a highly oral, myth-generating mechanism" (1 [pagination begins after 24 "items"]; 77) originating with modernism that would serve as the bridge between the mechanical culture of print and the new organicism of electronic culture. Chief among these mythmakers were the Futurists, who proposed a dynamic cultural model based on the use of *parole in libertà* – words liberated from the mechanical constraints of print (a legacy Harley Parker continued in *Explorations* with his use of Flexitype). However, as Papanek notes, it was "the abstract design of the machine, rather than its dynamism, which appealed to the largest group of artists" (1; 77). Of these, the most significant were the Dadaists, who "pushed the veneration of machine-culture the furthest, ending up with a curiously pre-Existentialist concept of man as a machine without will or meaning" (2; 78), the ultimate expression of which would be the "biomorphic and mechanomorphic" experiment of Duchamp's *Bride Stripped Bare*. The ambiguities of technology, which confers power at the price of humanity, are exemplified (writes Papanek) in Le Corbusier's concept of the house as a *"machine à habiter,"* such that "the actual human requirements of the occupants have been rigidly truncated to mold human needs into a pattern more acceptable to the machine" (4; 80). This would be the crux of a bifurcation within *Explorations* itself, **E8** ending with the nihilism of Jack Jones's "Dada in the Drugstore," and **E9** (*Eskimo*) flipping the mechanomorphic around via the Inuit understanding of the machine organically, as an ecology of interrelations.

Papanek's concerns about technology were shared by the other "Cold War salon" that contextualizes the Explorations seminar, the Macy Conferences (the first of these salons being Ray Birdwhistell's Culture and Communications seminar). *Explorations* is directly linked to the Macy Conferences through co-founder L.K. Frank, whose work appears in issues 4 and 5, and by Margaret Mead, present both at Birdwhistell's seminar attended by the Explorations group and at the Macy Conferences. Held in the aftermath of World War II, the Macy Conferences sought to explore the relationship between humans and machines based on an awareness of the "biomorphic and mechanomorphic"[20] shift highlighted by Papanek, the goal of the conferences being nothing less than an anthropology of the machine. While the Macy Conferences were deeply concerned with communications, their interest was not defined by the linear model of sender and receiver proposed by the Shannon-Weaver theory of information that excluded "noise" from the communication process. Rather, their focus was on feedback, as Margaret Mead had highlighted in her comments on the photographic documentation of Birdwhistell's seminar. Not only did feedback produce a circular model of communication, but it also supported an organic or ecological understanding of the communication process that was relational, underwriting thereby a sense of the crucial importance of the medium in any process of communication. David Riesman had highlighted this concept as the major contribution of Innis to media theory: a focus on the sheer materiality of the medium, which is also the theme of the Borges story, "Mutations" (**E4**, 21; *16*), in which symbolic structures such as "cross, cord, and arrow" ultimately reveal themselves in terms of their material substrates. This notion of the materiality of cultural production was of signal importance to Carpenter, and especially to his collecting of Indigenous artifacts, which for him were not artifacts at all but media – elements within a complex media anthropology that signified as a totality. He would reproduce the Borges piece from *Explorations* as the epigraph to his editing of the Carl Schuster *magnum opus*.

The Macy Conferences were held from 1941 to 1960; cybernetics was their focus from 1946–53, with the machine taken as the model for human cognition, the "researchers convinced that humans and machines are brothers under the skin,"[21] as Katherine Hayles puts it, who argues that the conferences were focused on information "as a disembodied medium" such that they "made information seem more important than materiality" (50). It is precisely here that Carpenter (and McLuhan) took their distance, both (following Innis) asserting that information media were fundamentally material and humanistic, Carpenter asserting in his 1970 book that the relationship between humans and technology was one in which we become what we behold, thereby also identifying the role of the observer as crucial in anthropological inquiry, as in his research in Papua New Guinea, where the media being used to analyze the Indigenous population were also changing that population. As Hayles puts it, "Information moves only through signals and ... signals have existence only if they are embodied" (62). Norbert Wiener, one of the key cyberneticians, foregrounded the tensions within the cybernetic model in the title of his book *The Human Use of Human Beings*,[22] the utilitarian overtones inescapable even for the author, who "struggled to envision the cybernetic machine in the image of a humanistic self" (86), as Hayles puts it. For Carpenter the anthropologist, however, the human could not be an afterthought.

Cybernetics posed an immense challenge to anthropology in its dislocation of the human into the technological. The human now became a question. No longer was the human the transcendent point of reference that, since Leonardo's *uomo universale*, had informed the human sciences. The human was now understood to be a historical phenomenon mediated by human technologies (or technologies of the human). As Claus Pias puts it, "Whereas before ... such things as life, language, or work were united in the concept of the human being, they now encountered one another beyond human limits in control circuits of information, switching algebra, and feedback."[23] As Pias goes on to note, "The anthropological illusion consisted in ignoring the complex of power and knowledge involved with creating the very notion of 'the human,' and in covering up, by means of self-naturalizing, the fact that this is a product of technologies of power" (19). Anthropology, however, had already lived through this scenario in the transition from the primitivism of Sir James Frazer and Lord Raglan, based as it was on the idea of a sovereign self gendered as male and racialized as white, to the cultural relativism of the Franz Boas in whose lineage Carpenter was himself represented. Far from ending anthropology, cybernetics enshrined it as the anthropocene; "man" has become universal in precisely the same way that media have merged with the human in the singularity of the *inforg*. The fact that everything is now on a digital platform has not put an end to the concept of media, as Friedrich Kittler proclaimed, but made it the total and inescapable environment in which we now live. It is within these complex interstices that Carpenter's career as an anthropologist played out.

Technologies of "Man"

The tensions between the technological and the humanistic are evident throughout *Explorations*, and especially so at the end of the series. The covers of the issues themselves tell this story. Issue 1 has three Indigenous masks on its cover from the 1948 film *The Loon's Necklace* (127), directed by F.R. Crawley. The film itself enacts a myth told "all across Alaska, Northern Canada, and Greenland,"[24] adverting, thus, to Carpenter's area of research. Issue 2 is in sharp contrast, with its spoof front-page headline "New Media Changing Tempo[ral and] Spatial Orientation." With issue 3 we're back to a "Northwest Coast" (149) Indigenous mask, again from *The Loon's Necklace*. Kandinsky's 1938 biomorphic artwork, *Comets* (its colour scheme somewhat altered), with its juxtaposition of the biological and the mechanical, appears on issue 4. Issue 5 superimposes the front page of the *Toronto Daily Star* with a "Mother Goddess, Our Lady of the Sports and Muse of Unofficial Poetry, blessing the arena. Cretan, 16th century B.C." (152).[25] The allusion to unofficial poetry recalls Lamartine's statement that the newspaper has replaced the book,[26] a concept that McLuhan embedded in *The Gutenberg Galaxy*, which was set in Linotype Times, a newspaper face.[27] Issue 6 excerpts Hokusai's *Great Wave Off Kanagawa*, a woodblock print. The cover of issue 7 was designed by Harley Parker using "native pigments and feather brushes at a Congo mission" (**E7**, 1). The cover of Issue 8 is explained as deriving from "the spherical nature of the oral world. Verbi-Voco-Visual standing for the word as sound ... and as sight (hieroglyphs). The hieroglyphs are placed on a curve, the lower curve, reading from left to right means 'looking for the ways' and the top curve reading from right to left means 'speech,'"[28] whereby speech is technologized as writing. The preponderance of masks on these covers is contextualized by Carpenter in "Eternal Ones of the Dream" (**E7**), its title alluding to Geza Roheim's book of the same title, an anthropological study of Indigenous Australian tribes. In "the preliterate world," the ear is foregrounded, rather than the eye, and this reversal of figure and ground is exemplified in this article by white lines of type on black pages. The mask, writes Carpenter, is inseparable from the singer who wears it; these masks sound, and thus they are living – "the mask, like the modern mobile, is four-dimensional, living in acoustic space" (75). Rather than concealing, the mask reveals, because it is functionalized by ritual and ritual belongs to the community. In this regard, if displayed in a museum, the mask becomes "empty of value" (75).

The tensions between museology and anthropology also emerge via the cover of *Explorations* 5, which bears special scrutiny. The figurine of the "Mother Goddess" on its cover was featured prominently in the Royal Ontario Museum (where members of the Explorations seminar often met) until 2001, when the consensus deemed it to be a fake, and the figurine was moved to storage. C.L. (Kate) Cooper claims, however, using an "object biography" methodology, that "the *afterlife* of the figurine – its collection history since it came to light in 1930 – is more interesting than the information which this particular artefact could have yielded when considered simply as a Minoan antiquity" (79). Cooper contextualizes her argument by noting, "In recent decades there has been a shift in the way that material culture is envisaged and discussed. The idea that objects are passive, functional possessions has been replaced by an understanding that they are part of a complex relationship with people which renders them active indicators, and even enablers, of social transformation" (79).[29] Cooper goes on to note that "object biography" explores the changing roles played by an object over time, the life of objects having "multiple stages ... from their initial production to their final place in an anthropological collection or museum" (80). In the case of the Minoan Bull-Leaper, Cooper seeks to show how "modern concerns have shaped the object itself, conceptually if not physically" (83). Claimed as authentic by Sir Arthur Evans, the figurine had some doubt cast upon its authenticity in the 1930s, but authenticity was reconfirmed in that same decade. As a result, the figurine influenced research on female costume and the role of women in Minoan society for half a century. But by 2001, Kenneth Lapatin[30] was able to demonstrate that the figurine and those like it were fakes that had been designed precisely to coincide with Evans's theories about Minoan culture:

> At this stage of its "life" the ROM Bull-Leaper was devalued in monetary terms, considered an ivory and gold objet d'art rather than a Minoan artefact, and lost its rarity value as a well-preserved antiquity. Yet its intellectual value had been enhanced as a result of Lapatin's work. At a time when Evans' opinions were being criticised and his authentications doubted, the "Bull-Leaper as Minoan figurine," without information about its archaeological findspot or Bronze Age function, could only really be admired for its appearance and remarkable preservation. However, Lapatin's work furnished the Bull-Leaper with another dimension (as well as far-reaching publicity). It was now seen as an example of early 20th-century taste, attractive and intriguing as a fake. Yet again, the ROM Bull-Leaper's identity had been shaped by scholarly opinion, and again it was instrumental in changing aspects of contemporary scholarship. (90–1)

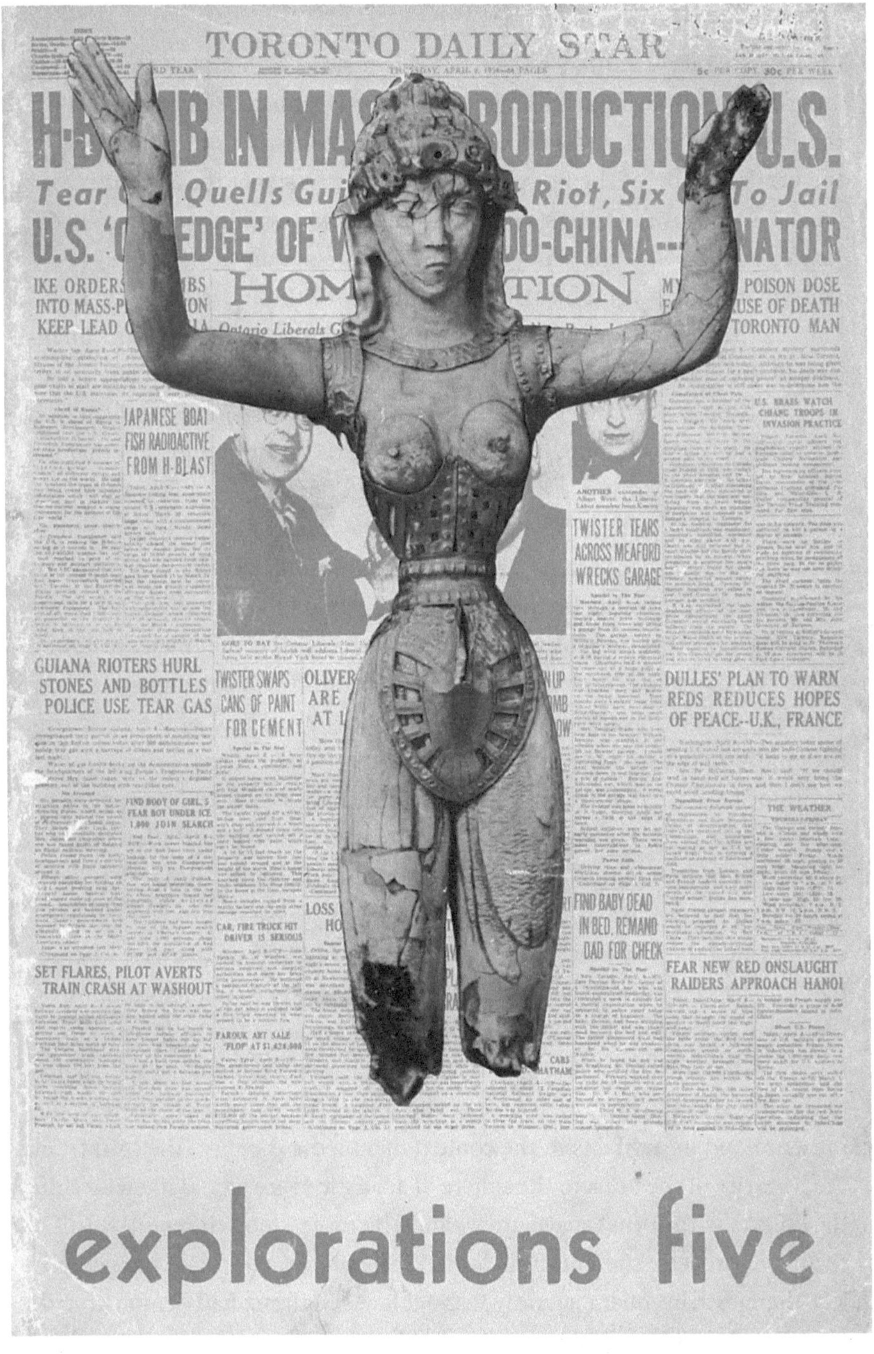

Figure 2.2 Cover, *Explorations* 5.

The cover of *Explorations* 5 is part of this history, although it throws into relief aspects of the figurine's "object biography" not considered by Cooper that derive from its mediated nature, an aspect brought out powerfully by the juxtaposition of the figurine with the front page of the *Toronto Daily Star* (8 April 1954). One aspect of that mediation was the museum itself. Harley Parker, who contributed the Flexitype section (*Anna Livia*) of **E5**, and the innovative graphics of **E8**, was head of exhibit design at the Royal Ontario Museum from 1957 to 1968; the museum was at that time ancillary to the University of Toronto, and hence members of the Explorations seminar would often meet there. The idea of acoustic space that galvanized the seminar was taken up by Parker, who had the profound insight that the museum was a medium – that it transformed the objects in it, rather than merely displaying them. The museum in the electronic era was a conundrum, however, because its display tactics were decidedly a product of print culture, including the information appended to the individual works on display. Parker sought to change this by making the museum into a multi-sensory space, rather than one oriented toward vision alone. As Gary Genosko puts it, Parker's goal was "to achieve a 'synthesis' of the 20th century museum visitor with an aural-tactile-kinetic perceptual orientation in a curatorial space marked historically by linearity and visual perception of a disciplined academic speciality."[31] He achieved this in his "Hall of Fossils" exhibition of 1967, which included "16 wall mounted, dial-less telephones delivering pre-recorded messages" (Genosko). These proto-audiophones transformed the museum into an acoustic space that was likewise interactive, and gained international fame through a Yousuf Karsh photo showing McLuhan in front of them. Karsh's photo demarcates a media history, from the shell that speaks when you put it to your ear, to the book, to the photograph itself, to the acoustic space of the audiophones, placing thereby the museum and its artifacts in the context of a media ecology. The shift from the linearity of the book to the sphere of acoustic space would likewise shift the objects within that space; they would be understood differently. This a recursive process: the museum changes the object, and that changed object changes subsequent narratives about it. As Malraux had demonstrated, photography had produced a profound change in the understanding of the art object, and of anthropology itself. This is brilliantly foregrounded by the cover of *Explorations* 5; the juxtaposition of figurine and front page remind

Figure 2.3 Yousuf Karsh, *Marshall McLuhan*, 1967. Reprinted with permission of the Yousuf Karsh Estate.

us that both are artifacts, both are media, both are information. By 1970, information had itself become the subject of a museum exhibition at New York's MOMA.[32] The mediated notion of cultural production allows us to understand museum objects such as the Mother Goddess (whether "real" or "fake") in terms of a media anthropology – the object as complex process rather than static product.[33]

Parker, with his notion of the museum as medium and the object as process, and Carpenter, with his notion of acoustic space, were thus far in advance of an anthropology that was still museum-oriented, albeit heading for a textually focused practice, which Carpenter likewise critiqued with his focus on the sensorial. Paradoxically, when anthropology caught up with him he was nowhere to be found. In good measure, this had to do with

Carpenter's spatial analysis of the anthropological object. Johannes Fabian's discussion of the denial of coevalness in anthropological research, drawing on McLuhan, among others, in his book *Time and the Other*,[34] critiques the notion of a "primitive" art that exists in a temporal zone different from that of the "modern" anthropologist (or colonizer, as Walter D. Mignolo argues in *The Darker Side of the Renaissance*). To this temporal analysis of anthropological practice, Carpenter added a spatial analysis, both at the level of the individual object and at the level of the museum. The acoustic space that he proposed constituted a methodology. At the level of the individual object, Carpenter argued that an Inuit carving was a process, both because it was interactive with its environment (as nomadic art would be) and because it represented the mediation of the person who produced it. And because it was not static, its being would be violated by traditional museological exposition (on a shelf, for example). Hence Carpenter's "Witnesses" room in the Menil Collection: objects are everywhere – up, down, in drawers, on the ceiling, all around, emphasizing the agency of the object to produce meaning.[35] In effect, Carpenter was putting the digital museum into place *avant la lettre*, or, more accurately, *après la lettre*.

Parker's design work at the ROM had foregrounded this galactic aspect of acoustic space: it was a form of constellated information, rather than the lineal, sequential, connected, teleological space produced by print culture. It was a cognate space that Carpenter encountered among the Aivilik. His article on "Space Concepts of the Aivilik Eskimos" (**E5**) refers to this as an "ecological space" (**131**; *126*), strongly implying its constellated character. The space where the Aivilik live – "the northwest boundary of the Hudson Bay" (**131**; *126*) – is changeable, shifting with the seasons – "distance between camps can only be understood in relation to climate" (**132**; *127*). Thus, "Aivilik do not reckon distance between points by miles or other abstract, inflexible units of measure, but regard it as fluctuating" (**133**; *128*); "there is no middle distance, no perspective, no outline, nothing the eye can cling to except thousands of smokey plumes of snow running along the ground before the wind – a land without bottom or edge" (**138**; *133*); "reference points ... are not actual objects or points, but relationships" (**138**; *133*). Most significantly, Carpenter's comments on the art of the Aivilik would map out the contours of the rest of his career:

In Aivilik art each experience is confined to its own space-time life, without reference to wider spatial relationships. For the most part visual representations are limited to single spatial units and their comprehension is not connected with the understanding of the surrounding space. Each element lives in spatial independence ... Asked to draw everything that had taken place in the interval since I had seen him last, a hunter sketched many independent scenes, often unrelated, not in sequential order, but scattered about on the paper without any particular orientation. At times, when figures overlap, they are endowed with transparency. An egg may be shown inside a bird or a child in a womb ... *This transparency implies more than an optical characteristic; it means the simultaneous perception of different spatial locations.* Space fluctuates in continuous activity ... Thus Aivilik artists do not confine themselves to the reproduction of what can actually be seen in a given moment from a single vantage point, but they twist and tilt the various possible visual aspects until they fully explain the object they wish to represent. They may draw a tent from one side and include as well, an end view of the tent in order to show its shape. Or they may draw the tent from one angle and other objects from another ... The hierarchy of size is intimately associated with the hierarchy of power, strength and importance: spatial scale has a structural correspondence to the scale of values ... Art is subservient to the ear, not the eye. (**140–4**; *135–9*; emphasis added)

These comments on acoustic space would ultimately inform Carpenter's masterworks, the exhibitions *Upside Down*.

Sigfried Giedion cites Carpenter's "Eskimo Space Concepts" in his article on "Space Conception in Prehistoric Art" (**E6**, 33–54) to support his central argument that horizontal and vertical spatial orientation is not universal, and that the distinction between up and down is not characteristic of "primeval art" (**42**; *41*).[36] *Explorations* 8 turns this into a headline and states the theme of issue 8 in cognate terms: "After thousands of years of written processing of human experience, the instantaneous omnipresence of electronically processed information has hoicked us out of these age-old patterns into an auditory world" (**item 24**; *76*). Edited by McLuhan and

NO UPSIDE DOWN

IN ESKIMO ART

Figure 2.4 "No Upside Down in Eskimo Art," *Explorations* 8.

written by him in good part, *E8* presents itself as the last gasp of print culture before it dies and is reborn as acoustic space, the overall theme of the issue being orality. Reminiscent of Marinetti's *parole in libertà* ("words in liberty"; the Futurist Manifesto is quoted in **item 14/31**), words in **E8** are wrenched out of their linear order by Harley Parker's use of Flexitype; as a note on typography states at the end of the issue, "inherent in the visual distortion of the word is the possibility of its sounding" **(63; 139)**. The use of colour printing further hoicks the typography out of its traditional domain of black and white signification (already explored by Carpenter in issue 7, where the black and white of the page are reversed) and moves it toward the multisensual integration of the auditory world.

Explorations 8 does not depict that world in universally positive terms, however. Item 14 states, "When information moves instantly to all parts of the globe it is chemically explosive ... Today the normal movements of information have the effect of armed invasion on some culture or group ... The new media normalize that state of revolution which is war" (*27*). Jack Jones[37] takes up this idea in the last essay in the issue, "Dada in the Drugstore." Prefaced with a quotation from Maurice Blanchot – "Truth becomes violence, and a passion for the end"[38] – the essay asks why nihilism disappeared from intellectual discourse precisely at the moment when "the full implications of contemporary political and technological totalitarianism sank in" **(43; 119)**. Hence, if the Futurists were giving words their liberty to return to the condition of orality, they were also offering "a blackboard demonstration of the invasion of the artist by mechanical rigidity" (**47**; *123*), such that "a speeding automobile is more beautiful than the Victory of Samothrace" (Marinetti, *Futurist Manifesto*, quoted **1**; *77*) and war a form of political hygiene.[39] Art became increasingly isolated from the world around it, "dependent upon and subservient to a non-creative and anti-organic society" (**48**; *124*). Only the Dadaists were willing to critique "the inviolable sanctuary of art" (**48**; *124*), but to do so they had to embrace nihilism itself – and to do so nihilistically:

> It seemed no longer possible to make any sense out of life, and it was the horror of this situation that the Dada movement tried to communicate. This was the situation which gave their chaotic 'art' its peculiar quality: it was not really art since art cannot arise in the absence of some irreducible quantity of faith; but on the other hand it was paradoxically closer to the true situation than the work which did manage to get created regardless of its abstract value ... Here the more profound attachment to art consisted in precisely the power to negate it. (**48**; *124*)

The choices are stark: negation or repression of negation. The avant-garde in art disappears, engendering nihilism, which is then repressed.

But a new art form emerged, suggests Jones, which was not subject to this process, a "vulgar and despised medium, the comic-book" (**53**; *129*), and specifically MAD *Magazine* (with the switch from comic book format to magazine taking place in 1955). What the creators of that magazine realized was that "the real world mattered less to people than the sea of sounds and images that the ever more powerful mass media were pumping into American lives."[40] MAD became the avatar of the new "polytechnic popular culture" (**53**; *129*) for which "all the cosmic, the fundamental questions no longer exist" (**61**; *137*), and thus nihilism becomes a commodity that one can purchase at the drugstore newsstand. Jones suggests that the creative person can respond to this nihilism "only with the concomitant affirmation of a new set of values which he believes it possible to create. Thus to him the situation of total or near-total disbelief created by the nihilist is only a *hypothetical* or possible attitude – possible if he himself should lose faith in regenerative or recreative power" (**44**; *120*). It was this faith that

Carpenter sought in his embrace of ancient cultures and through his editing of Schuster's vast project; unlike McLuhan, he was not a proponent of an art defined as "anything you can get away with."[41]

The last word of Jones's article is "hell" (**62**; *138*), and in this context the contrast between *E8* and *E9* couldn't be greater. *Eskimo*,[42] written and edited by Carpenter, is, in the first instance, materially different from the eight uniform volumes of the journal. Oversize (57 cm. [22.5 in.] when open, and 31 cm. [12 in.] wide), and landscape oriented (which takes on special significance in this book, with its white, glossy paper), it presents itself as an anti-book, a book that doesn't quite fit, a book (unpaginated) that is not organized in linear, teleological fashion, and a book that proclaims its originality in terms of form, not content. Its content is a remediation of the material from Carpenter's essay on spatial concepts among the Aivilik (**E5**), along with images of Inuit sculpture collected by filmmaker Robert Flaherty (1884–1951) and paintings by Group of Seven painter Frederick Varley (who had made a trip to the Arctic in 1938). There are also resonances with Carpenter's article in **E2** on concepts of the self and of the life process among the Aivilik, both of which are characterized by process and flow.[43] Carpenter's text seeks to undermine stereotypical understandings of northern peoples; his Aivilik are not "the noble savages of Rousseau's political theories."[44] Writing about the igloo, for example, Carpenter states that "the igloo is 'open,' a labyrinth alive with the movements of crowded people. No flat static walls arrest the ear or eye, but voices and laughter come from several directions and the eye can glance through here, past there, catching glimpses of the activities of nearly everyone." Similarly, works of art do not exist as "objects" separate from their creators or from those who interact with them, nor is there any sense of "realism." A carving of a seal, for example, does not seek to represent the shape of a seal, but to liberate the seal shape from the material being carved. This is a holistic sense of the artwork, one that "obeys the ear more than the eye" and asserts the connection between the organic and the artistic. In this context, the most paradoxical aspect of *Eskimo* is the section on "Mechanical Aptitude." Carpenter responds, here, to the nihilism of technologization that entered into the Canadian Arctic through the building of the DEW line[45] with the counter-intuitive observation that the Aivilik are excellent mechanics,[46] but they are so not through an embrace of technology. Rather, their expertise

In its topography, the eastern Canadian Arctic ranges from great glistening, coloured cliffs to flatlands that roll away, mile after empty mile, featureless and undifferentiated, save for quiet inland pools that blue-so mingle its monotonous expanse. The wind seems never to stop. It is a hard land, with few extras.

The fleeting weeks between the passing of one winter and the coming of another witness temperate and even warm weather. Snow melts, flowers bloom, birds flock from the south. The land becomes sombre brown, not colourless, but dead in colour, save for the brilliant orange of lichen-covered rocks

Figure 2.5 Carpenter, *Eskimo*, double-page spread.

emerges from their ability to perceive holistically – the machine is not a product for them, but a process: "Aivilik do not conceptually separate space and time, but see a situation or machine as a dynamic process." The machine is thus a set of interrelationships, not a collection of separate parts, "a spatial ecology of relations,"[47] as Raviv Ganchrow puts it. If the machine represented the dehumanizing effects of technology, as Papanek and Jones had suggested, Carpenter perceives the reversal of this dehumanization in *Eskimo*, where the machine among the Inuit becomes an exemplar of organic interconnectedness. *Explorations* thus comes full circle, from the proposal that electronic media are producing an acoustic space to the encounter with that space in an ancient culture via the paradoxical mediation of a machine. These interests are reflected in a study that Carpenter was at work on at this time, titled "Time and Space in a Primitive Society,"[48] its subject cognate with the discussions of acoustic space in *Explorations*, as well as Edmund Leach's "Cronos and Chronos," published in the first issue of the journal (**15–23**; *10–18*).

Eskimo was given a stellar review by Dorothy Lee in *American Anthropologist*.[49] She notes (characteristically) that "Carpenter has avoided, to a degree, the lineality of discursive writing, and has employed instead the simultaneity of television," and states that "Carpenter has the rare ability of spotting what is not 'present to the senses' of Western man," giving the book "the refreshing, unfinished quality of process" (166). Lee writes, "There was a time that I feared that Carpenter was reaching a point where he would feel that to write a monograph about his friends would constitute a betrayal or a violation of their integrity. He wrote to me from Fury and Hecla Strait: 'I have never been with friendlier companions. It would be very difficult for me to record many texts ... and as for giving tests, it just couldn't be done. They accept me ... but I could never 'hire' an informant or even find an informant. But just by looking and listening I've had some vivid impressions; beyond that I have not penetrated" (166). Lee claims that *Eskimo* is not an ethnography but a work of art, and that Carpenter "participates but does not observe in the usual sense of the word" (166). She concludes that in *Eskimo* "we see the role of man, indispensable to the actualization of the universal design" (167). Lee's comments are acute, especially as a contextualization of the metaphysically oriented articles about the Aivilik that Carpenter was publishing at this time in the *American Journal of Psychiatry*.

Carpenter's studies of Indigenous peoples in the Arctic were not at all similar to contemporary ones. Charles Campbell Hughes, for example, sought to summarize the current state of Arctic studies in his 1965 article "Under Four Flags: Recent Culture Change among the Eskimos."[50] As Hughes notes, the "Eskimo has been a stock figure in anthropology since its beginnings as a discipline in the last century" (3), though the tendency had been to ignore their cultural diversity (Canadian "Eskimos" serving as models for the various Indigenous communities in the Arctic [12]), as well as the effects of World War II and its aftermath on them, especially the 3,000-mile DEW line, whose greatest effects were on the Canadian Arctic (12). These effects paralleled the ones emerging from the earlier introduction of guns and the advent of the fur trade (17). It was the rifle that had contributed to the great decline in the caribou population that led to the famine among the Padleimiut in 1952 that was documented by Richard Harrington (subsequently reprinted by Carpenter in *Padlei Diary*). By the 1960s, thus, the Indigenous peoples of the Canadian North were having to adapt not only to the northern climate but to the introduction of southern ways of living (48).

Carpenter, invited (with other scholars) to comment[51] on Hughes's article, takes a highly idiosyncratic and deeply personal approach to the issues raised by Hughes (which he would revisit nearly a decade later in his self-assessment as an "unconventional anthropologist").[52] Carpenter writes that his fieldwork in the Arctic was comprised of "intense happenings"; "words failed, images failed, even memory failed" (55). As a result, he became "indifferent to the cold reports coming out on the Eskimo: they were alien to all I had experienced" (55). To the changes in the Arctic noted by Hughes, Carpenter adds the advent of anthropologists, "exhausting the traders' liquor and misinformation" (56). Meeting these anthropologists at conferences, Carpenter was struck by the fact that they reaffirmed "concepts that arose solely from professionalism, unencumbered by those thrilling insights that pierce the heart of those who care nothing for professionalism" (56).

Academic Twilight

Carpenter was critical of academia from the outset of his career, and became ever more critical over the subsequent years. In an address to Toronto's First Unitarian Church, titled "Twilight of the University," delivered in February of 1958, Carpenter states that the "tragic absurdity of our times" is a "moral failure ... to give leadership" that he locates in the university's "humanities and social sciences," such that they "can no longer be trusted to be the representatives of western thought."[53] Taking the example of literature, Carpenter argues that unless it becomes part of students' "everyday thoughts," it is "useless." Yet, far from awakening a love of literature, "the main achievement is to kill that interest ... The fact that serious literature survives at all simply indicates that education is not yet universal" (1). The attempt to broadcast on television a course in psychology given at a major Canadian university produced "the usual tranquilizer ... Professors hastened to explain that their subjects don't lend themselves to presentation over the new media. This is only partly true. More important is that very few professors have anything to say" (1). Carpenter explicitly targets examinations and degrees as having turned the university from a place of "attention" to one of "detention," noting that these elements were absent in medieval universities but introduced with printing. Psychology and sociology are particularly critiqued by Carpenter as a "pseudo-scholarship of verbal cobwebs" (2). Much of the blame for the state of universities derives from the appointment of non-academics in the area of governance, while faculty members appointed to governance quickly becoming "administrators" (3). "In the last century," writes Carpenter, "scholarship was produced by men of independent means ... Such scholarship produced its dilettantes and fools, but scholars were there too, whereas our current screening process carefully eliminates them ... Too long we have judged intellectuals and scientists on whether they get on in a group or are free of traits objectionable to administrators" (3). Research grants began to drive scholarship, making universities into another form of big business. "A scholar," however, "is a man who is not for sale" (4). Carpenter is particularly scathing about the Canadian intellectual milieu, stating that the "really interesting thing about the Canadian commissars of education is not that they enjoy a monopoly, but that it is a monopoly that advocates nothing, save the desirability of having no opinion" (5). These comments are aligned with ones expressed earlier in Carpenter and McLuhan's *Counterblast* (1954) about the "cringing, flunkey spirit of canadian culture" [*sic*] and the "ivy-clawed adolescent, the creeper mind," and they would persist for the remainder of Carpenter's career. Given Carpenter's attitude toward academia, the Explorations seminar would have appeared as an especially fortuitous escape from the milieu he describes here.

Despite his negative view of academia, Carpenter continued to publish academically during this period (and throughout his career), and in journals that suggest his interests were interdisciplinary before becoming a member of the Explorations seminar. His publication venues in the 1950s (concurrent with *Explorations*) included *American Anthropologist*, *American Antiquity*, *Pennsylvania Archaeologist*, *Journal of the Washington Academy of Sciences*, *American Journal of Psychiatry*, and *Arctic*. Of particular interest are the articles in the *American Journal of Psychiatry*, the most widely read psychiatric journal in the world and one of the most influential over the last century.[54] Carpenter's connection to the journal likely came from Ashley Montagu (**E6**; see also "Sea," 244, 251), who reviewed *Eskimo* for that journal.[55] Carpenter's articles are noteworthy for their metaphysical concerns, which tended to work against the visual practices of anthropological research (*pace* the "visual anthropology" with which Carpenter is often associated), leading him to describe his research as "cognitive anthropology."[56] In a review of Marvin K. Opler's *Culture, Psychiatry and Human Values*, Carpenter states that, in bringing psychiatry and anthropology together,

Opler "rejects polarity between personality *and* culture, and sees one as simply an aspect of the other."[57] "Witch-Fear among the Aivilik Eskimos,"[58] published in 1953, derived from research funded by the Arctic Institute of North America and the University of Toronto that took place from June to November 1950 and in November 1951 and January 1952 (194). During this period, Carpenter was also making a film about Dorset ivory carvings[59] that remained incomplete (although it was restored for the *Upside Down* exhibitions). In the *AJP* article, Carpenter notes that witchcraft replaced the longstanding practice of magic among the Aivilik, which by the 1950s had largely disappeared. "Bewitching was a constant threat," Carpenter states (194). Whereas in a communal culture misfortune was shared, the break-down of that communality put the focus on the individual. "Instead of com-munity cooperation to appease a deity or drive out a ghost, now there was interpersonal strife" (195).

In keeping with his ongoing project "Time and Space in a Primitive Society," Carpenter turned to time in another article, "Eternal Life and Self-Definition among the Aivilik Eskimos,"[60] having addressed the topic of space in *Eskimo*. "Time," writes Carpenter, "has been said to be the great problem for philosophers ... How, and with what, does man fill time? How, and how far, does he pass out of time? ... The Aivilik Eskimos have remained faithful to the problem ... They have sought the meaning of life in the prob-lem of time" (840). "Alcohol in the Iroquois Dream Quest,"[61] published in 1959, explores "mystical faculties" among the Iroquois, who incorporated alcohol into their dream quests after colonization. The goal of such quests was to get outside the self; the Iroquois believed that "by getting outside the ordinary human order, they would get inside a higher spiritual order" (148). This did not square with the Jesuits who sought to convert them, an aspect of Carpenter's article that is noteworthy, given that he was a professor at a Roman Catholic institution; while the Jesuits are not directly critiqued, their incomprehension of Iroquois beliefs is evident throughout.

While Carpenter's articles for the *AJP* do not focus on media, his re-view of J.C. Carothers's *The African Mind in Health and Disease: A Study in Ethnopsychiatry*[62] is exceptional, since it is a scathing account of a scholar who looms large in the first thirty pages of McLuhan's *The Gutenberg Galaxy*. (It was Carpenter who drew Carothers to McLuhan's attention.)[63] Carpenter writes that the "African" whom Carothers repeatedly invokes in terms of "the African mind," "the African mentality," "the African personality," and so on, is "apparently any colored man of African ancestry, living either in that continent or the United States." Carpenter laments the fact that scholars such as "Hallowell, Lee, Whorf, Sapir, Griaule and Spiro, who might have put the author on a scientific track, are not cited in the bibliography," and concludes his review with the comment that the author's warning in the last chapter of his book that "the reader who insists on close adherence to fact and well-established theory might be well-advised to read no further" unfortunately "comes too late." Here we witness the disciplinary differences between Carpenter and McLuhan that persisted, mostly covertly, throughout their careers. As Carpenter stated in "Sea," McLuhan was ready to siphon up anything that came his way, whereas Carpenter was much more conservative in his response.[64] Put another way, Carpenter's focus was on empirical evidence, whereas McLuhan's was on theory.

3

The *Wanderjahre*

RESPONDING IN 1982 to a request from Margaret Mead's biographer, Jane Howard, to characterize the early years of the anthropology department at the University of Toronto[1] (when Mead had been married to a member of its faculty), Carpenter replied that under its head, Thomas McIlwraith, junior colleagues tended not to last "more than two years. All later went on to international recognition. Toronto's Anthropology Department was noted solely for those who left."[2] Carpenter was one of those; describing himself in the biography appended to *Eskimo* as a "wanderer,"[3] he began his *Wanderjahre* in earnest after resigning from the University of Toronto in 1958.[4] Leaving behind the university did not, however, mean leaving behind the journal. Although he claimed in "Sea" that he sought to "bury" *Explorations* at the end of its run, it refused to die,[5] and he was among those who kept it alive.

Eskimo was published in 1959, after Carpenter had taken a position teaching anthropology at San Fernando State College (subsequently California State University, Northridge). By 1961, he would be chair of anthropology. In that year, Carpenter and Claude Lévi-Strauss were planning a publication on Inuit art; because the publisher had just issued a book on Native American art by Frederick Dockstader (whom Carpenter would encounter during his time on the board of the Museum of the American Indian), the publisher sought to delay the proposed publication, which ultimately failed to materialize.[6] This proposed collaboration between Carpenter and the greatest living anthropologist was made in the context of the international attention Carpenter had achieved the year before with the publication of the anthology *Explorations in Communication*,[7] published under Carpenter

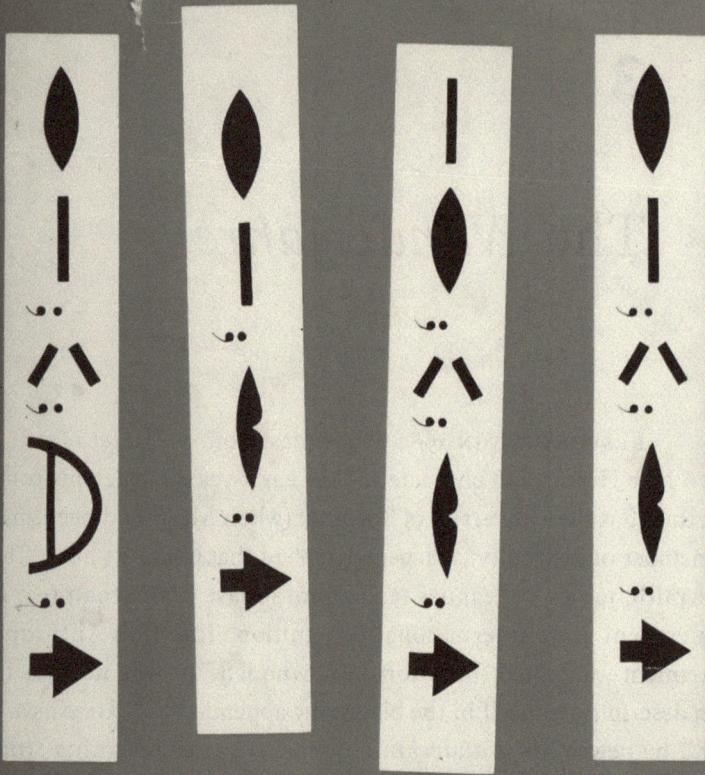

Figure 3.1 Cover, *Explorations in Communication*, 1960.

and McLuhan's editorship.[8] This publication is significant, because it remains the chief way in which the journal is known, given that the original issues now, as then, are "rare collectors' items" (ix). Reproducing Ray Birdwhistell's diagrams of kinemorphs on its cover (displaced from the horizontal to the vertical), the majority of the anthology's excerpts (sixteen) are from issues 4 and 7 (eight each), with three excerpts each from issues 5 and 6, and one from issues 2 and 3. Explorations 8 and 9 are not represented (8 would be reprinted seven years later, at the height of McLuhan's fame), and there are no excerpts from the first issue. Other than McLuhan and Carpenter (who published Carleton Williams's "Acoustic Space" [E4] under their own name), the only author represented more than once is Dorothy Lee; none of Carpenter's anthropological essays are included. The anthology thus fails to represent the anthropological orientation of the journal, giving the impression that it had an exclusively communications studies bent – in fact, the introduction to the anthology (which appears to have been written by McLuhan)[9] identifies *Explorations* as "a journal on communications" (ix). The reference in the introduction to "the Eskimo" takes a different tack from Carpenter's writing on the subject in the journal. "The Eskimo has been de-tribalized via print, going in the course of a few years from primitive nomad to literate technician ... The literacy we abandon, he embraces; the oral language he rejects, we embrace" (xi–xii). Carpenter's view, expressed at the end of *Eskimo*, was far more committed to the idea of cultural continuity:

> Though outside influences have at times changed, even replaced traditional arctic art, this ancient tradition, sometimes long slumbering, has on different polar seas repeatedly reasserted itself, and will probably continue to do so as long as fur-clad hunters roam this timeless, spaceless landscape. How far into past ages this tradition may reach back, I dare not even surmise, but the fact that it can stir us, even today, suggests it touches something universally human.

Ironically, this appeal to the "universally human" would increasingly become the major problematic in anthropological study in the 1970s and 1980s, and precisely at the moment when Carpenter was editing Carl Schuster's massive archive of materials.

The appeal to the universal is evident in Carpenter's other 1959 publication, *Anerca*,[10] a book of Inuit poems in translation, together with commentary by Carpenter, and drawings by Enooesweetok, credited as being "of the Sikosilingmuit, Fox Land, Baffin Island" (unpaginated).[11] Carpenter writes in a short preface to the book (quoting material in the attributions list for *Eskimo*) that "The poems come from Eskimo groups distant in time and space, but there is a basic unity which only a common tongue, common interests, and a common delight could foster. Some were created spontaneously ... others are age-old and belong to all. In neither do poets take care to be remembered as individuals, but simply disappear, as it were, behind their works; the poems, therefore, have been assigned to neither singers nor makers." The question of translation does not emerge here (there are only eight lines of transliterated Inuktitut), but is acknowledged in a note at the end of the book. Most of the poems were translated by Knud Rasmussen (1879–1933) in his fifth Thule report, based on a three-year trek beginning in 1921 that was led by two Inuit across the Canadian Arctic and Alaska to eastern Siberia.[12] The other major translator was William Thalbitzer (1873–1958), professor of Eskimo studies at the University of Copenhagen. Writing about the "Eskimo" language in 1968, Carpenter states that "The principal feature of Eskimo grammar is sometimes called 'case,' though it's unrelated to possession, in our sense, and cannot fairly be called 'tense,' because it doesn't emphasize temporality. Nor is 'position' entirely fair, for this implies pure space, devoid of time, action. Rather, it concerns transactions. Just as physicists explain that electricity is not something conveyed by, or contained in, anything, but the condition observed when there are certain spatial relations between things, so Eskimo grammar stresses what occurs when two bodies, in special position, interact. It indicates the position of each, relative to the other, and can also show position of speaker and listener."[13] Carpenter stresses the cultural differences between English and "Eskimo": "English emphasizes nouns, things that are there, apart from us. Eskimo, in contrast, makes little distinction between 'nouns' and 'verbs'; rather, all words are forms of the verb 'to be' which itself is lacking in Eskimo. That is, all words proclaim in themselves their own existence. Eskimo isn't a nominal language; it doesn't simply name things that exist, but rather brings things-actions (nouns-verbs) into being" (470). In effect, Carpenter is arguing that, as is the case with oral cultures generally, the language of the Inuit is concrete and situational. Inuit stories focus on actions; they do not express an "inner" life, which is largely the product of literacy. This discussion echoes, at a certain distance, the one that opens *La Pensée Sauvage*, where Claude Lévi-Strauss writes that "the words 'oak,' 'beech,' 'birch,' etc., are no less abstract than the word 'tree,' and given two languages of which one possesses only the more abstract term, while the other lacks it but has several dozens or hundreds of words for species and varieties, it would be the latter and not the former that, from this point of view, would be the richer in concepts."[14]

Carpenter translated two of the poems in *Anerca*, noting, "In Eskimo the word to make poetry is the word to breathe; both are derivatives of *anerca*, the soul, that which is eternal; the breath of life."

Weather Chant
Cold, Cold,
Frost, Frost,
Fling me not aside!
You have bent me enough.
Away! Away!

and

Who comes?
Is it the hound of death approaching?
Away!
Or I will harness you to my team.

The second of these poems is prefaced with an account of a myth about the "hairless dog-husband of Sedna, goddess of the fruitful sea" and how he "periodically rises from the nether world to bring death and disaster." The book as a whole is contextualized with an epigraph from Herodotus ("The whole of the country which I have been speaking of has so hard and severe a winter, that there prevails there for eight months an altogether unsupportable cold") and another from John Ross's *An Account of the Discovery of the Polar Eskimo* (actually *A Voyage of Discovery, Made*

Under the Orders of the Admiralty, which contains an account of the "Arctic Highlanders"), which records a conversation with an Inuit who cannot conceive that Ross comes from the south: "That cannot be, there is nothing but ice there." The idea of prevailing ice is conveyed in *Anerca* (as in *Eskimo*) by the largely "empty" pages where the drawings by Enooesweetok appear. These drawings were collected and privately published by Robert Flaherty in 1915; of the two portfolios known to be extant, one is in the collection of the Royal Ontario Museum. Lithographs on stone, these images represent one of the earliest efforts to produce such images via printing.[15] The artist was in fact Nungusuituq (Noogooshoweetok, Noasweeto).[16] It is not known why Flaherty decided to rename him, but this colonialist act resonated through much of Flaherty's work, most controversially with his film *Nanook of the North* (1922), a controversy in which Carpenter found himself involved through various interactions with Flaherty's legacy, including the reprinting of the drawings of Nungusuituq in 2001.[17] *Anerca* was given a lukewarm review in *American Anthropologist* by Margaret Lantis, an "Eskimologist" who taught at the University of Kentucky. The terse, two-paragraph review noted that "All except possibly two (from Carpenter's own collection) of the 22 poems and prose passages have been published elsewhere, chiefly in Knud Rasmussen's *Fifth Thule Expedition Report*, and several, according to the editor, have been 'modified.'" Lantis concludes, "Since all but one of the poems are reproduced without Eskimo text ... and since most of the drawings show rather dimly, one must agree with Carpenter's statement that this is not a book for specialists but one that 'has no purpose other than delight in making and reading it.'"[18]

Carpenter continued to write about the Inuit after his move to California, and among his first publications there was an account of his main native informant during his time in the Arctic. "Ohnainewk, Eskimo Hunter" was published in an anthology of essays by some of the most illustrious anthropologists of the twentieth century, including Raymond Firth, Margaret Mead, and Victor W. Turner.[19] Carpenter had overwintered with Ohnainewk in 1951–52, and the essay is comprised of Carpenter's recollections after the Inuit's death in 1954. In his telling, Carpenter is particularly concerned with the question of the native informant. As Carpenter relates, "Months later, at a trading post, I heard the details of his death. The whites sat around, familiarly discussing a man they had shunned in his life. His marriages and their failures, his troubles with the traders, were all described, not from his point of view, but the point of view of strangers" (418). Ohnainewk ultimately turned his back on the trading post and moved to a desolate "landscape of infernal grandeur" (421). It was there that Carpenter spent time with him and his family and became audience to the man's stories:

> He delighted in recitation, and the genius of the Eskimo language, which is highly expressive, full of onomatopoeic effects, favored him. He used hierarchic expressions: "The man his son," and he could say "bear" in such a way that we were awed as if in the presence of some wondrous ursine power. Statements often began with a *non sequitur,* best translated "So ... ," used not as a conjunction but as a magic conclusion that had no logical reference to the preceding statement. He spoke only of things we could touch and see, constantly choosing the concrete word, in phrase after phrase, forcing us to touch and see. No speaker so insistently taught the general through the particular. He had mastery over the definite, detailed, particular, visualized image. But the mythic abstract air of the telling blurred the sharp contours of these images, the has-been and the to-be became the now, and particular places, particular people, faded as he recited his litany of the great mysteries – birth, death, famine, water, sky. (421–2)

Teaching the general through the particular was likewise Carpenter's *modus operandi,* and as one reads through his account of Ohnainewk, one perceives a considerable degree of identification between Carpenter and the stories about Ohnainewk, "his marriages and their failures," his "troubles," and the fact that "there was not one hint that he was strong and brilliant and complex" (420).[20] It was Ohnainewk's stories that accompanied Carpenter on his journey from Toronto to California.

A unique aspect of the anthropology department at San Fernando Valley State College was that "each appointment of a traditionally trained anthropologist was matched by one from the performing arts: jazz composer, folksinger, dancer, etc.,"[21] as Carpenter noted in 1965. "These appointments were not peripheral, part-time, visiting lectureships – not fruit on the branch but part of the trunk: tenured, senior appointments in anthropology, the point being that the arts offer a primary approach for the experiencing of man" (453–4). Dorothy Lee left Harvard to join Carpenter there ("Sea," 252).[22] "A fabulous faculty!" wrote Carpenter subsequently. "Free-lancing had given me some contact with media, but here we were testing & playing, right at the edge ... Several innovations gained wide acceptance. Several films took international awards" ("Sea," 252–3).

One of Carpenter's anthropologist colleagues in California was Raoul Naroll, who published *Data Quality Control – A New Research Technique*[23] in 1962. Naroll's concern in this book was the reliability of data. "Surely every social scientist who works with oral or written reports needs to be concerned about their accuracy. The historian or political scientist who works with records, letters, memoirs, and chronicles; the ethnographer who works with native informants; the comparative ethnologist who works with the reports of ethnographers; ... all need to be suspicious of the reliability of the reports from which they compile data" (1). In effect, Naroll is stating that all research demonstrates bias, even in "the selection of the problem itself" (29). His solution is to transform research findings into quantitative data. While this position is naive – as Lisa Gitelman has argued, there is no such thing as unbiased data[24] – it points toward a tendency within ethnographical research in the 1960s to distrust the concept of the "native informant" as a colonialist invention,[25] and to realize that the theoretical position on which the research was based – be it "functionalism," "diffusionism," or "culture-and-personality" (Naroll 94) – would profoundly influence the research results. These concerns would lead to controversies about anthropological research in the 1970s and '80s, raising questions not only about colonialism but also about ethics. As Carpenter realized, the concerns also raised questions about mediation. If culture were to be considered data, or information, this perception would have to issue from the realization that, in the words of Pamela Sandstrom, "Information is part of an ongoing, organic cultural system, not a commodity that can easily be divorced from its meaningful context or content."[26] Sandstrom goes on to note that some anthropologists, such as Roy Rappaport, in his study of the Tsembaga people of New Guinea,[27] invoke the cybernetic model of culture as feedback in order to understand the relations between the human and the environmental. Carpenter anticipated this approach in his focus on technology as the third, mediating, factor in the relationship between the human and the environmental. Context is crucial in determining the relevance of data, and that context includes the mediation of the data. If an analytical approach is derived "from book culture" it will have "little relevance in a world shaped by electronic media, and little appeal to a generation ... interested in pattern, not atomized detail, and seeking relevant approaches to deal with existing data, not more data."[28]

These comments alluded, albeit indirectly, to the cracks that were beginning to appear in the facade of anthropological research. In 1961, Michel Foucault had contemplated the "death" of "Man" in his complementary (and unpublished) thesis,[29] a notion to which he would give iconic status in 1966 via the concluding words to *Les Mots et les Choses* that "Man" had been written in sand at the edge of the ocean and that this writing was in the process of being washed away. What Foucault did not grant attention to in that conclusion, however, was the writing itself – the idea that the epistemic changes in discursive practices that he had articulated were in fact the product of shifts in media. McLuhan, following Innis, had made this point forcefully in *The Gutenberg Galaxy* (1962): "By the meaningless sign, linked to the meaningless sound, we have built the shape and meaning of Western man" (50). Two years later, he proposed that "Man" be understood as relational to technologies of mediation, and it is arguably to Carpenter that he owed the anthropological extension of this insight, which goes some way to addressing why *Understanding Media* took such a broad approach to mediation – from clothing to clocks, from cinema to TV. Carpenter would likewise focus on media in his response to the questioning of anthropological practices that emerged in the ensuing decades.

Understanding McLuhan

While Carpenter was teaching at San Fernando, McLuhan published two major books, *The Gutenberg Galaxy* (1962) and *Understanding Media* (1964). The latter was a revised version of McLuhan's *Report on Project in Understanding New Media*, prepared for the United States Office of Education on behalf of the National Association of Educational Broadcasters. Carpenter often claimed a degree of authorship of *Understanding Media*, stating that there is a variation in tone in that book that

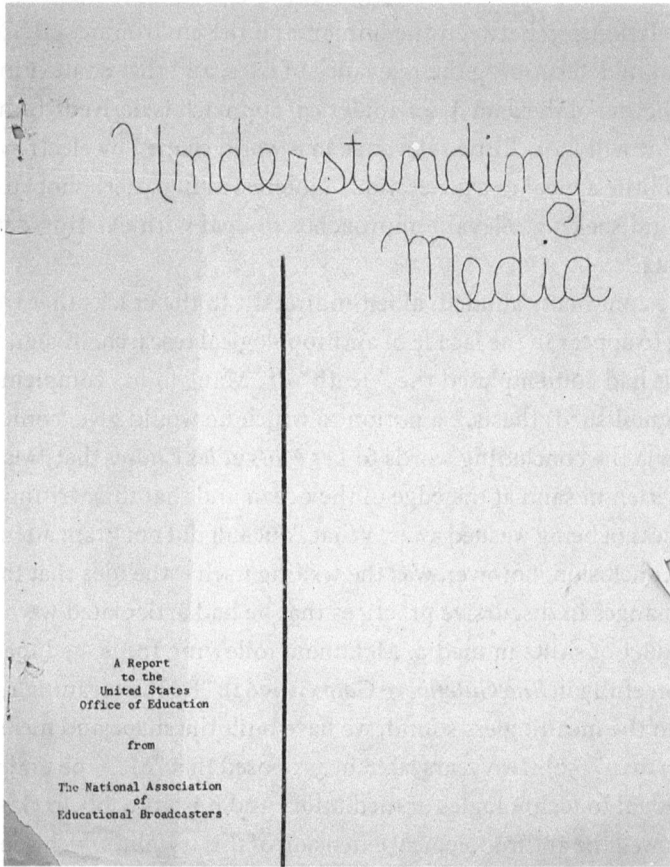

Figure 3.2 McLuhan's *Report on Project in Understanding New Media*, prepared for the United States Office of Education on behalf of the National Association of Educational Broadcasters, 1960.

is accounted for by the unacknowledged revisions he made to McLuhan's drafts. Carpenter's papers, deposited in the National Anthropological Archives held by the Smithsonian Institution, contain two copies of the report, but neither is annotated by Carpenter. There is underlining in red and blue pencil, and "X"s in the margins, but nothing else. Nor is there evidence of Carpenter's revisions to the drafts of *Understanding Media* that McLuhan was sending him. This was not for lack of importuning by McLuhan. He repeatedly wrote to Carpenter, asking for comments on the work in progress. On the draft of the section about "Money," McLuhan writes, "Dear Ted, will try to send you these drafts of the sections of the McGraw book. [McGraw-Hill published *Understanding Media*.] Haven't got rolling yet. Do comment."[30] In the section about "Number," McLuhan writes, "Check me out on this, Ted." In a letter dated 29 May 1961, McLuhan writes, "Am working on Understanding Media for hard covers. Be glad of your suggestions." On Thursday, 5 July 1962, McLuhan asks Carpenter to "give [him] any hints about form of these sections that you can do without bother ... Should I <u>avoid</u> inter-relating? Dont [*sic*] see how its [*sic*] possible. Is it good idea to bang away at the visual as child of literacy and father of the mechanical? ... Do you think of ways of strengthening the fact of technology as <u>extension</u> of our physical bodies? ... Have just done section on the wheel but Corinne [McLuhan's wife] hasn't typed it. Must have about 30 sections. Tell me titles of any that occur to you that I'm not likely to have selected."[31] On 14 September 1962, McLuhan writes, "Hey Ted Help! What's the best order for <u>all</u> the chapters? Please give an opinion before they get frozen."[32] On 9 October, McLuhan writes to Carpenter, "Haven't even heard whether you got the last 10 or so chapters of Und. Media. Had hoped to have some comments and suggestions from you before it got sent off to type-setters. Reassure us that you are all OK there Ted!"[33] On 5 November 1962, McLuhan writes to Carpenter, "Am now finalizing media mss. so really need prose comments and suggestions you have made as you read the thing."[34] In January of 1963, in a letter about the "tribal force" of electronic media, McLuhan writes, "You could help a lot in these matters for <u>Und Media</u> book Ted. Hope you get a breather to make a note or two on that mss."[35] In February of 1963, McLuhan writes, "Please send along comments on Und. Media soon, since I've got to finalize it for McGraw-Hill right away. They plan it for September."[36] On 2 June 1963, McLuhan tells Carpenter, "Corinne is right now beginning the final typing of <u>Und</u>. <u>Media</u>: <u>The Extensions of Man</u>. Or do you prefer: <u>The Ext of Man</u>: <u>Understanding Media</u>? Have to get it done before June 17."[37] Carpenter replied (as noted above, in chapter 2) that McLuhan should use the subtitle as the title, but McLuhan ultimately demurred. McLuhan's blandishments came to an end with a letter written from Detroit on 4 July 1964 telling Carpenter that "Und. Media sold out (4000 copies) in less than a month."[38] One can understand that Carpenter would have had a sense of ownership about the *Report*,

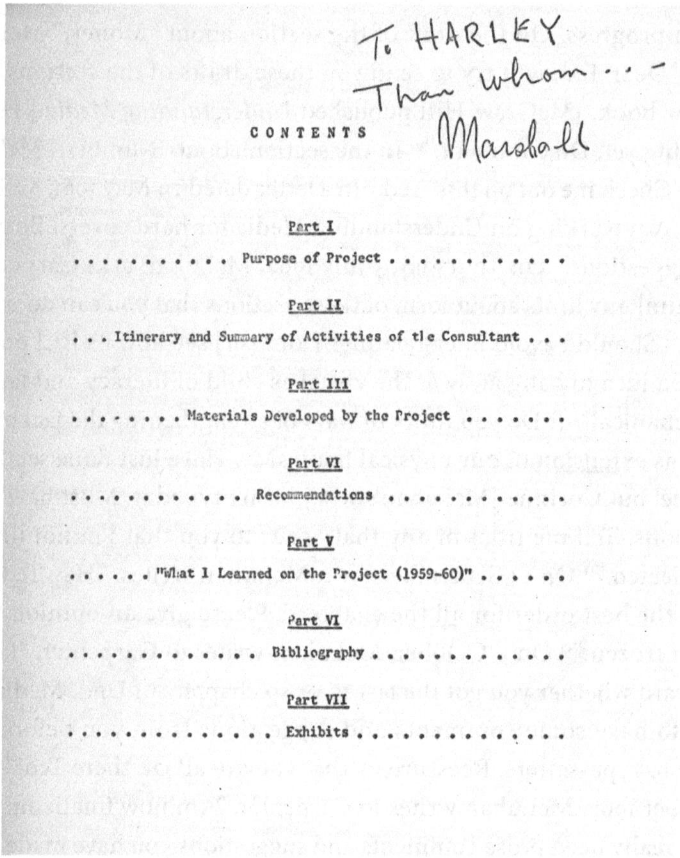

To HARLEY
Than whom ... -
Marshall

C O N T E N T S

Part I
. . . . Purpose of Project . . . .

Part II
. . . Itinerary and Summary of Activities of the Consultant . . .

Part III
. . . . Materials Developed by the Project . . . .

Part VI
. . . . Recommendations . . . .

Part V
. . . . . . "What I Learned on the Project (1959-60)" . . . . . .

Part VI
. . . . Bibliography . . . .

Part VII
. . . . Exhibits . . . .

Figure 3.3 Handwritten dedication to Harley Parker
in *Understanding Media*. Copy in the collection of the
Koerner Library of the University of British Columbia.

in that the media experiment conducted at Ryerson Polytechnic formed a significant part of it, and that a text written by Carpenter as part of that experiment is reproduced in the report as "material used in briefing the students" but without Carpenter's name attached. (Carpenter is nowhere mentioned in the *Report*.) This may have led to Carpenter's comments about authoring parts of *Understanding Media* (which is the handwritten title on Carpenter's copy of the *Report*).[39] Yet it was not to Carpenter, but to Harley Parker, that McLuhan dedicated a copy with the handwritten words "To HARLEY - - Than Whom ... Marshall."

Explorations Redux

Although Carpenter claimed he had wanted to "bury" *Explorations* after his move to California, it continued to haunt him, and he published a
number of items in the etiolated version of the journal edited by McLuhan
for the *Varsity Graduate* alumni magazine of the University of Toronto.
"Eskimo Masks: The Audience as Artist" was published in the Summer
1964 issue ("E" 10) and relates Carpenter's attempt to make a film about
masks he had encountered in the Arctic. (He had that same year worked
with Jacob Bronowski on the film *College* that encouraged college students
to pursue the "classroom without walls" concept in higher education.)[40] In
the article he writes, "We make machines in our own image. They are not
neutral instruments, but extensions of ourselves, with our biases, our ways
of perceiving and responding. The standard movie camera is designed and
used with all the visual conventions of our society. Even when we film a
totally alien subject, we do to it what we have already done to nature: we
record it in our own visual language. Our task, then, was first to experience
Eskimo [sic] masks, then to create instruments and techniques which could
record that experience without violation" (54). Carpenter articulates here
the fundamental paradox of anthropological study, namely that when a
non-native enters a native society, that society is immediately changed, rendering problematical the proposed research. "Here was the film problem.
It was easy enough to film the masks as if they were book illustrations or
gallery displays or dining-room décor, letting our eyes inspect them as they
were made to move for us. But letting them move on their own terms, en-
gender their own relations, make their own statements – this proved far
more demanding" (55). What Carpenter specifically added to this debate
was the focus on recording media, with the argument that they are not at all
neutral in the records they produce. What he did not envision at this point
was fieldwork done in collaboration with those the anthropologist was
studying, although in Papua New Guinea he would move in that direction.

In a film Carpenter contributed to while at San Fernando Valley State
College, the response to this problem is framed in terms of the removal
of the filmmaker (and anthropologist) as much as possible from the film.[41]
The documentary film *Georgia Sea Island Singers* (1963) presents African-
American songs and dances performed on St Simon's Island off the coast

of Georgia (USA)[42] as a form of cultural retrieval, the performances said to be a direct inheritance of nineteenth-century practices. The film begins in acoustic space with voice-over from one of the performers, and a text scrolls describing St Simon's Island as being a haven, until recently, for African-American communities, noting that it is still possible to hear on the island "spirituals ... as they were sung, perhaps a century or more ago." The singers then perform a number of these spirituals and also dance; one performer uses a stick to keep time. From time to time, singers' images are superimposed on the action; the overall effect of these techniques is a film that is much more "cinematic" than "documentarian." Describing the joy of spiritual renewal, one of the performers says, "When you sing, you sing; when you pray, you pray; when you dance, you dance; but when you shout, you shout" (7' 53"). One of the songs is preceded by the text: "God gave Noah / The rainbow sign, / Saying, No more water. / Fire next time" (11' 54"), taken from the spiritual "Mary Don't You Weep," which provided James Baldwin with the title of his 1963 book of essays *The Fire Next Time* that, like the film, was produced during a period of heightened protests against segregation.[43] The film ends with all the performers being identified with text while drumming, singing, and handclapping continue on the soundtrack: John Davis, Emma Ramsay, Henry Morrison, Mabel Hillary, and Bessie Jones.[44] The names of the filmmakers then appear: Archer Goodwin, Edmund Carpenter, Bess Lomax Hawes, Alan Lomax, Stanley Croner, Isidore Mankofsky, Fred Hudson, and William Varney.[45] Bess Lomax Hawes was Carpenter's colleague at San Fernando Valley; like her brother, Alan Lomax, an ethnomusicologist who had studied with Ray Birdwhistell, she was a folklorist who specialized in folksong.[46] In her memoir, *Sing It Pretty*, Bess Lomax Hawes writes of her encounter with "a brilliant anthropologist [who] was developing an experimental curriculum for the teaching of undergraduate anthropology based on examinations of and experiences with the art forms of all societies. His name was Dr. Edmund Carpenter ... I learned an incredible amount from Ted ... foremost of all to take pleasure and strength from my unusual background and not to worry so much about my lack of standard academic preparation ... 'By doing, you learn to do.'"[47]

Carpenter reflected on a number of the critical issues in anthropology that had come to the fore during his time at San Fernando Valley College in his comments on a lecture series presented at the Museum and

Laboratories on Ethnic Arts and Technology, UCLA, during the 1965–66 academic year. The lecture series, "Individual Creativity and Tribal Norms in Non-Western Arts,"[48] was convened on the occasion of a considerable donation of tribal arts by the Wellcome Trust to the university. Speakers included Robert Goldwater, professor of fine arts at NYU and director of the (now defunct) Museum of Primitive Art in New York ("Judgments of Primitive Art, 1905–1965"), William Bascom, professor of anthropology at Berkeley ("Creativity and Style in African Art"), Ignacio Bernal, director of the Museo Nacional de Antropología in Mexico City ("Individual Artistic Creativity in Pre-Columbian Mexico"), William Fagg, deputy keeper of ethnography in the British Museum ("The African Artist"), Adrian Gerbrands, professor of cultural anthropology at the University of Leiden ("The Concept of Style in Non-Western Art"), and Jean Guiart, directeur d'études (Religions Océaninnes) at the École Pratique des Hautes Études in Paris ("The Concept of the Norm in the Art of Some Oceanian Societies").

Daniel Biebuyck, who introduces the volume of published lectures,[49] states that one of the major issues in addressing tribal art is that of classification: the "methodology that underlies stylistic classifications is often lacking in consistency and rigidity" (1), a key problem being the tendency to focus on similarities at the expense of differences, and to associate tribal art with a timeless past. Another problem is acculturation: "some component groups are more exposed to outside influences and eager to incorporate some of the extraneous art elements than others" (5), an issue that Carpenter flagged repeatedly with reference to Inuit art.[50] Citing Malraux's *The Voices of Silence*, Biebuyck notes that tribal artists tend to create forms, and not merely reproduce them (6). A contentious issue is the word "primitive," which Robert Goldwater argues has positive connotations among art historians, but less positive among anthropologists, and he seeks to resolve "the profound misunderstandings and the assorted antagonisms that have divided anthropologists from artists and from art historians in their discussions about the primitive arts" (25). Another problem that arises is the lack of documentation of tribal art. "Thousands of pieces that are in collectors' hands or in museum vaults have never been made public" (95), comments Jean Guiart, and Ralph Altman (one of the commentators, along with Carpenter) states that "even famous collections made by men as prominent as Captains Cook or Vancouver have never been published" (187–8).

The focus in this introduction and in the book as a whole is on art as occupying a category distinct from other aspects of culture, an assertion with which Carpenter takes issue in his comments. Altman likewise notes that Thomas McIlwraith (Carpenter's former head of department at the University of Toronto) does not use the word "art" in the 400 pages of his two-volume study *The Bella Coola Indians* (188). As Carpenter states, "The concept 'art' is alien to most, perhaps all, preliterate people" (203). Carpenter quotes a comment made by Claude Lévi-Strauss about the "Kwakiutl [Kwakwaka'wakw] Indian whom Boas sometimes invited to New York to serve him as an informant" (203). Uninterested in the city's skyscrapers and automobiles, "he reserved all his intellectual curiosity for the dwarfs, giants, and bearded ladies that were at the time exhibited in Times Square, for automats, and for the brass balls decorating staircase bannisters; all these things challenged his own culture, and it was that culture alone he was seeking to recognize in certain aspects of ours."[51] "Are we equally restricted," asks Carpenter, "in our approach to ethnic arts?" (203). Whereas in literate societies, "art is viewed as a storehouse of experience" (203), in the tribal contexts with which he is familiar, art is a factor of everyday experience. "When Andy Warhol recently offered to sign any object, including dinners, clothes, and what-have-you, he illustrated a point tribal peoples have never doubted: Art and Life are interchangeable" (204). By this, Carpenter means that the "distinction between art and custom is not nearly so great among tribal peoples as it is with us" (204). One way in which to observe this would be to film a given ritual:

I mean *film*, in the full sense, exploiting the bias of the medium itself. The *effect* of such a film would be quite different from the effect of the standard artbook or museum display; I suggest it could be closer to the one experienced by the original participants. All translation is imperialistic, film no less than print. But certain media lend themselves kindly, and others do not, to rendering particular experiences, and the problem is to know the media and the experiences. This involves more than simply utilizing new media. Older media have been recast in new roles. Joyce's *Finnegans Wake* and Eames's multiscreen exhibit warrant the most intensive study by anthropologists and curators. (204)

This is a key statement of Carpenter's anthropological principles in its insistence on the role of media in anthropological documentation. Carpenter acknowledges that all media have biases and that film's "bias may turn out to be equally marked. Our recent awareness that print is not, as we once believed, a neutral medium for recording 'reality' has made us conscious of the bias of other media as well, and of the complexity of all cross-media translation" (213). Ultimately, as he puts it, "Boas is more Boas than Haida" (212). Carpenter's position regarding the role of media in anthropology is markedly more nuanced than the one put forward half a decade later by Margaret Mead. Writing about "Visual Anthropology in a Discipline of Words," Mead seeks to place the anthropological enterprise squarely within the context of "preserving records of the vanishing customs and human beings of this earth," whether they be "inbred, preliterate populations" or "in the depths of a Swiss canton."[52] Film could do this so much better than note-taking, writes Mead, yet film remains under-used in anthropological research. In part, this is because anthropologists tend to rely on the words of informants, in part because they lack the technical skills for filmmaking, in part because of a feeling that films should be artistic rather than scientific, and in good part because the discipline does not support "new" technologies of research. Mead notes the problematics of ethnographical film that simply reproduces the cultural assumptions of the filmmaker, noting, however, the beginnings of a trend toward "the articulate, imaginative inclusion in the whole process of the people who are being filmed – inclusion in the planning and programming, in the filming itself, and in the editing of the film" (8). Part of the reason for the urgency with which she is making these proposals is the threat of global homogenization represented by "a planetary communications system" (9), placing "the little traditions" (9) in grave danger of disappearing. Mead concludes by addressing the bias of media, arguing that if a move camera or tape recorder is set up and left to run on its own, such bias will be eliminated. Here is the greatest difference in her position and that of Carpenter, who was aware that the bias resided in the medium itself.[53]

Anthropology's disciplinary bias toward the visual was itself a product of media history, Carpenter argues in his essay on "primitive" art. Citing McLuhan's *Gutenberg Galaxy, Understanding Media,* and *Counterblast*

(1968), as well as Carpenter and McLuhan's *Explorations* journal and *Explorations in Communication*, Carpenter states that the medium that defines "primitive" is literacy. The phonetic alphabet and the printing press initiated an enthronement of sight that "destroyed [the] harmonic orchestration of the senses" (206), a process that was reversed by the accession of electronic media. "The telegraph, for example, when mated with the printing press, created the newspaper format with its discontinuous juxtapositions of simultaneous images" (207). It was precisely this re-orchestration of the sensorium that "attracted Parisian and Bauhaus artists to African art ... not ... love of primitivism" (206). There is a parallel here with current debates in anthropology, writes Carpenter, arising from the increasing involvement of anthropological subjects in their own social and cultural analyses. "Anthropologists, most of whom are nineteenth century in outlook, do not know what to do with such data ... So they put them in a new category: Native Autobiographical Reports. One cannot read these inside reports, with their descriptions of sensory awareness and involvement, without realizing how misleading the traditional, outside 'observations' have been. My impression of much African art is that it should be embraced, all senses involved, not simply viewed" (207–8). This notion of sensory involvement would become the driving force behind Carpenter's *Upside Down* exhibitions half a century later. As he states, "Once, with visibility zero, I traveled rapidly along a dangerous coastline, guided by an Eskimo who navigated by the feel of the wind and the smell of fog, by sounds of surf and nesting birds, and particularly by the feel of the pattern of waves and currents against his buttocks. With such interplay and interpenetration of senses, there can be no isolation of one sense" (208).

In his comments to the tribal art volume, Carpenter also refers to his 1966 publication in "Explorations," "If Wittgenstein Had Been an Eskimo,"[54] where he writes about the famous duck/rabbit perceptual conundrum, referred to by Ludwig Wittgenstein, and by E.H. Gombrich in his *History of Art*. (Carpenter included the image in the "Witnesses" room that he curated for the Menil Collection; see chapter 8 below.) The relationship between figure and ground demands that we see this image either as a rabbit or a duck, the oscillation between the two being a defining element of surrealist art according to Gombrich. Carpenter asks, however, if these assumptions are cross-cultural, would they have held up "If Wittgenstein Had Been

FIGURE 2

IF WITTGENSTEIN HAD BEEN AN ESKIMO

EDMUND CARPENTER

FIGURE 1

According to the philosopher Wittgenstein and the art historian Gombrich, we cannot see both rabbit and duck simultaneously. Illusion, Gombrich says, consists in the conviction that there is only one way of interpreting the visual pattern in front of us. Though we may switch rapidly from rabbit to duck, we cannot experience alternate readings at the same time. A shape cannot be seen apart from its interpretation.

Discovering the rabbit in the duck produces, according to Wittgenstein, a surprise not produced by the recognition of either image alone.

"Ambiguity—rabbit or duck?—is clearly the key to the whole problem of image reading," writes Gombrich. "I had a hunch when I wrote *The Story of Art* that the explorations by surrealist artists of the ambiguity of shapes, the game of 'rabbit or duck?', would provide the best possible entry into the labyrinth of representation."

The situation provides opportunity for comparison. Here two men, both famous for their analytical investigations, choose the same illustration for intensive analysis and agree on its interpretation. Each reader can play the game himself and test the Wittgenstein-Gombrich conclusions.

However, instead of asking if Wittgenstein's students perceive as he does, let us ask how someone from a different background, say an Eskimo, perceives visual puns. Can he see the rabbit and duck simultaneously?

Occurrence of Visual Puns

I showed Dali's *Paranoiac Face* (Figure 2) to several Eskimo hunters. Painting was alien to them, but visual punning was not: they showed the craftsman's appreciation of skillful work.

Visual punning is immensely popular in certain preliterate cultures (e.g., Figures 3, 4). It was practiced by Surrealists and is employed occasionally in advertising and in Pop Art (Figure 5). A number of books for children are punning exercises, including one where the puns are simultaneously visual and verbal. A comic strip series in the *New York Herald*, 1903-1905, was designed to be viewed from left to right, then turned upside down to finish (Figure 6). In a recent French film, the camera closes in on a traffic sign reading *Danger*, until it reads *ange*, and separates *Passage* into *Pas sage*.

FIGURE 3

FIGURE 4

50

51

Figure 3.4 Carpenter, "If Wittgenstein Had Been an Eskimo," 1966.

an Eskimo"? Far from being an anomaly in Inuit culture, visual punning is common, based on a simultaneity of perception outside the fixed point of view of literate culture. "Preliterate peoples often integrate grammars we conceptually separate ... The visual aspect is often only part of a pattern involving several senses" (54). Many Indigenous cultures engage with a juxtapositional epistemology – this *and* that, as with the Trickster figure,[55] who is both life *and* death, here *and* there, male *and* female. This is the domain par excellence of visual punning – of having two non-aligned images within the representational plane. In Inuit art, there is no motivation "to abstract single visual images, one at a time, from the dynamic flux of experience" (59). Referring to a composite mask (which Carpenter identifies in *Eskimo* as "Magemut Eskimo, south of lower Yukon River, Alaska"), Carpenter suggests the "soul" is configured here as an eye that would be perceived as a composite whole, its multivalence asserting itself through movement when

Figure 3.5
Composite mask
/ visual pun.
Magemut mask,
reproduced
from Carpenter,
Eskimo, 1959.

the mask is worn. What encouraged visual punning among the Inuit is their attunement to acoustic space, which is simultaneous in its sensory interrelations. This multisensuousness presents itself as a problem for traditional anthropologists when they encounter anthropological studies produced by natives. Carpenter also finds this mode of representation to be present in surrealist art (an intuition he would realize in the "Witnesses" room at the Menil Collection), and in marginalized modalities of non-Indigenous art, from surrealism to children's books to comic strips, such as one in *The New York Herald* (1903–05) that "was designed to be viewed from left to right, then turned upside down to finish" (51). As with these works, Inuit artistic modalities were intentional: "their existence and form were artistic decisions" (63), albeit decisions taken within a specific mediatic context.

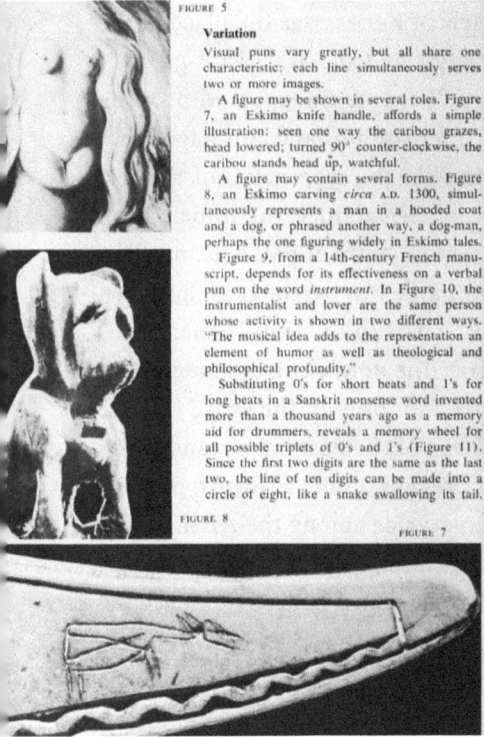

Figure 3.6 Carpenter, "If Wittgenstein Had Been an Eskimo," 1966.

The "Cold War Avant-Garde"

The developments in electronic media in the mid-1960s, with special reference to computation, were having a dramatic effect on the understanding of art, including tribal art, as Carpenter had suggested. *Image Sign Symbol*,[56] edited by Gyorgy Kepes (**E1**), takes up this shift, though essays by Carpenter, Lawrence K. Frank (**E4**), Siegfried Giedion (**E6**), and others do not consistently support Kepes's thesis that the move toward "the world as a communication network" (1) was being accompanied by an increasing dominance of the visual. John Blakinger's study of Kepes, *Undreaming the Bauhaus*, argues that Kepes was the fulfilment of McLuhan's prophecy that "the artist tends now to move from the ivory tower to the control tower of society" (11, quoting McLuhan, *Understanding Media*). The central question this posed for the post-WWII artist, in the view of Kepes, was the place of the artist in an increasingly technocratic society, the "Cold War avant-garde."[57] For Kepes, fields such as anthropology "became unexpected proving grounds for aesthetics, often through interdisciplinary languages that seamlessly crossed intellectual boundaries, like the cybernetics of Norbert Wiener, the systems theory of Ludwig von Bertalanffy, the information theory of Claude Shannon, and the common study of patterns, models, and symbols" (12–13). The Cold War avant-garde was paradoxical, however, since it sought to preserve values from the past in order to "[defend] society against the effects of the future" (11). The new, electronic media, in other words, presented a rearview mirror, not only in the sense that we perceive the present through the modalities of the past but because electronic media perform a vast retrieval of previous cultural forms, making them new again. This was Carpenter's experience among the Aivilik, who encountered the machine not as a mechanical sequence (intake, compression, power, exhaust) but mythically, as a constellated pattern of interfaces.

The methodology through which Kepes sought to address this multifoliate network was "the matching of seemingly unrelated images and ideas through a common visual or intellectual relationship ... [producing] a concatenation of visual ideas" (16). As Blakinger notes, "It may be tempting to reject this particular [form of] comparison as false equivalence" (16), as in fact many of Kepes's contemporaries did, starting with McLuhan, who argued that in the electronic era, art had become a matter of making (poiesis), not matching: "Making sense is never matching or mere one-to-one correspondence[,] which is an assumption of visual bias. For the *ear* makes an 'acoustic space structure' ... like a musical surround."[58] Tensions between visual and acoustic space are evident in *Sign Symbol Image*. Blakinger notes, for example, that John Cage sought overtly to undermine Kepes's focus on the visual in *Sign Symbol Image* with a musical composition, *Cartridge Music* (1960);[59] while the "score" is certainly a sign, it signifies as acoustic space, rather than as the linear, sequential, teleological space of literate culture.

The essays in *Sign Symbol Image* are contextualized by cybernetics and information theory (6): Lawrence K. Frank's lead-off chapter, "The World as a Communication Network," references Norbert Wiener in its first sentence; Heinz von Foerster (originator of second-order cybernetics) writes about "biological computation" (42); Ludwig von Bertalanffy (one

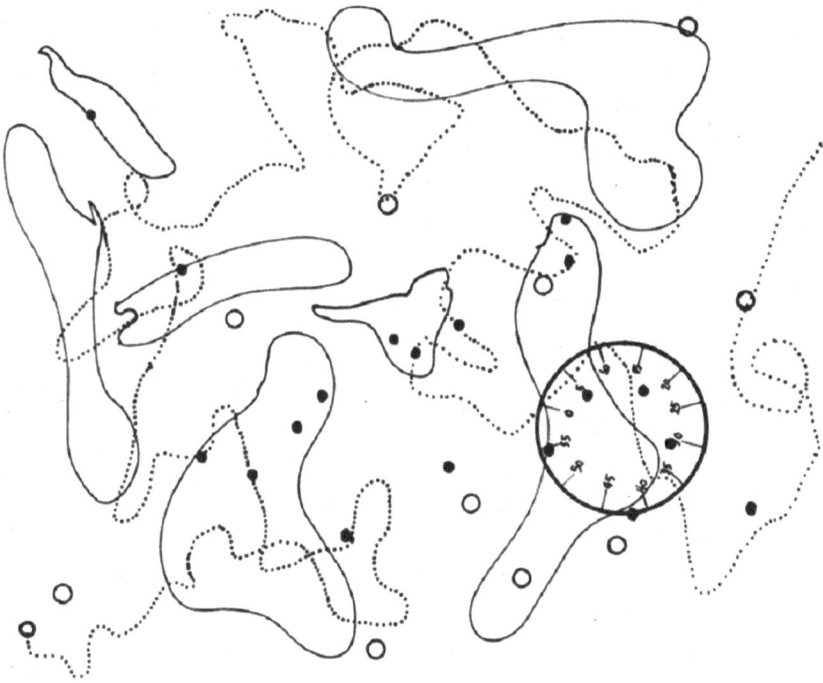

Figure 3.7 John Cage, *Cartridge Music*, 1960.

of the founders of general systems theory) invokes algorithms (276) in a discussion of symbols. A number of the contributors are psychologists; a major theme of the volume is the role of signs and symbols in cognition, the cognitive function in humans discussed as a technology, as in von Foerster's chapter, and in von Bertalanffy's reference to "psychological technology" (278). The bias throughout is towards the visual, however; while Frank makes reference to the "cosmic noise" (1) produced by the infinity of signs characteristic of modern life, that noise ultimately enters the visual domain, as in Pavlov's experiments, where "the bell became a *sign* to alert the dog" (1). Ultimately, thought is deemed to be visual.

Sigfried Giedion sounds a different note, however, writing, "Ours is a period of transition: a transition from the mechanistic age to the electronic age; a transition from the tangible, logical laws to intangible, irrational phenomena of the invisible world, from the normal bodies to the particles of the atoms, which cannot be seen by our eyes, but only the effect evaluated" (78). Carpenter's chapter discovers this new world in the mythic past of the Inuit. "Image Making in Arctic Art"[60] implicitly critiques the cultural bias inherent in the volume's valorization of the visual, while redirecting the volume's discussion of visual space to a consideration of acoustic space:

> To Western minds, the "monotony" of snow, ice, and darkness can often be depressing, even frightening. Nothing in particular stands out; there is no scenery in the sense in which we use the term. But the Eskimos do not see it in this way. They are not interested in scenery, but in action, existence. This is true to some extent of many people, but it is almost of necessity true for the Eskimos, for nothing in their world easily defines itself or is separable from the general background. What exists, the Eskimos themselves must struggle to bring into existence. Theirs is a world which has to be conquered with each act and statement, each carving and song. (208)

The key factor that distinguishes acoustic from visual space is literacy, a distinction that emerged powerfully to Carpenter in his study of Arctic art in Siberia:

> The contrast was remarkable: here was the most completely non-literate art tradition known, seen against a setting of total literacy. For Soviet Russia is the final, most sterile expression of literacy ... Everything is segmental and replaceable – especially people ... Everything visual requires a single point of view ... One cannot enter into an experience, complete it, modify it, interpret it ... Literacy creates a "middle distance"; it separates observer from observed, actor from action; it leads to single perspective, fixed observation, singleness of tone, and introduces into poetry and music the counterpart of three-dimensional perspective in art, all, of course, artistic expressions of the Western notion of individualism, every element being now related to the unique point of view of the individual at a given moment. (214)

Whereas the phonetic alphabet induced a "one-thing-at-a-time analytic awareness in perception" (214), the "Eskimo artist emphasizes all-at-onceness ... His mythic forms of explanation explicate all levels of any situation at the same time" (216). Carpenter stresses the tactility of Inuit art, designed to be held in the hand and felt, consistent with the "non-optical structuring of space" characteristic of Inuit culture. Carpenter likens this art to modernist works by Paul Klee, who sought to "[structure] space by sound" (220); for the Inuit, "the oral tradition is so strong as to make the eye subservient to the ear" (220). Even the architecture of the igloo is sub-servient to the "'wrap-around' aspect of auditory space ... Eskimos, with a magnificent disregard for environmental determinism, open up rather than enclose space" (221). Although Carpenter had made these arguments in other works, the context of *Sign Symbol Image* gives his arguments a new direction, especially in the context of the Cold War avant-garde. Taken in this context, Carpenter's insights into Inuit art constitute a critique of the technologization of the human (whose spectre Jack Jones had raised in **E8**) that underpins Kepes's volume, as well as the Western-centric orientation of the volume, its failure to incorporate media theory into its arguments, and its disregard of the concept of acoustic space.

4

The Fordham Affair

A YEAR AFTER THE PUBLICATION of *Sign Symbol Image*, the San Fernando Valley program in anthropology and art was closed. McLuhan, however, provided Carpenter (who was on his way to work at the Nationalmuseet, Copenhagen ["Sea," 259]) with an opening of sorts by inviting him, along with Harley Parker and Eric McLuhan (McLuhan's son), to Fordham University as part of a research team to be funded through his appointment as the Schweitzer Chair in the Humanities. The result, however, would be a rift in the relationship of Carpenter and McLuhan as the result of a controversy over the authorship of an article in a fashion magazine, a rift that led to larger questions of provenance in the work of Carpenter and McLuhan that emerge powerfully, if obliquely, in "That Not-So-Silent Sea."

McLuhan's work had been promoted at Fordham since the late 1950s by Father John Culkin, director of its Center for Communications, who became instrumental in McLuhan's accession to the chair in 1967. That year began productively for McLuhan. He had published the hugely successful *The Medium Is the Massage* (with Quentin Fiore and Jerome Agel), had *War and Peace in the Global Village* (again with Fiore and Agel)[1] and *Through the Vanishing Point* (with Harley Parker) in press, republished *Explorations* 8 with Something Else Press as *Verbi-Voco-Visual Explorations*,[2] and while at Fordham made the experimental film *Picnic in Space* (with Harley Parker). That same year, Princeton University put forward an offer to microfilm *Explorations* 1–6.[3] This hardly supports Carpenter's statement that the "Fordham effort collapsed" ("Sea," 258). The Schweitzer Chair[4] awarded McLuhan a research grant of US$100,000 – worth over US$850,000 today.

Although McLuhan's salary would be US$40,000 (equivalent to circa US$330,000 today), this was at a time when English professors were earning US$14,000 (circa US$120,000 today).[5] These figures were controversial, as was the increasing disorganization of McLuhan's lectures, which presaged McLuhan's diagnosis with a brain tumour. Immediately scheduled for surgery, McLuhan asked Carpenter to complete an article he was writing for *Harper's Bazaar* on fashion. The result was the most controversial aspect of the relationship of the two scholars. Philip Marchand, McLuhan's principal biographer, writes that the *Harper's Bazaar* article, "although blazoned with McLuhan's name ... was almost entirely the work of Ted Carpenter" (198), while adding that the piece was comprised of "shrewdly counterfeited McLuhanisms" (198). This recalls the heady days of the Explorations seminar, when ideas were being traded with intellectual abandon and without any sense of academic ownership, but those days were over.

If a fashion magazine appears to be an odd venue for a media philosophical disquisition, we need to remember that philosophers such as Sartre were introduced to America in the pages of *Harper's Bazaar*.[6] "McLuhan Looks at Fashion" begins with a reference to "tribal men," as McLuhan's chapter on "Clothing" in *Understanding Media* begins with a reference to "tribal societies," but the article as a whole is more reflective of ideas in Carpenter's writings on tribal art. The reflections on women in the article could not have been written by McLuhan, who was incapable of describing the body of a woman as "firm, but filled with tremulous spirit" (148). There are comments which recall McLuhan's article on "The Future of Sex": "Today, as we re-enter the tribal world, sharp differences between the sexes ... disappear rapidly ... Men and women dress more alike. They share hair-styles. Men wear jewelry. They are interested in scents, hair dyes, cosmetics. This disturbs older, literate types who keep saying 'You can't tell the difference,' and then slap their knees" (148–9).[7] A reference to the "visual pun" repeats Carpenter's observations elsewhere on Inuit art. "To the blind, all things are sudden" is referenced by McLuhan in *Understanding Media*. Allusions to the "Banibara of Africa" (157) clearly draw on Carpenter's anthropological orientation. The distinction between "light on" and "light through" is made by McLuhan in *Through the Vanishing Point*. The discussion of a "Kwakiutl [Kwakwaka'wakw] mask" (162) once again references Carpenter's anthropological research. Overall, one has the sense of a dialogue of ideas associated with Carpenter and with McLuhan. It was Carpenter himself who confirmed this interplay of ideas in a comment he attached to the copyright page of *They Became What They Beheld*, a book that reproduces a number of passages from the *Harper's Bazaar* article: "The text owes much to Marshall McLuhan, who, in fact, co-authored portions of an earlier version,"[8] although this comment raises more questions than it answers. Perhaps Carpenter is referring to the fact that McLuhan had drawn Carpenter's attention to Mark Schorer's *Blake: The Politics of Vision* in a letter dated 14 January 1961, commenting that Schorer "strikes media theme which he pursues throughout. Blake poet of perception: 'They became what they beheld' his theme. Not mysticism. Saw technology as extended sense and faculty."[9] McLuhan adds that he will draw on Blake in the epilogue to *The Gutenberg Galaxy*, telling Carpenter he will send him page proofs of *Galaxy* and "carbon of the Understanding Media job as rewritten for McGraw Hill [*sic*]."

An interview given by McLuhan to Gerald Emanuel Stearn that was published in *Encounter*[10] (one of the more notorious little magazines of the Cold War avant-garde, given its CIA funding) in 1967 and reprinted that same year, along with a letter from Carpenter to McLuhan, in *McLuhan: Hot and Cool*,[11] a collection of essays on McLuhan's work, is valuable for the light it casts on the McLuhan/Carpenter dialogue. McLuhan had written to Carpenter on 2 June 1963, asking Carpenter, "How about the Dell Hymes review of <u>Galaxy</u> in <u>Amer</u> <u>Anthrop</u>? Worth taking him up? ... He is bluffing. He is defending his own unconscious literate stake in a field that he doesn't understand ... Why didn't he tackle JC Carothers?"[12] *McLuhan: Hot and Cool* has a section devoted to *Explorations* that reprints a number of pages from **E8**, and the interview includes McLuhan's reflections on *Explorations* a decade after it ceased publication. What is extraordinary about the interview, however, is McLuhan's focus on anthropology, deriving in part from the hostile review in *American Anthropologist*[13] that is reprinted in the book. Hymes was a practitioner of linguistic anthropology associated with the focus on performativity in anthropological studies, and worked with Ray Birdwhistell at the University of Pennsylvania to develop a research field in the ethnography of communication that included electronic media. Reviewing *The Gutenberg Galaxy* under the rubric "Linguistics," Hymes states that the book "cannot be trusted as more than stimulation," with its "over-simplified view of types of society" that "gets facts wrong" (479) and that McLuhan takes "the contrast between oral and typographic communication ... to ludicrous extremes" (479). The review of a book subtitled "The Making of Typographic Man" ends with the uncomprehendingly naive comment that "it is good to see how attractively the book makes use of typographic resources" (479).

McLuhan, asked by Stearn how he became interested in media studies, replies that he was led in that direction by "artists [and] the new anthropological studies. As you become aware of the different modes of experience in other cultures – and watch them transformed by new, Western technologies – it is difficult to avoid observation" (266). In response to a question about *Explorations*, McLuhan replies, "We started *Explorations* when we felt we had something to say. We stopped it when we felt we had said it" (270). In reference to criticisms of the journal, McLuhan states that the "complaints about irregular, disconnected, irrational elements in *Explorations* show a complete unawareness. Connected sequential discourse, which is thought of as rational, is really visual. It has nothing to do with reason as such ... In the electric age we are moving into a world where not the connection but the interval becomes the crucial event in organization" (270). Stearn then moves on to Hymes's critique of *The Gutenberg Galaxy*, to which McLuhan replies, "One of the more unfortunate features of the entire anthropological enterprise in the twentieth century is that its practitioners are almost entirely and unconsciously literate. They approach structures of nonliterate and oral societies with many of the expectations and patterns which they have acquired from their own highly literate society. Margaret Mead and I have discussed this at some length ... Anthropologists, for example, assume that vision, as they perceive it in their Western mode, is normal to mankind, that other people see this way too" (272–3). In support of his critique of Hymes, McLuhan quotes a long letter from Carpenter:

Hymes is bluffing. He pretends that much is known about the shifting of sense ratios by the new extensions of man. The authorities he cites make no contribution to this subject, nor do anthropologists or linguists generally. They cannot even be trusted to recognize the significance of such an approach when they encounter it. Hymes is merely defending his own unconscious, literate stake in a field he doesn't understand.

Anthropologists see themselves as daring explorers, way out in front. Most are actually nineteenth century in outlook. They deal with data atomistically and feel free to abstract them and create regularities for them. Their visual models are highly ethnocentric, totally ill-suited to understanding non-literate patterns. Models offered by Joyce, Klee and Pound are ignored. The alienation theme of Man vs. Environment, so dear to the nineteenth century, survives among them like a watch ticking in the pocket of a dead man.

Yet anthropologists hold a monopoly on a body of data of prime importance to the understanding of environments as natural extensions of man. Their models blind them to the significance of these data; professionalism prevents them from accepting ideas which threaten existing management. Hymes' review is a classic example of this combined blindness and fear.

In objecting to McLuhan's forceful style, Hymes misses the point that technology is explicitness ... The sudden interest in linguistic decorum during the reign of James I arose when print made grammar clearly visible ... It was Western man, not McLuhan, who carried the individualizing capacity of print, and the lineal nature of thinking it fosters, to "ludicrous extremes" ... McLuhan suggests that lineal thinking alone is not capable of grasping and understanding our world in a global manner. He offers no single-minded, oversimplified exegesis, but opens the way for multiple models simultaneously applied. One obstacle to such an all-at-once analysis is the single-minded, oversimplified, obsolete approach which Hymes seems to be saying offers "an adequate view of human history." (273–4)

Carpenter had made a similar critique of anthropology and anthropologists in his essay on tribal art; what is significant here is his apparent repudiation of the linguistic model that had underpinned earlier work published in *Explorations*. While at Fordham, Carpenter had lectured on "Language and Culture as Ritual,"[14] where he expresses a performative theory of language that draws on the work of Alan Lomax and Bess Lomax, work that underpinned the film *Georgia Sea Island Singers*, a film suggesting that embodied communication precedes the development of speech. We are becoming aware of this now, suggests Carpenter, because we are in retreat from verbal communication as other modalities (such as mathematics) gain precedence. "Reality now begins for the scientist outside of verbal categories." Relatedly, the involving nature of electronic media reinvigorates ritual as a way of knowing, and "ritual is not ordered and ruled by words ... In the tribal world, the eye listens."

Carpenter's Fordham lecture suggests the confluence of Carpenter's and McLuhan's thinking about mediation. "Years ago," states McLuhan in the Stearn interview, "when I was working with Carpenter on anthropological matters, I used acoustic and auditory space frequently as a basic counterploy to visual Western man ... The Eskimo world is an ear one. When asked to draw maps, they draw areas they've never seen. From their kyacks [sic] they've heard water lapping against shores. They map by ear and it later proves quite adequate when checked by aerial photo ... Carpenter has remarked that anthropological materials are now beginning to be made up and published by natives themselves – their own stories are being retold by natives themselves. And the results are totally different from what the anthropologists said earlier" (275; I have changed the order of the quoted material here). This summarizes the central theme of Carpenter's *They Became What They Beheld.*

Wedded to the Mystery

An "Explorations" article that in many ways anticipates *They Became What They Beheld* was published by Carpenter in the Summer 1968 issue.[15] "We Wed Ourselves to the Mystery" continues Carpenter's polemical critique of anthropology with a *cri de coeur*: "I accept the old fashioned notion that the ethnologist is the twice-born spiritual adventurer whose fieldwork is nothing less than the spirit quest; that he exposes his dearest beliefs & habits to doubt & diversity, and returns changed by this intellectual ordeal. If he tells the truth about these experiences, he writes what is ultimately an autobiography: the metaphysics of me. If he carefully conceals what really happened to him, those experiences – inward & outward – he actually underwent or failed to undergo, then he writes the sort of intellectual foolishness currently popular in academic anthropology" (66). In an article that begins with a quotation from Claude Lévi-Strauss, Carpenter's critique of anthropologists for whom "the real world is not what is lived, but rather ... the underlying structures (laws) that govern appearances" (67) is pointed, and sets him at odds with both structural anthropology and its greatest living exponent. He was not alone in this evaluation. Edmund Leach (published in the first issue of *Explorations*) wrote in his 1970 introduction to the work of Lévi-Strauss, "Lévi-Strauss is a visionary, and the trouble with those who see visions is that they find it very difficult to recognise the plain matter of fact world which the rest of us see all around ... Lévi-Strauss seems to be more interested in an algebra of possibilities than in the empirical facts. "[16] What concerns Carpenter is that scientific study "leads to a rejection of the sensate world" (67); what is studied, in fact, is an "equivalent" to that which is being studied, but not the thing itself. For Carpenter, tribal art must be studied in context, that is, in terms of what it meant to those who produced it. And the first point that had to be made about that context is that it was not "art." Art in tribal contexts is environmental: every act takes on the role of art. Under the totalizing effect of electronic media, art is now assuming that role in Western culture, "environments" being a form of installation art, taking over an entire room in a gallery or an entire exhibition space. "To put a tomato can in the Guggenheim Museum, or to bring the unintended noises of the ordinary environment into the concert hall, is an important way of announcing that the environment itself is an art form, and that the total human condition can be considered as a work of art" (69). This is to understand art as a process, and not as an object. Carpenter quotes Laura Riding to the effect that "movement is strictly the language of life. It expresses nothing but the initial, living connotations of life. It is the earliest language'" (70). To greet the mystery of life is to engage with it outside the constraints of literacy. "We wed ourselves to the mystery," not "to conquer it or be conquered by it, but to greet it" (73). This is where anthropology should begin. "When the native artist combines color with sound, design with dance; when he mutes one sense while exploiting another; when he skilfully mixes & structures these varied sensory elements – let us credit him with intelligence and not condescendingly assume that what he has done might have been done better in words" (74). One might respond to that artwork with a film, or perhaps juxtapose it to other artworks from other cultures, both of which were procedures adopted by Carpenter.

Carpenter's critique of anthropology as an academic discipline was, ultimately, a critique of academia, which goes some way to addressing his increasing distance from university teaching. Having resigned from San

Fernando Valley State College "after an unseemly and bitter quarrel with the administration,"[17] Carpenter took up a one-year position in 1968 at the University of California, Santa Cruz, which had opened in 1966. The position, funded by the Carnegie Corporation, was in some ways an extension of the academic experiment he had been involved with at San Fernando, in that it sought to examine the role of the visual arts in post-secondary education, and this at a time when students in many parts of Europe and North America were agitating for university reform. "The New Languages" had been republished under Carpenter's name in *Readings on Creativity and Imagination in Literature and Language*[18] in 1968 (as had McLuhan's "Classroom Without Walls"), and in 1969, "The New Languages" was republished (along with McLuhan's "Classroom Without Walls" and "The Medium is the Message") in the more forcefully titled *Selected Educational Heresies*.[19] The volume published under the aegis of the Carnegie Corporation, however, was more comprehensive, and considerably more radical.

Proposals for Art Education (1970)[20] appeared under the editorship of Carpenter, Christopher Cornford (British artist and writer involved in nuclear disarmament campaigns and the early ecological movement), Sidney Simon (war artist and art teacher), and Robert Watts (British film producer who later worked on the *Star Wars* and *Indiana Jones* film series). The editors state that the volume seeks to address the questions *"What is art becoming? Why? What should art studies therefore become?"* and that "new urgencies demand new kinds of statement" (2). These new urgencies were visceral, manifesting themselves as "teargas drifting across the campus and students charging the administration building" ("Sea," 257). The volume consists of a section of era-defining quotations from a number of speakers invited to the university to contribute to the project, including James Ackerman (historian of Renaissance architecture), Rayner Banham (British architectural critic who wrote landmark studies of architectural ecologies in Los Angeles), Jacob Bronowski (Polish-British mathematician and philosopher famous for his BBC TV series *The Ascent of Man*), John Cage (artist, philosopher, and composer of aleatory music), Merce Cunningham (choreographer), Dan Flavin (minimalist artist who produced light sculptures with fluorescent tubes),[21] Allan Kaprow (creator and theorizer of Happenings), George Segal (pop artist), Leo Steinberg (American art critic), and Colin Young (British film educator). Quotations from these and other speakers appear under a number of rubrics: "World As

Is," "New Art," "Criticism and History," "University System," "Curriculum Structure," and "Art Curriculum." This section is followed by "Dialogues," which consists of transcriptions of tape-recorded conversations with students about the preceding topics. Essays by editors and speakers follow: Simon and Watts on "A Proposal for Higher Education," George Maciunas (founder of the Fluxus art movement) on "A Preliminary Proposal for a 3-Dimensional System of Information Storage and Presentation," Carpenter on "Art and the Declassification and Reclassification of Knowledge," Simon on the "Case History of a Course," followed by a very long article transcribing students' comments that includes a section on "McLuhan," and ending with a short essay by Watts titled "Ex-perimental Workshop." The volume is punctuated by large fold-outs that function as graffiti/commentary on the book as a whole, with quotations from 1960s luminaries such as Jann Wenner of *Rolling Stone* fame (founded in 1967).

The section comprised of quotations ("World as Is") reflects the general malaise of the time: rampant technology, increasing neuroses, capitalism gone mad, dissent, the generation gap. Buckminster Fuller is quoted as stating, "We will accelerate as rapidly into *yesterday* through archaeology as we do into *tomorrow* with astronautics" (4). Carpenter notes that, "Like sound, electricity penetrates walls, dissolves barriers" (3). McLuhan tells us that "The artist tends now to move from the ivory tower to the control tower of society" (4). Yves Klein urges us to "forget art altogether" (5), and Pete Townshend talks about why he decided to smash his guitar at the end of a performance (5). Abbie Hoffman offers the opinion that "only creeps listen to criticism" (6), and Sidney Simon laments that "ours is an age of overstatement" (8). Ackerman, referring to McLuhan, states that "The sure way to success in academic life is to be a little bit crazy" (10). And Susan Sontag argues that "Art today is a new kind of instrument, an instrument for modifying consciousness and organizing new modes of sensibility" (15).

Declassification and Reclassification

Carpenter's contribution, "Art and the Declassification and Reclassification of Knowledge," begins on a personal note: "It's easy to lose perspective in California. The sun is warm & life is casual. I knew a woman who, unwilling to wait to have her car washed, drove across the street to a paint shop

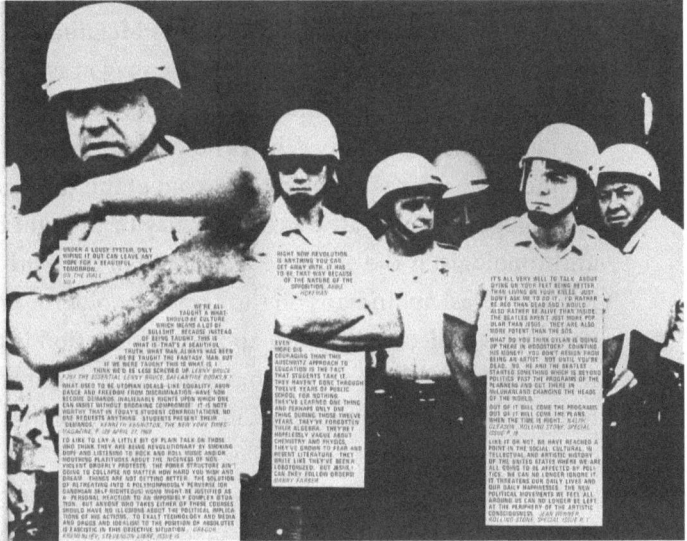

Figure 4.1 Foldout from Carpenter et al., *Proposals for Art Education*, 1970.

where there was no waiting line" (27). Carpenter then references the political moment, asserting that "The decision to pull out of Vietnam wasn't made on the Senate floor. It wasn't made in the White House. It was made on campuses" (27). He argues, "The activists ... achieved most of their major goals ... [through] the effective, often inspired use of media" (27). This observation leads Carpenter to his central point: "It makes no sense to me to discuss art in the lives of undergraduates in terms divorced from the bloodless revolution America is now experiencing. I see that revolution largely in terms of media changes, with artists & activists playing leading roles, and campuses operating as service environments for the equipment & resources employed in this revolution" (27). Carpenter laments the fact that, although he and his colleagues were invited to UCSC, the senior administration was not interested in meeting with them, and that the experimental courses that he and his colleagues taught were not incorporated into the curriculum, nor were any of the invited speakers encouraged to apply for positions at the university.

The major ill afflicting universities, suggests Carpenter, is classification, which restricts and controls knowledge. Whenever classification breaks

down, a "breakthrough" is achieved. "As McLuhan points out, every break-
down is a potential breakthrough. The 1929 crash revealed the economic
structure to the entire community. The breakdown of segregation revealed
the nature of racism" (29). When a new technology comes into being, the old
technology becomes a junkyard, but out of this junkyard a new art emerges
… What goes into an attic as useless may be brought back out as art … The
anthropologist is the *old rag & bone man* of the world, a title, in fact, con-
ferred by Naskapi Indians on the great ethnologist, Frank Speck" (29). The
procedure of declassification and reclassification is thus also a theory of
(re)mediation. "Every culture has a primary medium for the classification
of that culture's basic cliches. When a new medium replaces it, the old
one is freed and takes up its role as a declassifier" (32). Echoing McLuhan
and Watson's *From Cliché to Archetype* (1970),[22] Carpenter states, "Cliché
is whatever is in use & whatever is in use is environmental, hence largely
invisible. The moment a new cliché arises to surround it, the old cliché
becomes useless, hence very visible. Art is often shaped out of the useless
archetypes that come from junkyards; they are obsolete clichés, rearview
mirrors" (29). The process that informs this transition is remediation:
"Every new medium takes as its content the medium it has just rendered
obsolete: scribes recorded oral legends; printers set in type old manuscripts; Hollywood filmed books; radio broadcast concerts and vaudeville;
TV showed old movies; magnetic tape was used to copy LP records" (30).
New technologies create new perceptions. Referring to the work of Robert
Flaherty, Carpenter states that "Flaherty didn't begin with a script or a
point of view, but let the camera see everything, avid as a child, filled with
childlike wonder" (31).

"Declassification" emerges when the private becomes public, a tendency
exacerbated by mass media. "Recently the SDS [Students for a Democratic
Society] rifled Harvard's files and published a letter from the Dean to the
President … Last year, *Who's Who in the CIA*, published in East Berlin, listed
American agents by name … Last month the *Los Angeles Free Press* pub-
lished sections from this register, which was originally compiled with the
aid of Soviet Intelligence" (31). Carpenter himself turned to the *Los Angeles
Free Press* in 1969 to publish an early version of *They Became What They
Beheld*, declassifying a project he had been recruited for by the Australian
government. Carpenter traces the procedure back to *Explorations*: "Fifteen

years ago *Explorations*[23] reprinted items lifted from the files of broadcasters & publishers, e.g., Proctor & Gamble's rules on TV censorship, *Life* editor's instructions on creating news, etc. Printing this may have been illegal, but no action was ever brought. By declassifying the audience, the power of restricted information is neutralized and those who once sought to control it are rendered impotent & clownish" (31). Carpenter sought to enact this process on the political level, supporting Eugene McCarthy's bid for the Democratic nomination by using the technique of "crossing media" (32), or intermediation:[24]

Last summer I approached the McCarthy campaign staff with a suggestion for crossing media ... I proposed that the New York-New Jersey area be offered a night of radio sound & TV picture. Five of us were going to supply the commentary: John Culkin [a professor of media at Fordham], Jean Shepherd [radio and TV personality], Marshall McLuhan, myself, & Tony Schwartz [sound designer], who originated the idea & had a sound studio equipped to handle the project ... The plan was that we would announce in the New York newspapers that, at 7pm on a certain night, we would provide an evening's entertainment via two media. The audience merely had to tune in on a particular radio station, and we would advise [them] which TV station to turn to. If we saw a cigarette commercial, for example, we might suggest that everyone turn to that station & we would play one minute of coughing. Then we might suggest that everyone turn to Channel 7 where there was a laugh-show, and we would point out that the laugh-tracks were copyrighted in 1935 & that most of the people one heard laughing had been dead for some time ... Finally, and this was the whole point of the project, we would urge listeners to watch Hubert Humphrey [McCarthy's rival for the Democratic nomination] speaking. During his speech, we planned to read the four letters he wrote to his Draft Board gaining exemption from duty in the Second War ... while in the background we would play Hitler's ranting, bombs, & cries; then Humphrey's pro-Vietnam War speeches ... while in the background the guns & screams continued. The McCarthy team, mostly literary men, saw something profoundly immoral in the suggestion. (32–3)

The reference to "literary men" is contextualized by Carpenter in terms of the end of literacy: "The syntheses of understanding which once made common speech possible, today no longer work. As George Steiner points out, large areas of meaning are now ruled by non-verbal languages such as mathematics or symbolic logic or film. Little or nothing is verbal in modern music or art ... The monopoly, even tyranny, language enjoyed under literacy was shattered by electricity ... Literacy & its attendant technology promoted detachment & objectivity, detribalization & individuality. Electric circuitry has the opposite effect: it involves in depth. It merges individual and environment" (35–7). Carpenter quotes from a speech that Margaret Mead had recently given, in which she comments:

> *An essential and extraordinary aspect of man's present state ... is that at the moment when we approach a world culture ... we have available to us for the first time examples of the way in which men have lived at every period over the last fifty thousand years ... Some fifty thousand years of our history lies spread out before us, accessible, for this brief moment in time, to our simultaneous inspection ... All of us who grew up before the war are immigrants in time, immigrants from an earlier world living in an age essentially different from anything we knew before ... We have crossed a line, immigrated into an age for which we are essentially unprepared, and we are trying to make do with outmoded forms ... The young people who are rebelling all around the world, rebelling against whatever forms the government and educational systems take, are like the first generation born in a new country. They are at home here. Their eyes have always seen satellites in the sky. They have never known a world in which war did not mean annihilation. They know that computers are programmed by human beings and do not anthropomorphize them as their parents do. They believe that contraception is possible, and necessary, and that our capacity to feed the world will not last. They realize that if the pollution of air and land and water is allowed to go on, this planet will be uninhabitable. They know that, as members of one species living on one planet, all invidious distinctions based on race must vanish ... They no longer think in linear sequences dictated by print, but live again in a world in which events are presented to them in all their immediacy.* (33, italics in original)[25]

Mead's comments pinpoint with acute accuracy the issues that were manifesting themselves socially, politically, culturally, and economically, precisely through the increasing globalization of media inaugurated by television and by the immense powers of retrieval vested in electronic media, such that the cultural components of the past were now inescapably present in a world that was seeking to adapt to the "all-at-once-ness" required to comprehend this ahistorical present that was increasingly globalized spatially. The word "anthropomorphize" is of crucial importance, suggesting both the crisis of an anthropology forced to turn back on itself (such that the subject of anthropology became anthropology itself) and a realization that the *anthropos* itself had been remediated by electronic media – the extensions of "man." Juxtaposed to Mead's observations are Carpenter's own, with their vast range of literary references –Shakespeare, Yeats, Homer, T.S. Eliot, Blake, Shaw, Pound, Robbe-Grillet, C.S. Lewis, Whitman, Milton, E.M. Forster, Tolstoy, Coleridge, De Quincey, Baudelaire, Rimbaud, Cervantes, Joyce, Conrad, and Nabokov – as well as references to popular music, from Vanilla Fudge to Procol Harum to Jefferson Airplane, the juxtaposition indicative of the cultural shift that was occupying Carpenter and his colleagues at that time.

In addition to publishing *Proposals for Art Education* in 1970, Carpenter also published one of his major works, *They Became What They Beheld*.[26] Carpenter had been circling around the ideas in this book for a number of years, and published excerpts from it in the *Los Angeles Free Press* in 1969. This was an odd venue for what was putatively an academic text, although Carpenter's critiques of academia suggest that this choice of venue was meant to be controversial. Founded in 1964, the LAFP was a radical, underground newspaper that reflected the political turmoil of that time. As Mike Davis writes in *City of Quartz*:

The Endless Summer of the avant garde ... came to an abrupt end in August 1965. Southcentral Los Angeles exploded in rage against police abuse and institutional racism, creating for a few days the "barricaded commune" ... and "burning city" ... that Los Angeles intellectuals had frequently dreamt about as a kind of liberation from the Culture Industry. In fact, the Watts Rebellion, as well as the police attack on peaceful anti-war demonstrators at Century City in July 1967, politically galvanized artists and writers on the first broad scale

since the Hollywood witch-hunt. [Thomas] Pynchon wrote a stir-
ringly sympathetic and unpatronizing piece called "A Journey into
the Mind of Watts" (really a meditation on urban segregation). [Ed]
Ruscha painted *The Los Angeles County Museum on Fire* (1965–68),
[Budd] Schulberg organized a Watts Writers' Workshop, anti-war
artists contributed scores of pieces to the "Artists' Peace Tower" on
the Sunset Strip, the underground *Los Angeles Free Press* flourished,
and [Ed] Kienholz's tableaux denounced war.[27]

Not Since Babel

This was the context in which Carpenter began publishing in the *LAFP*, beginning in 1968 with "Not Since Babel" (5.192, March 22–28, 1968, 7, 9),
a rather tame contribution to a newspaper that was strewn with ads for
dominatrices and gay dating services, and appearing across the page from
Lawrence Lipton's review of Eldridge Cleaver's *Soul on Ice*.[28] Carpenter
returns to a number of points made in the *Proposals* volume, with particular
reference to the end of literacy. "We know almost nothing about the origin
of language ... It was once rather loosely believed that man was an alienated
ape who, after becoming erect, commenced talking. This early walkie-talkie
roamed several continents, producing pebble tools that remained nearly
changeless for hundreds of thousands of years. Then, less than fifty thousand years ago, man burst forth with a plurality of tools and art that pre-
supposed, it was assumed, the existence of fully developed language" (7).
Regardless of the veracity of this theory, what interests Carpenter is the
reversal of this process. "Some of the undergraduates I teach in California
... remind me, in their incapacity for formal speech, of Lancelot Andrewes's
'The Word, and not to be able to speak a word' ... This retreat from language
is surely one of the more interesting phenomena of our time. As George
Steiner points out in 'Language and Silence,' the synthesis of understanding
which made common speech possible, today no longer would ... Not since
Babel have words and thoughts clashed in such protesting combination" (7).
Language achieved its hegemony through its valorization of the visual, but
electronic media shifts this orientation to the invisible. Carpenter quotes
Buckminster Fuller to the effect that "in World War I industry suddenly

went from the visible to the invisible base, from the track to the trackless, from the wire to the wireless" (9). As literacy wanes, so does the individual, who begins to retribalize. Paradoxically, it is among dropouts that literacy survives, and it does so as a mode of critique. "In California, bookstores are feared as subversive centers; the underground press is written by and for drop-outs; the Word, not film, has become the medium of dissent ... In contrast, the classroom presupposes an audience ignorant of all literary traditions ... We live in a scene where a large percentage of college presidents come from Physical Education, but dropouts read Elizabethan verse and Greek Drama" (9). Carpenter concludes with the observation that, "When Constantinople fell, its scholars fled West, carrying their manuscripts with them ... Today's hippies are much like those fleeing scholars. They've taken the classics and fled from campuses which have fallen to weapons development, the CIA, and schools of Social Work" (9).

Another version of this article, published in an academic journal under the same title in 1970, is much longer and more redolent of McLuhan's media theories.[29] Here Carpenter expands upon possible theories for the origin of language, arguing that this question has been made much more complicated, "largely as a result of new fossil discoveries, as well as the findings of ethology and somatology" (81). Alan Lomax, the ethnologist of music, has suggested that song is "danced speech" (81), and Bess Hawes (with whom Carpenter worked on *Georgia Sea Island Singers*) has proposed that "music is a dance executed while standing still" (81). These comments suggest that if music and art can be considered languages, they nevertheless do not function linguistically; this had far-reaching implications, including and especially for anthropology, in the era when structural linguistics held sway. What raised the question of language is the shift toward total involvement posed by electronic media, a shift that is cognate with the function of ritual. "One comes to know a thing by being inside it. You get an inside view. You step into the skin of the beast, and that, of course, is precisely what the masked and costumed dancer does" (83). There is a degree of methodological self-reflexivity in Carpenter's comment that "the knower as observer and the knower as actor behold different worlds and shape them to different ends, and it's senseless to condemn one for failing to meet the standards of the other" (83), and this may go some way towards understanding the differences that arose from the Fordham affair. "As we become increasingly tribalized in art and outlook," writes Carpenter, "and draw closer to the Eskimo and Trobriander, anthropologists lose their best tool – the comparative method: its built-in shock, its challenge" (87). This notion would be reiterated a decade and a half later by James Clifford in *The Predicament of Culture*.

Carpenter published a second article in the *LAFP* during 1968 that was anomalous in its focus on the design of public buildings, although these topics had been raised in *Explorations* by Jaqueline Tyrwhitt. "On Designing Public Buildings for Play" (31 May 1968, 26) argues that "Play = involvement = happening = direct sensory experience." Illustrated by a model of the Art Center in Aalborg, Denmark designed by Alvar Aalto, the article asserts, "Information processing is replacing production as the principle human enterprise. Today more attention is directed toward production, packing and distribution of ideas associated with commodities, than with production of the commodities themselves, which is now done largely by machines. We have shifted from food-gatherers to data-processors; from work to play." Carpenter takes on the unwonted role of prognosticator in this article, predicting that "Increased use of computors [sic] will reduce human labor effort, especially in offices. An increasing number of tasks, especially in research and development, will be done by temporary teams ... Such efforts will be designed as networks maintained through modern media, rather than as face-to-face organizations within building enclosures ... Buildings ... will be largely habitats, not work plants." The McLuhanesque thrust of these predictions is confirmed by Carpenter's bio, which identifies him as an "anthropologist associate of Marshall McLuhan."

The McLuhan association is writ large in the excerpts from Carpenter's work in progress, *They Became What They Beheld*, printed from April to August, 1969 in the *LAFP*, since McLuhan is listed as co-author.[30] These excerpts are almost exclusively from Carpenter's essay in *Proposals for Art Education*. McLuhan's "contributions" are indirect, and are more "McLuhanesque" than "McLuhan," if in fact they are McLuhan's at all – there is no evidence that McLuhan contributed to these publications. Carpenter rarely cites from any of McLuhan's books or articles, and there is clearly a conflicted sense of "ownership" of the ideas that Carpenter is putting forward. Carpenter writes in "That Not-So-Silent-Sea" that he was the author of the *Harper's Bazaar* article on fashion that appeared under McLuhan's name, and that "three years later it appeared as a book, *They*

Figure 4.2 (*right*) Carpenter's "On Designing Public Buildings for Play" on front page of *Living Arts, Los Angeles Times* supplement, 31 May 1968.

Figure 4.3 (*below*) "Play = Involvement: On Designing Public Buildings for Play," *Los Angeles Free Press*, 31 May 1968, 26.

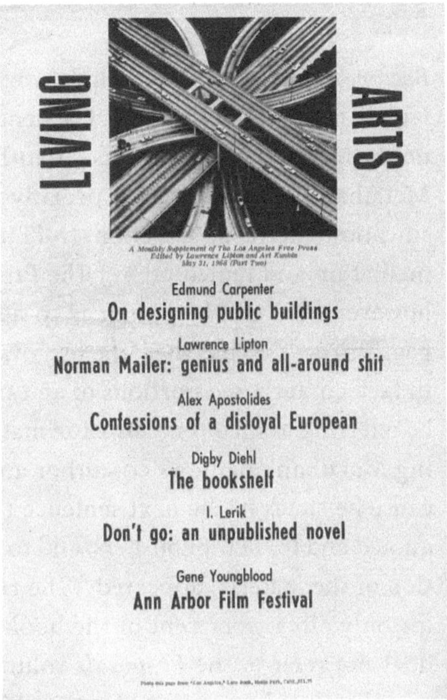

LIVING ARTS

A Monthly Supplement of The Los Angeles Free Press
Edited by Lawrence Lipton and Art Kunkin
May 31, 1968 (Part Two)

Edmund Carpenter
On designing public buildings

Lawrence Lipton
Norman Mailer: genius and all-around shit

Alex Apostolides
Confessions of a disloyal European

Digby Diehl
The bookshelf

I. Lerik
Don't go: an unpublished novel

Gene Youngblood
Ann Arbor Film Festival

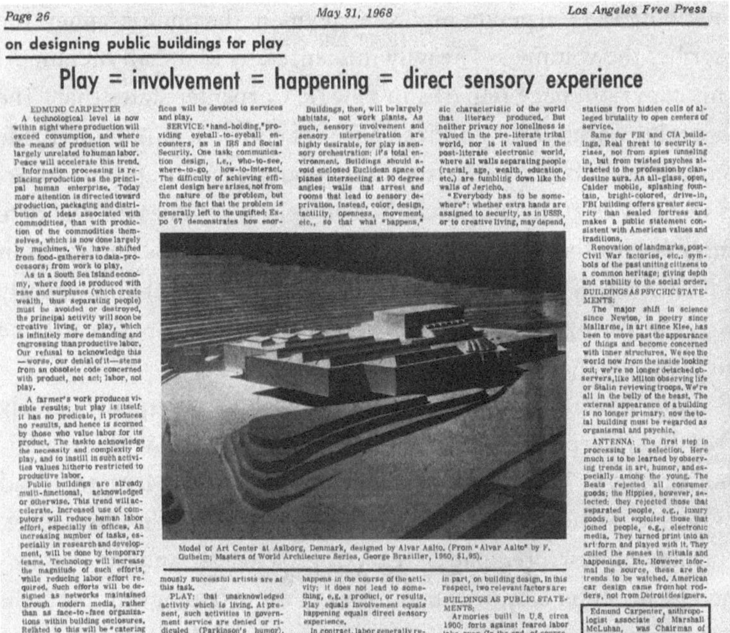

Page 26 *May 31, 1968* *Los Angeles Free Press*

on designing public buildings for play

Play = involvement = happening = direct sensory experience

EDMUND CARPENTER

A technological level is now within sight where production will exceed consumption, and where the means of production will be largely unrelated to human labor. Peace will accelerate this trend.

Information processing is replacing production as the principal human enterprise. Today more attention is directed toward production, packaging and distribution of ideas associated with commodities, than with production of the commodities themselves, which is now done largely by machines. We have shifted from food-gatherers to data-processors; from work to play.

As in a South Sea Island economy, where food is produced with ease and surpluses (which create wealth, thus separating people) must be avoided or destroyed, the principal activity will soon be creative living, or play, which is infinitely more demanding and engrossing than productive labor. Our refusal to acknowledge this—worse, our denial of it—stems from an obsolete code concerned with product, not act; labor, not play.

A farmer's work produces visible results; but play is itself: it has no predicate, it produces no results, and hence is scorned by those who value labor for its product. The taskto acknowledge the necessity and complexity of play, and to instill in such activities values hitherto restricted to productive labor.

Public buildings are already multi-functional, acknowledged or otherwise. This trend will accelerate. Increased use of computors will reduce human labor effort, especially in offices. An increasing number of tasks, especially in research and development, will be done by temporary teams. Technology will increase the magnitude of such efforts, while reducing labor effort required. Such efforts will be designed as networks maintained through modern media, rather than as face-to-face organizations within building enclosures. Related to this will be "catering services" providing vast range of professional and clerical services (in L.A., engineering teams are available for rental), either on a temporary or long-term basis.

Such trends mean that more time and effort in government offices will be devoted to services and play.

SERVICE: "hand-holding," providing eyeball-to-eyeball encounters, as in IRS and Social Security. One task: communication design, i.e., who-to-see, where-to-go, how-to-interact. The difficulty of achieving efficient design here arises, not from the nature of the problem, but from the fact that the problem is generally left to the ungifted: Expo 67 demonstrates how enormously successful artists are at this task.

PLAY: that unacknowledged activity which is living. At present, such activities in government service are denied or ridiculed (Parkinson's humor), i.e., they are seen through the eyes of the Age of Production, with much resulting confusion and conflict. Such activities must be accorded dignity: "If you want to render a man into nothing," says Dostoevski, "give to his efforts a character of uselessness."

Buildings, then, will be largely habitats, not work plants. As such, sensory involvement and sensory interpenetration are highly desirable, for play is sensory orchestration: it's total environment. Buildings should avoid enclosed Euclidean space of planes intersecting at 90 degree angles; walls that arrest and rooms that lead to sensory deprivation. Instead, color, design, tactility, openness, movement, etc., so that what "happens," happens in the course of the activity: it does not lead to something, e.g. a product, or results. Play equals involvement equals happening equals direct sensory experience.

In contract, labor generally requires sensory disengagement and fragmentation. Labor, by definition, is sensory fragmentation and specialization. Similarly, highly abstract research often requires alienation and the loneliness of privacy. Privacy is a prerequisite of literacy and a basic characteristic of the world that literacy produced. But neither privacy nor loneliness is valued in the pre-literate tribal world, nor is it valued in the post-literate electronic world, where all walls separating people (racial, age, wealth, education, etc.) are tumbling down like the walls of Jericho.

"Everybody has to be somewhere": whether extra hands are assigned to security, as in USSR, or to creative living, may depend, in part, on building design. In this respect, two relevant factors are:

BUILDINGS AS PUBLIC STATEMENTS:

Armories built in U.S. circa 1900: forts against feared labor take-over. (In the end, of course, labor joined the Establishment).

Police station: all-glass, brightly-lighted, near intersection, comparable to all-glass, see-through, California banks. All activities are under constant surveillance by citizens. Would change public image of police stations from hidden cells of alleged brutality to open centers of service.

Same for FBI and CIA buildings. Real threat to security arises, not from spies tunneling in, but from twisted psyches attracted to the profession by clandestine aura. An all-glass, open, Calder mobile, splashing fountain, bright-colored, drive-in, FBI building offers greater security than sealed fortress and makes a public statement consistent with American values and traditions.

Renovation of landmarks, post-Civil War factories, etc.: symbols of the past uniting citizens to a common heritage; giving depth and stability to the social order.

BUILDINGS AS PSYCHIC STATEMENTS:

The major shift in science since Newton, in poetry since Mallarme, in art since Klee, has been to move past the appearance of things and become concerned with inner structures. We see the world now from the inside looking out; we're no longer detached observers, like Milton observing life or Stalin reviewing troops. We're all in the belly of the beast. The external appearance of a building is no longer primary: now the total building must be regarded as organismal and psychic.

ANTENNA: The first step in processing is selection. Here much is to be learned by observing trends in art, humor, and especially among the young. The Beats rejected all consumer goods; the Hippies, however, selected: they rejected those that separated people, e.g., luxury goods, but exploited those that joined people, e.g., electronic media. They turned print into an art form and played with it. They united the senses in rituals and happenings. Etc. However informal the source, these are the trends to be watched. American car design came from hot rodders, not from Detroit designers.

Model of Art Center at Aalborg, Denmark, designed by Alvar Aalto. (From "Alvar Aalto" by F. Gutheim; Masters of World Architecture Series, George Braziller, 1960, $1.95).

Edmund Carpenter, anthropologist associate of Marshall McLuhan, was Chairman of Anthropology at San Fernando Valley State College and Professor of Communications Arts at Fordham University. He has recently been appointed to the Chair of Carnegie Professor at the University of California at Santa Cruz.

Became What They Beheld, under my name" (258). That book, however, is largely identical to the essay Carpenter published in *Proposals* that does not bear McLuhan's name as co-author, and bears little resemblance to McLuhan's own writings, especially the overriding metaphor of declassification and reclassification. (McLuhan was at that time writing about mediation and remediation.) The *Proposals* items published in the LAFP, however, do credit McLuhan as co-author, while a note on the copyright page in TBWTB states that "the text owes much to Marshall McLuhan who, in fact, co-authored portions of an earlier version." Here, Carpenter must be referring to the *Proposals*/LAFP material (largely identical, but one bearing McLuhan's name as co-author and the other not crediting him), because he states in the next sentence that "we are indebted to the authors quoted and to their publishers, and to *Harper's Bazaar* in which some portion of the material appeared." The *Harper's* material, however, accounts for only circa 5 per cent of the book, and the copyright page comment does not refer to the *Proposals* volume or to the LAFP material. Further complicating the question of authorship is the inclusion of the book's opening pages in a 1976 volume titled *The Director in a Changing Theatre*,[31] where they are attributed to Carpenter and Ken Heyman, the photographer; the editor describes the volume as "heavily influenced by Marshall McLuhan" (262). In his copyright page remarks in TBWTB, Carpenter states that "The Tribal Man who walks through these pages is composed, like the Bride of Frankenstein, of bits & pieces from many sources." This appears to describe his working relation with McLuhan as well. What does differentiate Carpenter's essay in the *Proposals* volume from the excerpts published in the LAFP is the page layout, which is highly juxtapositional and visually compelling, suggesting an exacerbated concrete poetry that is clearly the product of Carpenter's sensibility.

They Became What They Beheld, published in 1970, draws equally (largely word for word) on Carpenter's essay in the *Proposals* volume, with the addition of photographs by Ken Heyman, who had worked with Margaret Mead for twenty years.[32] Mead provides the blurb for the front of the dust jacket, which is printed on mirrored paper, reflecting the reader and thus underlining one of Carpenter's central principles in anthropological research: that anthropology is about the subject, not the object, of study. The book, writes Margaret Mead in her jacket blurb, is an "astute staccato comment on

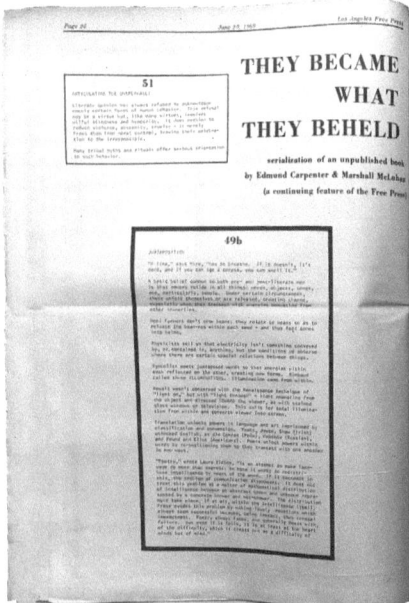

Figure 4.4 Full double-page spread, "They Became What They Beheld," *Los Angeles Free Press*, 20 June 1969.

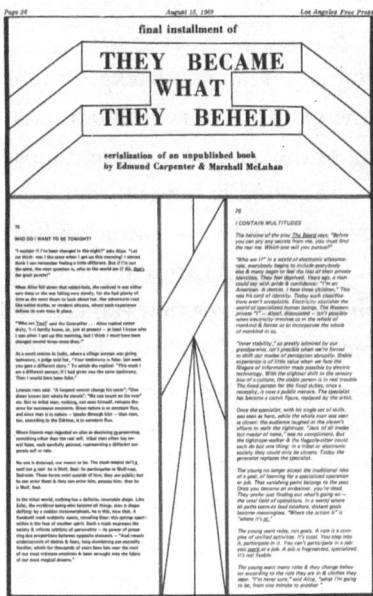

Figure 4.5 Final installment, "They Became What They Beheld," *Los Angeles Free Press*, 15 August 1969.

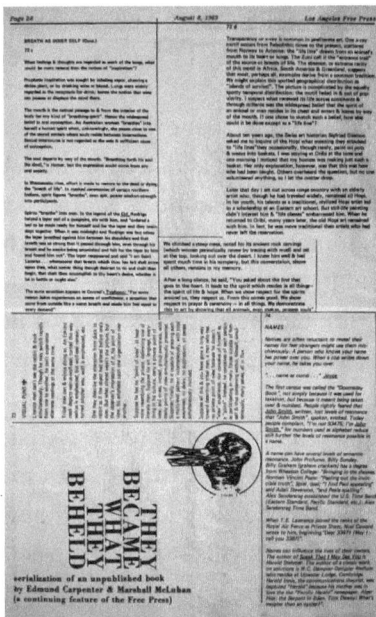

Figure 4.6 Rabbit/Duck, "They Became What They Beheld," *Los Angeles Free Press*, 8 August 1969, 28.

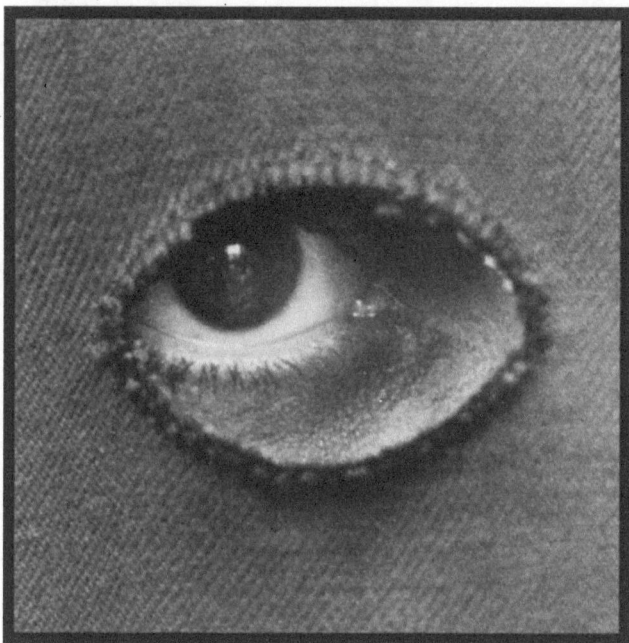

Figure 4.7
Eye framed by
canvas from
Carpenter,
*They Became
What They
Beheld*, 1970.

present and needed changes in sensory modes, against a background of fantasied primitive life, annotated by some extraordinary photographs." "Staccato" encapsulates the snapshot effect of the text, which is juxtapositional rather than linearly argumentative. The notion of the anthropologist as someone searching through the midden of twentieth-century culture and proceeding in an unscripted fashion is conveyed through the juxtapositional style of the text, each paragraph introducing a new subject, and topics circling back on themselves. This recursion derives from the "speed up" afforded by electronic media: "Condensing time & data – speeding up experience – reveals process. Archaeology & history are instant playback … Information overload requires speed up which permits recognition." Our lives are mediated, and the ethnographer's task becomes that of discerning patterns of mediation. The subjects of the photographs are unidentified but largely portray contemporary American culture, together with other images of tribal life, recurring, thus, to the book's overall theme of retribalization. The opening image of an eye framed by canvas[33] highlights the single point of view produced by visual culture that this book seeks to critique – the book is structured in such a way that it can be opened at any point, and lacks a teleology. The back cover blurb is by McLuhan: "Carpenter is one of the rare anthropologists who understands that the study of man is not based on matching but making. He makes sense," which is to say that Carpenter deciphers the shift from mimesis to poeisis, from product to process, from passive reception of a text to active engagement in its production, remediating the book thereby, in the words of Raviv Ganchrow, as "an entire ecology of situated relations."[34] It was McLuhan who had invoked William Blake's *Jerusalem* in the conclusion to *The Gutenberg Galaxy* (1962) in order to explicate "the changing patterns of human perception" (265). "Determined as [Blake] was to explain the causes and effects of psychic change, both personal and social, he arrived long ago at the theme of *The Gutenberg Galaxy*: ... 'they became what they beheld'" (265; the verse appears three times in the first two paragraphs of *Jerusalem*, part 2, section 36[35]). McLuhan goes on to state, "Blake makes quite explicit that when sense ratios change, men change. Sense ratios change when any one sense or bodily or mental function is externalized in technological form ... When the perverse ingenuity of man has outered some part of his being in material technology, his entire sense ratio is altered. He is then compelled to behold this fragment of himself 'closing itself as in steel.' In beholding this new thing, man is compelled to become it. Such was the origin of lineal, fragmented analysis with its remorseless power of homogenization" (265–6). "Blake," McLuhan goes on to note, "had the insights but not the technical resources for rendering his vision. Paradoxically, it was not through the book but through the development of the mass press, especially the telegraph press, that poets found the artistic keys to the world of simultaneity, or modern myth" (267–8). These distinctions emerge in Carpenter's book through the affectlessness of many of the highly posed subjects in Heyman's photographs of North Americans, bringing out the mechanization of their lives, which contrasts markedly with the vitality of the "tribal" photographs. This opened up Carpenter's work to a theme that would increasingly dominate it: the depredating effects of media technologies.

5

An Unconventional Anthropologist

IN THE SAME YEAR that he published *They Became What They Beheld*, Carpenter published a preview of his next book, *Oh, What a Blow That Phantom Gave Me!*, in "Explorations."[1] The point of departure for the article was the commission Carpenter undertook from the administration of Papua and New Guinea to advise on the "use of radio, film, even television" (90) in a place that existed in multiple temporalities simultaneously: "Port Moresby," writes Carpenter, "the capital, resembles a southern California town with air-conditioned offices, supermarkets, and drive-in theatre. Three hundred miles to the west, isolated bands practice cannibalism" (90). It was precisely this non-linear history that attracted Carpenter, a non-linearity that would ultimately lead him to his "quixotic adventure"[2] there. "I accepted the assignment because it gave me an unparalleled opportunity to step in and out of 10,000 years of media history" (90), writes Carpenter, alluding to *Ten Thousand Years in a Lifetime* (1968), the autobiography of Albert Maori Kiki, a Papua New Guinean pathologist and politician.[3] (Tellingly, the work was recorded on tape, and then transcribed.)[4]

Commenting on Carpenter's experiences in Papua, McLuhan remarked, "The Anthropologist, E.S. Carpenter, has performed experiments in New Guinea in which, by the use of photographs and movies made on the spot, he carried people ... through countless centuries of evolutionary cultural development in a few hours."[5] What lay behind the invitation of the Australian government (whose administration of Papua New Guinea would end in 1975) was the attempt to understand political tensions that had suddenly emerged in places such as Rabaul and Kieta. "The people of Rabaul had been in close contact with Westerners since 1885, and now suddenly they were marching in the streets" (90).[6] Carpenter had a theory that the introduction of media such as photography, film, and voice recording had initiated a moment of "self-discovery, self-awareness." While the Australian administrators focused their use of such media on content – "democracy, purity, and a Personal God" (90) – they were unaware of the *effects* of these media. "Those who had listened most attentively to these sermons were now in angry revolt" (90–1), largely because these media "were changing the environment itself" (91). Carpenter may have been aware, as Raviv Ganchrow suggests, that the Australians were engaged in a colonialist implementation of media strategies to obtain an administrative foothold through an "applied media theory, tried and tested in rural Soviet Union," while Carpenter himself "was clandestinely trying to understand the operations and perceptual transformations that take place through media contact."[7]

Arriving at an isolated area between the Sepik River and the Highlands, Carpenter distributed Polaroid photographs of villagers.[8] "At first there was no understanding. The photographs were black and white, flat, static, odorless – far removed from the reality these natives knew. They had to be taught 'to read' photographs ... Gradually recognition came into their faces. And fear." (92). Likewise with film, which produced "the terror of self-awareness" (92). David MacDougall has commented on this aspect of photography: "Carpenter's notion is that photography confronts us with our own individuality, forever alienating us from collective social experience," while arguing that there is another aspect of photography that "offers us the chance to add something to ourselves and review our varied appearances. It takes nothing from us; indeed, every image increases us and attests to the possibilities within us."[9] Carpenter did not share this philosophical approach to media in which "to look carefully requires strength, calmness, and affection" (7). He was astonished by how quickly the Indigenous peoples adapted to the new technologies, noting that soon "these villagers, including children and even a few women, were making movies themselves, taking Polaroid shots of each other, and endlessly playing with tape recorders" (93). However, the effect of this was "Instant Alienation. Their wits and sensibilities, released from tribal restraints, had created a totally new identity: the private individual" (93). Carpenter argues that the transformation

among the Indigenous peoples who encountered new media has its parallel
in "what electronic media, especially television, have done to all of us, with
much resulting anxiety and psychic alienation" (93). Carpenter advised the
government of Papua New Guinea "to restrain the use of electronic media
and if not, to prepare for chaos" (93). As for the film he shot while in Papua,
he later stated that "it had caused him so much trouble that he just put it
away."[10] Nevertheless, by giving recording media to the "native informants,"
Carpenter had found a way to surmount the ineradicable barrier faced by
the anthropologist who seeks to study cultures from an insider perspective.
In doing so, he effectively brought the traditional practice of anthropology
to an end, while at the same time demonstrating the fundamental role of
mediation in anthropological research. As Harald Prins has noted, the role
of mediation in this context was double-edged: although it had the potential to threaten ancient ways of life, media could also be used as instruments
of empowerment.[11]

By 1970, Carpenter had done research not only in Papua New Guinea, but
also in the Arctic, Siberia, Borneo, Outer Mongolia, and Micronesia, and he
claimed that his films had received awards in Cannes, Edinburgh, and
Venice.[12] The ghost of *Explorations* continued to haunt him, however. In a
one-page article published in "Explorations" (Spring 1971) titled "Media and
Moral Progress"[13] (posted from Adelphi College, Long Island, New York),
Carpenter writes, "About three weeks ago, during a brief period of about ten
days, I did a CBC-TV network show, a CBS-TV network show, a radio show for
both the U.S. and Canada, published an article for TV Guide, gave a public
lecture to an audience of several thousand people in a New York hotel, and
finally had the same material (all of it dealing with a preliminary statement
on the New Guinea research) printed in a newspaper." Carpenter goes on
to note that the response to the TV shows was a single letter, whereas in
response to the radio show he received several letters from former students.
In response to the *TV Guide* article, however, he received bundles of letters.
These letters consistently questioned "the desirability of using electronic
media in underdeveloped areas," although the primitivist assumptions inherent in this questioning had been addressed by Carpenter for decades.

The Papuan research inaugurated the most productive period of
Carpenter's career. It also marked a life change through his collaboration
with, and eventual marriage to, ethnographical photographer Adelaide de

LIKE HERALDIC CRESTS,
THESE POLES TOLD
OF THE MYTHOLOGICAL BEGINNINGS
OF THE GREAT FAMILIES,
AT A TIME BEFORE TIME,
WHEN ANIMALS AND MYTHIC BEASTS AND MEN
LIVED AS EQUALS,
AND ALL THAT WAS TO BE
WAS ESTABLISHED BY THE PLAY
OF RAVEN AND EAGLE,
BEAR AND WOLF,
FROG AND BEAVER,
THUNDERBIRD AND WHALE.

Figure 5.1 Page spread from Reid and de Menil, *Out of the Silence*, 1971. Reprinted with permission of the Bill Reid Estate.

Menil,[14] with whom Carpenter had begun to film a documentary in 1969 on modern media influences in Papua New Guinea, although the film was not completed.[15] In 1971, Carpenter commissioned *Out of the Silence*, photographs of Pacific Northwest Indigenous artifacts, particularly totem poles, largely taken *in situ* by de Menil, and published in 1971 with a text by William ("Bill") Reid.[16] Photography and anthropology grew up together, as Eliot Weinberger has noted,[17] both seeking to record a moment that will not return. If photography was first incorporated into anthropological research in the notorious interests of anthropometry, it soon became harnessed to the "vanishing peoples" trope, making of anthropology "a discipline that has appealed to the discontents of technological civilization, those who long for something else, a something forever receding" (16). Reid and de Menil subtly critique this trope, however, invoking the domain of acoustic space as a critique of visuality. Beautifully designed by Arnold Skolnick,[18] the book's clear acetate dust jacket conveys the idea of looking through – not only looking through a camera aperture, but also looking through another culture, a culture that speaks through the silence, exerting its presence uncannily, both there and not there. As Reid writes, "Whenever we look at a particular work of Northwest coast art and see the shape of it, we are only looking at its after-life. Its real life is the movement by which it got to be that shape" (8). The camera functions in this context less as a photographic device than as a spirit catcher. "The book," writes Robert Bringhurst, "was a subterranean success, quickly issued under five different imprints in two countries."[19] Although not credited in the book, Carpenter commissioned Reid's text, edited it, and subsequently claimed to have written much of it.[20] Bringhurst, who has translated Haida works extensively, and was a close associate of Bill Reid, has commented that Carpenter

> May actually have believed that he wrote Reid's poem *Out of the Silence* – a claim he made more than once in my hearing. But there is a manuscript of the text in Reid's hand (partially reproduced ... in [Bringhurst's edition of Reid's selected writings] *Solitary Raven*). I reproduced the manuscript largely because I had heard Ted say that he himself was the principal author. But the manuscript in itself isn't proof of very much, since the handwriting appears to post-date the published book ... I think it's entirely possible that Carpenter suggested the free-verse form of *Out of the Silence*, and I would not be surprised if he did this by retranscribing or even rewriting one of Bill's earlier prose drafts. And so I think it's possible that the text went back and forth between them. I don't believe it is originally or fundamentally Ted's. But these are just opinions, based on personal knowledge of both men, including a fair bit spent with the two of them together. I have never seen documentary evidence that would confirm these hunches or refute them.[21]

This does suggest, however, that Carpenter's understanding of "authorship" was dialogical, an understanding that emerges both in his relationship with McLuhan and in his editing of Carl Schuster's work.

By 1972, Carpenter was referring to himself as an "unconventional anthropologist" having a "tenuous position within the profession,"[22] a self-assessment he made in a 1972 article published in *Audience* magazine.[23] Illustrated with masks and sculptures from Carpenter's own collection, the article begins with an account of Carpenter's experiences in the South Pacific, on the Rajang River in Borneo. Carpenter describes an encounter with the Chief of Chiefs, who berates his fellow chiefs; pointing to Carpenter, he tells them, "You with your spears: he has come to collect them to show to children. You with your *parangs* [swords]: he is unarmed; he mocks you. Why? *He reads*" (90). As Carpenter comments, "Here's a man who recognizes that power today lies in media, not weapons" (90). Carpenter's tone is somewhat mocking of the anthropologists hosted in New Guinea by the Australian National University; he notes that the village houses built throughout New Guinea to house the scientists look identical on the outside, but inside they stock "dinner candles, Danish cheeses, German wines, though there were faint suggestions of ordeals suffered in the cause of science" (91). He notes further an incident where a New Guinean was fined "for eating an anthropologist's cat" (91). A long section of the article is devoted to Pidgin English, which had become the lingua franca of New Guinea, Carpenter commenting on the absurdity of many phrases in a Pidgin phrase book, such as "Please give me a pair of warm gloves" and "I like skating" (91). The effect of Pidgin is to put "a backspin on many words, thus slowing down information transfer and making communication easier to follow: *lakim* (like him) instead of simply *lak* (like); *bikpela* (big fellow) instead of simply *bik* (big). A few suffixes, used repeatedly, provide loose rhymes and rhythms that also aid in communication" (91). Unlike a language system that "is a kind of corporate dream [that] involves every member of the tribe all of the time in a great echo chamber" (91), Pidgin "offers no such depth" (91). Carpenter describes the rise of tourism in New Guinea, the banks of the Sepik River being lined with shops turning out masses of souvenirs. "Figures with erect penises are especially popular. One Los Angeles department store, unable to sell figures with dangling penises, donated them to local universities" (92). Carpenter mentions the ironic possibility that film, in its ability to preserve cultural expression, may ultimately become the most valid source of ancestral records, even if the film is inaccurate (such as one made by travelogue writer Lowell Thomas that Carpenter scathingly critiques).[24]

Carpenter next turns to Hollywood, California, and Prince Modupe, who entered the Hollywood milieu from French West Africa in the mid-1930s,[25] producing a musical titled *Zungaroo* at the Los Angeles Philharmonic in 1935, and advising Hollywood studios on representations of Africa in their films. "To avoid offending African governments," writes Carpenter, "MGM

WEST AFRICA

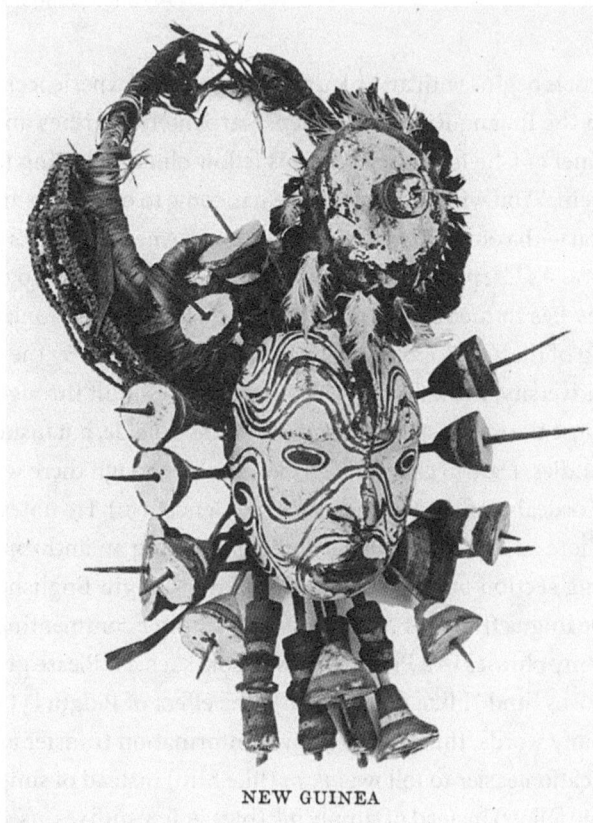

NEW GUINEA

CANADA

Clockwise from top left:

Figure 5.2
West African mask.

Figure 5.3
New Guinea mask.

Figure 5.4
Mask from Canada.

Carpenter Collection, "Notes of an Unconventional Anthropologist," *Audience Magazine.*

insisted that no film on Africa resemble Africa. Modupe's task was purely creative: to design buildings, songs, shields, dances, masks, even 'languages,' all of which Americans would accept as authentic but which no African would recognize as his" (93).

Finally, Carpenter turns to the Arctic, where his anthropological research was largely focused throughout his career. Carpenter begins with an extended confession:

> Though I have written, over a period of twenty years, on a variety of topics concerning my life with the Eskimo, I have never, until recently, attempted to describe those experiences that touched me most ... I've wondered whether this failure derived from personal censorship or from poverty of expression ... The few times I tried, in relaxed moments, to tell someone what it felt like to undergo intense happenings, I faltered ... Words failed, images failed, even memory failed. The whole key and rhythm of my life had been altered forever by a handful of experiences that left no communicable mark. And even now, as I wait for the right words, I wonder how accurate, how honest, these descriptions will be, and to what extent I work them up a little afterward. For months after I first arrived among the Aivilik I felt empty, clumsy, I never knew what to do, even where to sit or stand ... I had done extended fieldwork before, in the tropics, and did more later. But this was different. I recall an afternoon with an Eskimo whom I admired and his daughter whom I loved. She was betrothed. I was married. He once sent her to me, an act that embarrassed me and hurt her ... Such experiences left me indifferent to the cold reports coming out on the Eskimo: they were alien to all I had experienced. I gradually stopped taking the wrappers off my copies of *American Anthropologist*; I let my membership in that organization drop; I listed my occupation as "teacher," not "anthropologist." In the early fifties there was only limited interest in Arctic research and even less backing. So I helped dig the Toronto subway and worked nights in a brewery to finance trips, a breach of faculty etiquette my colleagues never forgave. But soon the Canadian Arctic was drawn into the world battleground and anthropologists settled about the posts ... They published voluminously, and they all took one another's

publications very seriously. Almost all of these reports I judge to be based on casual observations, full of heavy theory, fusty kinship data and pretentious claims to insights into self concepts, all badly written and few of lasting value ... I see anthropology as far more than the study and presentation of man. It's experiencing man: sensing, apperception, recognition. It's art. (93–4)

Carpenter's awareness of himself as "other" in Inuit culture heralded an increasing unease within anthropological research that derived from the awareness that anthropology was ultimately a valorization of non-Indigenous modes of understanding. Carpenter brings this out in an exchange he had with his guide, Ohnainewk. "The wind is cold," says Carpenter. Ohnainewk laughs. "How ... can the *wind* be cold? You're cold ... But the wind isn't cold" (94).

Not for the last time, Carpenter takes up the question of "authentic" Inuit carvings, noting that what passed for authentic Indigenous sculpture in the post-war era was the product of the teachings of James Houston and dates to the late 1940s.[26] Charles Taylor's account of Houston in his classic work of Canadian identitarian culturology, *Six Journeys*, credits Houston as "prime mover in the renaissance of Eskimo art."[27] After a first trip to the Arctic in 1948, Houston began to collect small soapstone carvings that attracted the attention of the Canadian Handicraft Guild in Montreal, which commissioned Houston to acquire more carvings on his next trip. "By the mid-fifties, Eskimo art had become a national, even an international craze" (84), as Taylor notes. Houston's success in the field of art led to his appointment by the Canadian government as federal administrator for West Baffin Island, a territory of 65,000 square miles that housed more than a dozen Indigenous encampments. Houston encouraged the Inuit in and around Cape Dorset not only to carve but also supplied them with printmaking materials with which they became equally successful. Yet, as Taylor states, "There are those who scoff at his achievements ... According to the scholar and Eskimo enthusiast Edmund Carpenter: 'Eskimo stone art was made for, used by and believed in, solely by Westerners ... Having deprived him of his heritage, and even the memory of his heritage, we offer him a substitute which he eagerly accepts, for no other is permitted'" (92).[28] Houston left the Arctic in 1962 to work as a designer for the Steuben glass company in

Manhattan, and it is this tendency toward commercialism that Carpenter decries in the art deriving from Houston's northern interventions, as well as the way in which the artwork promoted by Houston obscures the history of traditional Inuit artifacts. "Traditional perspective is gone: stability and single perspective have replaced mobility and multiple perspective. Traditional notions of discovering and revealing are gone: asked by the Queen how he decided what to carve, an Eskimo replied that he consulted Mr Houston because he had no desire to produce anything unsalable" (95). While Carpenter understands the propaganda value of this art in the context of Canadian nationalism, his major concern is the way in which anthropologists have tended to authenticate it as Indigenous art, and the extent to which the Inuit have been exploited in this process. "In addition to carving stone, Eskimos were trained to make totem poles, pottery, and prints, though all were alien to Eskimo culture ... Prints proved enormously popular. They combined Siberian designs with techniques learned directly from Japanese printmakers. By error, Siberian designs were included in a booklet on Canadian native designs and Eskimos were given this booklet for reference. Many Eskimo prints displayed in art museums and printed on Christmas cards owe their form to this error" (95).

This notion of cultural difference is the one on which Carpenter ends. "Consider that best-selling photography book, *The Family of Man*. Superb photographs of people from around the world were combined with quotations from great poets to make an overall statement: that there is absolutely no difference between anybody. Though people differ in color and creed, they all love, quarrel, protect their children, etcetera, exactly as we do. The message is clear: we should love them because they are like us. But that statement has its troublesome corollary: what if they aren't like us?" (97). Carpenter here sounds a note that would be heard with increasing intensity through the 1970s and '80s: "the ineluctable Otherness of the Other" (18), as Eliot Weinberger has succinctly put it. Edward Steichen's enormously popular exhibition and book, *The Family of Man*,[29] "a kind of pop anthropology," as Weinberger writes, sought to assert that "we are all like us" (18), but there was the rub. The exhibition and book were a response to the antinomies of the Cold War that sought to assert the oneness of humans while, ironically, being a product of the United States Information Agency, itself an American instrument of the Cold War, although, as Eric Sanden puts

it, the usia did not have to manipulate the exhibition for its international
tour since "its sentimental earnestness offered a congenial co-optation."[30]
There were further ironies in the exhibition's Western, Christian, patriar-
chal, heterosexist ideologies. Roland Barthes, who saw the exhibition when
it reached Paris in 1956, wrote in *Mythologies* (1957)[31] that the exhibition de-
historicized and depoliticized the material it presented, thus undermining
its attempted response to the Cold War. In a contemporary review,[32] Hilton
Kramer decried the exhibition's universalist tendencies: "If Steichen had
been the least bit susceptible to what anthropologists call 'culture shock' –
that sudden, brute intuition of the 'otherness' of cultures different from our
own – he would have had to ... hold open the possibility that the 'essential
oneness of mankind' is continuously held at bay by the nagging details of
our actual lives."[33] Kramer's highlighting of the particular accorded with
Carpenter's response to the overarching theories of conventional anthropology: rather than families, he sought out kinships.

Angelization

The increasing homogenization of cultural differences is explored by
Carpenter in *Oh, What a Blow That Phantom Gave Me!*, which reproduces a
number of passages from the *Audience* article and includes photographs by
Adelaide de Menil. Whereas *Don Quixote*'s phantoms were the product of
print, the ones Carpenter explores here are the product of post-literate media and their tendency to separate mediated spirit from real flesh through a
process Carpenter calls "Angelization" (3). "In preliterate societies," writes
Carpenter, "the separation of spirit from flesh is thought to occur in the
surrealist realm of dream, art, ritual, myth. Daily life, in the field or on the
hunt, is intensely sensate, with all senses alert & the spirit imprisoned in the
body. We reverse this. Our electronic workaday world divorces images from
physical reality" (11). The implications are serious. "Newsmen long ago discovered that news could be used as a hook from which to hang prejudices.
They rarely reviewed current events or films or books; they merely orna-
mented opinions with them. For them, reality was an irrelevancy, something best avoided; what mattered was opinions about reality" (14), which
sounds presciently like Twitter (now known as "X"). Drawing on the work
of Dorothy Lee (**E2; 3, 4, 6, 7**), Carpenter writes that in non-literate cultures,

symbol and thing are taken to be one, whereas in literate cultures, the symbol is taken to be a representation of that thing. Extending this insight to an observation impinging on anthropological research, Carpenter states, "Even in science the observer is recognized as enmeshed in observed fact. Newton may have been confident that 'facts' have a stable eternity outside the contaminating range of our psyche, but we are less confident. We accept that culture & language & other man-made patterns alter experience. Even to observe is to alter, and to define & understand is to alter drastically" (18). The rise of literacy "favored the eye at the expense of all other senses ... Where other senses were employed, it was with the bias of the eye" (24). Modernist art seeks to undermine the primacy of the visual by invoking tactility through "abrupt edges with intervals" (25), as in a comic strip. This is an art of the interface, as opposed to an art of separation, an art "full of abrupt encounters – sudden interfaces" (26), which is also the world of happenings, of performative events where everything is happening at once, and of electronic music that "favors interface & interval" as opposed to "the acoustic continuity of symphonic music" (26). It is the poetry of Pound and Eliot, and above all the prose of Joyce. It is akin to hearing rather than seeing: "The eye focuses, pinpoints, abstracts ... In contrast, the ear accepts music from all directions simultaneously" (29). This acoustic space is "resonating, in flux, creating its own dimensions moment by moment" (31). Carpenter calls this "danced-song" (52) and likens it to Indigenous art of the Pacific Northwest. "Bill Holm, a student of Northwest Coast Indian art & dance, speaks of 'a certain physical satisfaction from the muscle activity involved in producing the characteristic line movement of this art'" (52–3). Holm goes on to state that the "constant flow of movement, broken at rhythmic intervals by rather sudden, but not necessarily jerky, changes of motion-direction, characterizes both the dance and art of the Northwest Coast" (53). Carpenter sees analogies with Kuskokwim masks, "complex mobiles with extensions & moving parts" (31); significantly, these masks were not valued in the West until they were championed in the 1940s by surrealist artists such as Max Ernst, André Breton, Roberto Matta, and Enrico Donati.

Addressing the phenomenon among young people who "find nothing incongruous about conflicting reports in the press, radio, TV, etc." (44), Carpenter cites anthropologist Lucien Lévy-Bruhl's notion that pre-literate peoples have a "'pre-logical mentality'" such that "they weren't bothered by the coexistence of contraries" (44), a state that Carpenter argues is close to the contemporary way in which "media [exist] as self-contained environments, having little correspondence with other realities or environments" (44), and hence the title of the first part of the book, "Worlds Within." Media function as a form of "spirit possession" (50) in their ability to produce total, all consuming, environments akin to the "binding power of the oral tradition" (53) or the dreamworld. "Unlike print, TV doesn't transport bits of classified information. Instead it transports the viewer ... [who] participates solely as a dreamer ... All TV becomes a dream. This is the inner trip, the inward quest, the search for meaning beyond the world of daily appearances ... Sight surrenders to insight, and dream replaces outer reality" (64–5).

The second part of the book is a "Media Log" constituted by random notes made by Carpenter on various field trips (the first of which, he writes, was taken in 1935 when he was thirteen years old [69]). The 1950 Zuni *katchina* figure on the cover of the book is the presiding spirit for this section; ignored by anthropologists, it was collected by surrealist William Copley, and Carpenter likens his media log to this figure, in that the events the log records "belong to the world of surrealism where events are experienced from within, not observed from without" (69). "We live in different communities of time," writes Carpenter, "different personalities of time. The electronic world is the tribal world of interpenetrating space & all-contemporaneous time, but one of many times going on at once: the world of Magritte and Ernst" (85). This surrealist *entrée* to the inner world is equally a reproach to the ineluctably visual (and conservative) bias of the anthropological discipline.

Entries in the log are datelined Borneo, Indonesia, Papua, Northwest Territories, Canada, USSR, New York, and California (a number of them familiar from the *Audience* article). An entry datelined "Bau, Indonesia; 1957" strikes the surrealist note immediately in recounting an "insignificant" village with a one-room school whose only text is *Geological Strata of York County, Pennsylvania* (71). Yet the meaning of the book as a medium is not lost on the teacher. "He understands what a book is, what it means to capture words & suspend time; what it means to organize all perceptions & experiences using the format of a book as a model. This seemingly irrelevant book ... couldn't be more appropriate, for it tells him that the true mapping of the universe begins below the surface & that for scientists, truth

Edmund Carpenter

Oh, What a Blow That Phantom Gave Me!

ZUNI KATCHINA FIGURE, CIRCA 1950

ZUNI KATCHINA FIGURE, CIRCA 1890

Figure 5.5 Cover, *Oh, What a Blow That Phantom Gave Me!*, 1973.

lies in the underlying structures (laws) which govern appearances" (71), an account that clearly channels the structuralist anthropology of Lévi-Strauss that he had elsewhere critiqued. Carpenter bears witness to examples of "incipient writing" (73), such as the singing (or talking) boards of Easter Island. Noting that these boards first emerged almost a century after European contact, he also cites examples from his time in New Guinea when natives who were exposed, however briefly, to writing, sought to produce their own, allowing Carpenter to glimpse "men moving almost unaided from speech to writing" (74). A bartender encountered in Angoram, New Guinea, is desperate for reading material until he encounters "a set of the collected works of Aquinas, abandoned by a mad-missionary-turned-deale[r]-in-pagan-art. Late conversations usually end on some fine Thomistic point" (75). The photographs by Edward Curtis of the "vanishing Indian" are equally surreal, in that they were staged. "Curtis built sets. He supplied wigs. Subjects weren't posed so much as staged, and though the costumes were accurate, the staging was false. A film he made on Kwakiutl [Kwakwaka'wakw] life, as he imagined it was lived prior to European contact ... was embarrassingly theatrical" (91). Carpenter goes on to state that, "Behind the mask of 'Noble Savage' or 'Victim as Hero,' Indians are simply exploited, their identities stolen from them like land and furs" (92). It is comments such as these that gave *Phantom* "a cult-like following among visual anthropologists."[34]

Carpenter's allusion to structuralist anthropology channels one of the most important intellectual debates of the twentieth century, one which in many ways drew on distinctions, especially of speaking and writing, that had been raised in *Explorations*. Lévi-Strauss's claim, in *Tristes Tropiques*, that he introduced writing to the Nambikwara, became the focus for one of Jacques Derrida's most famous deconstructions, arguing that, far from introducing writing into an oral society, speech is always already written. Specifically addressing anthropology (although usually read in a philosophical context),[35] Derrida (who had been a subscriber to *Explorations*, as Carpenter noted in "Sea") argues that the privileging of speech over writing is a particularly Western gesture that imbues speech with a fullness of presence denied to writing; this becomes the overriding position he takes in the various analyses comprising *Of Grammatology* (1967). Lévi-Strauss responded to Derrida by stating that Derrida had taken rather too seriously the law of the excluded middle – Aristotle's notion that a statement must be either true or false, with no velleities of nuance intervening; the Nambikwara were far from being a "pure" oral culture that fell into "impure" writing. This reading points to another understanding of the "middle" that is often "excluded" from consideration, however, that of *tò metaxú*, or the medium, likewise theorized by Aristotle, meaning the relationality inherent in all oppositions.[36] From this position, the twenty-eighth chapter of *Tristes Tropiques*, ambiguously titled "A Writing Lesson" (but who is giving the lesson to whom?) becomes an intriguing meditation on what Lévi-Strauss calls "a mediatory agent" (298), precisely the blindspot of Derrida's analysis, its focus on language failing to recognize that language, whether written or spoken, requires a material medium. It is this that emerges from Lévi-Strauss's analysis, rather than writing (or speaking) itself. Derrida critiques Lévi-Strauss for failing to recognize as writing the "few dotted lines or zigzags on [the Nambikwara's] gourds" (296), but what Derrida fails to recognize are the gourds. Similarly, what Lévi-Strauss observes when he gives paper and pencils to the Nambikwara is that they draw "wavy, horizontal lines" (296) on their paper. Whether or not this is writing, it is definitely a foregrounding of the act of mediation. But the scene becomes even more extraordinary when the chief begins "reading" this wavy writing out loud, his speech itself becoming a pure act of mediation, the chief himself acting as "an intermediary agent" (296). Lévi-Strauss's chapter thus goes beyond the speaking and writing duality to include that aspect of anthropology whose importance Carpenter relentlessly averred, particularly in the third section of *Phantom*.

This third section of the book, "The World Turned Upside Down," records the effects of media such as mirrors, photographs, films, and voice recordings, on native peoples Carpenter encountered in Papua, New Guinea. When Carpenter writes, "I wanted to observe ... what happens when a person – for the first time – sees himself in a mirror" (113), he invokes the famous passage in Lévi-Strauss's *Tristes Tropiques*, where the budding ethnographer writes:

I was about to relive the experience of the early travellers, and, through it, that crucial moment in modern thought when, thanks to the great voyages of discovery, a human community which believed itself complete and in its final form suddenly learned, as if through the effect of a counter-revelation, that it was not alone, that it was part of a greater whole, and that in order to achieve self-knowledge, it must first of all contemplate its unrecognisable image in this mirror, of which a fragment, forgotten by the centuries, was now about to cast, for me alone, its first and last reflection.[37]

What is significant in Carpenter's account is the materiality of the mirror, and its mediatic extensions into photography and film. Carpenter was troubled by the "self-conscious performances" (138) of the Papuans when they were aware of being recorded, causing him to reflect on ethnographic films: "Since most ethnographic films profess to record just that – people going around doing things – the question arises: do they? Or has the camera produced changes in behavior we can't see because they are so common among us, so much a part of our lives that we fail to recognize them as alien in others? Do we take self-awareness for granted?" (138). Carpenter explores this idea in an entry on photographs taken in Papua by Irving Penn in 1970. "These photographs aren't anthropological documents in the usual sense. They don't record moments out of daily life ... One thing is certain: on every face, even the faces of children, there is fear. Not fear of camera or cameraman. Not ordinary fear ... The terror in their eyes is the tribal terror of being recognized as individuals" (141).[38] The changes imposed by media on the Papuans are not unique to them. "Knowledge of media alone is not sufficient protection from them. The moment Marshall McLuhan shifted from private media analyst to public media participant, he was converted into an image the media manipulated & exploited" (162).[39] This was the clearest statement of the rift which had grown between Carpenter and McLuhan after the Fordham affair.

Misanthropology

At the end of *Oh, What a Blow That Phantom Gave Me!*, Carpenter returns to the theme of anthropological research in a section tellingly labelled "Misanthropology."[40] As Carpenter states, anthropology is "an offspring of colonialism" and reflects what Claude Lévi-Strauss calls "a state of affairs in which one part of mankind treats the other as an object" (189). In the twentieth century, Carpenter continues, "the trend has been toward the manipulation of peoples in the very course of studying them," and adds that he is not referring merely to "American anthropologists working on CIA counterinsurgency projects" (189).[41] What concerns Carpenter is "the anthropologist's role as translator" (189). He agrees with the position of Paul Radin, who argued, "The only acceptable ethnology was the life history, self-told by members of indigenous society. But those who undertook such efforts found themselves far removed from the mainstream of anthropology" (189). Relativism was not the answer; Carpenter quotes Stanley Diamond (founder of the journal *Dialectical Anthropology*), who states that relativism is a "perspective congenial in an imperial civilization convinced of its power ... Relativism is the bad faith of the conqueror, who has become secure enough to travel anywhere" (189). Very little of anthropologists' work could serve the purpose of keeping an Indigenous culture alive. "Every category [of their research] came from the dominant culture. The indigenous culture wasn't preserved & presented: it was swallowed" (190). Aware of this, Carpenter found himself presented with a dilemma when working in Papua: "I had been asked to find more effective uses for electronic media, yet I viewed these media with distrust" (190–1). While the government administrators believed media were "neutral tools" (191), Carpenter had come to realize that they "are so powerful they swallow cultures" (191). "What was everywhere needed," he writes, "was the sort of media sophistication which comes only with detachment, dislocation, study" (191). His solution was to produce this book, avoiding the "information control" of standardized publications.

Carpenter's concern about "misanthropology" was echoed in the same year by one of the landmark publications in the field, Clifford Geertz's *The Interpretation of Cultures*,[42] which collects a number of essays Geertz wrote in the 1960s, together with a new one articulating the concept of "thick description." While this chapter has a theoretical orientation, Geertz, like Carpenter, confesses that he grows "uncomfortable" when he gets "too far from the immediacies of life" (vii). Geertz's particular focus is culture, and how it might be made theoretically more manageable by reducing and thus intensifying its scope. His argument is that culture is semiotic, a system of signs, and that as such it is subject to interpretation (5). This act of interpretation requires "thick description," a drilling down that takes into account all available phenomena, or signs, in order to arrive at the correct reading. What is noteworthy about Geertz's discussion is its use of mediated terms.

Describing two boys, one of whom has an eye twitch, and the other of whom twitches his eye to send a message, Geertz states that the difference between a twitch and a conspiratorial wink is "unphotographable," yet that difference constitutes a cultural difference, because the wink is a form of communication, a "socially established code," a "message" (6) that, when understood in its culturally complex context, produces "a stratified hierarchy of meaningful structures" (7). To fail to understand this complexity, argues Geertz, is to understand "anthropological research as rather more of an observational and less of an interpretive activity than it really is" (7). Anthropological interpretation, thus, is "like that of the literary critic" (9) because "doing ethnography is like trying to read ... a manuscript ... written not in conventionalized graphs of sound but in transient examples of shaped behavior" (10).

By this point in Geertz's argument, one can begin to anticipate the objections that an ethnographer such as Carpenter would make: that signs require a medium; that photography is not a neutral medium; that anthropology has largely been oriented toward what can be observed visually; that literacy is a medium having vast cultural implications; and that sound is likewise a complex medium that has been overlooked in anthropological research, especially in its articulation as acoustic space. Anthropology for Geertz is ultimately the articulation of anthropological principles of thick description; like semiotics, it is a closed circle, restricted to reiterating its own principles of interpretation – the "anthropological" is "a system of scientific analysis" (15) that exists "in the book, the article, the lecture, the museum display, or, sometimes nowadays, the film" (16). Anthropological phenomena are produced by the anthropologist: "The ethnographer 'inscribes' social discourse; *he writes it down*" (19). Writing, in this anthropological articulation, becomes anthropology itself. Geertz quotes Paul Ricoeur in support of this position. For Ricoeur, it is "not the event of speaking, but the 'said' of speaking" that is important; "what we write is the *noema* ['thought,' 'content,' 'gist'] of the speaking. It is the meaning of the speech event, not the event as event" (19). The medium is not meaningful, only the message. Yet in the same breath (albeit in a footnote), Geertz can write that "*Self-consciousness about modes of representation ... has been very lacking in anthropology*" (19n3, emphasis added).

Geertz's description of the anthropological process is an indirect way of saying that the anthropologist is part of the ethnographical project; to pretend otherwise would be "bad faith" (20n4).[43] In addition, he asserts that anthropological research must be "microscopic" (21). In this way, anthropology would escape its universalizing tendency: "To set forth symmetrical crystals of significance, purified of the material complexity in which they were located, and then attribute their existence to autogenous principles of order, universal properties of the human mind, or vast, ahistorical *weltanschauungen* [*sic*], is to pretend a science that does not exist and imagine a reality that cannot be found" (20). The "typical" is not the universal, nor is there a "purity" in the findings of the ethnographer, that somehow ethnographical research gets closer to the bone than other types of research. This will fail, of course, to solve the dilemma of cultural variance with biological unity except by acknowledging that there is only cultural variance – "another country heard from" (23). If such research is to make any claims worth heeding, it will do so theoretically; the goal of this theoretical orientation is to enable a conversation that dwells upon "the delicacy of its distinctions" rather than "the sweep of its abstractions" (25). What this conversation will produce is a "refinement of debate" (29): "The essential vocation of interpretive anthropology is not to answer our deepest questions, but to make available to us answers that others ... have given" (30).

In addressing the conflict between universals and particularities that has haunted anthropology, Geertz turns to a mediatic metaphor: "Culture is best seen not as complexes of concrete behavior patterns – customs, usages, traditions, habit clusters – as has, by and large, been the case up to now, but as a set of control mechanisms – plans, recipes, rules, instructions (what computer engineers call 'programs') – for the governing of behavior ... Man is precisely the animal most desperately dependent upon such extragenetic, outside-the-skin control mechanisms, such cultural programs, for ordering his behavior" (44). "Extragenetic" reads like a run around the Boasian genetic universal, while the mediatic metaphor is a stand-in for culture itself. Geertz notes that he is advancing these notions in the context of areas such as cybernetics and information theory, which lead him to argue that "there is no such thing as a human nature independent of culture" (49). The *anthropos* is not an origin point of culture but a product of it, and what produces that culture (and the *anthropos* itself) are technologies. This, writes Geertz, is not typological "Man," but empirical "man" (51). However, the Explorations seminar was more radical in its response to the cybernetic challenge. For McLuhan, "man" was a product of technology, whereas for Carpenter "man" was displaced into the technologies of his aesthetic objects, an involution that would ultimately reveal the concept of "man" as upside down, not the origin of culture but its product. Writing about the carvings of Indigenous peoples of the Pacific Northwest in the catalogue produced for the opening of the Menil Collection, Carpenter states that "Coastal people focused their vast energies on technical problems which they solved artistically … When you go to sea, you need technology to a degree never demanded on land."[44] What is lacking in Geertz's argument is precisely this sense of mediating technologies, as well as and including orality and literacy. In this context, Carpenter's focus on media within anthropological practice must be considered a major contribution to the discipline.[45] It was also a major contribution to media studies.

The disciplinary articulation of media within anthropology has been given the name "visual anthropology," and Carpenter is often associated with this sub-category of research, although there is a degree of unsuitability attached to this association, since Carpenter critiqued the concept of visual culture throughout his career; his theoretical and critical orientation was much more toward acoustic rather than visual space. The movement within anthropology to establish the use of media such as film and sound recording in field research was concretized by the 1975 publication *Principles of Visual Anthropology*, to which Carpenter contributed a chapter.[46] Margaret Mead wrote an impassioned introduction to the volume, wherein she represents anthropology as a mode of preserving disappearing cultures and laments the refusal of the discipline to employ contemporary media, preferring "the hopelessly inadequate note-taking of an earlier age" (4). Anthropology, writes Mead, has become "a science of words" (5); Lévi-Strauss, she notes, "has devoted all of his mature years to an analysis of that part of myth and folklore caught with a written translation of a written text" (5). Mead notes the power of film to affect a culture's sense of itself (as Carpenter had done repeatedly), arguing that this justifies the restriction of such films to "scientific" use. She adds that involving ethnographic subjects in the process of filming does not eliminate the need for restrictive safeguards "although it is often sentimentally claimed to do so" by invoking "shallow claims of culture-free procedures" (8). To avoid these, Mead suggests setting up a tape recorder or camera and leaving them in the same place to gather material on their own, as if recording device or camera were neutral mediators of what they recorded; in fact, the sense of media as mediators of meaning is completely absent from Mead's text. Mead sees a danger in the coming "planetary communications system," in that it will homogenise the multiplicity of cultural traditions, and expresses the hope that "before such planetary systems of thought are developed, the Euro-American tradition will have been broadened and deepened by the incorporation of the basic assumptions of the other great traditions and by the allowance for and recognition of what we have learned from the little traditions" (9). The colonialist position expressed here could not be further from Carpenter's own position, which he sets out in a chapter that reproduces the opening section (circa 113–42) of "The World Turned Upside Down" in *Phantom*. "The Tribal Terror of Self-Awareness" documents the incursion of new media into tribal culture as anything but neutral, the chief effect of such media being to "individualize" members of the tribe, hoicking them out of their communal existence. "A camera holds the potential for SELF-viewing, SELF-awareness, and, where such awareness is fresh, it can be traumatic" (455). When seeing themselves on film or hearing their voices on tape, "tribesmen responded alike: ... they ducked their heads and covered their mouths" (451). Tribespeople seeing their images in a mirror for the first time are "paralyzed" (452). Carpenter notes that a Polaroid picture of a tribal person is anything but a picture of reality: "The photographs were black and white, flat, static, odorless – far removed from any reality they knew" (454). The projection of films caused "pandemonium" (454). Hearing their voices on tape recordings, the villagers "leaped away" (454). Perhaps even more startling was how quickly these media became normalized among the tribespeople: "In an astonishingly short time, these villagers ... were making movies themselves" (454). Carpenter includes an image (plate 10), taken by Adelaide DeMenil [*sic*], that shows a tribesperson in Biami, Papua, taking a photograph. Consistently, Carpenter's focus is not on the use of media such as photography, sound recording, and film to capture a "vanishing culture," but as cultural artifacts themselves – as media, rather than as devices to record messages. "Since most ethnographic films profess to record ... people going around and doing things – the question arises: do they? Or has the camera produced changes in behavior we can't see because they are so common among us, so much a part of our lives, that we fail to recognize them as alien in others?" (456). Carpenter returned to this question in a foreword he wrote to Julia Blackburn's 1979 book *The White Men: The First Response of Aboriginal Peoples to the White Man*.[47] Carpenter writes that, "When ever people meet the unfamiliar, they at once translate it into something they already know, and that means they never face the unfamiliar directly" (7). Carpenter asks, "Do we ever really know how natives see us? We seldom ask ... We love stories about our machines being mistaken for animals and our media being mistaken for gods. The truth is less flattering" (8).

While stationed in Papua New Guinea, Carpenter wrote a review, published in *American Anthropologist*,[48] of *Literacy in Traditional Societies*, edited by Jack Goody, that brings out the theoretical dimensions of his chapter in *Principles of Visual Anthropology*. Goody was a social anthropologist who, with Ian Watt, had published a paper in 1963 arguing that the philosophical and scientific achievements of classical Greece derived from the alphabet; like Carpenter and McLuhan, Goody attached great significance to technologies of communication in their ability to effect social and psychic change. Carpenter's review was scathing. Not only does he find an "air of casual assembly" in the book, but he also asserts that "one is left with the impression that none of the authors is primarily interested in this field, nor acquainted with its literature" (430). Carpenter calls upon the distinction he made in the *Proposals for Art Education* essay between declassification and reclassification to argue that Goody's claim that literacy in traditional societies is often overlooked by anthropologists derives from the fact that media environments are invisible to those who inhabit them. The literate anthropologist, thus, fails to see literacy. "What they see is the past, because they're not involved in it. It requires alienation – some degree of alienation – before I can see my own environment ... The past is visible because it's obsolete. Like a junkyard, everything in it is declassified. This makes it splendidly attractive, because the moment anything is declassified, all its resources, hitherto concealed and restricted by classification, become visible and accessible. The past serves as an antienvironment to the present, permitting perception and awareness" (431). In this context, the anthropologist can be likened to W.B. Yeats's "old rag and bone-man" (431), which was "the title ... given to Frank Speck by the Naskapi" (431). Yet now that electronic communication has made literacy available for anthropological study, anthropologists have tended to ignore it, and those who do study literacy "are said by their colleagues to have 'left anthropology'" (431). Although Goody et al. cite Harold Innis and Eric Havelock, and the "'extravagant'" McLuhan, they appear unaware that the questions they address have been explored earlier and in far greater depth. Goody fails most significantly to distinguish between orality and literacy as media. "To Goody, writing is simply speech made visible" (431). Alluding to *Explorations*, Carpenter states, "Poets have long been at home where anthropologists are strangers. Fifteen years ago I asked Ezra Pound, Robert Graves, Wyndham Lewis, Laura Riding, T.S. Eliot, E.E. Cummings, and Roy Campbell to comment, relative to literacy, on four of Dorothy Lee's articles, including her study of lineality. All did and their comments were superb, but an apprehensive university president buried that venture after proofs had been passed" (432). Carpenter concludes that "*Playboy* magazine recently published an article on this subject that was far more scholarly than what Cambridge University Press offers for $12.50" (432), referring to the interview with McLuhan published in the March 1969 issue.[49] In that interview, McLuhan states that a "basic characteristic distinguishing tribal man from his literate successors is that he lived in a world of *acoustic* space, which gave him a radically different concept of time-space relationships ... Literacy propelled man from the tribe, gave him an eye for an ear and replaced his integral in-depth communal interplay with visual linear values and fragmented consciousness" (59). These themes, first worked out in *Explorations*, remained important for both McLuhan and Carpenter in their various spheres of enterprise. The currency of the research produced by the Explorations seminar was confirmed by the 1977 reprinting of "The New Languages," with Carpenter as sole author, in the eponymously titled *The New Languages: A Rhetorical Approach to the Mass Media and Popular Culture.*[50]

The Limits to Media

The concerns Carpenter had expressed about media in the *Visual Anthropology* volume reappeared, albeit in a North American context, in an interview published in a book that collected responses to the landmark 1972 publication of *The Limits to Growth*,[51] a study, commissioned by the Club of Rome, that used computer modelling to forecast challenges that limited resources and an increasing population would pose for the future of the planet. While skeptics critiqued the modelling employed by the study, environmentalists hailed the report for addressing concerns about resource conservation and about pollution and for making proposals about sustainability. One such response to the book was produced by Willem L. Oltmans,[52] who conducted a large number of interviews on the topic, spurred by "a rising consciousness that generations of today or tomorrow have no right whatsoever to leave the children of tomorrow or the days after tomorrow one huge garbage pile" (vii). The interviewees constituted an illustrious body of public intellectuals and world figures, including U Thant, secretary-general of the United Nations, Margaret Mead, Arnold Toynbee, Marshall McLuhan, Lewis Mumford, Carpenter, Claude Lévi-Strauss, Julian Huxley, Barry Commoner, Edward T. Hall (published in **E3**; 4), Maurice Strong, Ivan Illich, Noam Chomsky, Edward Teller, Herbert Marcuse, Mary McCarthy, Linus Pauling, and Kenneth Boulding (published in **E5**).

Given the Club of Rome's focus on holistic responses to global change, a number of interviewees highlighted the importance of this approach in their response to *The Limits to Growth*. Mead comments that "without computer models we have very little chance of handling the complexity of the problem that we are going to be facing" (19). McLuhan spoke about figure and ground, praising the club's "recognition that survival now depends upon an ecological balance of all factors simultaneously," (77) but critiquing the "systems-development" approach of the report produced by investigators who are "*unconsciously* alphabetic and literate men who can think of no other strategies of investigation except in terms of quantitative assumptions by means of yes-or-no or 'two-bit' programs" (76). Lévi-Strauss stated that the club's report was "too cautious and too weak," and that, twenty years ago, in *Tristes Tropiques*, he had "tried to express exactly the same kind of ideas, fears and warnings" (154). Commoner critiqued the report in terms similar to those put forward by McLuhan – that "computer models are ... misleading because they force you to select the data in such a way as to leave out any information which cannot be put into strictly mathematical terms" (167), arguing as well that the chief cause of pollution was not population increase but economic profligacy that requires technologies that are "insanely counterecological" (168). Anthropologist Edward T. Hall argued that the "problem that man is facing right now is that he inevitably confuses his extensions with the thing that is being extended, in other words, extensions with reality" (186–7). Chomsky stated that the "major problem of *Limits to Growth* is not posed by the under-developed world. It's posed by the advanced industrial societies, where people are literate, where people are committing their vast resources, material and intellectual, to destruction" (289). Teller argued, against the "prophets of doom," that "nuclear explosives ... could stimulate gas reserves which are contained in rock of small pore size and which cannot be pumped out by conventional methods" (311), thus addressing predicted shortages in energy. Marcuse praised the report because it demonstrated "the destructiveness and aggressiveness which is inherent in the capitalist system" (334). McCarthy laments that television, unlike print, does not encourage "an informed body known as public opinion" (347). To Oltmans's statement that "Marshall McLuhan tries very hard to find what on earth television does to our minds," McCarthy responds, "Yes, but he is for it, and I am against it. I am completely against television. I think it could be abolished" (345). Boulding is skeptical about the report, and about computer modelling, stating that we are hampered in our predictions by "our inability to predict the future of knowledge" (437).

Carpenter's interview comments are markedly different from those given by the other interviewees. He does not address computer modelling, pollution, or political economy. Rather, he takes a culturalist approach, arguing that the greatest dangers to the continuance of humankind are posed by electronic media: "If you want to destroy a culture, the strongest weapons you have ... are electronic media" (137). He critiques anthropological research for ignoring this aspect of cultural production, stating that such research "belong[s] to an Alice-in-Wonderland world" (137). His particular concern is that "electronic media obliterate culture. They replace cultural environments with media environments. It's no longer Captain Cook stepping in and out of different cultures; we now step in and out of media" (137). Citing his own work in Papua New Guinea, Carpenter states that when supplying native peoples there with media such as cameras, his hope was that these media would be used to reflect the "culture," "perceptions," and "values" (138) of the Indigenous peoples. It was the medium that dominated, however, not the message: "What they made were *films* ... Media swallow cultures. The native left his culture totally behind and stepped into the world of the camera" (138). In a hypermediated period, culture becomes "a myth maintained by anthropologists ... a thing of the past" (138). Media tend to produce "spirit divorced from flesh," a tendency sensed by young people, who "turn back and try to rediscover their bodies" (138–9). This same cohort has abandoned univocal ideas of truth. "They accept many universes, many realities. To them, television does not reflect the world outside. It is not supposed to" (140). Meanwhile, suggests Carpenter, the world outside is collapsing. Interviewed in his sixteenth-floor apartment in Manhattan (Carpenter had begun teaching anthropology at the New School for Social Research in 1970 ["Sea," 258]), Carpenter notes, "The sound level is so high, it is difficult to do a tape recording ... The sound level in New York City has reached the point where people are going insane ... I have never before seen a culture where the environment is driving people insane" (140). Of particular concern to Carpenter is that "anthropologists have never dealt with media" (141). He states that his own studies of media "have been wholly unacceptable to anthropologists ... To them, media have no existence. But they find nothing disturbing about putting a culture in a book" (141). Ultimately, the media image of a culture takes precedence over the culture itself. Whereas with print culture "there is an urge always to refer back to the flesh, to the physical thing" (143), this is not so with electronic media. As a result, Western civilization is losing its direction. In an interview published in *Television Quarterly* that same year, Carpenter makes similar points, stating that television "records a world within ... Television, far from expanding consciousness, repudiates it in favor of the dream ... In the pre-literate world, 'spirit possession' is thought to occur rarely, under circumstances fraught with mystery and danger. With us, it occurs daily."[53]

Arctic Realities

In contrast to this hypermediated world was the one that Carpenter repeatedly returned to in the Canadian Arctic, and it was to this area of research that he had recourse after he completed his project in Papua New Guinea, publishing *Eskimo Realities*[54] in the same year as *Phantom*. Drawing on *Phantom* and on *Eskimo* (vol. 9 of *Explorations*), as well as on *Anerca*, *Eskimo Realities* (designed, like *Out of the Silence*, by Arnold Skolnick in a format resonant with the *Eskimo* volume) reiterates a number of Carpenter's key interests, including Inuit "cosmography" (13);[55] spatial orientation based on the directions of winds, rather than land mass or stars (23); the lack of a concept of "enclosed space" (24), such that "visually and acoustically the igloo is 'open'" (25); how perception is performative rather than observational (26); the powerful mnemonic sense among the Inuit (27); and acoustic space (33–7).

What is new in *Eskimo Realities* is a discussion of the concept of "sila," an ambiguous notion, in that it can refer both to outer and inner realities. Sila is a "goddess of the natural order" and "goddess of thought" (45), the way in which form is brought out of nature, and this concept leads to the second distinctive quality of *Eskimo Realities*, which is its pronounced focus on Inuit art, the book containing many more images of Inuit art than does *Eskimo*, some of which were provided by Carl Schuster, whose work Carpenter had known since at least 1966 and would edit later in his career. Carpenter also drew on the studies of Jorgen Meldgaard, ultimately establishing the Carpenter-Meldgaard Endowment (through the Rock Foundation) in 2009 at the National Museum of Denmark to register and make available to the public Meldgaard's archive of northern research.

In writing about Inuit art, Carpenter emphasizes that the term "art" is a misnomer: "No word meaning 'art' occurs in Eskimo [*sic*], nor does 'artist' ... Carving, like singing, isn't a thing. When you feel a song within you, you sing it; when you sense a form emerging from ivory, you release it" (58–9). Art, for the Inuit, is a process, not a product, "a ritual, not a possession" (75). Inuit art, like Inuit language, is "polysynthetic" (78), and reached an apogee of sorts with the work of the Dorset people (800 BCE–1300 CE), whose art "was the finest. They excelled in carving tiny, exquisite effigies, probably amulets and shamans' gear" (83; cf. the cover image of a hand holding some sculptures). The tininess of the artifacts is significant: they are the products of a tactile culture, the objects made not simply to be held in the hand, but felt and experienced by and through the hand. The complexity of this experience is evident in the tactile maps employed by some northern peoples.[56] These maps do not function within the domain of visual space; they are meant to be held in the mitten and felt, a multi-dimensional form of sensory perception allied with audile-tactile space. As Carpenter remarks, the small carvings are not made to stand upright, which would make them subject to a single point of view. In this way too, they are made to conform to tactile

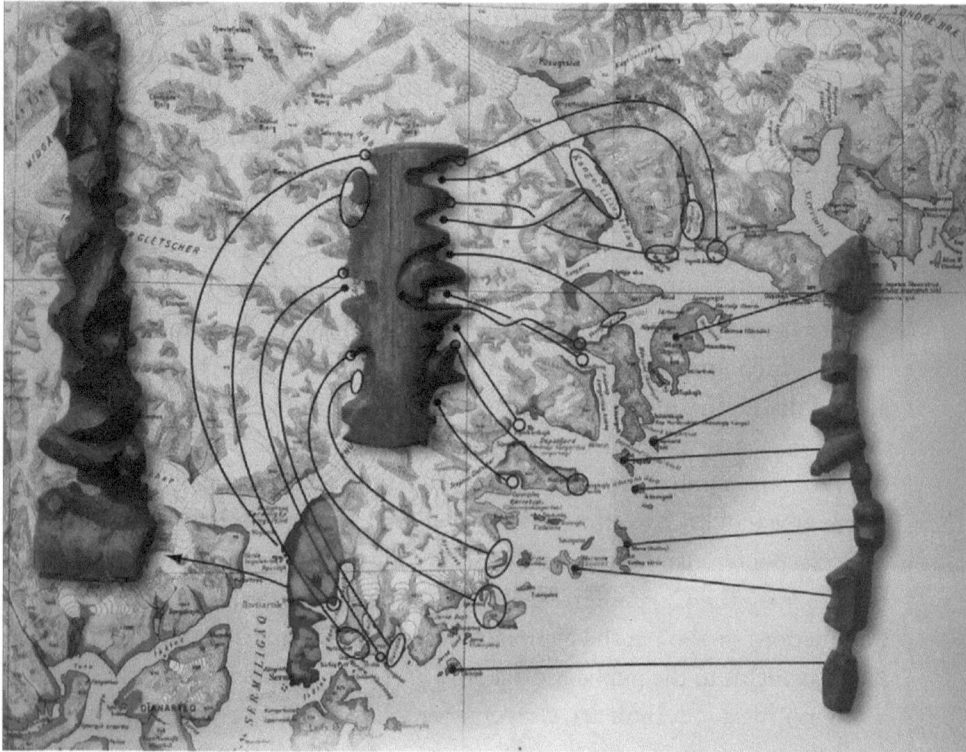

Figure 5.6 Hand-held shoreline maps.

rather than visual encounters. For the Inuit, "delight comes from the simultaneous perception of multiple meanings within one form" (145). Inverted figurines, meant to be worn upside down as a pendant, are of particular interest to Carpenter. Some anthropologists have suggested that these figurines represent deceased beings – people and animals; others suggest that they were worn by women to ensure a good birth. As Carpenter comments, "In many oral and manuscript cultures, reversal is employed as a magical technique, at once sacred and profane" (149). The embodied sense of art extends to tattooing, suggesting that the "Eskimo know themselves and others through art" (160). This traditional relationship to art was changed dramatically, however, by the interventions promoted by James Houston in the late 1940s. The resulting carvings "are massive, heavy, and fragile, designed to be set in place and viewed by strangers. The traditional role of art is gone:

object has replaced act" (192). Carpenter does not condemn this art, since it represents financial security. What he does condemn, however, is the notion, promoted even by anthropologists, that this art is historically genuine. "We let the Eskimo [sic] know what we like, then congratulate them on their successful imitations of us" (195). These observations are brought together in Carpenter's retelling of the myth of Sedna, giver of life and bringer of death. "In a life where neither reason nor strength prevail, where cunning counts for little and pity least of all, the Eskimo [sic] sings of life, for only art prevails, and even then, not always" (217). The dominant focus on art in *Eskimo Realities* represented a decisive turn in Carpenter's anthropological research toward aesthetics, while questioning the application of Western notions of art to non-Western artifacts. In this he anticipated the interest in objects as sites of cultural mediation, as opposed to understanding such objects as "texts" to be read.[57]

Eskimo Realities was reviewed by Bruce Cox in 1974, along with Richard Nelson's *Hunters of the Northern Forest: Design for Survival Among the Alaskan Kutchin* and Joseph Senungetuk's *Give or Take a Century: An Eskimo Chronicle*, in *American Anthropologist*.[58] Accorded a single paragraph, Carpenter's book was not well received. *Eskimo Realities* is described as "an augmented edition of *Eskimo*, which Carpenter published in 1959" (418),[59] the reviewer lamenting the absence of Frederick Varley's illustrations and the photographs from Robert Flaherty's collection that had appeared in the earlier book: "The earlier book had a unity of purpose which *Eskimo Realities* lacks ... Text and illustrations seem oddly assorted. For example, pp. 88–91 show Dorset pendants opposite Knud Rasmussen's account of collecting amulets among the Netsilingmiut. The unstated implication is left that Netsilik amulets ... have the same function as the small animal replicas on the Dorset pendants. The pendants shown, however, did not come from the Netsilik area" (418). The review concludes with the comment that Carpenter sees his role in the book as "to pose evocative, if far-fetched, questions with which the reader must puzzle" (418). Based on the articles published by Carpenter that advocated a radical pedagogy, one has the impression that he would have agreed with this assessment.

More than a quarter century after *Eskimo Realities* was published, Tim Ingold returned to it in a chapter of *The Perception of the Environment*,[60] suggesting that Carpenter's Arctic research had retained its currency into the next millennium. Ingold is particularly concerned with the speaking/ seeing dichotomy as a definitively Western phenomenon that occludes anthropological research into sensory relations. Taking up Carpenter's Arctic research, an interest that he shares, Ingold argues that Carpenter, along with McLuhan and Ong (all three published in *Explorations*), "effectively laid the foundations for a currently vibrant field of inquiry that has come to be known as the anthropology of the senses" (250). This is so only orthogonally; what they founded was media studies, though the confluence of sensory anthropology and media studies as Carpenter articulated it is a reminder of the anthropological element in Carpenter and McLuhan's foundational contribution to media theory.[61]

Turning to "Carpenter's seminal study of Inuit sensory experience" (253), Ingold asks, "Why, in the face of overwhelming evidence for the centrality [*sic*] of eyesight to the Inuit perception of their environment, did Carpenter nevertheless insist to the contrary that, for them, the eye is subservient to the ear?" (253). Answering his own question, Ingold continues:

> Could it be because he took with him into his study a preconceived notion of vision, as analytic and reflective rather than active and generative … that was fundamentally incompatible with his fine appreciation of the dynamic potential and spherical topology of the Inuit lifeworld? And if, as Inuit ethnography suggests, it is perfectly possible to combine the perception of a lifeworld of this kind with a thoroughgoing ocularcentrism [*sic*], albeit of a kind radically different from that with which we are familiar in the West, then how can we any longer attribute such perception to the predominance of hearing over sight in the balance of the senses?

This can only be described as a wilful misreading of Carpenter, who theorized acoustic *space*.[62] Acoustic *space* is a theory of spatial mediation, not a theory about hearing. It seeks to articulate a modality in which the entire sensorium operates in specific ways; visual space is likewise a modality in which the entire sensorium operates in specific ways. Carpenter makes this abundantly clear in *Eskimo Realities*: "Reading tracks involves far more than just knowing where to look. *Everything smelled, tasted, felt, heard can be as relevant as anything seen.* I recall being out with trackers once and when I stooped to scrutinize the trail, they stepped back, taking in the whole. *Interpenetration & interplay of the senses are the heart of this problem*" (22, emphasis added).[63] Carpenter anticipates, here and elsewhere, that "fusion of the sensible and the intelligible" that Paul Stoller considers to be of central importance to an evolved anthropological practice. Writing in *Sensuous Scholarship* (1997), Stoller states that:

> It is especially important to incorporate into ethnographic works the sensuous body – its smells, tastes, textures, and sensations. Such inclusion is especially paramount in the ethnographic description of societies in which the Eurocentric notion of text – and of textual interpretations – is not important. I have noted elsewhere why it is representationally and analytically important to consider how perception in non-Western societies devolves not simply from vision (and the linked metaphors of reading and writing) but also from smell, touch, taste, and hearing. In many societies these lower [*sic*] senses, all of which cry out for sensuous description, are central to the metaphoric organization of experience.[64]

This is much closer to Carpenter's *modus operandi* than Ingold's account of it, albeit that, for Carpenter, the sensorial hierarchy invoked by Stoller did not exist. Carpenter's position has more in common with that elaborated by Constance Classen: "The thought of speech as a sense seems odd to us moderns. This is partly because we conceive of the senses as passive recipients of data, whereas speech is an active externalization of data. It is also because we think of the senses as natural faculties and speech as a learned acquirement. The ancients, however, had different ideas on the matter. They were apt to think of the senses more as media of communication than as passive recipients of data."[65]

These differences in sensorial engagement were important to Carpenter because they also produced different understandings of art – was art a special cultural category or was it fully integrated with social practices? Carpenter questioned the category of "art" as having the same status cross-culturally, and this emerged with considerable force in a symposium organized by the magazine *artscanada* on "the sacred in art" that was filmed by the Canadian Broadcasting Corporation and shown on the

TV series *Man Alive* in May of 1971. The editor of the article established a broad framework for the discussion, invoking "the collective psyche" and its "memories of a primordial and primary garden of primitivism."[66] Joining Carpenter in this discussion were Vancouver media artist Gary Lee-Nova; Toronto artist Ronald Bloore; medical ethicist Father Benedict Ashley; Gregor Goethals, who wrote about the interface of television and religion; and Gene Youngblood,[67] media theorist and author of *Expanded Cinema* (1970). Lee-Nova opened the discussion by arguing that the concept of the sacred must, of necessity, be accompanied by the concept of the profane. Father Benedict argued that things cannot be sacred unless they ask questions. Youngblood asserted that all artworks pose questions. Bloore stated that a Kwakiutl [Kwakwaka'wakw] mask expresses a universal humanity. Goethals responds that this ignores cultural specificity. To this discussion Carpenter responded, "I tend to avoid the word sacred and the word art too because I'm never sure of the meanings. Other people have clear meanings for them but I never agree with those meanings and I don't have any of my own so I shun these and native peoples generally do too" (21). As an example of the sacred in Inuit culture Carpenter cites the story of Sedna, "the most sacred story told by the Eskimo [*sic*] and probably Canada's oldest myth" (21). Bloore notes in response that sacred art need not be of museum quality; it only needs "aura" (23). Youngblood added that such objects that are now in museums should be returned, because their context defines them. Father Ashley stated that the concept of creator has shifted from the sacred to the secular, and that "technology has given contemporary man control over nature and I think pretty soon even over changing himself – man is going to create himself in a sense" (23). To this, Youngblood responded, "Mr McLuhan himself has said something about television, that once you put the world inside a man-made environment, you're in charge of the whole show and you must program it all" (23), a concept that filled Youngblood with horror. To Bloore's comment that the sacred in art is divorced from "the socio-political structure" (25), Carpenter responded that one can only understand the "grammar" of such art by understanding how art functions contextually. "In anthropology I'm fascinated by the way people unhesitatingly go into the arts and talk about primitive art as if it could be experienced with some gut reaction" (25). To Bloore's question, "What's the matter with having a gut reaction to art?" Carpenter asks, "Would you have a gut reaction to Dostoevsky printed in Russian if you didn't read Russian?" (25). Bloore replies that his comment applied to visual culture. Lee-Nova concludes the discussion with the hope that the environment itself can be made sacred.

Responding to this notion of the complexities and differences within artistic production in a catalogue essay for a massive exhibition on art of the "far North" curated in 1972 by the National Gallery of Art in Washington, DC, Carpenter (then teaching at Adelphi University) contributed an essay titled "Some Notes on the Separate Realities of Eskimo [sic] and Indian [sic] Art,"[68] as well as about a dozen catalog entries (287). His inclusion in the book along with pre-eminent anthropologists such as Frederica de Laguna (an expert on Paleoindian art of the north) and Henry B. Collins (the leading American prehistorian of the Arctic), indicates that by the early 1970s, Carpenter was recognized internationally as an expert on northern Indigenous peoples and their culture and (perhaps to a lesser extent) on Indigenous art of the Pacific Northwest. His contribution to the volume seeks to differentiate these two areas of artistic production. Carpenter begins by articulating the *modus operandi* of anthropological research: "To experience the unfamiliar in tribal art, we must step outside the patterns of perception of our culture and explore new worlds of images, new realities. We must study alien perceptions and codifications by experiencing them. Anything less merely confirms previous convictions" (281). Pragmatically, however, this is impossible. To fully know a people, one would have to relinquish one's identity, and even that would not constitute a surety. "'We wed ourselves to the mystery,' not to conquer it or be conquered by it, but to greet it" (281). In these terms, "the ethnologist is the twice-born spiritual adventurer whose fieldwork is nothing less than the spirit quest ... he exposes his dearest beliefs and habits to doubt and diversity, and returns changed by this intellectual ordeal" (281, as he had written in the Summer 1968 issue of "Explorations"). This understanding of ethnology is a far cry from the notion held by "some anthropologists" that "the real world is not what is lived, but rather the underlying structures (laws) that govern appearances. Thus they are bent on making anthropology a science of the same type as the physical sciences, for these, too, reject appearances and insist that reality is not in them but in the laws that govern them" (281). The problem with this approach, Carpenter argues, is that it rejects "the sensate world" (281), which is to say the entire domain of perception which was so important to the scholars involved in the Explorations seminars.

Carpenter finds that intellectualism characterizes most studies of tribal art, whose "gravity and jargon erode the living edge" (282). These anthropological accounts of tribal art create a scientific "equivalent" of tribal art, and then study that, the reality escaping their grasp. This, however, is not science; it is "imperialism" (282). The anthropologist must recognize that "all symbolic systems are implosive, and therefore must be experienced from within" (282). Not to do so renders tribal art as "mere trophies – loot displayed in a pirate's wardroom" (282), Carpenter alluding here to Stanley Edgar Hyman's article in E2 arguing that tribal art must be understood holistically, as part of a ritual process. Harkening to his "Notes of an Unconventional Anthropologist," Carpenter states that, although similarities may be observed among the artifacts in the "Far North" exhibition, "This should not mislead us. These groups differed from one another and these differences were vital to each" (283). The art of these groups is also differentiated internally. While Inuit sculpture is incredibly detailed, when the same sculptor turns to "the world of dream ... he replaces realism with surrealism, and structures space with the ear, not the eye" (283). It is not surprising, then, that surrealist artists such as Breton, Ernst, and Matta et al. should have been so taken by the art (especially masks) of the Inuit. The key factor linking surrealism with acoustic space (space structured by the ear) is simultaneity, of more than one spatial vector interfacing with others. "Like sound, each mask creates its own space, its own identity; it makes its own assumptions" (284).

Turning to Haida art, Carpenter distinguishes between the simultaneity that characterises Inuit masks, and the idea of metamorphosis that underpins the transformation masks of the Haida. "Unlike the Eskimo [*sic*] artist, the Haida artist ... doesn't create space; he *fills* space" (285). Carpenter quotes Bill Reid (whose poem "Out of the Silence" Carpenter commissioned for the volume of that name, referenced here by Carpenter [288]) to the effect that, in Haida art, "all is containment and control, and yet always there seems to be an effort to escape" (285). While some northern art appears "poorly executed" (286), such as certain examples of Athabaskan art, the question this art poses fuses the aesthetic with the ontological, having to do with the ability to call from within one's self "images powerful enough to deny [one's] nothingness" (287). The differences noted here by Carpenter informed his collecting practices for himself and for the Menil Collection, practices which ultimately took the form of the radical juxtaposition that he associated with surrealism.

6

The Menil Connection

AFTER THE PUBLICATION OF *Out of the Silence*, Carpenter commissioned a second study of Northwest Coast Art,[1] published in 1975 as *Indian Art of the Northwest Coast*,[2] by Bill Holm and Bill Reid, with an introduction by Carpenter. The book was connected to an exhibition titled "Form and Freedom" at the Rice Museum in Houston, Texas, in the fall of 1975 that focused on work from John and Dominique de Menil's collection of Northwest Coast Art, as well as from the collections of Christophe de Menil, Adelaide de Menil, Carpenter, and Francesco Pellizzi.[3] The central feature of this art, writes Carpenter in his introduction, is "transformation" (9), through which a single image can occupy multiple spaces via what Carpenter had previously termed "visual puns," a quality (again, as he had noted before) much appreciated by the surrealist artists who were exiled in New York in the early 1940s. Anthropologists, however, deemed such multiplex forms of representation to be errors, largely because their approach to art was functionalist, an approach that ultimately reduces tribal art to the status of souvenir. As Lévi-Strauss told Carpenter, even the New York dealer who supplied the surrealists with a number of tribal artifacts considered them to be akin to "quaint curios of the *Gemütlich* type."[4] It was surrealists and abstract artists who first expressed a kinship with Indigenous art of the Pacific Northwest; Max Ernst, along with Barnett Newman (as Carpenter notes) arranged an exhibition of "Northwest Coast Indian Painting" in 1946 at the Betty Parsons Gallery in New York. Of key importance for both Newman and Carpenter was that Indigenous artifacts be understood as aesthetic objects that spoke to the present moment. As Newman wrote in the catalogue to the exhibition, "Does not this work rather illuminate the work of those of our modern American abstract artists who, working with pure plastic language we call abstract ... are creating a living myth for us in our own time?"⁵ W. Jackson Rushing has stated that Newman was well-read in ethnological studies of "primitive" art and in anthropological theory; what is significant about his work is the notion that contemporary art functions in many ways parallel to tribal art. As Newman puts it in his catalogue essay, "Just as modern art stands as an island of revolt in the narrow stream of Western European aesthetics, the many primitive art traditions stand apart as authentic aesthetic accomplishments that flourished without benefit of European history" (quoted by Rushing, 189).

One of the lenders to the Parsons Gallery was George G. Heye's Museum of the American Indian. It was precisely the *refusal* to understand Indigenous art aesthetically, however, that was at the heart of the animus that Carpenter had for Heye, who would become the object of Carpenter's tellingly titled *Chief and Greed*, published in 2005. "Every piece" in the museum's collection, writes Carpenter, "was classified and labeled as a scientific specimen. Tribal carvings were housed with seashells and minerals as objects of natural history ... Part of the gap [between the scientific and the aesthetic] derived from the anthropologists' insistence that ethnological specimens had meaning solely in terms of the social matrices from which they came" (11). Drawing on his concept of declassification and reclassification, Carpenter points out that by removing the eighteen objects from the museum and putting them in the Parsons Exhibition, the surrealists were able to reclassify these objects as artworks. Carpenter credits Lévi-Strauss for articulating the appeal of Northwest Coast Indigenous art to the surrealists, namely "the almost monstrous faculty to perceive as similar what all other men have conceived as different" (quoted by Carpenter, 11).⁶ This juxtapositional quality was likewise spatial, allowing for multiple points of view rather than the single point of view associated with visual space.

Carpenter traces the collecting of Northwest Coast art to traders in the eighteenth and nineteenth centuries: "By 1820, the demand for curios had created a souvenir industry" (13), evidenced by the number of identical masks produced during this period. Collectors formed an international cadre – Captain Cook from England, James Magee from the US, Alejandro Malaspina from Spain, Captain Urey Lisiansky from Russia. A number of later collectors were personally known to Carpenter (he states), such as

George Thornton Emmons, Charles F. Newcombe, and John R. Swanton, all of whom "lived, by choice, between two worlds" (16), that of the Indigenous cultures they researched, and that of non-native culture. They had a profound understanding of native iconography that escaped artists such as Emily Carr. These anthropologists were also collectors, some having become active in acquiring objects for the World Columbian Exposition in Chicago (1893), while also commissioning work for this exposition, thus producing the "anthropological specimen" (16). Ironically, Indigenous artifacts had little market value until the mid-1950s, as Carpenter observes, and thus such artifacts were rarely exhibited, anthropologists likewise ignoring this work because they did not deem it to be art. Among the collectors, Louis Shotridge stands out as Indigenous, ultimately employed by George Gordon of the University Museum, Philadelphia, as a collector of note. Shotridge also studied under Franz Boas, working as a linguistic informant, and at the University Museum in Philadelphia he worked with Edward Sapir and with Frank Speck, Carpenter's doctoral supervisor. Shotridge's collecting career was complex, because he was considered a traitor to his own culture for removing artifacts at the behest of museums. Carpenter recalls spending time in Klukwan, at the Whale House, a magnificent example of Tlingit art, where the tribe rejected large financial offers for the house while leaving it exposed to the elements; Carpenter himself prevented children, on one occasion, from damaging it. This difference in the understanding of "art" suggests that many great works were lost, while what can be found in museums represents "mere merchandise" (24).

Carpenter recounts that Dominique de Menil, mother of Adelaide, and collector, with her husband John de Menil, of works now housed in the Menil Collection in Houston, Texas, had asked him to amass Northwest Coast artifacts for their collection. Since the late 1950s, Dominique de Menil had been associated with the art department at St Thomas University, a small Basilian college in Houston,[7] organizing exhibitions there, teaching, and ultimately becoming chair of the department, while also collecting and curating for the Menil. At St Thomas, the de Menils had created a "teaching collection." As the de Menils' biographer William Middleton describes it, the "historical range was tremendous: a carved relief of the Egyptian deity Horus (1314–1197 BC) rubbed shoulders with an ancient Greek painted terracotta amphora (520 BC) and *The Borghese Warrior* (seventeenth century), a

HOLM: Ladle of wood. It's hard to determine the material at first glance, but if you look closely, you see the growth rings and grain of the wood.

REID: The main attraction is the patina, which gives the ladle almost the quality of horn. Its overall form is relatively pleasing. I prefer ladles with bowls tapering down a little more. This one rounds off at the end. It might have been different once. Perhaps it broke off when the artist was making it, or he may have decided to make it that way. But it hasn't got quite that canoe-like element of some of the other ladles here. This handle has a strange structure: the hollowness of the bowl extends right up the handle to the head, so that the handle is almost hollow. That has nothing to do with any function I can perceive. But perhaps he just carried out the adaptation of the canoe shape to the spoon.

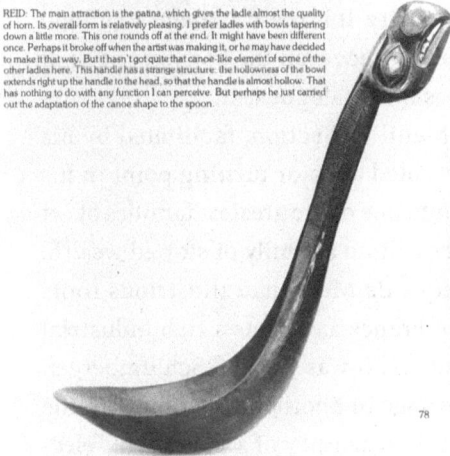

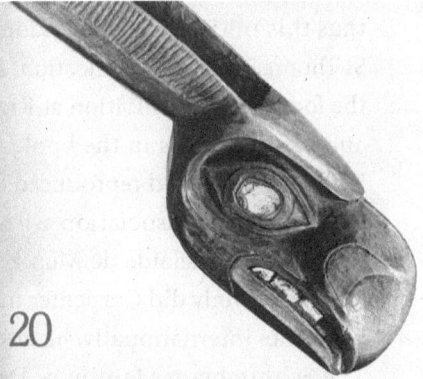

20

The eagle head on the end is well brought out and has abalone inlays for the eyes and teeth. Strange how a person who could do good carving on the head would get so sloppy with the striations on the handle. Why didn't he take an extra ten minutes to put those lines on straight? It was a simple thing to do.

HOLM: I agree—its color and general form are its high points. When he hollowed out that handle, he didn't stop at the eagle's head, but continued right through its mouth. I can imagine somebody looking at that and saying, "Gee, look at all that work—he's carved right down to there!"

The hole through the head doesn't seem to be anything, yet there it is. Maybe it was to lighten the spoon, or to prevent it from cracking.

78

Figure 6.1 Eagle-headed wooden ladle, Kwakwaka'wakw, Menil Collection. Reproduced in Holm and Reid, *Indian Art of the Northwest Coast: A Dialogue on Craftsmanship and Aesthetics*, 1976.

miniature of a work in the Louvre. The grouping went from pre-Columbian terra-cotta bowls to nineteenth-century American folk art, from an eagle-headed wooden ladle from the Kwakwaka'wakw peoples of the Pacific Northwest to a standing female figure of carved wood by the Bambara people of Mali. And there were recent works to reflect contemporary concerns such as *Vietnam* (1965), an antiwar, painted collage on stainless steel by Michelangelo Pistoletto, a major figure in the *arte povera* movement" (417). By 1968, however, the de Menils had cut their ties to St Thomas, finding it too conservative in its approach to art, and decided to begin an association with Rice University, where Dominique de Menil became director of the Institute for the Arts.[8] Based on her interest in Pacific Northwest art, "Dominique de Menil expressed [to Carpenter] the desire to exhibit such masterworks. The plan was to search everywhere and select the best" (24).[9] However, writes Carpenter, "this proved unfeasible." Mme de Menil then suggested "exhibiting the Shotridge collection" (24), but this proposal was not supported by the tribes from whom the artworks had been taken and thus this initiative was abandoned. As a result, the artifacts collected for St Thomas's teaching collection, such as the ladle referred to above, became the focus for an exhibition at Rice University. It is these artifacts that Reid and Holm discuss in the book; Carpenter recorded the conversations of Reid and Holm and reproduced them as the catalogue text.

Carpenter's association with the Menil Collection, facilitated by his marriage to Adelaide de Menil, represented a major turning point in his career. Not only did Carpenter marry into one of the greatest families of art collectors internationally, he also married into a family of storied wealth. The Schlumberger family of Dominique de Menil had illustrious roots in the political and cultural history of France as well as a rich industrial heritage deriving from the textile industry. It was Conrad Schlumberger, Dominique's father, who took that heritage in another direction with the invention at the beginning of the twentieth century of a method of "electrical prospecting"[10] that could be used to find petroleum deposits. By 1926, the company Schlumberger founded was prospecting four oil fields in Houston. (Carpenter became an expert on the Schlumbergers' history; Middleton's biography lists a dozen items about the family conveyed to him by Carpenter.)[11] Dominique's husband, Jean de Menil, fourth Baron Menu de Menil, had an equally intellectual background; a graduate of Sciences Po, he became a banker in Paris and subsequently took up a position with Schlumberger. Having made a trip around the world as a student, he acquired a small collection of African ceremonial masks, records of Tahitian music and Polynesian traditional clothing. After their 1931 marriage, Dominique and Jean began collecting objects such as a Punu mask from Gabon and painted loincloths from Papua New Guinea (*DV*, 169–70). Thus began a life of collecting both tribal and Western art, the latter primarily American and European, with an emphasis on surrealism. The one comparable mid-century American collection that likewise sought to place ancient art in dialogue with modern art was that assembled by Louise and Walter Arensberg in Los Angeles,[12] resulting in a collection that influenced the Menil's founding director, Walter Hopps (*DV*, 547). Comparing the two collections, however, it is immediately evident that the one in Houston is superior, both for its breadth of circa 12,000 plus pieces (the Arensbergs' focused on pre-Columbian sculpture and modernist art, with an emphasis on Duchamp, that could fit in their LA house), and for resolving the question of a museum, a question that remained unresolved for most of the Arensbergs' lives. The Menil building, designed by Renzo Piano, was opened in 1987. A number of its holdings belong to the Adelaide de Menil and Edmund Carpenter Collection and include Yup'ik, Haida, Tsimshian, and Tlingit masks. Other items are from the Edmund Carpenter collection, including Ulu knives, needle cases, and a comb, all of walrus ivory, as well as artifacts associated with harpoons; most of these derive from St Lawrence Island (Alaska).[13] Owing to his considerable ethnographic knowledge, Carpenter became invaluable to the de Menils in their collecting of tribal art; in the double-page photograph at the beginning of *Art and Activism: Projects of John and Dominiqude Menil*, Carpenter is pictured with them.[14]

In 1962, Schlumberger was listed on the New York Stock Exchange (*DV*, 399), and the de Menils at that time established trust funds for each of their children amounting to circa US$30 million each (equivalent to about ten times as much in 2023). Marrying into this wealth had six major impacts on Carpenter: he could work as an independent scholar; he could publish outside the constraints of the academy; he could avail himself of funding from a research foundation, the Rock Foundation[15] (founded in 1976 by Adelaide de Menil as president, and Carpenter as vice-president, with a ledger value, in 2018, of US$5,454,071);[16] he could take on the massive (and expensive) editing project posed by the Carl Schuster archives, which he eventually published under the aegis of the Rock Foundation;[17] he could extend his collection of tribal art; and he could advise the de Menils on art acquisitions and exhibitions. As William Middleton writes, "Adelaide and her husband, Edmund Carpenter, were instrumental in Dominique's acquisition of many important sculptures and objects from Oceania and the Pacific Northwest, and many works from their own collection were included at *Rhyme and Reason*" (*DV*, 580). *La rime et la raison*, held in Paris at the Grand Palais in 1984, was the first extensive exhibition of art collected by the de Menils. Carpenter wrote an essay for the catalogue on "*Art de la mer de Béring et des Eskimo*" (Art of the Bering Sea and of the Eskimos [*sic*]) in which he distinguishes the art produced around Bering Strait from 500 BCE to 800 CE by its use of metal, acquired through Asiatic trade: "*Il est indéniable que l'art de la mer de Béring reflète les influences de l'âge du métal*" (It is undeniable that the art of the Bering Sea reflects the influences of the age of metal).[18] Design elements associated with these artifacts, particularly representations of animals and birds, were shared with works using ivory. Carpenter goes on to note that the artifacts were miniature, given that the people who created them were nomadic, and it was this art (especially works in ivory) that Carpenter celebrated in the *Upside Down* exhibitions.

Carpenter had been collecting Arctic and Pacific Northwest artifacts for the Menil Collection since the mid-1970s, and in the decade preceding the Paris exhibition these acquisitions were being made in an increasingly politicized environment. The collecting of Pacific Northwest Coast Indigenous artifacts was further complicated by Canada's creation of the Cultural Property Export and Import Act. In the fall of 1977 the Victoria (British Columbia) *Daily Colonist* published a series of articles by Stephen Hume about the sale of Indigenous artifacts from Canada to the United States, and in particular to the Menil Collection. Writing on Sunday, 4 September 1977, in the first of three articles, Hume states that, "For months, a syndicate of Indian-art dealers has been working feverishly to beat Tuesday's proclamation date of a federal law that will regulate the export of Canadian heritage, Provincial Museum officials say. One of those involved is a former University of Toronto anthropology professor."[19] Alan Hoover, assistant ethnology curator of the British Columbia Provincial Museum, is quoted as stating, "International Indian-art dealers in BC have known about Bill C-33 for a long time. They knew before the museums did. They're making a killing while there's still time" (1). Peter McNair, ethnology curator of the museum, commented that "some artifacts are going to the Menil Foundation in Texas, which has a significant Northwest Coast Indian art collection" (1). Howard Roloff, a dealer in Indigenous artifacts based in Victoria, remarked that Bill C-33 would "change things," and that he was "working overtime to 'liberate' as much art as possible and offer it to US buyers such as the Menil Art Foundation" (1). The article goes on to note that "Edmund Carpenter, an agent for the Menil Foundation, spent about $350,000 for two masks and about $175,000 for a rattle this year – all in one week" (1). The museum could not compete with these prices. Carpenter is described as "a leading agent for the Menil Foundation," and that he is "sometimes referred to as the foundation's 'consulting anthropologist.'"[20] Carpenter was involved in negotiations for the purchase of the Crosby Collection of artifacts gathered in BC in the late nineteenth century. While the Menil Collection sought to buy the collection, Carpenter stated that "He would be happy to let a Canadian institution acquire the collection if the institution could come up with the money. Carpenter subsequently put a time limit on his offer to sell to Canada."[21] Canada raised the funds, and the collection went to the (then) Museum of Man in Ottawa.

Carpenter told his side of the story in a 22 May 1977 letter to William N. Taylor, Jr, director of the Museum of Man, stating, "We would not bid against a Canadian museum," and adding, "Adelaide and I are not collectors. Nearly everything we acquire goes directly to a museum."[22] Carpenter also said that he and Adelaide de Menil had "a dream ... to create somewhere, perhaps in some remote, beautiful spot, a temple of Northwest Coast art, a place that will touch visitors by its form, its integrity ... So that's what our 'collection' is all about. But, in spite of this interest, we are sensitive to other needs and have no desire, ever, to frustrate efforts to return objects to the descendants of their creators."[23] In response to the articles in the *Daily Colonist*, Carpenter wrote again to Taylor, stating that the articles "create serious problems. In the United States, government agencies keep careful watch over foundation activities. Federal and state officials would not look kindly upon the activities alleged here, if true."[24] But, adds Carpenter, "they are not true ... Every statement made by the Daily Colonist is false ... No specimen was ever acquired from Howard Roloff. The Menil Foundation has never had any connection with him." This would not be the last time that Carpenter encountered the complexities of collecting in the era of decolonization. While Carpenter had enjoyed collecting from his student days,[25] by the time of the 1968 founding of the American Indian Movement, the collecting of Native American and Indigenous Canadian artifacts had become increasingly politicized as well, a politicization that also hovered around the controversies associated with the Museum of the American Indian in which Carpenter would become personally involved. In addition, there was a vast ontological gulf between Indigenous and non-Indigenous notions of an artifact (as Carpenter himself often pointed out) which extended to museum display. Bill Reid and Adelaide de Menil's *Out of the Silence* represented this difference starkly, with its images of totem poles returning to the earth. Douglas Cardinal's National Museum of the American Indian in Washington, DC, likewise interrogated colonialist aspects of collecting with its limited exhibition spaces versus the vast void at its centre, painted white, that is the negative involution of the capitol that it faces and a sombre reminder of the genocide of Native Americans.

Museological Controversies

Collecting controversies characterized the museum landscape in the 1970s and '80s. In 1984 the exhibition *Primitivism in 20th Century Art*, staged at MOMA, caused a ruckus. Responding to the broader implications of the controversy, James Clifford stated in *The Predicament of Culture*[26] that he "does not see the world as populated by endangered authenticities" (5) in good part because "people and things are increasingly out of place ... After 1950 peoples long spoken for by Western ethnographers, administrators, and missionaries began to speak and act more powerfully for themselves on a global stage" (6) in which "dwelling and ... travel ... are less and less distinct" (9). It is with these sentiments that Clifford approached the MOMA exhibition, suggesting that what the MOMA exhibition proposes is a "Family of Art" concept similar to that of "The Family of Man" that Carpenter had implicitly critiqued at the end of his *Audience* article. Picasso, for example, is said to have had a "profound identity of spirit with the tribal peoples" (quoted, 191). Clifford notes that "Anthropologists, long familiar with the issue of cultural diffusion versus independent invention, are not likely to find anything special in the similarities between selected tribal and modern objects. An established principle of anthropological comparative method asserts that the greater the range of cultures, the more likely one is to find similar traits" (191). This observation goes to the heart of critiques made about Carl Schuster's vast ethnographies, a project on which Carpenter was then working. What is said to connect the "tribal" and the modern is "abstraction," but as Clifford points out, what this really means is that "tribal" art appears to coincide with the rejection of the pictorial illusionism instaurated in the Renaissance. At no point, however, does Clifford attend to media shifts in this version of art history, which would go a considerable distance in adducing a historical, as well as mediatic, foundation for proposing affinities between the "tribal" and the "modern." Instead, Clifford frames the MOMA exhibition in terms of "the restless desire and power of the modern West to collect the world" (196). Carpenter was well aware of this conundrum, and confronted it directly in the major exhibitions he produced at the end of his career, in which "upside down" was not only a reference to a spatial differentiation that identified a cultural pattern and a media history, but also a pedagogical position that sought to invert the

Western concept of collecting, forcing the viewer to adapt to the context in which the art was produced and in which it acquires meaning. Carpenter was also aware that what produced the "affinity" between "tribal" and "modern" art was the process of reclassification. Clifford echoes this insight when he states that the MOMA exhibition presents "a history not of redemption or of discovery but of reclassification" (196). Clifford cites Carpenter only once in *The Predicament of Culture*, when writing about Lévi-Strauss's New York sojourn and his encounters there with "tribal" objects and their surrealist collectors. "According to Edmund Carpenter, the surrealists felt an immediate affinity with these objects' predilection for 'visual puns'" (238). Carpenter would expand this notion to suggest that anthropology is itself surrealistic insofar as it seeks to produce meaning through a calculated juxtaposition of the "tribal" and the "modern," and Carpenter would take up this configuration when he established the "Witnesses" installation in the Menil Collection.

The complexities of ethnographic research emerged in another controversy in which Carpenter intervened, with reference to Robert Gardner's film *Forest of Bliss* (1986), which examines funerary practices in Benares (Varanasi), India and their intersection with daily life. The Rock Foundation had previously supported Gardner's film *Altar of Fire* (1977) about the Vedic ritual in Kerala, India. In producing this film, Carpenter "brought two of [his] closest friends together: Frits Staal, a Vedic scholar at Berkeley, and Robert Gardner, the filmmaker at Harvard."[27] Staal's research was published in 1983 as a massive, two-volume slip-cased production titled *Agni: The Vedic Ritual of the Fire Altar*[28] that includes tipped-in colour and black-and-white photographs by Adelaide de Menil as well as cassette recordings of the chanting, and was funded in part by the Rock Foundation (xxv).[29] During the filming of *Altar of Fire*, Carpenter "assisted with the technical organization, made sketches and measurements of sacrificial implements, and collected information of various kinds" (I, xxvi; II, 744). He also assisted with the sound recording. While *Altar of Fire* was received without controversy, *Forest of Bliss* was excoriated by some for its eschewing of subtitles and (English) voice-over narration, and praised by others for its filmic qualities. Tellingly, Gardner has stated, "I thought that the audience would not simply wait for the mysteries to be dispelled but would come up with their own solutions, supply their own answers, and so, in that way, *they would be doing their own anthropology"* (emphasis added),[30] a comment that could be applied equally to Carpenter's *Upside Down* exhibitions, which likewise sought to invert the anthropological equation, putting the onus of "interpretation" on the participant by eliminating labels for the artifacts. (Gardner in fact claimed Carpenter as his filmic mentor.)[31] Because the central issue had to do with the use of film within an ethnographic context, the controversy took flight in the pages of the *Society for Visual Anthropology Newsletter.* The controversy began with Alexander Moore's article "The Limitations of Imagist Documentary: A Review of Robert Gardner's *Forest of Bliss,*"[32] which claims that Gardner's film, while beautiful, is anthropologically deficient because "it relies on only one perceptual mode, vision, to convey information" (1) and "illuminate the universal human condition" (3). This is an odd critique to be making in a newsletter devoted to *visual* anthropology (over and above the appeal to the "universal"), and highlights the unease within the discipline about media, as well as the lack of critical reflexivity in a discipline that, historically, has been ineluctably immersed in visual culture. The critique is also incorrect; the film makes exceptional use of acoustic modalities to convey its information, modalities heightened by the lack of voice-over and subtitles. (As Susan Sontag noted in a review of the film, "Life has no subtitles or voice-over commentary.")[33] Even though there is much speech in the film, Moore deems it "mute" because he does not understand the language, which is, again, a telling comment on the anthropological enterprise.

In a letter responding to Moore's review, Gardner stated, "I wonder if the time may not have come for members of certain orthodoxies in Anthropology to rethink their threadbare doctrines" (3). Jonathan P. Parry, who had done ethnographical research in Benares, echoed Gardner's comment with the suggestion that the film seeks to counter "the singularly sanitized and idealized picture of the city which emerges from certain recent works of Western scholarship."[34] If the Ganges is the source of purification, this is clearly not to be understood in Moore's terms of hygiene; part of the resonance of the film is its juxtaposition of Western and non-Western sensibilities, as Moore unconsciously testifies when he laments the filming of a dog fight because it could upset the sensibilities of Westerners who love their pets. As Ákos Östör, co-producer of the film, states, the negative reviews of the film reveal "an incredibly literal ... bias"[35] which fails to understand how film as a medium produces meaning. The most damning review issued from Jay Ruby, considered to be a major figure in "visual anthropology."[36] Ruby's opening gambit is that anthropologists "have too easily accepted ideas about film generated by non-anthropologists."[37] Ruby's major complaint about Gardner's work is that it seeks to be anthropological while ignoring "all of the hallmarks of ethnography" (10), a critique that he extends to the work of Robert Flaherty. As a result, all of Gardner's films are "useless ethnography" and *Forest of Bliss* "a failure as film art" (11). Carpenter, who had taught with Gardner at Harvard and whose wife, Adelaide de Menil, had done still photography for Gardner's film on Vedic ritual, *Altar of Fire*,[38] took particular umbrage with Ruby's assessment. The tone of Carpenter's response to Ruby is evident in his title: "Assassins and Cannibals or I Got Me a Small Mind and I Means to Use It."[39] Referring to Ruby's article as "latrine gossip" (12), Carpenter states that "Professor Ruby can't write, can't think, can't tell the truth. His comments on *Forest of Bliss* remind me of complaints about difficulties in understanding Pound and Joyce. Forty years ago *The Saturday Review of Literature* developed a whole readership around such complaints. Since many of those readers were teachers of literature, we may safely assume that the class-room damage was considerable" (12). Carpenter extends his critique mediatically: "Today's speedup of information, with consequent information overload, forces us to abandon analysis in favor of pattern recognition. This shorthand is really a dismemberment of history in which all context is lost. History survives only as an art form in print culture. The public has already lost the sense of chronology, once fundamental to Western education. The right approach is more important than all the details" (12). Carpenter contrasts this loss of historical memory with the "shared codes" of traditional cultures (the topic of *Materials for the Study of Social Symbolism*), in which cultural memory is maintained homeostatically. As Carpenter puts it, "the differences between 'important ideas' [quoting Ruby] and ideas important in anthropology is often considerable" (12). If Professor Ruby seeks to critique "false cultural images" (12) he should start with nationalism, which, in the Canadian context, "reinvented the Eskimo [*sic*]: renamed them 'Inuit,' taught them an alien art, groomed them for new media roles, and ridiculed contrary accounts. Anthropologists cooperated, including Professor Ruby" (12).

This comment refers to Ruby's contribution to the exhibition catalogue *Robert Flaherty: Photographer/Filmmaker,* for which Ruby wrote the essay "'The Aggie Will Come First': The Demystification of Robert Flaherty." "In the pages of the book," writes Carpenter, "Flaherty was charged with racism, romanticism, dishonesty, falsification, insensitivity, and much more" (12).[40] In fact, Ruby refers to *Nanook of the North* as "one of the most influential films in the development of an anthropological cinema," and states that "Flaherty espoused a view of film as a medium for communicating ethnography which is very modern,"[41] yet Carpenter notes that the catalogue's ethnographic acuity is indicated by the misattribution of a glass negative attributed to Flaherty that appears on the book's cover; the photographer was actually Bert Chesterfield, notes Carpenter. The catalogue is filled with such errors, he states, adding that "Professor Ruby should distance himself from this disaster" (13). Instead, adds Carpenter, "Now I'm asked to believe that what I admired was false, and not just *Nanook*, but all of Flaherty's films, and all of Gardner's as well: full of racism, sexism, colonialism, romanticism, ignorance, arrogance. These denunciations sound like echoes from the Chinese Cultural Revolution" (13).[42] In opposition to those who critiqued a film such as Robert Flaherty's *Nanook of the North* as a colonialist venture,[43] Carpenter calls it "the best film ever made of the Eskimos [*sic*]" because "Flaherty photographed people as they saw themselves" (55).[44] To argue for an unmediated ethnology, Carpenter states, is to forget that "no traditional culture survives untouched. The most remote village has long since been drawn into the world economy" (55). When the exhibition travelled to the International Center of Photography in New York (4 April to 18 May 1980), Carpenter gave a lecture in Manhattan countering exhibition organizer Jo-Anne Birnie Danzker's focus on "the 'demystification' of Robert Flaherty" with "the demystification of anthropologists and film critics." Carpenter argues, "Anthropologists, insisting on context and chronology, stand flat-tired by the highway … Other questions and other methods now occupy a transformed world" (56). Such anthropologists, writes Carpenter, "talk of the accuracy of science and the errors of art. That merely betrays an ignorance of both … Those who knew the Eskimos [*sic*] first-hand praised Flaherty. Who, then, are his critics [?] One who comes to mind, who wrote 'Alas, for Flaherty,' is not an anthropologist, not a filmmaker[,] not a film historian. She belongs, rather, to a new genre of film philosophers who, with limited exposure to film and no exposure to Plato, ponder reality, preferably in California.["]⁴⁵ Asking his audience why they are attending this exhibition, Carpenter replies, "It's Flaherty's ghost that summons us ... His concern was human dignity. That's what his films are about. That's why we love to watch them over and over. Those proud faces will not go out of mind and be forgotten ... To which his critics reply: romanticism; life was never so ennobling. I disagree. The Eskimo [*sic*] I knew were proud people.["]⁴⁶

Connecting Patterns

It was in the wake of museological controversies such as these that Carpenter began to publish a monumental work that in many ways appeared to fly in the face of the "postmodern" turn in anthropology. *Materials for the Study of Social Symbolism in Ancient and Tribal Art: A Record of Tradition and Continuity, Based on the Researches and Writings of Carl Schuster, Edited and Written by Edmund Carpenter, Assisted by Lorraine Spiess*⁴⁷ was literally Carpenter's magnum opus, given the twelve massive volumes in each set weighing 97 pounds ("Sea," 260) that were magnificently produced, although the study's provenance, as with other works by Carpenter, was complex, as the subtitle ("edited and written") suggests. Carpenter had 600 sets printed, which he distributed *gratis*, largely to scholars and libraries outside North America (3.453). The frontispiece, unidentified in the book, reproduces an engraving of Prince Jeoly (or Giolo), an enslaved Miangas Islander who was purchased in Mindanao, Philippines, in 1690 by William Dampier, who brought Jeoly to Oxford and displayed him there until Jeoly's untimely death a few months later from smallpox. Carpenter's elision of Jeoly's biography evidences a racial insensitivity that also manifested itself in his refusal to accept "Inuit" as a legitimate moniker for Indigenous peoples of the Canadian Arctic, and in his characterization of the Minik affair in terms of scientific research.⁴⁸

Schuster's massive study of cultural artifacts, which, owing to his sudden death (in Carpenter's presence ["Sea," 260]), he was unable to publish in a coherent form, had a simple thesis: that cultural patterns are ultimately connected, regardless of how widely dispersed they might have become. Jorge Luis Borges's "Mutations," published (as Carpenter notes) in *Explorations* 4 in 1955, provides one of the epigraphs to the study. It is a parable about how

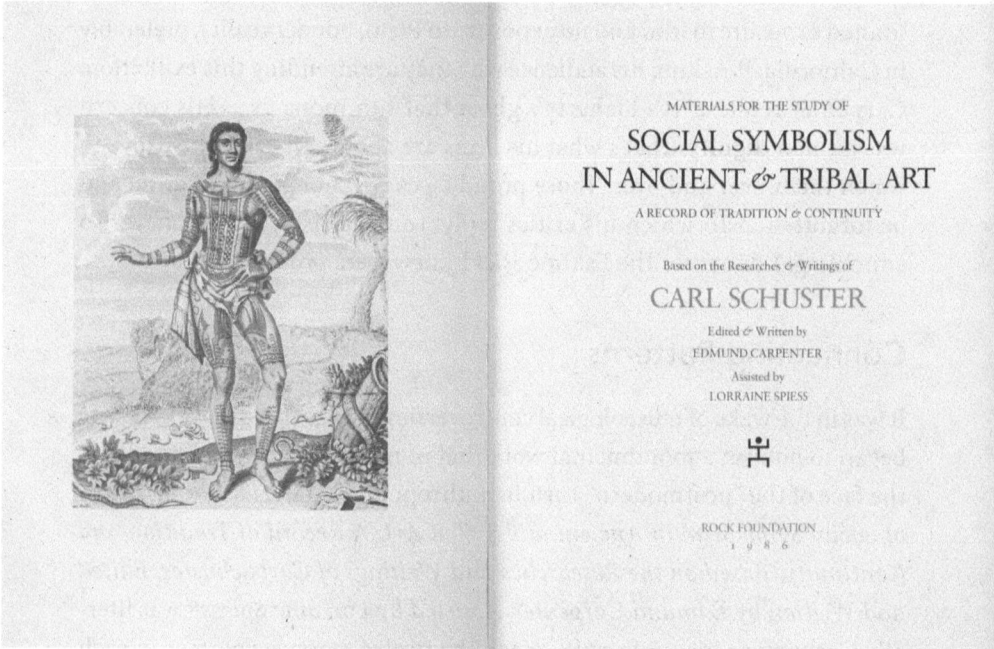

Figure 6.2 Frontispiece and title page, Schuster and Carpenter, *Materials for the Study of Social Symbolism.*

symbolic forms ultimately erode into their material substrates, the cross into the marble it was carved from, the horseman's cord into a cinch on a dress, an arrow into a piece of iron. The task of the ethnographer in this context is to discern the patterns that underlie these materials. Another epigraph is provided by a longtime friend of Schuster (3.13), Ananda Coomaraswamy,[49] an expert on the art of India, who was deeply critical of the literate bias of academia, which he claimed resulted in an inadequate response to the ways in which ideas were communicated in oral cultures.[50] The epigraph reads: "The folk has thus preserved, without understanding, the remains of old traditions that go back sometimes to the indeterminably distant past, to which we can only refer as 'prehistoric' ... Had the folk beliefs not indeed been once understood, we could not now speak of them as metaphysically intelligible, or explain the accuracy of their formulation" (1.10). The internal quotation is from René Guénon, and the concurrence of Coomaraswamy and Guénon is significant in that they promulgated the

notion of the *philosophia perennis*, or perennial philosophy, that argued
the universal connection of religious beliefs and motifs. As William W.
Quinn, Jr, writes in *The Only Tradition*, "To Coomaraswamy and Guénon,
the establishment of primitive wisdom or mythology qua philosophia perennis was based on perceiving the difference in modes of thought and
apperception, and, by extension, their ontological predicates. Primitive
peoples tended to think in images and symbols, unlike moderns, who are
used to empirically based scriptural or graphic abstractions and models
by which they adjudge all other forms of thought and expression."[51] The
distinction between the "primitive" and the "modern," thus, is a mediatic
one, and the role of the anthropologist is to get behind the mediatic pre-
suppositions of modernity in order to understand the thought of those
deemed to be "primitive." The images and motifs of "primitive" peoples
represented a totally unified system of thought and being, and thus, "to
Coomaraswamy and Guénon primitive culture was Traditional culture"
(178), where "Tradition" means *a group of interdependent metaphysical
principles and a concomitant cultural worldview*" (4, emphasis in original).

The notion of the *philosophia perennis* contextualizes Carpenter's comment in the introduction that Schuster sought to "decode" the "ancient
system" of "man's earliest iconography" as a "memory link from the present
back to paleolithic times" (33), an enterprise that Carpenter terms a success.
"When he juxtaposed specimens from New Guinea & South America, medieval Germany & modern Africa, his concern was not historical, but the
underlying principles which govern their forms & meaning" (33). Schuster's
ultimate goal was to produce "evidence of continuity in cultural history"
(33); he was "not really interested in proposing any specific theory of contact, but simply in demonstrating affinities in the field of traditional design"
(Carpenter quoting Schuster, 3.259). Schuster's research was not held in es-
teem by his colleagues, writes Carpenter. "Their criticism derived partly
from the American bias against tradition. They saw history in terms of invention & diffusion ... Younger colleagues also questioned broad comparative studies which sought to demonstrate common denominators among
cultures" (34). But Schuster's research was oriented differently, suggests
Carpenter. "This iconography isn't some vague variable like totemism. It's
closer to chess: self contained, unrelated to food-production or warfare,
technology or grammar ... Truly conservative traditions, [Schuster] felt,

were transmitted internally, from generation to generation, not externally between alien peoples" (34–5). Schuster did not claim to be a diffusionist, writing in 1948, "I am not really interested in proposing any specific theory of contact, but in simply demonstrating affinities in the field of traditional design" (quoted, 37). So massive were Schuster's archives that Carpenter claims he used only a fraction of them to produce the twelve volumes of his edition (37); "his archives contain incalculable riches from a world now forgotten" (40). Carpenter tells how he met Schuster: "Somehow, in 1959, he learned that I had recently returned from studying collections in Irkutsk [one of the largest cities in Siberia]. He just appeared, knocking at my door in desert California. Over the next ten years we met irregularly and corresponded frequently. I enjoyed sending him 'fresh' evidence. After his death I discovered that he already had nearly everything I sent" (40–1).[52] Those archives contained circa 80,000 negatives, about 185,000 prints, circa 800 rubbings, about 2,500 drawings, a bibliography of 5,670 items, and 18,000 pages of correspondence in more than thirty languages (41; also Appendix 2, "Archives & Editing," 1.934-8), and were donated at Schuster's death to the Museum für Völkerunde, Basel. Carpenter's friend Bernard Fontana, an anthropologist based at the University of Arizona, urged Carpenter to redeem the tragedy of Schuster's early death by getting his efforts into print (43), and the result was these twelve volumes.

Carpenter had long had an interest in the history of artifacts, especially when those histories extended over vast periods of time and of place. In some senses, this flew in the face of traditional anthropological research, which tended to focus on specific times and places, rather than making the large claims associated with Schuster's research. In 1950, when *Explorations* was about to be launched, Carpenter wrote a short essay titled "The Story of a Sacred Grove,"[53] which he published privately as *Serpent on the Hill*, about a "great snake constructed of earth and rocks on a hill overlooking Rice Lake" (northeast of Toronto, in the vicinity of Peterborough, Ontario).[54] Its origin, suggests Carpenter, contains the prehistory of the province, peopled by Beringian nomads who eventually moved as far as South America. "We're dealing here with thousands of years and the sweep of two continents."

Equally vast was the range of Carl Schuster's research. Editing such a massive fonds posed problems that Carpenter elucidates in the first volume. "My plan was to use only Carl's own words, omit none of his ideas

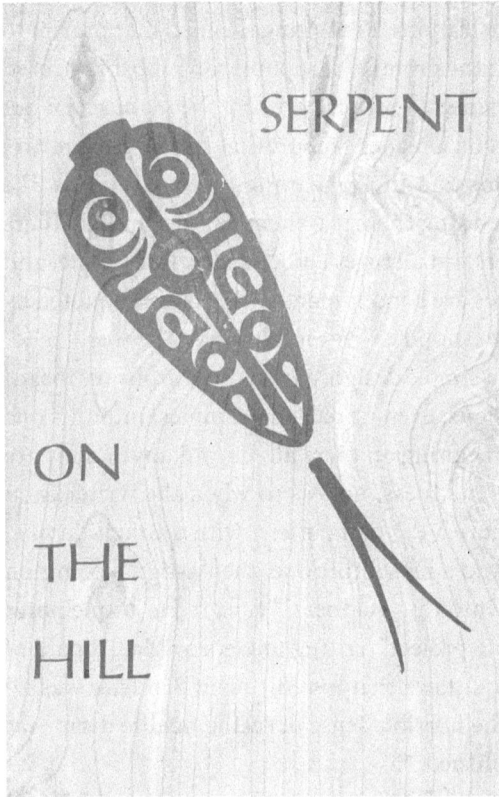

Figure 6.3 Cover, *Serpent on the Hill*, 1950.

and exclude all of my own judgements. I spent several years assembling such a text. It was unreadable. But out of that effort I came to know the data. Patterns emerged ... Wherever I could, I used Carl's own words. About twenty percent of the text comes directly from him, sometimes with only minor editing. Most of this appears in Volume 1, Part 2, often word-for-word from his published texts. Elsewhere I use little; in some chapters, nothing. At first I tried to distinguish between Carl's writings and mine, but soon gave up. I had to decide what to use, how & where; what to emphasize, modify, contradict; what to weave into the whole and what passages to keep intact. Throughout the text, 'I' refers to me, to my judgements, though many of these come directly from Carl's writings. A strange way to edit someone else's work! But, after years of frustration, I saw no alternative ... The final text, I believe, is wholly consistent with what Carl might have written" (1.942). Yet Carpenter also states that he omitted much – "whole areas of study," including 60,000 illustrations. Presenting the final manuscript to Harvard University Press, with the promise of support for publishing costs, its editor of social sciences declined to read it. MIT sent the manuscript out for review, but rejected it based on a reader's report that stated, "[There are] absurd relations between forms and their meanings ... Reading it is like reading a dictionary and pretending there is a theme or plot in it ... There are those who believe in universal structures embedded in form, style, and human behavior. These volumes are a monument to this belief" (quoted by Carpenter, 1.948).[55] Carpenter responds, "We rightly apply the word 'mad' to any enthusiast who chooses a simple design, assigns it an arbitrary meaning, then forces all similar designs, even unrelated examples, into this one category, bestowing the same meaning on them all ... Art & mythology are always at the service of man's madness, no less so when the writer is an anthropologist. When I compare a Papuan pattern with a Brazilian one, or juxtapose a modern motif and a mesolithic one, then assign a common origin to them all, don't I fall into this madness?" (1.949). He at one point despaired about completing the project, writing to George MacDonald of the (then) Museum of Man in Ottawa that his editing of Schuster was an "obsession" and that he had "the horrible sense of seeing my life disappear in trivia, with nothing accomplished."[56]

Carpenter elucidates Schuster's basic premises in the first section of volume 1, "Descent & Relationship" (47). "Paleolithic peoples invented an iconography to illustrate their ideas about genealogy ... Thus the same intelligence lies behind all genealogical patterns. No matter how varied the art style, the rules governing their composition are everywhere alike" (47). With the rise of city states, however, and the invention of writing, assumptions about tribal genealogies were largely lost, although they still existed palimpsestically "as deep metaphors in urban cultures" (47). Carpenter elaborates in volume 2 that "Many people equate the branching of a tree with the genetic union & division by which every family, clan or tribe perpetuates itself. They express this 'natural' association of ideas in language & myth, and visually depict a 'family tree' as anthropomorphic, providing it with appropriate human attributes" (2.21). Because the iconographies emerging from this process represent genealogies, their basic building blocks are "conventionalized human figures" that are "designed to be joined limb-and-limb with adjacent figures, the intention being to illustrate descent &

relationship" (48). In the same volume (2), Carpenter addresses the question of origin versus diffusion. Discussing the motif of the double-headed figure, he writes that either it was "repeatedly reinvented, or so ancient that it everywhere enjoys a common origin, for it occurs on all continents" (2.99). Carpenter states categorically, "I doubt that [the motif] was independently invented over and over again. I believe this motif derived from anthropomorphic Y-posts" (2.99). Part of the problem in determining origin versus diffusion has to do with the difference between "a participating symbol and a referential symbol ... In tribal societies ... the symbol is recognized as an inextricable component of that which, to Western thinking, it merely represents ... Literacy promoted the shift from reverential to referential ... There is a world of difference between saying 'three generations' and reciting ancestral names individually" (2.1201). However, "secularization was never total. No one who has ever observed gaming among North American Indians could ever regard that activity as purely secular. The emotional commitment alone can be awesome. And the game itself is always ritualized, with cosmic interpretations" (2.1201). Rather than developing these ideas into a coherent and systematic argument, however, the books proceed in very short paragraphs that accompany illustrations. One has the impression, at times, of George Eliot's Mr Casaubon, looking for the key to all mythologies, except that in Schuster's case, he believed he had the key. What he was looking for was even more empirical evidence: as Carpenter states, he "suffered, he confessed, 'from CONSTANTLY EXPANDING HORIZONS'" (3.260). As Carpenter notes, however, "the incontrovertible truth he hoped to find always eluded him" (3.322). To which Carpenter adds, "it eludes me" (3.322). Perhaps as a result, many of the particularities of interpretation are inconclusive: "Do these zigzags share a common meaning, or at least a common origin in genealogical patterns? Perhaps not all of them" (307). Nevertheless, Claude Lévi-Strauss asserted in his 1965 Huxley Memorial Lecture on "Kinship" that, "If social anthropologists were half as interested in material culture as they ought to be, they would probably have paid more attention to Carl Schuster's fascinating survey of the world-wide occurrence of a type of geometrical pattern which, from its geographical distribution and from known early examples he thinks goes back to paleolithic times ... If Schuster is right, not only the facts of kinship, but the theory as well, may be scores of thousands of years old. What we have painstakingly unearthed

The basic 'bricks' used in the construction
of genealogical patterns are conventionalized human figures:

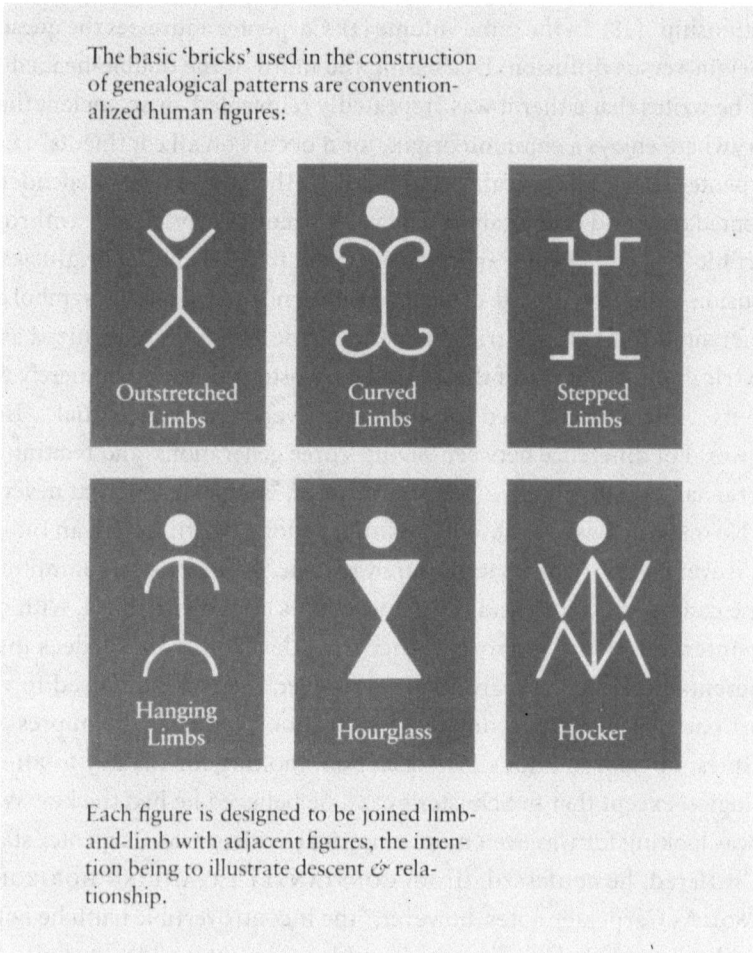

Outstretched Limbs	Curved Limbs	Stepped Limbs
Hanging Limbs	Hourglass	Hocker

Each figure is designed to be joined limb-
and-limb with adjacent figures, the intention being to illustrate descent & relationship.

Figure 6.4 Iconographies, Schuster and Carpenter,
Materials for the Study of Social Symbolism.

beneath the facts might be nothing else than this age-old theory" (quoted
by Carpenter, 1:683).[57] Other than Lévi-Strauss's comment, Schuster's work
was met with silence, although Carpenter records a correspondence he
had with the art historian Leo Steinberg, who, having read Schuster and
Carpenter on "Genealogical Patterns," confessed that, while at first he believed that Schuster was "wildly overinterpreting," he was finally won over
by Schuster's "sweep of ... imagination" (1:685).

Volume 2 of the study "reorganizes, under new headings, data outlined in Volume 1. The argument remains the same. I even re-use some of the same illustrations & interpretations ... Few readers will start with Volume 1:1 and continue through 3:3. Even those who do may find it difficult to recall previous explanations. So I repeat them, over & over again, often verbatim. No reader is ever expected to remember previous explanations, nor asked to flip back to earlier illustrations. This repetition may irritate, but the alternative would be unreadable" ("Preface," 2.15). If this sounds anti-academic, Carpenter confirms that it is. "I continue in the same non-academic style: telegraphic sentences, ampersands, abbreviations, vulgar forms, minimal text. This is deliberate. The polished essay was invented by an older generation to keep a younger generation from thinking too much. It was also designed to contain reality within language. Since most of the evidence here doesn't fit comfortably into language, I devised a format more congenial to it" (2.15). Carpenter claims that Schuster would be delighted by the format but disturbed by Carpenter's style. "My vulgar style would certainly have disturbed him. He was very courteous. He avoided friction. He hoped for academic recognition. This was denied him, principally by archaeologists who saw themselves as 'hard-rock scientists'" (2.15). Further on in volume 2, Carpenter states that he does not give "deference to academically-established boundaries between artistic provinces & periods" but rather to "inherent form & content. This isn't the route to academic popularity, but it does illuminate dark areas of prehistory, accessible by no other means" (2.295). Carpenter clearly identifies with Schuster the outcast researcher here, while exhibiting a disdain for the academy that has putatively rejected them both. Yet his procedure does not derive simply from personal disposition; it reflects Carpenter's belief that "proposed analogies are more real than the boundaries which they transgress and that certain preconceptions of cultural history need revision, not the evidence that violates them" (2.299).

The general title of volume 3 is *Rebirth*; the volume was to have begun with an essay by Schuyler Cammann (an anthropologist whose field of study was Asia) on cosmic games. Because that essay did not materialize, Carpenter produced a "scissors-and-paste text" deriving from Cammann's and Schuster's work, noting that while this "violates a number of academic conventions," it "ends a long publication delay" (3.13). Carpenter redrew a number of the illustrations in this volume, and as he did so he "noticed that particular forms favored particular rhythms, both of hands & voice. So I composed tunes & lyrics to accompany their production" (3.13). This leads Carpenter to explore the theory that Celtic interlaced ornaments encoded melody.[58] At Carpenter's urging, musicians sought to make reconstructions of these melodies; they were performed at Lincoln Center, New York, in 1986, "and received a standing ovation" (3.107).

The third book of volume 3 is titled "The World Turned Upside Down," a theme that had preoccupied Carpenter since the days of *Explorations* and that would continue to dominate his thinking to the end of his career in the exhibitions prepared for the Branly and the Menil. In the introduction to this third book, Carpenter addresses the question posed by Borges's "Mutations" story that is cited at the beginning of the Schuster/Carpenter magnum opus: how is it possible to determine the meaning of Paleolithic geometrical artworks when the consensus is that "the cultures in which they arose ceased utterly to exist" (3.452). Carpenter disagrees: "I believe that certain paleolithic objects, customs, modes of thought, even institutions, survived in recognizable form into later periods, and that this was true, perhaps especially true, of paleolithic 'geometric' art. Much of it never ceased to exist at all. We simply didn't know where to look for its survivals, or failed to recognize them for what they are" (3.452). The reasons for this misprision are many: "specialists unwilling to venture beyond their specialties; prehistorians unfamiliar with tribal art; ethnographers unfamiliar with prehistory; anthropologists regarding every culture as a special creation" (3.453). It is also the case that "archaeology creates ... lacunae. Confined to imperishable materials, it by-passes language & lore, ignores music & dance, and turns its back on most of women's art. Only when women's designs were transferred to imperishable materials do we glimpse what must have been, in its time, the most popular of all arts ... Continuity in the traditional arts of women offers a reasonable explanation for similarities that must otherwise be dismissed, or attributed to recent diffusion or independent invention" (2.518). Carpenter concludes that "The schematic art of modern tribesmen clearly has significant roots in the past. This goes unrecognized when viewed through a microscope. Carl Schuster's telescopic vision reveals grand continuity" (3.453). As an example of this "grand continuity," Carpenter cites resemblances between "the art of the Eskimo [*sic*]" and "that of the prehistoric hunters of paleolithic times in Europe & Asia" (3.457). Acknowledging that the "gap in time between the horizon of Eskimo [*sic*] archeology (at most a few thousand years ago) and the upper paleolithic of the Old World (from about ten to forty thousand years ago) is enormous," Carpenter nevertheless argues that "resemblances are unmistakable" and that "the Eskimo [*sic*] have ... somehow perpetuated paleolithic traditions into recent times" (3.457). "The World Turned Upside Down" strikes an appropriate note for the conclusion of this massive study, both because the trope of the *mundus inversus* resonates broadly across cultures, occupying studies as diverse as Giuseppe Cocchiara's *Il mondo alla rovescia* (1963) and Mikhail Bakhtin's *Rabelais and His World* (1940; 1965), and because Schuster and Carpenter are able to extend the trope to the inverted figures of totemic representations based on "the mythic notion of inversion as a prelude to rebirth" (3.449). The topic of inversion as a prelude to rebirth would occupy Carpenter for the remainder of his career.

Collecting Butterflies

Despite distributing *Materials for the Study of Social Symbolism* broadly, it received little attention, as Carpenter noted in "Sea": "No reviews, no hype, no consumers" (260). Typical of the response to Schuster's project was a comment made by Adrienne L. Kaeppler that Carpenter included in the book. Kaeppler, an expert on Tongan dance and the ethnographical relationships between dance, music, and the arts, wrote to Carpenter:

> I really find this type of "butterfly collecting" objectionable. I would be hard pressed to say anything good about it – I find such comparisons farfetched and, indeed, uninteresting. I cannot see how it gets us anywhere. There is no analysis, no evidence, only speculation that shortly turns to fact. Each time a question is posed, my answer is, "No." Although it is stated that the intention is morphological, the outcome smacks of diffusion from (ultimately) a paleolithic source. At the end I only sigh and say, "So what." I suppose this will upset you, but I suspect most anthropologists will agree with me, unless they just want to be kind. (3.450)

A heavily redacted (at circa 300 pages) volume published a decade later did somewhat better with its (still few) readers. *Patterns That Connect: Social Symbolism in Ancient and Tribal Art*, by Carl Schuster and Edmund Carpenter, was issued in 1996 by the well-established publisher of art monographs Harry N. Abrams. The title was supplied by Mark Siegeltuch, who assisted Carpenter on *Materials for the Study of Social Symbolism* and who maintains the Wikipedia page on Carl Schuster. Writing in the cybernetics journal *Continuing the Conversation*, Carpenter quotes Siegeltuch as stating, "Today's speed-up of information flow, with consequent information overload, forces us to abandon analysis in favor of pattern recognition ... The central role of memory in perpetuating [traditional] cultures generates formal patterns of organization which are remarkably ancient and remarkably stable over time ... With the death of the comparative method after World War II, American universities embarked on a program of specialization in all areas of history, religion, and anthropology which has all but obliterated those 'patterns that connect'" (quoted by Carpenter, 9).[59] The book was given a one-page review in *American Anthropologist* by Harald E. Prins (who, along with John Bishop, would subsequently become one of Carpenter's unofficial "biographers"), Prins describing the book as "an etymology and archaeology of ancient motifs representing a grand theory of kinship symbolism in tribal art."[60] Prins summarizes Schuster's and Carpenter's main argument that the "cross-cultural existence" of similar patterns "is due primarily to very early prehistoric migrations, not cultural diffusion." Prins concludes his largely descriptive review with the comment that, "While [Schuster and Carpenter] may not be able to offer conclusive proof of their argument, their massive evidence and erudite interpretation flatten any lazy assumptions." What impressed Carpenter most about the book is that it became a cult object among tattooists. Writing to Oxford anthropologist Rodney Needham (whom he had asked to blurb *Patterns That Connect*), Carpenter recounted a story he had heard about students who had stolen one of the Schuster volumes to use its pictures as tattoo models. "This explains similar loses [*sic*] and mutilations at other libraries. Word of this source was spread via tattoo newsletters. How appropriate! Since many of these designs started as tattoos and then underwent changes & rebirths, now they're returning to their original form at the end of their last transmutation. In teaching

Schuster's work it will now be possible to skip slides and simply ask various students to step forward and strip."⁶¹

Carpenter presented material from the Schuster project (with most of the illustrations coming from Schuster's files) at the end of 1985 in Jerusalem, at a conference presided over by Claude Lévi-Strauss, on *Art as a Means of Communication in Pre-Literate Societies*.⁶² Lévi-Strauss's opening address distinguishes pre-literate art as communal, whereas art in literate cultures is said to be the product of individuals. Given that he was speaking in Jerusalem, Carpenter decided to take a local artifact, Megiddo (Armageddon) gaming boards, and seek parallels. These he found in Oceania, Europe, and West Africa. "I felt free to make such comparisons," he writes, "in the belief that the proposed analogies were more real than the boundaries which they transgressed and that certain preconceptions of cultural history need revision, not the evidence which violates them" (27). Consistent with the third volume of *Materials*, the theme of rebirth is central, as in the Jain boards of India, whose ladders (as in Snakes and Ladders) represent the *axis mundi* and whose snakes represent the "Cosmic Reptiles who swallow neophytes and dead souls, pass them through their joint-marked bodies, then void or vomit them, reborn" (28).

Returning to Schuster in 2006 via an article published in *Natural History* under the title "Decoding the Tribe," Carpenter once again remarks on how difficult it is to convince anthropologists of Schuster's theory of genealogical interconnections across cultures. "A person who bases a theory on bits and pieces from different cultures becomes the anthropological equivalent of Victor Frankenstein, assembling a monster by taking an arm from here, an ear from there."⁶³ Carpenter was particularly interested in the recurrence of "the inverted figure. Many Paleolithic 'Venus' figurines, some made as early as 30,000 years ago, were perforated at their ankles so that they could be suspended upside down" (44). These inverted figures occur across broad swathes of territory over millennia; from these figures Schuster sought not a psychic unity but a key to their decoding, leading him to an understanding of "the concept of many within one," a concept that is "alien to contemporary Western thinking" (46). Regardless, Carpenter is "convinced that Schuster's work bears witness to the survival of an ancient iconographic system … that crossed continents" (47). "People everywhere," he notes, "are pattern-makers and pattern-perceivers" (47).

Writing Anthropology

In the same issue as the Prins review of *Patterns That Connect*, Carpenter reviewed Laurel Kendall et al., *Drawing Shadows to Stone: The Photography of the Jesup North Pacific Expedition, 1897–1902*, about Franz Boas's joint expedition with Russian anthropologists to the Bering Strait.[64] Carpenter takes issue with the authors' statement that by collecting artifacts on this expedition the anthropologists hastened the demise of the people they were studying. On the contrary, writes Carpenter, collecting and displaying the artifacts ensured cultural continuity. He also disagrees with the assertion that natural history museums originated with cabinets of curiosity. Rather, natural history museums were a response to Darwin's assertion that "all life could be placed on a common basis ... They challenged freak cabinets (unnatural history) and relic shrines (supernatural history) ... Today we are urged to abandon natural history museums in favor of American Indian shrines. How quickly we forget" (771). Rather than produce a "grand comparative study" (772) after his expedition, "Boas redefined Culture as cultures, promoted ethnic dignity, and opposed racism. American anthropology became political."[65] Because of Boas's shift in focus, "the comparative method faded ... Carl Schuster, who took structuralism deep into prehistory, found his work ignored." Once again, universalism asserted itself in Carpenter's work, and precisely at the moment when anthropology was seeking to go in other directions that were both local and political.

Carpenter notes that the volume under review was published in connection with a symposium on the Jesup expedition held at the American Museum of Natural History in 1997. "For a week, scholars read papers. Many were excellent. The overall tone of the symposium, however, concerned ethnic identity, gender studies, *shamanitis*, even a whiff of Jung. Considering the state of race relations in America a hundred years ago, Boas probably made the right choice. But not now. Today Darwinian psychologists borrow from software. Linguists talk of universal wiring. These and other New Age claims enjoy wide acceptance, unencumbered by evidence. They should be tested. Our museums bulge with relevant data. Anthropologists still have the comparative method, however rusty. Are any willing to put their precious learning in jeopardy, ignore political pressures, bypass funding, and venture into the unknown? I hope my life expectancy extends that far" (772). These comments were made in the wake of James Clifford and George Marcus's 1986 book *Writing Culture: The Poetics and Politics of Ethnography*, the other book by Clifford that framed the publication of *Materials*. *Writing Culture* has been called "perhaps the single most influential anthropology book in recent decades."⁶⁶ The book focused discussions about "reflexivity and representation" (2) that had been circulating in the discipline for a number of years, and, in the process, politicizing these questions in a way that "seemed to threaten the traditional bedrock principles of truth, science, and objectivity with the relativizing epistemic murk of newfangled literary theory and other suspect influences" (2). The theory wars had begun in earnest. Carpenter – clearly out of step with his discipline – decided to head north.

7

Northern Preoccupations

ON 7 JUNE 1987, the Menil Collection opened its doors in Houston, Texas. In her foreword to the 320-page catalogue (which illustrates only a small percentage of the now 17,000 works in the collection), Dominique de Menil states that, beyond noting that the catalogue contains beautiful images, she hesitates to write anything else. "Events, people, situations, and works of art most of all are always beyond what may be said of them. Language restricts, limits, impoverishes ... Roland Barthes wrote, 'la parole est fasciste'; 'imperialistic,' would say Edmund Carpenter."[1] De Menil admits that "words can be illuminating," but "discourse must not take the place of art itself" (7). John and Dominique de Menil were said to have been influenced in the articulation of their collection by André Malraux's notion of the "museum without walls," producing in their museum what one of the curators has termed a "transmurality,"[2] a desire to go beyond the bounds of the museum itself to invoke a larger domain of art that, in this case, included the Rothko Chapel and subsequently the building housing the Dan Flavin installation, both on the Menil campus, as well as suggesting the living, human dimension of art that transcended any specific locale or time frame.

Carpenter contributed an essay to the Menil catalogue titled "Deeply Carved: Art of the Northwest Coast" (164–7) in which he emphasizes the connection between Pacific Northwest artifacts and the technology employed by native peoples to produce their huge (60 foot) canoes. Cognately, to create a sheep-horn bowl, it was necessary to carve out the horn, steam it and spread it, and then lock it in a mold to cool (164); Carpenter finds similar applications of technology in Alaska and Micronesia. The art of the

Northwest coast was comprised largely of "animal and human motifs serving as crests for moieties and clans, families and individuals. Artists distorted nature by reducing each crest to its essential parts ... then dislocating and rearranging them within the design. By accentuating particular features of crest animals, they created an iconography of recognized symbols. To this they added highly conventionalized design elements such as ovoids, u-forms, and s-forms. The total effect was formal, intellectual, austere" (165, paraphrasing Wilson Duff). Carpenter emphasizes that what appears representational in this art is in fact mythic. "Even crest animals, used solely for social events, possessed mythic attributes and engaged in extraordinary activities ... We can never translate such a myth perfectly because we lack an identical mind to grasp it" (167). As this comment suggests, writing about tribal art at this time was a complicated enterprise. In *The Predicament of Culture*, James Clifford had raised questions about the 1984 MOMA exhibition "Primitivism in 20th Century Art," framing these questions in colonialist terms of "the restless desire and power of the modern West to collect the world" (196). Four years later, again in New York, an exhibition of African art had included an Azande hunting net among the masks and sculptures on display, raising the question of what precisely constituted the "aesthetic." That exhibition had been curated by Susan Vogel, who, like Carpenter, contributed an essay to the Menil catalogue on "African Aesthetics and the Art of the Ancient Mali" (124–7). Vogel writes that it is possible to infer "a broad underlying African aesthetic sensibility" (124); her essay examines ancient Malian works in the Menil Collection as a way of interrogating this hypothesis and "the degree to which it is a valid concept in the wider area" (124). Vogel hypothesises that there is a "timeless, motionless quality normally associated with African art" (124). This, however, immediately invokes a stereotypical concept of Western classical sculpture established by Johann Winckelmann[3] that has been contested by scholars as diverse as Sergei Eisenstein and Hans von Trotha.[4] The language of Western aesthetics permeates Vogel's chapter: "emblematic" versus "individual"; "symmetrical, still, standing beyond gesture and event"; "man as a universal"; "African art is idealizing"; "perfect beings in their essence"; "anklets ... coquettishly on her hip"; "what is good is beautiful, and what is beautiful, good"; "moral perfection is ... essential to the aesthetically successful work"; "highly abstract and intellectual"; and so on. Here we have a precise example of what Carpenter referred to as the imperialism of language, and in this context, it is possible to conclude that Vogel's display of a hunting net in an exhibition of African art extends this colonialism to the artistic world itself. The anthropologist of art, Alfred Gell, has addressed "Vogel's net" directly; although he is largely supportive of the inclusion of the net in that exhibition, he does acknowledge that it was "a one-sided transaction in art-making, in the sense that essentially metropolitan concepts of 'art' would be in play, not [I]ndigenous ones."[5] Carpenter's repeated assertion that not all cultures have the concept of "art" must be taken into account in this context. As he put it in "Sea," "Picasso's art is not out of Africa" (250). The study of artifacts as aesthetic expressions was an approach established by A.C. Haddon (founder of the School of Anthropology at Cambridge) in his 1894 study *The Decorative Art of British New Guinea: A Study in Papuan Ethnography*.[6] What particularly rendered such studies important to a researcher such as Carpenter, who combined traditional anthropological interests with media studies, was the sense developed by Haddon and others that the value of these artifacts lay less in their status as individual works than in the ecology they formed within the context of their social and natural environment. This observation was articulated by Mary Douglas as the principle that "objects constitute social systems."[7] To house indigenous artifacts in a museum thus had the effect of changing their meaning completely by removing them from the cultural environment in which they made sense. This made museum spaces highly contentious in the ethnographical context.[8] It is not that a net cannot be aesthetically pleasing, but to posit that an aesthetically pleasing net functioned as a "work of art" is a major distortion of its context.[9] As George W. Stockton Jr notes, "The relativization (and universalization) of Western aesthetic standards ... have recontexualized the production of traditional items of material culture ... [such that] items that once had multiple functions, so that their aesthetic element could only be isolated by abstraction, have often had their functions reduced in scope by processes of acculturation."[10] It was based on this reasoning that Carpenter paid particular attention to the viewing context of the artifacts included in the *Upside Down* exhibitions – the *ground*, as well as the figure. In effect, he sought to turn the museum upside down (and with it anthropology), declassifying it as a visually-oriented museum space and reclassifying it as an acoustic space, where the centrality of the viewer is dethroned and where the museum object is presented in terms of the multiplicity of its functions, rather than as a singularly "aesthetic" and static object.

As the Menil Collection moved towards its 1987 opening, Carpenter was himself entering into a period of consolidation, both personally and professionally. The establishing of the Rock Foundation by Adelaide de Menil in 1976, with Carpenter as vice-president, provided him with the financial wherewithal to pursue major projects such as the Schuster edition, and to republish *They Became What They Beheld* in 1980. On the personal level, in the mid-1980s he and Adelaide de Menil took up residence in the Gainsborough Studios on Central Park South in New York City, in a loft that Carpenter described as "a one-room apartment with four bathrooms"[11] that became the seat of the Rock Foundation. Carpenter and de Menil also restored several seventeenth- and eighteenth-century houses on their East Hampton property; eight of these houses were given to the East Hampton township in 2007, with funding to move and maintain them as community buildings. The property itself sold for over US$100,000,000.[12]

Carpenter may have thought that he had put *Explorations* behind him by this point. McLuhan had died at the end of 1980; although he and Carpenter had not collaborated since Fordham, they remained friends, Carpenter providing a pipe band for McLuhan's funeral. In 1992, however, Canadian journalist Robert Fulford resurrected the journal once again in an article published in the limited circulation *Canadian Notes and Queries* (as discussed in chapter 1). Fulford's article prompted a response from Carpenter; it includes a number of priceless anecdotes and some moving scenes (especially of McLuhan after his aphasic stroke), but overall displays a surprising degree of animus, which becomes exacerbated in Carpenter's concluding comment that belies his statement that "we got along famously" ("Sea," 242): "Years ago, walking north through Central Park, I saw coming toward me, like a silent jet, the most handsome, graceful, powerful man I'd ever seen. Pure energy. He stared me right in the eye as he shot past. Muhammad Ali. Last year, in a hotel lobby in Islamabad, I saw him again: listless, witless, flabby. Strangers lifted his arms into boxing position and posed themselves for pictures while throwing mock punches at his jaw. He was then led to the water fountain and his head pressed down to drink. I thought of Marshall" ("Sea," 260). This is not at all how McLuhan appeared in the fall of 1978 to a junior fellow at Massey College (University of Toronto), who had been invited by Claude Bissell[13] to lunch with them. On entering the dining hall, conversations ceased when fellows caught site of McLuhan; clearly, he still had aura among a generation that had not grown up with him as a major cultural figure. At lunch he was animated, witty, and extraordinarily wide-ranging in his conversation, and energetic enough to go on talking for close to three hours. Asked at one point if television would bring down the Berlin Wall, McLuhan replied cryptically, "Joshua fit the battle of Jericho." When Bissell suggested that it was time to go, the curtain dropped on "McLuhan" and rose on a rather avuncular professor, who asked the graduate student what he was working on. Told that the dissertation topic was *erlebte Rede* (free indirect discourse), McLuhan asked informed questions and demonstrated his knowledge of the relevant theory, including that of the Mikhail Bakhtin who had recently been "discovered" by North American academics, which then led McLuhan to talk about Russian Formalism and the connections between parody and critique. In subsequent meetings, McLuhan was equally lucid and gregarious. While this may not have been the McLuhan whom Carpenter knew forty years before, it was also not the McLuhan that he portrays in "That Not-So-Silent Sea."[14]

Witnessing the Arctic

The retirement of Jørgen Meldgaard from curatorship in the area of "Eskimology" at the National Museum of Denmark in 1997 was celebrated by a *festschrift* (in part supported by the Rock Foundation) for which Carpenter wrote two chapters.[15] The first of these is on "19th Century Aivilik Iglulik Drawings" (70–92), dubbed by Carpenter a "fun essay. No novel theory underlies it. No massive documentation fills it. No grand conclusion caps it. It simply illustrates a handful of early Aivilik drawings from the many that lie forgotten in scattered archives" (71). Among these drawings are those collected by George Comer, a Connecticut whaler, for Franz Boas's research on "The Eskimo of Baffin Land and Hudson Bay." As Carpenter had observed in a number of his publications, "there are few inhibitions about shifting perspective when convenient" (77) in the drawings, suggesting once again the cultural specificity of three-dimensional representation. Similarly, "no hint of private identity marks these 'corporate' figures" (78),

Carpenter referencing here the idea that oral or acoustic cultures are communitarian, not individualistic (the latter a product of literate cultures). In this context, Carpenter states, "Tribes in this area take their identity, their everlasting identity, from names believed to be periodically reincarnated. Many of the names recorded by Parry's 1821–1823 expedition are still current among the Aivilik/Iglulik" (87). It is only Europeans who are given personal identities in the drawings Carpenter examines.

Carpenter's second essay in *Fifty Years of Arctic Research* is titled "Arctic Witnesses" (303–10) and focuses on Knud Rasmussen, Peter Freuchen (1886–1957), Robert Flaherty, Richard Harrington (1911–2005), and Bent Sivertz (1905–2000). What they all have in common is that their reputations have been subject to severe criticism in an era described by George Swinton in another essay in the volume as characterized by "political and ethnical correctness."[16] As Carpenter puts it, "Each bore honest witness to the events they observed. Unfortunately, later critics, without evidence, tried to discredit their work" (303); "each tells of honesty colliding with academia" (309). A "witness," for Carpenter, is someone who actually does something, rather than theorizing about it. Rasmussen, for example, was criticized as a "showman" who was guilty of "romantic exaggeration," especially in his translations of Inuit songs (303), even though he was a great explorer of the Arctic. Freuchen, who accompanied Rasmussen on the Fifth Thule Expedition, was dismissed as "a clown, a teller of tall tales, an embarrassment to the scientific community" (304), based largely on his novel *Eskimo*, although Freuchen's Fifth Thule publication on zoology "remains a classic" (306) and was praised by Meldgaard. Freuchen's chief critic was Kaj Birket-Smith (also a member of the Fifth Thule Expedition), whom Carpenter describes as a "plump aristocrat, self-styled scientist, new to the Arctic" (305) who "rose high in academia" (306), a "backhanded compliment," as Freuchen's biographer states.[17] Carpenter was a fervent supporter of Robert Flaherty, whom, he writes, had by 1982 been "charged ... with racism, colonialism, dishonesty, falsification, insensitivity, much more" (306), based largely on his 1922 film, *Nanook of the North*.[18] The distortions attributed to that film, argues Carpenter, mask the "real distortions – politically motivated, government financed, academically embraced, beloved by the media" (308).

Another Arctic witness, the photographer Richard Harrington (the only Canadian photographer to be included in *The Family of Man* exhibitions), photographed Inuit people in the 1948–53 period, documenting the severe famine at that time. Although his photographs were critiqued by scholars such as Maria Tippett, Carpenter mocks her assertion that Farley Mowat's *People of the Deer* provides a more accurate account of that period. "Of the limitless errors in Mowat's best-seller, my favorite is his charge that traders encouraged the slaughter of caribou solely for their tongues which were bundled & shipped South. A 'Deer's Tongue' is the popular name for an arctic plant (*Liatris* sp.) used to flavor tobacco" (308). Carpenter submitted a paper on Harrington to a 1996 British Museum conference titled "Imagining the Arctic." The paper was rejected because it lacked a measured tone, exemplified by Carpenter's comment about the conference's guiding principle, "*that photographs are neither truthful nor neutral 'analogons' of reality*" (quoted, 308) with the statement "I know no such thing" (308). Carpenter suggests that another reason his paper was rejected had to do with Harrington's photographs themselves, which failed to show the "bountiful" land that Inuit claimed they had been exiled from in the 1953 forced relocation of several Inuit families from Inukjuak (located on Hudson Bay in the province of Québec) to Grise Fiord (on the southernmost tip of Ellesmere Island) and Resolute Bay (on Cornwallis Island), both in the Canadian High Arctic and both circa 2,000 kilometres (circa 1,250 miles) north of Inukjuak. Carpenter was writing at the time when a claim against the Canadian government for compensation in the amount of Can$10,000,000 had been made by the exiled Inuit. (In 1996, the Canadian government established a trust fund in that amount for the relocated families.)[19] "Those seeking compensation," writes Carpenter, "described their former life at Inukjuak as an Eden of game, health, happiness, and their later life at Grise Fiord & Resolute Bay as a time of hunger, cold, misery. The fascinating thing about this view is that it sustains itself without evidence" (309). A major contextual factor in the relocation was the Cold War. "Those seeking compensation called relocation a political act designed to establish sovereignty. Nonsense," states Carpenter. "If human flagpoles had been needed, surely uniformed officials would have been selected, not a handful of starving Eskimos [*sic*], then publicly regarded as curiosities of uncertain affiliation. Academics created the sovereignty motive. That claim was [a] mere footnote in a national movement. After long delay, Canadians, like Americans, moved against racism, chauvinism, imperialism. This was most welcome.

Yet, here & there, reform got out of hand. Most misdeeds were real enough. But this was not. It never happened" (309). The consensus has been less apodictic.[20] When the Canadian government apologized to the Inuit in 2010, it referred to "promises that were made and not kept ... [The Inuit] were promised they were going to a more abundant place. They were promised they would remain in one community. They were promised that they could leave and return to their home communities after two years if they were unhappy. They were not provided with adequate shelter and supplies. They were not properly informed of how far away and how different from Inukjuak their new homes would be, and they were not aware that they would be separated into two communities once they arrived in the High Arctic. Moreover, the government failed to act on its promise to return anyone that did not wish to stay in the High Arctic to their old homes. The Government of Canada recognizes that these communities have contributed to a strong Canadian presence in the High Arctic."[21]

Carpenter published excerpts from Harrington's Padlei diary along with some of the photographs taken by Harrington in a book produced by the Rock Foundation in 2000. Carpenter writes in the introduction that "Westerners have been re-inventing Eskimos [sic] for centuries. Richard Harrington accepted them as he found them ... It seems incredible that photographs of this sensitivity should remain unknown, unhonored, and the events themselves forgotten or denied."[22] Carpenter stresses the implacable conditions that Harrington faced in the North (Padlei is on the west side of Hudson Bay) during the 1950 caribou famine, caused by a shift in migration patterns. The diary speaks of relentless cold and wind, of dogs who would be at your throat if ever you fell, and of the effects of famine. One Inuit, Pipkaknak, had "obtained enough cariboo [sic] to live moderately well" (52), Harrington writes, although his store of ninety caribou would not last the year. Government officials were "fed by plane traffic," but these officials "never see the hunger that stalks now" (80). The pictures of Inuit are not aestheticized in the manner of Edward Curtis; viewing them is harrowing and deeply disturbing. Only the rare photographs of snow dunes and of sled teams against a barren horizon suggest an aesthetic dimension. As Carpenter notes in the epilogue, it was in the area of Padlei that "America soon installed ... the world's most sophisticated electronic defense system, yet communication with local Eskimos remained almost paleolithic" (104).

PADLEI DIARY, 1950

An Account of the *Padleimiut Eskimo*
in the Keewatin District west of Hudson Bay
during the Early Months of 1950 as

Witnessed, Written & Photographed by
Richard Harrington

Edited by
Edmund Carpenter

Agartook, Sheneujuak Lake camp

Rock Foundation
2000

Figure 7.1 Frontispiece and title page, Harrington, *Padlei Diary*, 2000.

While Harrington's photographs eschew aesthetic effects, the same cannot be said for this publication, which is beautifully produced, cloth-bound
with sumptuous dust wrapper,[23] printed on heavy paper, and slipcased, its
design credited to Carpenter and two others (Jerry Kelly and Betsey Peare),
with printing at the Stinehour Press (a private press located in Lunenberg,
Vermont). This aestheticization is problematical in the light of questions
raised by reviewer Sarah Elder: "How should anthropologists prepare food
and eat during a food shortage? What function do we perform in a life and
death crisis? How do we cope with overwhelming personal helplessness? ...
Should we film people near death, too weak to give consent?"[24] Elder notes
that the book was distributed for free "to Nunavut communities, residents,
and libraries" (659). *The Globe and Mail* produced three articles about it,
received 500 letters in response, and Harrington, at the age of ninety, was
awarded the Order of Canada.

The last Arctic witness discussed by Carpenter is Bent Sivertz. Carpenter tells us very little about Sivertz, other than that he was, at the time of the Inuit relocation, head of the Arctic Division in the Department of Northern Affairs and National Resources (cf. J. Cavell, 140). Sivertz "claimed that the 1953 plan originated with him" (J. Cavell, 132). While subsequently Sivertz became aware of problems at Grise Fiord, "he used sovereignty as an excuse for leaving Grise Fiord in place ... perhaps because he feared having a project he once championed categorized as a failure. At the 1993 [Royal Commission] inquiry [into the relocation], Sivertz defended the relocation. When challenged by commissioner Mary Sillett, he coldly denied that there had been any hardship whatever" (J. Cavell, 141). Carpenter states that Sivertz was "passionately committed to the welfare & rights of northern Canadians ... Once the [health and starvation] crisis became clear, the government acted decisively. The ill were hospitalized. Families moved to government settlements. The Eskimos [sic] were saved. An exaggeration? No. The crisis was real, the outcome uncertain" (309). The 1953 relocation of "Eskimo [sic] volunteers" (309) was "uniformly applauded. Then, suddenly, forty years later, criticism arose, without benefit of evidence. Anthropologists, gender activists, journalists and government funded lawyers denounced this relocation as a violation of human rights" (310). Carpenter is particularly concerned about the role of anthropology in this controversy. "Anthropology is sometimes called a 'social science.' This legitimately applies only where it borrows from science, say carbon dating or genetics. Basically, anthropology is humanistic or political or both. Right now, politics dominate. So we ask: what political factors gave rise to this belated criticism? In America at least, political correctness has overwhelmed academia ... No academic discipline got scrubbed cleaner than anthropology" (310). Political correctness pervaded the Royal Commission, according to Carpenter: "Due process, justice, evidence, common sense, turned upside down ... None of this made sense until one realized: this was a TV psychodrama masquerading as a government in action. Real Commissioners, real Inuit, added a touch of verisimilitude" (310). Carpenter strikes a contrast between the "Eskimos" portrayed by Flaherty in *Nanook of the North* and the "Inuit performances at the Royal Commission" (310). "Did they [the Inuit] accurately portray Inuit?" asks Carpenter. "If so, then 'Eskimo' and 'Inuit' refer to different people. In those hearings, Inuit lied. All people lie, of course, but Eskimos lied so rarely, this astonished Whites. They had never before met people so truthful. Again & again one heard 'Eskimos don't lie.' Yet these Inuit lied. Inuit behavior differed from Eskimo [sic] behavior in another way ... Sobbing Inuit, fleeing the [commission] room, [appeared to be] coached. As they had ... They were, after all, raised on TV ... Inuit take their identity, their art, their entertainment, even their name, from the West" (310).[25] This leads Carpenter to a short excursus on the use of "Eskimo" versus "Inuit." He argues that the former is not "pejorative" and that the latter "gained acceptance only after official promotion, beginning in the late 50s ... Activists insist on the exclusive use of 'Inuit.' They condemn 'Eskimo' as racist ... My hope is they will return to that proud name ... To realize who they were, makes them what they are. When I'm in search of *me*, I don't want someone else's history. Rejecting your history means rejecting yourself" (310). Carpenter would return to this question of nomenclature at the end of his career when assembling the *Upside Down* exhibitions.

The Burial of the Dead

In 1992, Carpenter became embroiled in an international scandal that had originated one hundred years earlier with Franz Boas's request that Robert Peary bring back with him from his next Arctic journey an "Eskimo" who could be studied at the American Museum of Natural History. Peary brought back six; four died within a year, the fifth moved back to his native land, and the sixth became internationally famous as "Minik, the New York Eskimo." His story is told by Kenn Harper in the book of that title.[26] The most controversial event in Minik's New York life concerned the death of his father, Qisuk. In order to observe the proper mourning practices, Minik asked to be present at his father's burial. The museum, however, had already decided that the body would be dissected and the skeleton mounted for exhibition. In order to appease the boy, the museum staged a fake funeral, with Minik present. Boas subsequently confirmed this, adding that "he saw 'nothing particularly deserving severe criticism' in the act" (85; the internal quote is from the *New York Evening Mail*, 24 April 1909).[27] Minik ultimately learned of his father's fate, including the fact that his father's bones were displayed in the museum, from fellow students at school (93–4), who had read stories about the "Eskimos" in the newspapers, some of which dramatized Minik's discovery by stating that he had come across his father's skeleton while visiting the museum (a story discounted by Harper, and also by Carpenter). Minik and his story were eventually forgotten until Harper published his 1986 book *Give Me My Father's Body: The Life of Minik, the New York Eskimo*.[28] When Harper's story was picked up by Toronto's *Globe and Mail* and by the *Washington Post*, however, the museum came under pressure to return the remains of the Inuit "specimens."

It is at this point that Carpenter takes up the story in an article titled "Dead Truth Live Myth,"[29] published in 1997. Carpenter contextualizes Boas's desire to examine an "Eskimo" with the then prevailing position that "Polar Eskimos" were "living fossils" who had been "'arrested' at an early stage" (27), a position with which Boas, and Aleš Hrdlička, a practitioner of physical anthropology,[30] took issue. Carpenter acknowledges that northern peoples did not often survive their sojourns in the south, but argues that, "For every Eskimo buried in Europe or the Lower States before 1900, many more explorers and whalers filled arctic graves. Yet, Westerners volunteered to go North and Eskimos volunteered [*sic*] to go South" (27). Carpenter is very critical of Harper's account of Minik, suggesting that it was written with film rights in mind.[31] Particularly cinematic is the suggestion that Minik discovered his father's bones in the museum, states Carpenter, but, contrary to Carpenter's assertion, Harper does not accept this story (although newspapers did). Carpenter urged the museum to ship the bones back to Greenland; the museum replied they would need a formal request. To arrange this, Carpenter travelled to Greenland, and, with Jørgen Melgaard, succeeded, through the aegis of the Lutheran Church, to have a formal request for the remains to be issued, and in August of 1993, the remains were reinterred. Even though he initiated this process, Carpenter states that the Inuit belief in reincarnation means that "bones are irrelevant ... Polar Eskimos believed that the evil of a dead person remained in its corpse, its bones" (28). Yet Carpenter considered the service of burial "entirely appropriate. It made sense to the living, for it reunited them with the dead" (29). Carpenter's description of the service is accompanied with photographs by "Adelaide Carpenter" (28),[32] which show the procession to the cemetery and the raising of the cross. At the service, Carpenter read a statement in which he said:

Museums of natural history were founded on the belief that all life belongs to a common order subject to common principles. There is the further belief that science can contribute to human betterment. To this end, scientists gather information from many lands. It was in this spirit that citizens from this area visited New York nearly a century ago. There they contributed details of their customs and beliefs to this grand pursuit of knowledge. They did not live to know the importance of their contribution, but we do and it should not be forgotten. (28)

Harper takes issue with this account of Minik in the revised version of his book. "The service, and the printed remarks and press release that resulted from it, were carefully orchestrated by Edmund Carpenter and the American Museum of Natural History to secure maximum credit for themselves" (230), and Carpenter, with Adelaide de Menil Carpenter, were credited as "prime movers and couriers" (230). At the service, the mayor stated that the Inuit who were being reburied had "against their will, helped to write our history" (230). The vicar stated that, "When it became known that the dead had not been laid to rest, many questions came up" (230). As Harper notes, these statements are at odds with Carpenter's remarks: "'Visited?' 'Contributed?' These were not the sentiments that the mayor had just expressed on behalf of the community" (231). Harper goes on to state that "Carpenter, a wealthy patron of the museum, was a pushy man, and accustomed to using his wife's considerable fortune to buy his way into situations that fed his enormous ego" (231). Harper was puzzled by the attack on his book in Carpenter's "Dead Truth Live Myth," stating, "Perhaps [Carpenter] had forgotten the personal note he had sent me in 1987 congratulating me [on my book]" (231). Although Carpenter claimed that among the Inuit who knew Minik's story, Harper's book "was not their favorite reading" (29). Harper counters that "Among the Polar Inuit there was a profound sense of relief that the events that began over one hundred years ago had finally reached a conclusion" (232). Commenting on this affair in her biography of Franz Boas, who initiated the project to import living "specimens" from the Arctic for study in New York, Rosemary Lévy Zumwalt asks, "What remains for us of the stories from Qisuk, Atangana, Nuktaq, Aviaq, Uisaakassak, and Minik? Is it the pathos of these six Eskimos taken from their homeland by the explorer Peary? Is it outrage over the abuse of power by scientists and administrators with respect to the disposition of the dead bodies of four Eskimos? Is it recognition that the press both kept the story alive and sensationalized it for their readership? Or is it, as Edmund Carpenter reflects, knowledge triumphing over misbegotten belief? There are no easy answers to these questions, but there clearly was a trail of travesty, and the sad end to this trail leads to the cemetery in Qaanaaq, Greenland, where a bronze plaque declaims, 'They have come home.'"33

Polar Polemics

Two years later, in 1999, Carpenter entered into a polemic about the post–James Houston Inuit sculptures that he disdained when he critiqued French president Jacques Chirac's acquisition of such work on Chirac's visit – the first by a head of state – to the newly-formed Canadian territory of Nunavut. "It's not primitive, it's not very old. Is it even art?" blared the headline on the front page of Canada's newspaper of record, *The Globe and Mail*.34 "Art should express some freedom and independence of thought," Carpenter is quoted as stating, "but what is called Inuit art is essentially dictated from outside." "It is a synthetic form," he continued, "not unlike Disney world, where you create souvenirs to satisfy the buyer ... Inuit stonework is simply a cheap Henry Moore that everybody can have, and then feel warm inside in their feelings toward native peoples." Carpenter notes that the Inuit were nomadic, and thus large, heavy carvings were not part of their lives. "Soapstone carvings just weren't part of the traditional culture, said Mr Carpenter, who is now retired in New York, and who was once a colleague of Marshall McLuhan." Characterizing the pieces collected by Chirac as "souvenir art," Carpenter remarks that "The Danes, who go for trolls, got the Greenlanders to make troll-like things. The Americans favoured scrimshaw, and they got that [from Alaska]. The Russians went in for grand tableaux ... and the Canadians under Jim Houston got the Eskimo chipping away at stones." Chirac, however, was unperturbed; upon viewing one such carving he was heard to say, "*C'est superbe.*"

The year before (1998), Carpenter and Adelaide de Menil were involved in a controversy regarding two Aleut artworks: a mask dated 1510/1660 and a bentwood hunting hat consigned to auction at Sotheby's. Tribal leaders asked that these works be restored to them, but de Menil and Carpenter refused. In response to Allison Young, cultural director for the tribes, Carpenter wrote that a 1990 federal law "allows your organization to take possession of virtually any object relating to Aleut heritage in virtually every museum in the United States."[35] Private collectors, however, were not subject to this law, which was aimed at restitution. Carpenter added that he was motivated by his concern for the safety of such artifacts, which, at present, tended to fare better in private hands. "Tribal museums still lack adequate funding to guarantee protection," he wrote in a letter made available to *The New York Times*. "We agree on goals," he added; "we differ on immediate action." Carpenter acknowledged that "collectively the white culture has a lot to answer for," but that he did not support the "political correctness" that deems "all victims as heroes." While he agreed that "people should 'possess and identify with their own history,'" art is "not something you inherit; it's something you earn." He also noted that much art returned to tribal centres is subsequently looted. "On a recent visit to Point Hope in Alaska, where there was supposed to be a protected Eskimo [*sic*] site of Ipiutak house ruins dating from about A.D. 600–1200, he said he found ample evidence of recent looting."

The complexities and controversies of collecting with specific reference to Carpenter's practices were addressed in 1997, in the context of a study about a Nootka mask and its complicated trajectory from museums to dealers to collectors and auction houses. Writing in the journal of the Baessler Institute, Berlin, Christian F. Feest, an ethnologist who specializes in the study of Native North Americans, stated that "museum objects have an ambiguous past: they are part of the history of their culture of origin as well as that of its collectors."[36] Once an artifact leaves its original context it becomes subject to "the needs of collectors and museums ... the dealers, and the auction houses" (256). A Nootka mask (identified as such by Franz Boas) acquired by the Dresden Anthropological-Ethnographic Museum in 1881 is Feest's case in point. For the first hundred years after its acquisition, the mask aroused little interest, but when dealers began to market Indigenous artifacts, the mask took on a new life. One of those dealers was Everett Rassiga, who sought to effect a relationship with the Dresden Museum through a gift (eventually deemed fake) of an Aztec figure; as a result, the Dresden Museum opened up its collection to him in order to facilitate further exchanges. Rassiga then "happily informed an American customer that Dresden had opened all of its storage for him and offered to obtain specific objects that might be of interest to the collector, who immediately ordered *two* Nootka masks collected on James Cook's third voyage" (263). That collector was Edmund Carpenter. (It is not known why Carpenter ordered two masks, nor the reason he associated them with Captain Cook.) Carpenter obtained one mask in 1975 for US$15,000 (circa US$82,750 in today's currency), which he stated to Feest was "very cheap" (264). However, Carpenter was concerned about his acquisition; he wrote Dresden to ask for confirmation of the mask's provenance but received no reply. Despite his doubts, the mask was shown in the 1984 exhibition in Paris of artifacts from the Menil Collection. By 1997, however, Carpenter and Adelaide de Menil decided to send the mask to auction at Sotheby's. "It was their first sale of objects," writes Feest, "instigated by the increasing reluctance of museums to accept donations of American Indian material since the passing of the Native American Graves Protection and Repatriation Act of 1990" (267). The mask was described in the catalogue as being associated with "two other 18th century Nootka masks remaining in the Dresden collection. One of the latter is identical with a mask in the British Museum collected by James Cook and accessioned into the collection by 1780" (268). Feest remarks, however, that "almost every single assertion in this account of the object's 'documentation' is false" (268). He wrote to Carpenter to point this out, and Carpenter immediately alerted Sotheby's. An article published in *The New York Times* on 1 June 1997,[37] comprised of an interview with Carpenter and Ellen Taubman of Sotheby's, retracted the Cook association while focusing on the effect that provenance had on auction sales, especially if owners – "such as Captain James Cook, James Hooper, George Gustav Heye, Edmund Carpenter, or Adelaide de Menil" – were well known. The mask sold for US$525,000 (circa US$970,000 in today's currency), "the highest price ever paid at auction for a work of Native American art" (269). As *The New York Times* noted at the end of 1997, "In the realm of American Indian art, the collectors Adelaide de Menil and her husband, Edmund Carpenter, have celebrity status" (quoted, 269n4), to which Carpenter added that "celebrity-owned icons (Warhol, Jackie, Windsors, etc.), like holy relics, command astronomical prices at auction" (quoted by Feest from a personal communication by Carpenter, 269n4). In this way, suggests Feest, the mask transformed itself from an artifact to a work of art, and Carpenter would find himself increasingly occupying that fault-line as he continued to acquire objects for the Menil Collection, and for his own private collection.

Carpenter's ongoing interest in the status of "art" was reflected in a 2002 book published by the Smithsonian on eastern Arctic Archaeology, Carpenter contributing a chapter on "Tradition and Continuity in Eskimo Art" that drew largely on the *Social Symbolism* volumes. In revisiting those twelve volumes, Carpenter revindicates the comparatist methodology employed by Schuster to assert connections between Paleolithic Inuit art and contemporary artworks.[38] "Schematic art," he writes, "of pre-historic times will remain a subject of futile speculation as long as it is *not* placed on a comparative basis with modern tribal designs. The basis for this approach is simple: art begets art; if you seek the wellspring of traditional art, be prepared to dig deep."[39] Carpenter's particular focus is on the production of inverted images: humans, birds, and animals that were worn upside down on necklaces, with identifying features obscured, although female figures are often represented in terms of steatopygia. In typical Schusterian fashion, Carpenter finds connections between Paleolithic pendants produced in Italy and Dorset figurines produced in Canada, suggesting that the inverted human figures represent ancestors who were invoked as a form of protection. Carpenter stresses that he is less interested in interpretation than in form – the fact that very similar and at times identical forms appear in vastly separated times and territories. "Eskimo [*sic*] art resembles Paleolithic art generally; it has the same 'feel'" (73), and the reference to tactility emphasizes that this not merely or only a "visual" correspondence: "what goes out of sight need not go out of mind" (77). A Dorset bear effigy, for example, has a compartment that might have contained red ochre to convey that the bear was "living," a practice connecting it to the *pharmaka* of the ancient Greeks as well as to the Australian Aboriginal *churinga*. "Carving was like singing: those who felt a song within, sang; those who sensed a form emerging from ivory, released it" (76). Such art was not connected to shamanism; it was connected to the everyday. Carpenter makes similar points in his chapter "How an Upside-Down Lady Became an Upside-Down Bird," written for a *festschrift* honouring Renée Boser, an expert on textiles whom Carpenter often consulted when he was working on the Schuster project in Basel. Focussing once again on inverted figurines often worn as pendants,

Carpenter is interested in the connections between the pendants representing women and those representing birds. "Many tribesmen," he writes, "regard death as an inversion of life. They say a soul can be reconstituted ('re-membered') by reunion with its primary kin whose spirits reside in the joints of that soul's body. Once reunion is achieved, the body is turned, then left floating in limbo, head-down, in the position of childbirth, ready to re-enter the world. My guess is that ancient peoples, much like modern tribesmen, wore effigies of re-membered (therefore inverted) ancestors as protective chains of guardian spirits. Inverted-birds were once, I think, the inverted-ladies of such necklaces, their original meaning now forgotten."[40] From this thesis Carpenter extracts a moral: "Beware the vengeful ghost who walks like the living; greet warmly the flying ghost who will soon rejoin us; and shun, if you can, the bird-woman, for without meaning, there is no beauty" (445).

Carpenter's interest in the Arctic was sustained by a last project in Siberia. He wrote about this in a paper titled "Imagining the Past" that was published in the 2005 volume *Structure and Meaning in Human Settlements*,[41] with photographs by Adelaide de Menil and drawings by Enooesweetok. The volume as a whole, note the editors Joseph Rykwert and Tony Atkin, sought to find "social, productive and cosmological order embedded in the physical structure of every human community, even in those of the most marginal and unprepossessing hunter-gatherer societies."[42] Carpenter's focus is on Zhokhov Island, in central Siberia,[43] a frozen landscape that has not been inhabited for more than 8,000 years, its people perhaps "proto-Eskimo" [*sic*] (216). Carpenter notes that although archaeologists tend to frown upon the practice, he wishes to acknowledge that he is "reconstructing the past through personal experience" (212), drawing largely on his experience in the Arctic over the 1951–52 winter. There, the environment ruled all. "On the polar ice, when snow or fog fills the air, the horizon disappears and you are suddenly blind white, in a seamless balloon, no up, no down, no point of reference, nothing the eye can cling to … In the High Arctic, atmosphere can distort. Before your eyes, a coastline disappears. Dog becomes bear-sized; bear, dog-sized. What first seemed a stable landscape becomes, as you watch, something else" (212–13). Once again, Carpenter invokes the inverted figures worn on anklets as signs of rebirth, and, drawing on Schuster's comparatist bent, ends his article by noting that, in Zhokhov, he saw "a grave of an adult female, plus newborn infant ... marked by two feathers gracefully bound by split quill. A comparable grave of mother and child, in distant Denmark (same date, same tool kit, same lifestyle), lay on a bed of swan pelts, presumably to carry them to limbo and rebirth" (217). The Zhokhov dig was enormously complicated, involving international cohorts of researchers and the use of ice-breakers, bi-planes, helicopters, and a tractor. Carpenter writes about the dig in an unaddressed letter dated 11 September 2000 and sent from 7 rue Las Cases in Paris.[44] Writing in the lapidary style that increasingly characterized his authorial voice, Carpenter says Zhokhov was "bleak, beautiful, demanding. Less than 5 miles across. Outlier of the New Siberian archipelago, about 700 miles NE of Tiksi. Volcanic ridges. Flatlands of moss, lichens, poppies. No more than 20 flora, a few tiny spiders & gnats, if you look carefully. No mosquitoes. Polar bear breeding ground (one smashed our bath). 'Hey Steve, two fox in your tent.' A few walrus. No fish." This would be Carpenter's last archaeological project.

8

Collecting Memories

THE LAST DECADE of Carpenter's career was marked by an increasing interest in museum and gallery exhibition and practices. He had begun collecting for the Menil in the 1970s, and had also been amassing a personal collection since then, as is evident from the pieces reproduced in the *Audience Magazine* essay. In 1999, under Carpenter's direction, "Witnesses to a Surrealist Vision" opened in the Menil Collection, where it is now on permanent display.¹ The name of the exhibition derived from the surrealist notion that tribal artists had borne witness to a similar sense of radical juxtaposition that fuelled surrealist art – the lobster on the ironing board syndrome.² Carpenter also included astrolabes, anamorphoscopes, and other modes of ocular perception (or misperception), and a reproduction of the "rabbit/duck" that he wrote about in "Explorations" 12.3 (1966). While the room does not contain explanatory material, a pamphlet is available at its entrance containing notes by Carpenter. The pamphlet has an epigraph from André Breton: *"In Oceanic art, one finds the greatest sustained effort to express the interpenetration of the physical and mental to resolve the dualism of perception and representation."*³ The random juxtapositions of surrealist collections were made in the hope that "accident would reveal analogies that convention concealed." In this way, the surrealists sought to make "the unfamiliar familiar … This belief led to a particular interest in invisible art, silent music, and motionless dance." This critique of the visual is a significant part of surrealist aesthetics. "The invisibility of some tribal art appealed to the Surrealists. Ancient earth sculptures, for example, were visible only to gods; aerial photography revealed them to us" (as in the case of the Nazca lines that influenced minimalism).⁴ By "silent mu-

Figure 8.1 Installation view of *Witnesses to a Surrealist Vision*, Menil Collection, Houston, Texas. Photo by Paul Hester.

sic," Carpenter refers to African instruments that are "reversed at the lips, [and] vibrate soundlessly within the mouth, rendering music tactile." The surrealists believed that "the analogies they proposed were more real than the boundaries (such as space, time, and chronology) they transgressed. [Concomitantly], certain preconceptions held by anthropologists needed revision, not the data that violated them."[5] Two aspects of surrealism attracted Carpenter. The first was that the surrealists were greatly attracted to the "*arts premiers*,"[6] the arts of Indigenous peoples often characterized by radically juxtaposed elements, including spatial orientations, producing what Carpenter termed the "visual pun." The second aspect was the notion that anthropology itself was surrealistic in that it implicitly juxtaposed different spatialities and temporalities – that of the field and that of the study. The implications were considerable; juxtaposing different cultures destabilized the worldview that the ethnographer takes for granted – the idea that the ethnographer works from a stable cultural position and is studying a culture that is likewise stable. Ontology and epistemology are rendered uncertain through such juxtapositions, thereby unmooring ethnography as a practice and exposing its biases and assumptions. This was the point of *Witnesses*: the room did not contain ethnographical artifacts owned by surrealists.[7] The thrust of the room was a much larger exposition of anthropology itself, anticipating as such what has come to be called "art-ethnography."[8] As Kristen Laura Strange writes in her master's thesis on the *Witnesses* room, "Carpenter's style of writing and chosen themes reflect James Clifford's term 'surrealist ethnography... that moment in which the possibility of comparison exists in unmediated tension with seen incongruity'" (71, quoting Clifford, *The Predicament of Culture*, 146).[9] Strange concludes, "Carpenter acknowledges that there are problems with Surrealism's appropriation of [I]ndigenous cultures through the collecting and fetishizing of their spiritual objects. But he also recognizes that by defying modernist categories of objects, 'Witnesses' provides an alternative display method that rejects this limiting view of what constitutes high art" (105). This goes to the heart of the collecting ethos at the Menil. As Pamela G. Smart has written, "What [John and Dominique de Menil] collected was a thoroughgoing expression of their off-modern commitments. They viewed (however naively) the antiquities, Byzantine and medieval art, and 'tribal' objects, *particularly* from Africa and Oceania, as 'pure' expressions of tradition and humanity, innocent of the secular rationalism ushered in by the Enlightenment, embodying a nostalgia for an imagined pre-modern past ... The Surrealism in which they had developed a special interest manifested the dissonant, apparently incompatible elements of the off-modern."[10] It was these two elements – tribalism and surrealism – that particularly connected Carpenter to the collecting interests of the de Menils.

In 2002, Carpenter returned to his early research interest in Iroquois culture (drawing on a 1942 article in *American Antiquity*)[11] for a *festschrift* dedicated to William C. Sturtevant, an anthropologist whose field of expertise was the language and culture of Indigenous North Americans (and who had served with Carpenter as a trustee of the MAI).[12] "European Motifs in Protohistoric Iroquois Art"[13] pursues that research in the context of Carpenter's interest in cultural patterns, an interest inspired by Carl Schuster. Asking what caused "sixteenth- and seventeenth-century Iroquois to carve figurines of modest nudes, wear them as pendants, and bury them with their dead" (255), Carpenter answers that they were influenced by trade goods that accompanied European explorers and often preceded them into the interior, and were thus post-contact: "European goods reached the Iroquois well ahead of Europeans ... carried over vast distances via ancient networks of trade and alliance" (255; the order of these two clauses has been reversed). Once again, Carpenter returns to the inverted pendants that he had discussed elsewhere, the pendants suggesting that "the World Beyond is an inverted world where ancestors await rebirth" (255). Although the Iroquois did not wear inverted figurines, they would sometimes use this trope to represent the departed. Carpenter concludes that we may never know the origin of such figurines, but that he prefers "to imagine that somehow, by means unknown to me, Eve, perhaps the Virgin herself, appeared among the Iroquois, bringing solace and comfort to mothers in days of sorrow and anxiety" (261).

Dropping the Penny

Carpenter's interest in artifacts such as Iroquois figurines was not only that of an anthropologist, but also that of a collector. As a collector, Carpenter was scrupulous in terms of provenance (as with the Dresden mask); as he noted at the beginning of a lecture he gave at the New School in 1986, "One of the fun things of being a collector is that when you get stuck with a fake you remember it!"[14] Carpenter gives an account of his own encounter with a fake in "The Wondrous Head of Roscrea."[15] The head had been found in the 1830s on an island near Roscrea, County Tipperary, Ireland. Seeing it in 1977 for sale at a New York gallery, Carpenter "recommended the head to an American collector, Dominique de Menil" (41), who displayed it as Celtic in the 1984 Grand Palais Exhibition and then at the Menil in Houston. Subsequently, it was to be the subject of an essay in *The Menil Collection* (1987), but before the essay could be printed, experts in Celtic art dismissed the head as a forgery. It was then assumed that the head was Maori, based on its facial tattoos. "Could such a specific design as the Maori facial tattoo occur in both nineteenth-century New Zealand and ancient Ireland? Well ... yes," answers Carpenter, channelling Schuster here. "Possibly. Specific motifs occur worldwide and in many periods" (43). There was, however, a trade in the nineteenth century of fake Maori heads, and this turned out to be the denouement of the story, confirmed ironically by a local historian in Roscrea, who had himself created the myth of the Wondrous Head. "How could we have been so naive?" asks Carpenter. "The answer may be embarrassingly simple. We wanted that story to be true" (48).

Viking Visitors?

Beardmore Cache of Relics Resolves Into Battle of Archeologists

By ROBERT L. GOWE

Edmund S. Carpenter

Globe and Mail (November 26, 1956).

Figure 8.2 Carpenter pictured in Beardmore article, *Globe and Mail*, 26 November 1956.

Carpenter's passion for exactitude and rectitude in collecting (which dated to the Explorations years in his exposure of the Beardmore "relics")[16] emerged in two publications of the new millennium. The first was *Norse Penny*. Published by the Rock Foundation in 2003, the pamphlet takes issue with the consensus that this penny found in Maine was genuine.[17] Carpenter writes that in the mid-1950s, there was an explosion of interest in possible Viking settlements in North America, and that it was precisely then that the Norse penny was found – a coincidence that made him highly suspicious, especially since all the "artifacts" that had been claimed as genuine were subsequently exposed as fakes – including the Beardmore artifacts at the Royal Ontario Museum that Carpenter himself had exposed. Carpenter does not question the authenticity of the coin but its provenance – how it got to Maine, noting that many such Norse coins from a nineteenth-century find in Norway had gone to auction and were relatively easy to procure from coin dealers. Guy Mellgren, who found the penny, was a coin collector, worked at an auction house, and had an interest in pre-Columbian contact in North America. The coin was originally misidentified as English;

when it was then claimed to be a Viking artifact, international attention was focused on it, and the Smithsonian deemed it genuine. Yet Carpenter's doubts persisted. He asked if Guy Mellgren, who found the coin, could have been the victim of a prank (as the ROM was with the Beardmore find), but his widow deemed this to be impossible, since he did not identify the coin as Norse in his lifetime. Carpenter concludes on a skeptical note, nevertheless: "I prefer the Scottish verdict: Not proven" (18).[18] The scholarly consensus is divided, with Robert Hoge of the American Numismatic Society stating in 2006 that the find was a hoax,[19] and Norwegian numismatist Svein Gullbekk accepting the find as genuine,[20] while stating that "Carpenter's scrutiny of the evidence and circumstances around this find is impressive and overdue" (1).

Carpenter's interest in artifacts extended to those persons who collected them. In an essay written in 2003 for the *European Review of Native American Studies*, Carpenter told the story of Chief Red Thundercloud (1919–1996), whom Carpenter claimed to have known for many years. Carpenter first became aware of the chief through Frank Speck. Speck had grown up with a relative, "a Mohegan-Pequot widow who spoke Algonquian,"[21] an experience that shaped his career as an anthropologist. Speck introduced Thundercloud to George Heye, the founder of the Museum of the American Indian, who advanced Thundercloud money to purchase Native artifacts. Thundercloud eventually moved to East Hampton where he created a "Native" village that became popular with tourists and with people living in East Hampton (whose Fourth of July parade he led for many years); Carpenter would often encounter him there when at his East Hampton home. By this point, Thundercloud's identity as a Native was in dispute; genealogical research revealed that he had been born into a prominent African-American family. Like Archie Belaney, who lived as Grey Owl in Canada, the chief maintained the fiction of his Native identity to the end, posing in front of restaurants in hope of being invited for lunch. In the same issue of the journal, Carpenter published an account of the collector, printer, and maker of medicinal quackery Amos H. Gottschall (1854–1938), whose itinerant travels across the United States resulted in a vast collection of Native artifacts that were largely made for the souvenir trade. A major buyer of Gottschall's collection was George Heye.[22]

Chiefly Greed

Heye was very much on Carpenter's mind at this time. Carpenter's last major publication was *Two Essays: Chief and Greed*,[23] about Heye and the complicated legacy of his collecting, the Museum of the American Indian. The first free page of the book contains the quotation "Life is Positional Power & You Haven't Got It," said to Carpenter at a board meeting of the MAI at which he was physically assaulted. *Two Essays* appears to have been printed in part to demonstrate who precisely holds that power. As Carpenter writes in the preface:

> This book contains two essays: *Chief*
> *Greed*
> What links them is the Museum of the American Indian.
> What differs is the tone.
>
> Between chapters, I insert artifacts & ask:
> What each meant to those for whom it was originally intended?
> What motivated an "outsider" to collect it?
> What was its fate after Heye acquired it?
>
> This disrupts continuity, but serves as a reminder that utilizing & guarding this collection was the Trustees' primary duty.

Carpenter acknowledges at the outset that his portrait of "Chief" (George Heye, pronounced "high") is greatly indebted to Junius Bird, curator at the American Museum of Natural History, who gave a candid account of Heye to the *New Yorker* three years after Heye's death. Heye grew up in great wealth produced by shares in petroleum interests and began collecting Indigenous artifacts in the late 1890s when he was working in Arizona; he purchased a deerskin shirt from a Navajo woman, and from there moved on to collecting artifacts. Thus began an insatiable career of collecting items from North and South America that eventually amassed circa 700,000 artifacts. When the collection came to the attention of Franz Boas, he expressed his concerns about Heye's "dilettantism" (18) and about the storage conditions of the artifacts, although this had little impact on Heye. What concerned Carpenter about Heye's acquisitions were the implications for the Indigenous cultures from which they were collected. Carpenter quotes, in this context, Czech historian Milan [Hübl]'s comment that "The first step after liquidating a people is to erase its memory" (54), to which he adds, "when one culture rides over another, it destroys forever a unique way of being" (54). As Amy Lonetree remarks in *Decolonizing Museums*, the signal aspect of Heye's collection was that "the needs and interests of Native Americans were not considered primary during [Heye's] tenure at the MAI."[24] It was "people outside Indigenous communities [who] would produce the scholarly knowledge about Native Americans" (86). The implications of this disjunction were evident in the museum's display protocols. As Lonetree comments, "Culturally insensitive and older types of object-based ethnographic displays dominated the museum" (87).

Heye had founded the Museum of the American Indian in 1916, with an initial donation of 400,000 items, and appointed himself director for life. In its first decade, the MAI acquired an additional 300,000 items, many acquired unscrupulously, most inadequately catalogued, and all of them stored in a rudimentary fashion. The establishment of the museum had placed it within the public domain; when Heye could no longer maintain it, the museum should have been transferred to another public entity, likely the American Museum of Natural History. Heye refused to do this; rather, to cover financial shortfalls, he began deaccessioning material illegally. Among the buyers were surrealist artists then living in New York. "They raced to the Bronx," where Heye had his annex. "Now they could choose. They did. They first focused on Yup'ik masks. Imagine a cross between a Calder mobile & a Miro painting. The Yup'ik collection at the MAI was the finest in the world, numbering in the hundreds ... André Breton acquired [a] Kuskokwim mask ... from the Annex, as did Georges Duthuit, art historian for the Surrealist movement" (120). What they encountered in these artworks they transposed into their own creations, especially the notion of the visual pun. "True," writes Carpenter, "the Surrealists just stripped the MAI of one masterpiece after another. But they liberated American Indian art from centuries of neglect" (124).

The book's second essay, "Greed," focuses on the deaccessioning of items[25] from the collection, especially by Frederick Dockstader, an

Oneida-Navajo anthropologist who became director in 1960 (three years after Heye's death). "He sold, traded or gave away thousands of pieces each year ... Only a few can be reunited with their histories. Field records were discarded; catalog entries falsified; associated objects scattered" (136). Carpenter was appointed as a trustee of the MAI during this period of deaccessioning, serving from 1973 to 1985.[26] Appalled by the MAI's practices, he engaged in several lawsuits, from a high of eleven to four that were ongoing in 1978,[27] and made a complaint about the deaccessioning to the New York state attorney general. As reported in *The New York Times* of 3 March 1974, "A member of the board, Edmund Carpenter, an anthropologist, has charged the museum's trustees and its administration with mismanaging the museum's collection of 4.5 million pieces."[28] The story created a national and international scandal.[29] Dockstader stated in the article that "much of what Carpenter says is true, but things must be placed in context." That context was both the need for funds and the normal museum practice of deaccessioning and trading in order to improve the collection overall.

Members of the MAI board were not pleased that Carpenter had made his concerns public. One trustee at a dinner meeting held at New York's Century Club "left his chair, moved behind [Carpenter] & knocked [him] to the floor ... Most trustees looked stunned, but four smirked" (144–5). At the end of the meeting, Carpenter's motion that deaccessioning be suspended having been tabled, Carpenter asked a fellow trustee if he had time for coffee. "'Carpenter,' he replied, 'life is positional power, and you haven't got it'" (145). Dockstader was dismissed, but this did not resolve the MAI's problems, including dealings Dockstader had with Dr Arthur Sackler, whose central role in the opioid crisis has resulted in many museums dissociating themselves from him. The Rock Foundation agreed to support the creation of an inventory of remaining items, while acknowledging that it had previously acquired "a number of ex-Heye artifacts on the art market" (185n13). Dockstader's claim of 4.5 million specimens was proved wrong; 676,605 pieces were inventoried, 26,992 were listed as deaccessioned, and circa 16,000 as missing. While the inventory was being developed, 200 further works were secretly sold, and the MAI, given to the state of New York in Heye's will, had to fend off an offer from Ross Perot to relocate it to Texas. "In spite of 500 years of Indian rip-off, many trustees found the opportunity for greed or power irresistible, including Indian trustees" (156).[30]

(Carpenter himself voted in favour of the Texas relocation, acknowledging subsequently that "it was a mistake" [186n3].)[31]

With the intervention of David Rockefeller, the Custom House at the southern tip of Manhattan was deemed an appropriate location for the MAI; the New York location is now adjunct to the National Museum of the American Indian in Washington, DC, whose establishment was largely at the initiative of Senator Daniel Inouye. All of this is related in a text filled with blacked out names. As Carpenter puts it in his "NO INDEX," "The dead can't sue for libel. The living can" (176). In a 1989 letter to legendary Australian anthropologist John Mulvaney (who had helped Carpenter with identifications of Australian artifacts when he was working on the Schuster book), Carpenter laments the transition of museums from places of learning to places of entertainment. "I feel particularly depressed," he writes, "as I watch a museum where I served as a trustee for 13 years (and kept afloat financially for some of that time), become a silly tourist attraction under media pressure from Indian activists and their supporters."[32] Carpenter goes on to say that the "American Museum of Natural History offered to take over the bankrupt Museum of the American Indian, pledging over 160 million for a new building ... This offer was rejected ... & an alternative accepted, in which the Smithsonian would open two tourist centers, in NY & Washington, without academic responsibilities, and not connected to the National Museum of Natural History. One reason given concerned the title 'Natural History,' Indians objecting to the classification, and ignoring the fact that this classification grew out of the 19th century's greatest contribution: placing all life on a common basis governed by common principle."[33] Amy Lonetree tells another story about the NMAI, although one equally critical, of a lack of clarity and "truth telling" (112) in the early exhibitions, of a "postmodernist" approach to history that obscures "an Indigenous understanding of history" (112), and of the co-opting of the language of decolonization in the NMAI's self representations. "By producing a museum that features exhibits that only curators or those from the academy engaged in postmodern theory can readily appreciate," she asks elsewhere, "have we created a new institution of elitism? In my opinion, the museum misses an important opportunity to educate because of its choice to present a blurred abstract message to dispel those stereotypes about Indian history and culture that have long predominated in American culture."[34] The key way to address these shortcomings, she argues, is through "the privileging of the Native voice" (636) via the adoption of a collaborative model of curation and exhibition.[35]

Carpenter indirectly addresses some of these questions though the ethnographical accounts of objects collected by the MAI that are interspersed with his essays. In these short studies, Carpenter's staggering knowledge of provenance is everywhere evident. One of them concerns a seventeenth-century club, said to have been retrieved by John King during a 1675 raid (part of the King Philip's War) on a Native settlement:[36]

Depressions along the concave edge of the club once contained wampum. Each inlay represented a spinal vertebra. Many Woodland clubs, especially ball-headed clubs, were conceived as anthropomorphic, some explicitly so. It's a curious club, more symbolic than functional. The grip resembles a European sword. Its grip's finial depicts an open-mouthed creature, probably an Underwater Panther. If so, it is an appropriate symbol. In Woodland cosmology, death swallows victims. Did John King pick up the club in the Falls Fight? We know he was there. I suspect, however, it came by another route. In this iconographic system, clubs were deliberately left behind as boasts & insults. It was even specified that a club's head should point in the direction from which its owner came. Surely John King was preoccupied during the Falls Fight, hardly in a souvenir-collecting mood. Moreover, this club was no weapon & weapons were used in the Falls Fight. It was largely symbolic, designed as such & abandoned as boast & insult. I think King came by this club after visiting the smoking ruins of a successful Indian raid. A descendant of John King placed this club on loan to the MAI. She provided detailed family records. Someone discarded them. No loan record was prepared. The likely reasons for this can be inferred from the chapter on Deaccessioning. The club is now privately owned. Its alleged price: over $400,000. (86)

Another analysis concerns wampum belts and has a Canadian context. After the American Revolution, Indigenous leaders divided their wampum belts, four of them eventually being sold to the Ontario Provincial Museum, only to be bought back by Confederacy chiefs. "Pauline Johnson,

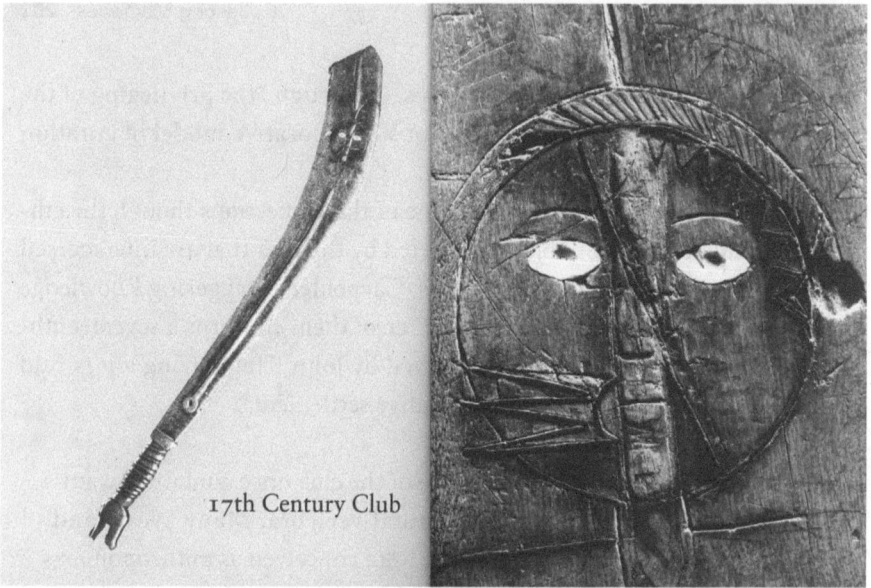

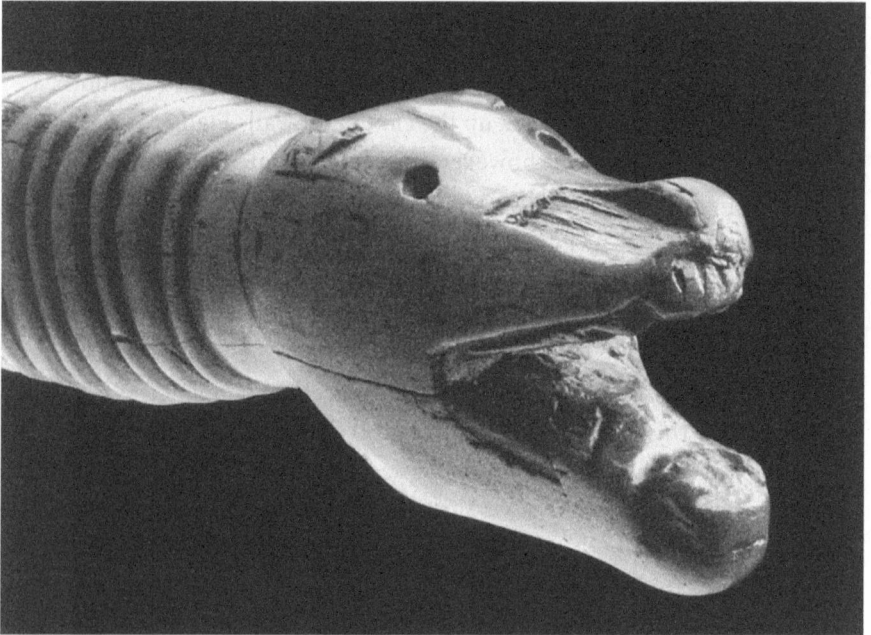

Figure 8.3 (*top*) Seventeenth-century club with close-up, from Carpenter, *Two Essays: Chief and Greed*, 2005.

Figure 8.4 (*bottom*) Detail, seventeenth-century club, from Carpenter, *Two Essays: Chief and Greed*, 2005.

poet-performer, acquired two or three. She sold one to Heye & gave another to the English romantic painter Frederick Leighton ... In 1900 ... [several such] wampum belts ... were now in the possession of a Mr T. R. Roddy, 271 Wabash Ave, Chicago, Ill. Civil servants wrote to civil servants. For nine years, nothing happened. Finally, the Secretary of Indian Affairs wrote directly to Roddy. No reply" (161). Heye acquired the belts in 1910. Carpenter continues his narrative:

> Frank Speck & Edward Sapir then worked for Heye ... In 1914, Sapir, now an anthropologist in Ottawa, wrote to Duncan [Campbell] Scott, Deputy Superintendent, Indian Affairs, advising him that "missing" belts were displayed in Heye's collection. Speck had identified them, but, Sapir added, Speck "might find it personally inconvenient" to be the source. Duncan Scott, at Sapir's suggestion, wrote to Heye ... [stating] "I will feel constrained to place this matter in the hands of the Department of Justice for advice" ... Without evidence of theft, Heye declined to return the belts. Scott asked the Six Nations chiefs for an affidavit: were the belts national or personal? The Chiefs provided sufficient information to identify them as stolen ... But by 1924, none of this mattered. Canada tried to seize the existing belts from the Confederacy Chiefs, whom Duncan Scott now sought to remove. Over 50 years of silence followed. Then, in 1977, Paul Williams, Director, Treaty Research Program, Union of Ontario Indians, Toronto, wrote to the MAI, asking about wampum generally & an Ojibway belt specifically. The reply ... essentially refused all information, but said ... a Board member would look into the matter ... [The ensuing report] admitted "dubious circumstances" surrounding the belts, but nevertheless recommended selling them to Canada for US$225,000 ... Williams asked for their return ... In 1986, the MAI Board met with the Six Nations chiefs in New York. Ethics & goodwill prevailed. The belts were returned, 1988. (163)

Carpenter's attitude toward stewardship and deaccessioning was complicated. In 1977 he was asked to provide an inventory of the MAI's wampum belts, and was offered proof that certain belts had been "stolen" from their Canadian Six Nations keepers. "Carpenter responded, 'I have no special knowledge concerning the subject which interests you,' and suggested the young man conduct research elsewhere." Carpenter then "propos[ed] a plan for the sale of the very belts" that had been the subject of the inquiry, proposing that the belts be sold back to Canada for US$250,000 (circa US$1,079,000 in 2019). He also stated, "Personally, I'd like to see these belts returned to their *traditional* owners."[37] Yet, at an auction held at the end of 1988 by Sotheby's New York of American Native artifacts, to which Adelaide de Menil had consigned an Aleut mask, Carpenter was quoted as deploring "the 1990 Federal statute that provides for the return of many Indian objects to the tribes, but makes no provision for housing or caring for the objects."[38] Carpenter and de Menil refused the tribe's request to withdraw the mask; it was sold for US$46,000 (circa US$85,000 in 2023) to a foundation that planned to return the mask to the Aleuts.

Neal B. Keating gave *Chief and Greed* a highly positive review in *Museum Anthropology*, noting that the "inter-chapters" span sixty years of Carpenter's ethnographical research.[39] Keating writes, "What is perhaps most useful about Carpenter's treatment of Heye's biography is the close attention paid to the social networks through which Heye moved hundreds of thousands of Native objects. These included networks of anthropologists and archaeologists, other collectors, dealers, and the wealthy elites of New York City" (80). In a handwritten letter to Carpenter, commenting on *Chief and Greed*, Claude Lévi-Strauss said, "You have made an invaluable contribution to the history of American anthropology."[40] Yet, despite the appalling accounts assembled in *Chief and Greed*, some scholars have reassessed Heye in a positive light in the ensuing years. What may have sparked Carpenter's ire, and led to the writing of this book, according to Ann McMullen, was the statement in the *Washington Post* by Richard Kessler that "but for [Heye's] 'boxcar' collection, we'd have no Museum of the American Indian today ... It is high time for the ingrates in charge of this museum ... to acknowledge and credit their benefactor."[41] McMullen goes on to state, "Those who have described Heye only as an obsessive and even nefarious collector have done so based on their own preconceptions or disregard for contradictory evidence" (66). With reference to Carpenter's *Chief and Greed*, McMullen remarks, "Unfortunately, suggesting that Heye's goal was to amass a huge collection identifies his motives by matching them with his results, rather than understanding the goals he set for himself" (74). McMullen goes on to state, "Heye's work has often been explained by reference to Boas's salvage anthropology paradigm; and although Boas urged Heye to focus on salvage, Heye resisted. While preservation was important to Heye, accumulating early objects was primary. Anthropologists, including Frank Speck and Edward Sapir, who documented 'memory culture,' could not understand Heye's frequent disregard for recent works they offered. These pieces were contradictory to Heye's agenda – he purchased them solely to document organic items or precontact technologies" (77).[42] Heye's collection constitutes 85 per cent of the holdings of the NMAI. Carpenter's comment on the new museum was characteristically laconic: "What impresses me most about the NMAI is its openness. Secrecy no longer prevails. The difference is overwhelming. The new staff knows little of the past or finds it mildly amusing. Just as well" (172). Amy Lonetree nuances this account with the comment that Vine Deloria, on the MAI Board during Carpenter's tenure, "linked the new museum and its educational mission to the larger American Indian self-determination movement that began in the 1970s ... Deloria believed that controlling the means of representation is a powerful step in exercising tribes' sovereign rights" (88). Carpenter was out of step with this thinking, and with the politicization of Indigenous cultural aspirations generally. What must be acknowledged, however, is Carpenter's own role in the coming into being of the NMAI through his dogged interventions at the MAI.

Anthropology Upside Down

While Carpenter was assembling what would be his masterwork, the exhibitions *Upside Down*, he was given a last occasion to remember McLuhan. Returning to Fordham University in 2005 in order to speak at a session of the Media Ecology Association Conference that honoured his legacy, where he was given three standing ovations,[43] Carpenter took this as an occasion to remember McLuhan. "Marshall," published the following year in *Explorations in Media Ecology*,[44] revisits much of the material in "That Not-So-Silent Sea," while adding material that was not present in either version of that article. In the EME article, Carpenter states that he gave McLuhan articles on spatial metaphors and Hopi metaphysics and that "Marshall was greatly influenced by Whorf" (180); however, these claims are not made in "Sea" (cf. 239), and the bibliography of Whorf's writings in *Language*

Thought and Reality: Selected Writings of Benjamin Lee Whorf [45] does not support the claim that Whorf first addressed spatial metaphors in his writing. When Whorf does write about space (as in "Gestalt Technique of Stem Composition in Shawnee"), he states that "everything unvisual is unspatial," a comment that is antithetical to Carpenter's and McLuhan's development of the concept of acoustic space. [46] Most of the new material in the EME article concerns Carpenter's and McLuhan's relations with Northrop Frye. [47] "One of the more amusing things on campus," writes Carpenter, "was an encounter between Marshall McLuhan and Northrop Frye. McLuhan was tall, handsome. He strode. Frye was mouse-like. He scooted ... McLuhan would intercept him, greet him warmly: black is white, stand on your head, eat hair, add crazy glue, 10,000 words, a fire hose in the face. Frye must have taken hours to recover. McLuhan and I called the then H.N. Frye, Hugo, for Hugo N. Frye. 'You go and fry' was then a euphemism for 'Go fuck yourself'" (182). [48] Carpenter also reiterates that "there was never a Toronto School of Communication," the rubric through which Carpenter gained a second life in Canadian media studies (just as "visual anthropology" was used as a recuperative label for his work in the US). In a 2005 interview, [49] Carpenter was more sanguine about McLuhan, noting that although they "differed in certain commitments," they "got on handsomely ... He was so much fun to be with. He could turn a phrase. He was basically a poet ... [McLuhan] was a comet in my life. He was the most interesting thing going in Toronto .... [The Explorations group] was like a jazz combo." Asked what it was that *Explorations* wanted to focus on, Carpenter replies "media," although the seminar was "all over the place ... it was pretty wild." Carpenter also remembers the moment the seminar encountered the concept of acoustic space, which he likens to "a Frank Gehry building." Carpenter describes the Explorations seminar as like "the Andy Warhol Factory," with members feeling "free to take anything ... There was no real authorship." Of the *Harper's Bazaar* article, Carpenter says he published it under McLuhan's name, but later under his own name. "There was no problem in the traditional sense of ownership ... I believed in McLuhan since the first day we met."

While the Media Ecology meeting offered Carpenter the occasion to return to his collaboration with McLuhan, the exhibitions *Upside Down* provided a return to *Explorations 9: Eskimo*. Shown first in Paris at the Musée du quai Branly in 2007 and then in Houston at the Menil in 2011, curated by Carpenter and his curatorial assistant Sean Mooney and funded in part by the Rock Foundation, the exhibition was a "testament to the scholarship of Edmund Carpenter and the unique place he occupies in the history of anthropology in America. His groundbreaking research, conducted over the past sixty years, sheds light on the ontology and epistemology of oral cultures, especially those of the Canadian Arctic, Alaska, and Siberia, as well as various ethnic groups living in New Guinea. His work speaks to the impact of modern media on these cultures as well as our own. Carpenter's scholarly contributions derive from a keen understanding of the synaesthetic, or multisensory, ways in which human beings conceptualize and process their relationship to the environment and to one another."[50] The exhibition comprised circa 300 artifacts made of metal, bone, and ivory, dating from 1000 BCE to 1400 CE, together with Yup'ik masks made in the 1800s, drawn from collections, public and private, in Canada, Denmark, France, New Zealand, and the United States. Carpenter had been mulling over the exhibition since he made his film about Dorset carvings in the 1950s, and was spurred into thinking about the exhibition again after seeing a show of Celtic art in Venice in 1993. Carpenter was impressed by the art but appalled by the "disastrous display," as he noted in a letter to Robert McGhee, of the (then) Canadian Museum of Civilization, who had proposed a Dorset exhibition to Carpenter.[51] Although the Venice exhibition struck Carpenter as a failure, it suggested to him "the idea of a walk-around case with multiple windows ... as one possible solution to exhibiting arctic ivories. He noted that the "case should not be square: no Eclidian [sic] space in Eskimo [sic] thought." He goes on to say that he "planned an entrance designed to cleanse visitors of all prior space conceptions. Borrowed (stole) the idea from the artist Doug Wheeler ... No 90 [sic] angles; no corners; no planes ... The whole exhibition should reflect a spatial world far removed from Euclid's."

Carpenter contributed four essays to the catalogue for *Upside Down*. "Arctic Realities" (14–25) draws on a number of Carpenter's previous writings, going back as far as "Space Concepts among the Aivilik Eskimos," published in *Explorations* 5, and including drawings by "Enooesweetok" that appeared in *Eskimo*. It is the conception of space in the Arctic that remains the crucial element in Carpenter's thinking over the decades: "There is no line dividing earth from sky. The two are of the same substance.

Figure 8.5 Installation view, *Upside Down: Les Arctiques*, Musée du quai, Branly, Paris, 2008–09, in Celant, *Doug Wheeler*, 208.

There is no middle distance, no perspective, no outline" (14). It is precisely the unity of earth and sky that distinguishes this space as something other than visual. "In our society, to be real, a thing must be visible ... Space is conceived in terms of that which separates visible objects. We call a gale-swept tundra 'empty' because nothing is visible" (15). This is acoustic space, a space that is configurational, where all elements are interrelated, a space in which there is no upside down, a space, as Carpenter remarked in an essay for the Beyeler foundation about a Yup'ik mask, that is "a song rendered visually."[52] As Mikhail Bronshtein and Kirill Dneprovsky write in their essay about "Ancient Eskimo Art of Ekven" (on the coast of Bering Strait near Cape Dezhnev), the Ekven artifact "illustrates Edmund Carpenter's well-known theory that Eskimo sculptures lack a top or base; in order to understand the object, one must hold it and study it from all angles."[53]

The keynote essay, "Upside Down" (27–43), returns to the theme of figurines made to be hung upside down, and concomitant connections (drawing on Schuster's theories and on "Tradition and Continuity in Eskimo Art") between Eskimo art and Paleolithic traditions that stretched from Eurasia to Polynesia and Arctic Canada (28). Once again, the theme is spatial as well as cultural: inverted figures suggested death and rebirth. "Dorset Film" (80–5) describes a film Carpenter produced in 1957 about the Dorset people. Fritz Spiess (a founding figure in Canadian cinematography) was at the camera, and while 107 reels of 35mm film were produced, the film was not completed and was housed in the Canadian Museum of Civilization (known now as the Canadian Museum of History). The film was restored for the exhibition and excerpts were projected in conjunction with the Dorset artworks. The fourth essay by Carpenter, "Old Bering Sea" (86–117, with twenty-eight photos of works from the Rock Foundation), documents artworks from Alaska and Chukotka (Siberia), such as an Okvik Doll with Head on Stomach in walrus ivory.

Carpenter's collaboration with artist Doug Wheeler on the design of the exhibition was inspired. Wheeler's aesthetic was one that appeared to have emerged directly from the pages of *Explorations*. As Germano Celant puts it:

From 1945 to 1950, a surge of energy after years of global conflict encourages new directions in visual art. Compared to the fracturing and fragmentation practiced by the historic European avant-gardes,

Figure 8.6 Okvik doll, Old Bering Sea, in walrus ivory, circa 200 BC to 100 AD, in Helfenstein et al., *Upside Down: Arctic Realities*, 2007.

many artists now turn to a sensory practice that addresses the totality of perception, no longer solely dominated by vision, but engaged with all the senses. Art seeks an experiential synthesis that moves beyond the traditional representative forms of painting and sculpture, beyond looking and touching to an expanded sensibility. Comprehension concentrates on the all-inclusive perceptible; art becomes total experience.[54]

This was the (re)discovery of acoustic space, a space that, even when it could be seen, did not conform to the dictates of visuality. It was open rather than closed; configurational rather than linear; spherical rather than flat. It was a space that began to dominate the art world at this time, from installations to environments, minimalism to happenings. "This was the era in which the Groupe Espace was formed, when artists were producing works based on a '*spazialismo* manifesto,' when avant-garde art galleries were named 'A Space,' where artists calling themselves 'Ace Space Co.' produced works titled 'A Space Atlas,' and where aesthetic discussion centred on questions of the performance of space."55 It was also when the Explorations seminar was discussing acoustic space. As Celant notes, this was the "period of gestation and development in the work of Doug Wheeler" (13), a time when "a series of writings and events emerge to emphasize light and the void" (14). One such writer was Daisetz T. Suzuki, whose essay on "Buddhist Symbolism" was published in *Explorations* 5. Suzuki, writes Celant, "encourages the individual's reappropriation of the inner breath, assuming it as the matrix of his/her own creativity ... It is an invitation to make contact with an inner spark that serves to exorcize the shadows and allow the reappropriation of 'light.' It liberates buried energy; it is the affirmation of a method that allows one to become aware of a nothingness that is translated into life-giving power" (14) – as if "the whole world ... sprung out of Nothingness," as Suzuki puts it (**E5**, 8; 3). One of its most significant manifestations was John Cage's 4′ 33″, a work, writes Celant, "that brings out the dialectical counterbalance of sound – silence" (14). Art becomes, in the context, "a 'journey' stimulated by the errant force of perceptiveness. As a result there is an assumption that art is a vector for sensory and visual rebirth" (14). The art produced out of this matrix "no longer exists solely as a fixed and stable object, but is fluid and dynamic. It sets in motion a dissociative flow of images and becomes mutable ... It is transformed into an intangible, radiant, almost esoteric state that incorporates a regenerated energy that can affect everyone, activating profound perceptual experiences" (17). The result is a concept of "art as stage and setting" (17), art as environment. "The declaration of art as a *total whole*, where all phenomena – sensory and conceptual – come together, presents an obvious contrast to a sensibility that maintains a bias toward the object, isolated and mobile, responsive to any requirement for manipulation, transport, market, and location" (23). It also presented a contrast to the practices of anthropology. Carpenter had been struck by the work of Robert Cannon, his colleague at San Fernando, whose "first anthropological film experiment combined live action, stills, animation, stop-frame, multi- screen, time-lapse, etc., imagery ... creating a world totally free from three dimensional perspective."[56] The key point is this freedom from three-dimensionality, which was the signal product of printed lineation.[57]

Carpenter had written an article in *Natural History* in 1978 on "Silent Music and Invisible Art"[58] in which he stated that although concepts such as silent music and invisible art are foreign to Westerners, to tribal cultures they make sense. "In many tribal societies, silent music is cultivated, even institutionalized. Singers sometimes plug both ears, converting sound into inner vibration. Or they may play small musical instruments inside closed mouths" (99). Silent music was also part of the "spirit quest" (99). The songs bestowed upon the initiate remained with him throughout his life, revealed just before death. Paintings, meanwhile, were often hidden, as in a cave. The sound of a spirit rattle was produced by something inside the rattle, and the rattle itself became a blur when shaken. "How do you paint a song?" asks Carpenter. "How do you carve a word? One way is to use an acoustic model: make the eye subservient to the ear by patterning space acoustically ... Auditory space has no favored focus. It is a sphere without fixed boundaries, space made by the thing itself" (98–9). Alaskan "Eskimo" masks, for example "were inspired by songs heard in dreams ... Used once, each mask was then burned" (99). Similarly, "Navaho sand paintings ... are generally erased as a final step in their production" (99).

"Nothingness" was Carpenter's characterization of the Arctic, a nothingness that was paradoxically a total ecology of human interaction. It was art, he wrote, that had the ability to call from within one's self "images powerful enough to deny [one's] nothingness" (*Far North*, 287). Although Wheeler had not travelled in the Arctic, his father's profession as a doctor in Arizona led to his introduction to Navajo sandpainting in a shamanistic ritual to celebrate a newborn:

> There's a shaman who's on his knees ... working on a sandpainting ... It's freezing weather. He takes the baby and lays it down on the painting. And his hand [is filled] with powder, different colors [between his fingers] and he continues [drawing] the lines over the body of

the baby ... Finally, the shaman picks up the baby and hands him to the mother ... I'm still watching and the shaman gets up and he has ... a big handmade broom. He just [sweeps the drawing away] and all those colors, they whirl and swirl up into [the sky]. It's cobalt end-of-daylight blue, you know, floating up like this spectral flash swirling around, and then it was gone ... I forgot about how cold it was. It was just the most beautiful thing I had ever seen. (Celant, 31, quoting Wheeler from a 2012 interview)

Ultimately, this would take the form, in Wheeler's art, of "an empty, or emptied-out territory, the negative of presence. It is almost a desert wilderness where the life of colors and images is suspended to leave room for nothingness, or something that is not there ... The aspiration is to arrive at a pure field, where what matters is the simple palpitation of color, preferably *achrome*, or of light, without falling into the three-dimensional object containing geometric or optical compositions" (44). Concomitantly, Wheeler seeks to produce "spatial disorientation" (123) in the viewer, including through the use of "anechoic material and an array of directional microphones that capture all ambient sound and project it back shifted by half a wave cycle, which effectively cancels it out, producing silence" (129). In other works, he strives for a sense of "dimensionless space" (190), a so-called Ganzfeld environment in which space appears uniformly unstructured.

This provided the performative context for *Upside Down*:

In early 2006, the anthropologist Dr. Edmund (Ted) Carpenter – an expert in Eskimo and Inuit cultures – begins preparing an ambitious exhibition of ancient objects made by [I]ndigenous peoples throughout the Arctic regions: small ivory carvings, iron tools, funerary objects, and large ceremonial masks from a group of international collections, to be shown at the newly opened Musée du quai Branly on the Left Bank in Paris. Following a recommendation from the collector Christophe de Menil, who in 1981 commissioned a ganzfeld environment from Wheeler for her residence in Manhattan, Carpenter invites the artist to create an exhibition design that can offer visitors a visual, spatial, and climatic experience of the Arctic. The exhibition,

entitled *Upside Down: Les Arcticques*, opens on September 30, 2008,
and includes an original Wheeler light environment that uses ice as
a material. (202)

In his proposal to Carpenter and Adelaide de Menil, Wheeler wrote, "I see
the design of the exhibition to be ... a spatial context in which the artifacts,
most humble in origin, are all we see ... We enter the exhibition in night
and exit in day. The presence of light and the lack of it controls and defines the spatial context ... There will be an unobstructed one-way flow or
route through the gallery" (quoted by Celant, 202).[59] According to Celant,
Wheeler was "inspired by the logic that informs Carpenter's theory: beginning with an analysis of many ancient carved ivory figurines – worn or
used – that represent the head at the bottom, one can deduce that ancient
Arctic cultures, from the Evken to the Ipiutak tribes, from the Yup'ik to the
Kukoskwim, shared a vision of an inverted world, without horizon, that
does not distinguish between up and down" (202). The floor was composed
of ice (kept frozen in the same way as in ice rinks), light was used to create a
Ganzfeld effect, and infrasonic speakers emitted sounds that created "sonic
'rooms'" (209) that drew on the research of Philippe Le Goff and his field recordings of Inuit songs, producing an effect described by Wheeler as making "the air, the whole volume of the space, alive. It's like it [had] a breathing
aspect" (quoted, 209). Some of the minute objects were represented in large
projections, a tactic that Wheeler said was inspired by Carpenter: "I was
doing this for Ted Carpenter, to try and show these things in a way that
would elevate them to how *he* sees them ... Ted wanted these objects to be
seen as art objects and not as an ethnographic survey show of old artifacts"
(quoted, 209). Wheeler also designed the exhibition's tenure at the Menil in
2011, where the effect, once again, was one in which the artifacts "appear to
float in space" (210). *Artforum* declared the installation to be one of the ten
best of the year, achieving the representation, in the words of Jay Sanders,
of "an unstable landscape that can fundamentally lose its horizon, merge
ground with air, and fully disappear" (quoted, 210).

The choice of very small artifacts may have reflected Lévi-Strauss's theory in *Wild Thought* that the miniature "might present, always and everywhere, the very type of the work of art. For it would seem that every scale
model has an aesthetic vocation – and whence would it draw this constant

virtue, if not from its very dimensions? ... What virtue is there, then, in re-duction, whether of scale or of properties? Its virtue results, it seems, from *a sort of reversal of the process of knowing* [emphasis added]: to know the real object as a whole, we always have a tendency to start from its parts. The resistance it confronts us with is overcome by dividing it. Reduction of scale reverses this situation: smaller, the object as a whole appears less daunting; from the fact of being quantitatively diminished, it seems to us to be qualitatively simplified. More precisely, this quantitative transposi-tion augments and diversifies our power over a homologue of the thing; *through it, the thing can be grasped, weighed up in the hand, apprehended in a single glance* [emphasis added] ... With a scale model *the knowledge of the whole precedes that of its parts* [emphasis in original]" (28). These comments contextualize the artifacts and the exhibition in *Upside Down* through their emphasis on perceptual reversal, tactility, and configura-tional knowing.

The Paris installation, however, was not received in a Lévi-Straussian context. One review expressed serious reservations, arguing that such ex-positions should be curated by Indigenous peoples themselves. Yannick Meunier, of the Centre for North American Studies in the Sorbonne Nouvelle, visited the exhibition three times, but found that his initial im-pressions remained unchanged. "L'atmosphère diaphane de la salle," he writes, "l'emporte sur un contenu culturel imprécis, au point où l'on peut se demander en quoi ces vestiges diffèrent d'une autre collection d'objets inuit"[60] (the diaphanous atmosphere of the room extends to the imprecise cultural content, at which point one has to ask what differentiates this col-lection of artifacts from any other). The *mise-en-scène* reminds the reviewer of Flaherty's *Nanook of the North*, rendering the representations of snow, cold, igloo, and so on as shopworn stereotypes. What he was looking for in the exhibition was "une vision moderne de l'écoumène inuit" (157) (a mod-ern vision of the Inuit environment), although not of the sort presented by Doug Wheeler, which struck Meunier as suggesting that Inuit culture grew up in a laboratory. The lack of expository material furthers this sense of the artifacts' detachment from their context. Meunier explicitly distinguishes the *mise-en-scène* of the exhibition from its contents, but to what ends does it work? While the objects in the exhibition are undeniably brilliant works, when that exposition ends, the works will go back to museums and become, once again, objects of study – except for those going back to the Rock Foundation. For this reason, writes Meunier, *"Upside Down – Les Arctiques* ne peut être considérée comme une exposition sur la 'culture esquimau ancienne,' mais ... sur une partie de la collection privée de l'anthropologue Edmund Carpenter"* (160) (*Upside Down: The Arctics* cannot be considered an exhibition about "ancient Eskimo [*sic*] culture," but ... about a part of the private collection of the anthropologist Edmund Carpenter).

Reviews of the Houston exhibition, however, were overwhelmingly positive.[61] Harald Prins and Bunnie McBride wrote in *American Anthropologist* of how visitors experienced the exhibition: "Entering the space we are immersed in white stillness. This is a clearing within an arctic whiteout. Edgeless floor curves up into wall, erasing horizon. Ground and sky merge. In the clearing there are hundreds of finely carved treasures to be found. Almost all are white ivory, antler, or bone carvings resting on thin translucent white shelves in waist-high glass cases, like surface finds unveiled by wind blowing away snow ... Listening intently, we notice sounds all around us – whistling wind, murmuring voices, groaning ice. Flanking one side of this space is a long curved wall punctuated by windows filled with a subtle spectrum of cold light, ranging from pale cerulean to bright white."[62] In a brilliant review essay, Marcia Brennan wrote that, "Much like the individual artworks displayed in *Upside Down: Arctic Realities*, the exhibition itself could be seen as a composite phenomenon that is best approached from multiple perspectives at once and 'turned this way and that.' In its creative conflations and inversions of Paleolithic and modern motifs, the show simultaneously cultivated the perspectives of ethnographic anthropology and contemporary art criticism, with their attendant conceptions of distanced criticality and aesthetic proximity. This perspectival hybridity revealed as much about aboriginal Arctic cultures as it did about the epistemological structures and aesthetic desires informing contemporary museum collection and curation practices."[63] Given that the Yup'ik masks had a "second life" in the surrealist movement, the exhibition suggested that these artifacts "are interwoven within the history of modernist aesthetics ... The dance masks thus instantiate multiple histories that encompass not only the ethnographic traditions of Arctic peoples, but the patterns of individual and institutional collecting, and the subsequent display practices, that underpinned the production of modernism's own canonical genealogies and its often contested histories." By means of the interventions of Wheeler and Le Goff, "the exhibition space evoked a complicated hybrid typology that blended exoticized connotations of the Arctic igloo with the sanctified associations of the modernist gallery's classic white cube." It was as if Carpenter was seeking to produce Dominique de Menil's ideal of an artistic exhibition, "an atmospheric miracle, which set the work of art in such a light that it would shine and talk to anyone who would care to look and listen."[64]

Ever the "trickster,"[65] Carpenter leaves us with a riddle at the end. If there is no upside down in Arctic art, what precisely is inverted in these exhibitions? Far from convening a "visual" anthropology, what the exhibitions opened up was a hybrid space that sought to engage the entire sensorium based on Carpenter's belief that the senses were primary media. *Upside Down* decontextualized the visual space that was the hallmark of anthropological research and reclassified it as acoustic space. What Carpenter had sought in Papua New Guinea was to invert the traditional order of anthropological inquiry through the act of encouraging the subjects of his research to use the media of that research, such as photography, film, and sound recording, thereby decentering the anthropologist and producing concomitantly an anthropology that reflected on its own coming into being. His interests were at once epistemological and ontological – they sought to study not only the what of anthropology but also the how. What he turned upside down in *Les Arctiques* was anthropology itself.

Conclusion

The Metaphysics of Me

EDMUND SNOW CARPENTER characterized himself at various
times in his career as someone who studied mineralogy and then "fell" into
anthropology,[1] as a madman,[2] and as a university professor who taught for
forty years at Toronto, Santa Cruz, and Harvard.[3] All of these statements
demand qualification. What need no qualifications are the characterizations of Carpenter as a "wanderer,"[4] as an "unconventional anthropologist,"[5] and, most acutely, as a believer in anthropology as nothing less than
a psychomachia:

> I accept the old fashioned notion that the ethnologist is the twice-
> born spiritual adventurer whose fieldwork is nothing less than the
> spirit quest; that he exposes his dearest beliefs & habits to doubt &
> diversity, and returns changed by this intellectual ordeal. If he tells
> the truth about these experiences, he writes what is ultimately an
> autobiography: the metaphysics of me. If he carefully conceals what
> really happened to him, those experiences – inward & outward – he
> actually underwent or failed to undergo, then he writes the sort of
> intellectual foolishness currently popular in academic anthropology.[6]

Here we have all of Carpenter: conservative, spiritual, intellectual, self-
questioning, provocateur, mythomane, and deeply critical of anthropology and its practices. If this *cri de coeur* strikes us as Romantic, it is inten-
tionally so. As Carpenter wrote, "Isaiah Berlin reminds us that: '*until the
Romantics came along, there was only one answer to any question. Truth was
one[;] error was many. You might not know it, you may be too benighted to*

find it, there must be one answer. The Romantics said the same question can have more than one answer."[7] There is no doubt that what Carpenter wrote about the spirit quest here is genuine, and that he lived by this credo. He was moved to self-assessment after Harald Prins and John Bishop published their extended account of his career in the *Visual Anthropology Review*. In a letter to Prins, he stated that he found the account "overly generous" and "painful to read."[8] "Self-loathing is one of my few virtues – rooted in realism … I have no interest in the past, only in current projects. Alive. Learning experiences. Open a drawer. Give everything within it (and nothing else) complete attention. Close the drawer." Carpenter's sojourn in the Canadian Arctic in the winter spanning 1951–52 was one such drawer, and it was clearly traumatic for him. He returned to this moment again and again in his writing, describing it in exactly the same words over the trajectory of half a century. Writing of that time, he stated that "the whole key and rhythm of my life had been altered forever."[9]

This personal approach to anthropology had a number of implications, and often led Carpenter into controversy. The Minik affair was undoubtedly the most controversial in Carpenter's career, as attested by the strong response that Kenn Harper issued to Carpenter's intervention in the burial of the "New York Eskimos." The Minik affair highlighted Carpenter's unease with the increasing politicization of Indigenous groups and the spin-off effects of that politicization on anthropology, collecting, restitution, and museology, all of which he encountered in his relations with the Museum of the American Indian and with his acquisitions for the Menil Collection. His understanding of the Arctic was deeply connected to his time with Ohnainewk, a time when Arctic politics were very much inflected by the Cold War, and when the personal and the political were not conjoined in the way they were in the 1960s and beyond. It was as if he was encountering the rewinding of the Alain Resnais et al. film *Les statues meurent aussi*: the Indigenous artifacts that had "died" and been laid to rest in the colonizers' museums were now coming to life again and insisting on returning home.[10]

Carpenter's deeply personal response to his time in the Arctic was a major factor in his career-long criticism of the anthropological enterprise. In 1961 he commented on Herta Haselberger's "Method of Studying Ethnological Art"[11] (in which the author equates "ethnological" with "anthropological"), which argued that "the art of ethnological peoples differs from other art only in degree" (341). Haselberger's essay is written within the idiom of "the higher cultures" and of "the 'great' arts" while arguing that "evolutionism can contribute little to such questions as the boundaries of art" (342). For Haselberger, aesthetics is the defining quality of an artifact: if it is utilitarian, it is not art. "Art is involved only when the action produces results defined to affect someone, and is not, like play, an end in itself" (342). It was Winckelmann, she argues, who made the study of art "scientific" (342) with his classicizing aesthetic that distinguished European art from non-European art. That "scientific" methodology leads to classification, which is Haselberger's chief focus. Of major interest in terms of Carpenter's aesthetic are Haselberger's use of the terms "haptic" and "optic," the latter defined as art at a distance, which, Haselberger declares, is "nowhere found among ethnological peoples" (346). Space concepts are complicated in ethnological arts, she continues; "ethnological art is far too alive, too real and corporeal, to be subject to mere aesthetic laws." Thus, "when a Baffinland Eskimo [*sic*] ... portrays an animal (Schaeffer-Simmern, 1958), his sculpture is intended to represent the living animal in all its reality. Base and main-prospect are superfluous for such a carving, and therefore neglected" (347).[12]

Carpenter's response to Haselberger focuses on "a consideration of the artistic act and the acoustic structuring of space, with illustrations of both from the Arctic" (361); much of the material is familiar from other publications (such as "Tradition and Continuity in Eskimo Art"). In response to one of Haselberger's categories, Carpenter remarks that Inuit carving "is generally utilitarian" (361); nevertheless, "a carving, like a song, is not a thing; it is an action" (361). Thus, one is not actually collecting objects when one collects Inuit art (and Carpenter, with Adelaide de Menil, amassed the largest collection of paleo-Arctic art in the United States).[13] The approach Carpenter takes to such art "is generally called 'mystical' or 'subjective' or 'insight without method' ... [not] 'objective' or 'scientific.' That competent fieldwork should be called 'mystical' and incompetent fieldwork called 'scientific' is one of the more remarkable features of our profession" (361). Inevitably, Carpenter tweaks Haselberger for citing Schaeffer-Simmern because she "fails to note that the souvenir art which this volume describes is strictly post-1948, Western-designed, Western-valued, and some of it Hong Kong-made" (361). Carpenter also critiques the use of a base in these post-1948 sculptures, stating that "a base, a favored point of view, three-dimensional perspective, etc. ... reflect growing individualism, an aggressive self-concept that seeks to possess and control the external world" (362), a shift in which "anthropologists-apologists" (362) are involved. As he had noted in *Sign Image Symbol*, the key element of Inuit art is "the structuring of space by sound" (362) thanks to "the binding power of the oral tradition" (363), and this "non-visual structuring of space" (363) consistently escapes anthropologists (363).

Carpenter even expressed his misgivings about the anthropological enterprise to Margaret Mead, whom Carpenter and Adelaide de Menil had invited to their East Hampton estate when Mead was nearing the end of her life. "'She was so American,' said Carpenter, 'that I think it was like coming home, for her to be here.'"[14] At one point, Mead summoned Carpenter for a conversation. "You go around saying all these bad things about anthropology," she says. "I know anthropology is full of little minds, but the remarkable thing about it is that if you put them in a room together and lock the door, I don't care how small they are ... they would come out with a statement that's valid and human." Carpenter demurs. "Margaret went on and argued that the method was larger than any of the people. What she was really implying was that anthropology is something like Euclidian [*sic*] geometry, and that you can take a small mind and come up with a competent surveyor. I'm not so sure that's true. I think anthropology is more than a simple method. It's an art – as much an art as a method. And art doesn't come out of committees and out of small minds."[15] As Dorothy Lee had noted in a letter to Carpenter dated "11.24.61," responding to Carpenter's disenchantment with San Fernando College, "for me, you are ... a leader that can help create a new definition of anthropology,"[16] and this comment productively places his critiques of the discipline in that context.

Carpenter's critiques of anthropology focused particularly on visuality, and this puts into question the characterization of him as a "visual anthropologist," a characterization elaborated by Prins and Bishop in various articles on Carpenter.[17] They themselves admit that Carpenter "found himself at odds with the growing academic cohort in visual anthropology."[18] Carpenter would be the first to note that the term "visual media" begs a number of questions, including the status of print as a visual medium. Yet it was precisely this questioning by the Explorations seminar that opened the door to a consideration of acoustic space that Carpenter claimed was a landmark moment in his thinking and was a consistent point of reference throughout his career, most powerfully in the *Upside Down* installations. Carpenter's theoretical reflections on visual and acoustic space led him both to a critique of anthropology as a discipline and also to the museum as medium, neither of which is addressed by the notion of "visual anthropology," even though both the discipline and museology are ineluctably visual. This was the crucial significance of "The New Languages": changing the medium changed the object of study. In this context, "visual anthropology" – a "troubled genre," in the words of Prins[19] – would be better named "media anthropology."[20]

Today the preferred term is "multi-modal anthropology," and it brings with it an increased sense of the problematics of mediation that Carpenter had insisted upon since the mid-1960s. Writing in a 2019 issue of *American Anthropologist*, Stephanie Takaragawa et al. state:

> Although the idea of multimodal anthropology may challenge dominant paradigms of authorship, expertise, capacity, and language, we argue that there is nothing inherently liberatory about multimodal approaches in anthropology. Therefore, as our discipline(s) increasingly advocates for the multimodal in the service of anthropology, there is a need for deep engagement with the multimodal's position as an expression of technoscientific praxis, which is complicit in the reproduction of power hierarchies in the context of global capitalism.[21]

The authors are careful to situate themselves inside this problematic, not outside it, with the understanding that media environments are encompassing, and this element of self-reflection is cognate with the issues that Carpenter was raising in *Oh, What a Blow That Phantom Gave Me!*, albeit that reflections on global capital were not within Carpenter's remit, and that he was insensitive to issues about race. It is only through his insistence on the ways in which media shaped what they mediated that he came close to addressing issues raised by Takaragawa et al. The authors' statement that knowledge and its generation "should not remain solely in the hands of scientific experts" (522) likewise resonates with critiques Carpenter was making half a century ago. In calling for "an *anthropology of the multimodal* premised on what we believe should be an ongoing obligation to try to make sense of the technologies and inheritances upon which multimodal practices depend" (522), the authors are effectively proposing a media anthropology in the sense that Carpenter understood it.

What interested Carpenter about media in anthropology was not primarily the use of film or photography or sound recording, but the need to reflect on the fact of mediation itself, a position articulated in *They Became What They Beheld* and in *Oh, What a Blow That Phantom Gave Me!* By mediation, he meant not only the visual sense, but the entire sensorium. While the senses are aligned in acoustic space, in visual culture the eyes dominate, but this does not eliminate other sensorial responses; indeed, these responses may be heightened. As Elizabeth Edwards remarks, photographs achieve their effects through "a form of 'figural excess,' which cannot be encompassed within linguistic and semiotic practices alone."[22] Recent studies of photography in an anthropological context have stressed the relationship of the visual to "other sensory modalities" such as "orality and sound," whereby "people use the material form of photographs as foci for telling stories and claiming histories, singing, and chanting" (229).

As David Howes has noted, the dominance of vision has not always prevailed culturally.[23] The post-war focus of Margaret Mead and Rosa Métraux on the senses as producers of meaning (rather than as fixed organs that could be measured) spurred renewed interest in the sensorium that was undermined, as Howes notes, by these scholars' insistence that the sensory organs operated like literate language. The analogy to language, Howes states, "whether it be to linguistics (Claude Lévi-Strauss), text (Clifford Geertz), discourse (Michel Foucault), or dialogue (Dennis Tedlock) proliferated and completely dominated the anthropological imagination" (440). Howes states, however, that there were exceptions. "Some managed to keep their senses about them, such as Edmund Carpenter. In company with Marshall McLuhan, he developed a theory of how the extension of any one sense by technology (e.g. radio as an extension of the ear, etc.) alters the way in which the other senses interact, and thereby impacts the way in which people think and act" (440).[24] As Howes suggests, Carpenter can thus be considered a progenitor of sensory anthropology, now a major field of anthropological research.[25] More broadly, if contemporary theorists can define media as "the operation of a deep, technoanthropological universal that has structured the history of humanity from its very origin (the tool-using and inventing primate)," such that media become "a tool for excavating the deepest archeological layers of human forms of life," [26] they can do so (albeit unawares) thanks to a discourse inaugurated by Carpenter and the Explorations seminar.

Carpenter's sensual approach to anthropology (which he articulated in relation to media biases) was summed up, in Carpenter's lexicon, by the word "witness," be it an Arctic witness (chief among whom was Ohnainewk) or a surrealist witness (who witnessed the reclassification of "objects" as "art"). Etymologically, a witness can be auricular, as well as visual, and can have a spiritual dimension; "witness" can mean "knowledge, understanding, wisdom," and it can advert to the "inward testimony of the conscience" (OED). What Carpenter meant by this word was empirical knowledge, as opposed to theory-based forms of knowing that characterized McLuhan and Lévi-Strauss alike. It was the empirical element that attracted Carpenter to the work of Schuster, even though Carpenter's editing, (re)writing, and reworking of Carl Schuster's immense collection of materials was ultimately a *folie à deux*. It was Schuster's madness to amass such a vast archive, and Carpenter's madness to seek to edit it into coherence. Carpenter clearly identified with Schuster the outcast, the researcher without an academic position, the misunderstood genius. The material Schuster left behind was largely intractable, leading Carpenter to make the same points over and over again, as he himself admitted. The lack of academic interest in the published volumes simply confirmed that a genius is misunderstood in his own time. Yet Schuster's research, especially in the context of Carpenter's highly selective editing, is a precursor of the ways in which memes are now understood to function within an anthropological context – essentially through declassification and reclassification. [27]

More broadly, *Materials for the Study of Social Symbolism* would today find a place within the global turn in historiography. Given impetus by the 2006 founding of the *Journal of Global History*, which publishes articles such as "Connecting the Afro-Eurasian World" and "Intertwined Maritime Silk Road and Austronesian Routes: a Taiwanese Archaeological Perspective," [28] the field argues that nomadic empires laid the foundations for modernity. A key aspect of the field's methodology (as the journal's inaugural issue puts it) is the comparative study of interconnections over vast spans of history. [29] The interest in cultures that are nomadic has given rise to books such as Anthony Sattin's *Nomads: The Wanderers Who Shaped Our World* and Kenneth Harl's *Empire of the Steppes*, both of which typify "a larger project of shifting histories away from nation-states and colonialist defamation and toward the peoples and processes that have knotted us together."[30] Schuster and Carpenter's enterprise sought to achieve this understanding in the cultural domain by redirecting our attention to the notion of culture as process, as something in the making, as something mediated.

The references to media that recur throughout Carpenter's career inevitably raises the question of Carpenter's relationship with McLuhan. It is clear that Carpenter experienced an anxiety of influence with reference to his former Toronto colleague that was complicated by the circumstances of the Explorations seminar, where ideas were bandied about without a sense of ownership, and where the role McLuhan played in founding the journal was more prominent than Carpenter allowed. In this context, Carpenter's sense of that "not-so-silent sea" is telling: members of the Explorations seminar were embarking on a truly original course of intellectual inquiry, and no one member could be ascribed "authorship" of an idea, even one so groundbreaking as "acoustic space," which belonged equally to Williams, Carpenter, McLuhan, Tyrwhitt, et al., each of them processing it in different ways. Carpenter's claim to having made contributions to *Understanding Media* must be understood in this context, especially if we remember that "Understanding Media" as Carpenter knew it was, in fact, the *Report on Project in Understanding New Media*. This report was McLuhan's but it incorporated ideas from the Explorations seminar, including the media pedagogical project undertaken by the seminar that included aspects of that project written by Carpenter, who is not referred to in the *Report*. However, McLuhan's repeated exhortations that Carpenter respond to McLuhan's revisions to the *Report* that resulted in *Understanding Media* were clearly not heeded by Carpenter, rendering moot his statement that one can discern a difference in tone in that book deriving from Carpenter's contributions to it. Carpenter truly did have a distinctive, lapidary style of writing, but it is not evident in McLuhan's work. When the two were not working together as closely, Carpenter had no qualms about including McLuhan as co-author of articles in the *Los Angeles Free Press* that bear little trace of McLuhan's interventions. Carpenter also employed ideas from McLuhan and Watson's work in progress, *From Cliché to Archetype*, in his own work, before *Cliché* was published, thanks to McLuhan's letters to Carpenter describing the book. Similarly, Carpenter asserted a sense of ownership with reference to the work of Carl Schuster and of Bill Reid. Carpenter's way of responding to ideas he encountered was ultimately environmental; he didn't claim ownership of his own ideas, as his students were well aware,[31] but the flipside of this position was that he did not hesitate to appropriate the ideas of others. Yet Carpenter's work was distinguished in its own right from McLuhan's; what distinguished it was Carpenter's empirical orientation, not a set of ideas. Carpenter was a witness; he was not a theorist. He was even a witness when he sought to reflect on himself as an anthropological researcher – "the metaphysics of me."

What, then, was his legacy? The connections between media and anthropology resonate to the present day, and Carpenter's stake in this orientation was foundational. He can also claim some credit for the National Museum of the American Indian, due to his unstinting criticism of the Museum of the American Indian and its deaccessioning practices (although he believed that the NMAI went too far in the direction of entertainment, rather than scholarship). In seeking to empower the Native people he encountered in Papua by affording them the use of cameras, Carpenter can also be considered a precursor of the "strategic traditionalism" proposed by Faye Ginsburg[32] as a way of understanding the use of media by Indigenous peoples. To argue that the use of media by Indigenous peoples would somehow diminish their cultural achievements, Ginsburg counters that this thinking aligns with Fabian's concept of the denial of coevalness – that "primitive" peoples should not consort with "modern" media. As Steve Loft has noted, Indigenous people embrace a "media cosmology" that includes "language, culture, technology, land, spirituality, and history."[33] The notion of media as translators accords powerfully with the notion of shapeshifting, whereby "storytelling" is "knowledge transference" (xvii). To this understanding, Jackson 2Bears adds that masks of the sort that so intrigued Carpenter are "animate artifacts ... sacred technologies that we used to access the spirit world"[34] in a way cognate with the functioning of computers and the internet. Steve Loft quotes Vine Deloria's remark that, "In a world in which communications are nearly instantaneous and simultaneous experiences are possible, it must be spaces and places that distinguish us from one another, not time nor history."[35] This, too, is acoustic space.

Carpenter did not leave an academic legacy in terms of students who continued his research trajectory, as Prins and Bishop remark,[36] although there were two major exceptions: Paul Heyer and Steven Feld, whose academic careers gave Carpenter's teaching heritage an international scope. Heyer taught communications studies at Wilfrid Laurier University in Ontario. The focus of his research was on *Communication in History*, the title of a textbook (co-edited with Peter Urquhart and originally with David Crowley) now in its seventh edition (carrying it over a twenty-five year span) that includes Carpenter's "The New Languages." Heyer (with David Crowley) also wrote a new introduction to Harold Innis's *The Bias of Communication*, originally published by the University of Toronto Press with an introduction by McLuhan, Heyer thus extending the legacy of both McLuhan and Carpenter through these introductions and his 2003 biography of Innis. In the obituary he wrote for Carpenter, Heyer states that, "It was Carpenter's writings, which I came to through McLuhan, that inspired me to pursue graduate work in anthropology and then later seek a career in communication studies" (513). Having enrolled at the New School for Social Research, Heyer carried with him *Explorations in Communications* as his *vade mecum*, but he never expected to study with Carpenter, given the latter's "enigmatic reputation, global wanderings, and disdain for the more formal constraints of academe" (513). Signing up for a course titled "Anthropology of the Present" with the instructor TBA, Heyer was delighted to find that Carpenter was teaching it, and they remained in touch over the years.

Carpenter's other noteworthy student was Steven Feld, whose *Sound and Sentiment* has been acclaimed as a "landmark," as "one of the greatest ethnographies ever written," a "masterpiece," a book that "undergirds acoustemology, or the anthropology of sound," and as a book whose influence extends across "cultural and linguistic anthropology, ethnomusicology, performance studies, media studies, history, and folklore."[37] An "ethnographic study of sound as a cultural system" (3), the book analyzes "modes and codes of sound communication ... in Kaluli society" (3), a group of people who inhabit the southern highlands of Papua New Guinea. In his introduction to the thirtieth anniversary edition of *Sound and Sentiment*, Feld looks back over his initial fieldwork and forward to the present moment, when what he studied then was present now "on a three-terabyte hard drive" (xxiii). It was at the New School that Feld studied "media anthropology" with Carpenter. "Erudite about art history and material culture, Carpenter ... was also a deep listener with a provocative approach to understanding the interplay of auditory, tactile, and visual senses in the Arctic. His radical text and visual productions [such as *They Became What They Beheld*, with Ken Heyman] inspired my interest in experimental crossings of anthropology and music ... Carpenter's involvement with sensory media studies equally convinced me to work in sound and visual media simultaneously" (xxv). In addition to his textually produced anthropological work, Feld has produced recordings following on from Canadian composer R. Murray Schafer's development of the idea of the soundscape (xxvii), his research drawing on Carpenter's studies of the Aivilik's "space awareness [as being] acoustic," to the extent that it "dominated visual space."[38]

All of this is a far cry from the claim that Carpenter was one of the founders of the "Toronto School of Communication,"[39] a notion that Carpenter himself repudiated ("Sea," 251). It was not only the linear underpinnings of communications theory (sender-receiver) that rendered it problematical as an anthropological mode of inquiry, but the lack of sensory engagement that emerged from that model's failure to theorise "noise." The recursive model of media theory was much more conducive to Carpenter's thought, because the notion of feedback opened on to Carpenter's meditations on the materiality of mediation in anthropological research. In this context, Feld's account of "ethnography as 'turned around' and 'turned over' Kaluli" (246), concepts that emerged from the Kaluli when they read his book about them, are highly resonant. For the Kaluli, to turn around a word is to give it a fresh metaphorical dimension, hiding the message while highlighting the medium. This leads to the notion that to fully understand a word requires one to turn it over: "Getting to the 'underneath' of what is implied is 'turning over' words to rotate or shift their multifaceted figure and ground possibilities" (249). For the Kaluli who examined Feld's book, this is what ethnography does: it turns around their culture into another language and then shows what's underneath, a "rather clever image of the intricacies of ethnographic work" (249). In *Upside Down*, the effect of Arctic art within an anthropological context was similar: it upset the traditionally visual approach to such artifacts (with its assumptions about dimensionality) and caused them to be inverted, not only to be seen in another way, but to be experienced acoustically, configurationally. Carpenter associated this upsetting of visual norms with surrealism, arguing that its juxtapositional modalities were characteristic not only of acoustic space but of anthropological practice generally, insofar as anthropology always juxtaposed the culture of the ethnographer with the culture being studied, and that these domains were ultimately incommensurable. As Carpenter put it in an interview:

> The Surrealists collected ethnographic art, but they didn't bundle it by culture area ... They were interested in juxtaposing these things to see if there were any patterns that connected ... They were interested in the chance encounter, not the systematic thing. This is where anthropologists have often totally misunderstood what the surrealists were doing. The anthropologists say an object takes its value from the culture that produced it, that it has no value outside that [culture]. Now it's no accident that the structuralists in anthropology accepted that pattern as well. Claude Lévi-Strauss and all these far reaching examples that he preferred to put side by side, fully aware of the fact that there was no historical connection between them ... He said there could be elements at work here, and the most basic one that he came up with is that the human brain is an electronic organ that operates on the basis of plus or minus, like a computer, yes or no, back and forth, and that the co-existence of contraries, the unity of opposites ... is not a genetical factor, it's just a function of the brain ... The Surrealists understood this ... It seems to me that Surrealism is the 20th century's main art form.[40]

Carpenter's comments resonate with current understandings of the museum as a space that mediates the knowledge held by the collection and the knowledge of the people who are represented by the collection.[41] Raymond A. Silverman writes in his introduction to the edited collection *Museum as Process*, "The notion of 'knowledge' that underpins the work presented in this book acknowledges its concreteness but asserts that its substance invariably changes as it moves through space (from culture to culture) and time (from generation to generation)."[42] This sense of process has been given impetus by the digitization of collections (though not unproblematically), emphasizing that the museum is increasingly a space of mediation as initially conceived of by Harley Parker and given iconic representation on the cover of *Explorations* 5, which superimposed the "mother goddess" with the front page of a newspaper. As Prins and Bishop argue, Carpenter's focus on media was motivated in part by the sense that reflection on the role of media in producing the object of research undermined the notion of scientific objectivity. In this, as Prins and Bishop state, Carpenter "was far ahead of his time. Margaret Mead, for instance, displayed a more naive faith in the objectivity of cameras as observational instruments."[43]

To discuss mediation at all in the context of anthropology is an index of how far the discipline has changed from the early days of Carpenter's fieldwork. The "silent sea" confronted by McLuhan in the Explorations seminar that was the "not-so-silent sea" described by Carpenter in 1992 has become for anthropologist Orin Starn "a dark dirty sea far from any sheltering shore."[44] Thirty-five years after James Clifford's *Writing Culture*, the practice of anthropology is characterized by "overspecialization" (5), the acknowledgement of "plural pathways" undercutting "simple disciplinary periodizations" (5). The concept of fieldwork has concomitantly shifted; the field is increasingly "here" rather than "there" – we have become other to ourselves, suggesting that what anthropology was always already studying was the culture from which it emerged, rather than the culture "in the field." As Starn puts it, "What anthropologists 'discover' in the field inevitably refracts, often mirrors, the discipline's agendas of the moment" (6). Many of these concerns were expressed by Carpenter throughout his career, though often from outside the mainstream discourse of anthropological disciplinarity, where they were either not heeded or rejected as lacking academic gravitas. He was aware, in particular, that "postcolonials [should] have their own say as opposed to being ventriloquized by the anthropologist," as Starn puts it (8). The most dated aspect of *Writing Culture* is writing itself, as Starn observes: "The very idea of writing, at least anything more than a text or tweet, can seem old-fashioned now in the age of multimedia, streaming video, and the avalanche of other digitized communication" (8).[45] Here, again, Carpenter was prescient with his articulation of "the new languages," which were post-linguistic and hypermediated. Even James Clifford, looking back on *Writing Culture*, has asked about that book: "Where are technology, communications media?" (25).

It was through his insistence on the *anthropos*, on the human,[46] in an increasingly mediated culture, that Carpenter produced an enduring response to what Mark Greif has called *The Age of the Crisis of Man*.[47] From the Boasian universalism of the Schuster project to the "misanthropology" of *Phantom*, Carpenter was involved in a debate that questioned the "humanity" of the "human" in the wake of genocides, invasive media technologies, and the decline of belief systems. As Greif writes, by the 1940s "the issue was no longer respect for plural human worlds (like those of the Zuni or the Kwakiutl [Kwakwaka'wakw]) but defense and diagnosis of a common human world" (44), a world that Carpenter understood had been made common (and suspiciously so) through global media. If the "moral anthropology" (45) of the time was raising doubts about the increasing reliance on "Reason," it was Carpenter's contribution to locate this rationality in a particular media form, namely literacy, and to illustrate through his anthropological research that there were other ways of knowing and of configuring human knowledge (and thus the "human"). This had the distinct advantage of addressing the broad question of "technics" while avoiding the prevailing abstractions in answering it. If "technik [had become] independent, inevitable, a force like humanity or culture" (47), Carpenter demonstrated that technics were in fact relational with the human, not an independent category. His studies of the human as it encountered technologies of mediation were much more sophisticated than the prevailing ethos of the "technology-as-organization narrative of the discourse of man" (228). Carpenter was highly cognizant of the fact that "as communications technologies grow in significance, alongside material leftovers and remnants, something unnerving happens – the immaterial circulation of signs crosses over with material circulation, until one witnesses a further denudation of values" (230). Carpenter's response was not to adopt the scientific analysis proposed by Lévi-Strauss, with its echoes of Claude Shannon's and Norbert Wiener's communicational theories (as Greif notes, 298). Rather, it was Lévi-Strauss's "anticolonialism, antiethnocentrism, and fundamental philosophical, moral, and political commitment to difference" (298) that resonated in Carpenter's work, and precisely because the basis for Lévi-Strauss's position was mediatic:

> There is no such thing as a people without history ... all cultures have histories. The ones that can't point out those histories to us, as we can point out ours, are cultures that don't have *writing*. In this sense,

Lévi-Strauss says, one can easily identify the mechanism of what we see as a greater development: some cultures, like that of the modern West, are self-consciously and visibly "cumulative." But more cumulativeness – pointing yourself in a single direction to maximally enhance one trait, with all its consequences – does not betoken superiority to cumulative cultures heading in some other direction, or less cumulative cultures whose dynamism is not as unidirectional. (Greif, 300)

The one great flaw in Lévi-Strauss's thinking, as Derrida was to point out, was its insistence on structural identity, rather than difference. But Derrida's critique was itself enmired in the notion of the sign; Carpenter's focus on media positioned him differently. Carpenter proposed an understanding of "man" as always already mediated, but by virtue of that fact, the human could be understood as a relational concept that put the human in touch with the media ecology – including the natural environment – where it had its being. This informs at once Carpenter's empirical orientation and his resistance to the cybernetic turn. In the mediated world, "man" was still present, albeit "extended," as McLuhan would have it. This concept of anthropomorphism has come under increasing scrutiny within media theory via the pronouncements of Friedrich Kittler about "so-called Man" ("der sogenannte Mensch"),[48] but in that "so-called" Carpenter would have been able to hear the call of the non-present presence that announces the *mediation* of the "human" and, in doing so, turns anthropology upside down.

Notes

Introduction

1 In reviewing the documentary (*Oh, What a Blow That Phantom Gave Me!*), Sigurjón Baldur Hafsteinsson writes that the film "offers no explanation or contextualization of Edmund Carpenter's work. We get glimpses of some of his work and his ideas but nothing of his background, intellectual development, or what happened to him after his Papua New Guinea year. Nor does the film discuss or indicate the influence of his teaching, films, or controversial ideas on his fellow anthropologists." See Hafsteinsson, "Review of Harald Prins and John Bishop," 77–8.

2 Carpenter, "That Not-So-Silent Sea," 260nn284–6.

3 See Serres, *Le Tiers-Instruit*.

Chapter One

1 Heyer, one of Carpenter's students at the New School for Social Research, states that *Explorations* was "one of the great intellectual experiments of the twentieth century" in his obituary for Carpenter, "In Memoriam Edmund Snow Carpenter," 513.

2 I am drawing here on Williams, *Cassell's Chronology of World History*, 550–61. For "inforg" see Floridi, *Information*, 43.

3 Edmund Carpenter, "That Not-So-Silent Sea," in Theall, *The Virtual Marshall McLuhan*, 236, hereafter referenced as "Sea." Originally published in a shorter version as "Remembering *Explorations*," 3–14.

4 See Spiess, "Edmund Carpenter," in Helfenstein et al., *Upside Down*, 228–9. Carpenter began at CBC with a weekly radio program that subsequently became a TV program. See Prins, "Obituary: Edmund Snow Carpenter," 24. Spiess was the main editor on the Schuster/Carpenter project.

5 Marchand, *Marshall McLuhan*, 119.

6 I am paraphrasing here and in the following paragraphs the Wikipedia entry on Carpenter, wikipedia.org/wiki/Edmund_Snow_Carpenter (accessed 11 May 2022); it and the biographical essay by Prins and Bishop (noted in the introduction to this volume) are the major sources for Carpenter's life story. Both are filled with numerous errors. As the current study makes clear, Carpenter did not found the journal *Explorations*; this was done at McLuhan's initiative. Nor did Carpenter co-write McLuhan's *Understanding Media* (1964). Prins and Bishop attribute a book to Carpenter titled *Time/*

Space Concepts of the Aivilik (1955), which Carpenter did not write, and their list of his publications is singularly incomplete. The complexities of the relationship between McLuhan and Carpenter appear in the present volume.

7   Grimes, "Edmund Carpenter."

8   Carpenter, "Iroquoian Figurines," 105.

9   Carpenter, "Recently Acquired Manuscripts," 166–8; "Five Sites of the Intermediate Period," 298–314; "Four Hopewellian Tumuli in Western New York," 209–16; "Tumuli in Southwestern Pennsylvania," 329–46.

10 Carpenter, "An Unusual Pottery Jar from East Milton," 38. The article is preceded by Carpenter's dissertation supervisor Frank Speck's "Reflections on the Past and Present of the Massachusetts Indian," in which Speck argues that assuming the "Indian" population of the US was extinguished by colonization is incorrect. "The blood of the Indian native peoples still continues to flow in the veins of a posterity bearing the names and conscious identities of the original nations" (33). The following year, Carpenter and Hassrick published "Rappahannock Games and Amusements," 29–39.

11 Speck, Hassrick, Carpenter, *Rappahannock Taking Devices*. These three authors also wrote a study of Rappahannock Herbals that was given a strong review by La Barre, who noted that "Frank Speck continues to astonish his colleagues with an extraordinary ability to draw sound ethnography out of apparently thin air," and notes that the co-authors "have made a significant contribution to our knowledge of increasingly acculturated and fragmentary groups" (466). See La Barre, "Review of Frank Speck, Royal B. Hassrick, and Edmund Carpenter, Rappahannock Herbals."

12 See Carpenter, "Frank Speck: Quiet Listener," 78.

13 Tyrwhitt had worked with Sigfried Giedion, and with Patrick Geddes (**E5**), the legendary town planner. In Berlin, she was associated with onetime *Reichskommissar* Gottfried Feder, author of the Nazistic *Die neue Stadt*. In 1951, she was appointed visiting professor of Town Planning at the University of Toronto and was befriended by McLuhan, to whom Giedion had introduced her. During her second year in Toronto she was invited by McLuhan to join him and some colleagues in their application to the Ford Foundation to establish an interdisciplinary seminar on culture and communication. See Shoskes, *Jaqueline Tyrwhitt*.

14 Shoskes, *Jaqueline Tyrwhitt*, 152.

15 As noted by Buxton, "The Ford Foundation and Communication Studies."

16 "From the very beginning it was apparent that there were irreconcilable intellectual differences in the group. Carl Williams stood as the champion of the traditional scientific reliance on quantitative measurement. McLuhan, of course, had a rather different approach to reality" (Marchand, *Marshall McLuhan*, 118). I would also argue that there were major differences that became exacerbated over the years between Carpenter and McLuhan, resulting in the somewhat animistic tone of the "Sea" article, especially its conclusion.

17 Michael Darroch and Janine Marchessault note that Carpenter was also influenced by A. Irving Hallowell's research on "'spatio-temporal orientation.'" Hallowell was, like Carpenter, a student of Frank Speck, and spent his career as a distinguished anthropologist. See Darroch and Marchessault, "Introduction," v, n1.

18 Tyrwhitt's "The Moving Eye" (**E4**, 115–19; *110–14*) argues that the Mughal city of Fatehpur Sikri had been planned in such a way that it did not privilege a single point of view, similar to a Chinese painting, which is appreciated through the moving eye, rather than the fixed point of view.

19 See Fulford, "All Ignorance Is Motivated," 3–8.

20 Carpenter, undated letter to Marshall McLuhan [circa 1957], Carpenter Papers, National Anthropological Archives, Smithsonian Institution, NAA.2017-27, Box 31 (hereafter Box 31).

21 Carpenter "quotes" the letter in "Sea" as follows: "Gee whiz Ted, what a breath of fresh hair. Let us up periscope and see if the concrete is hardening. Yep, it's hardening up and down the budget valley. Now don't go into a feminine flap. If I didn't think you could raise $50,000 in half an hour any time you set your mind to it, I'd do it for you" ("Sea," 243).

22 See Marchand, *Marshall McLuhan*, 138.

23 Carpenter's articles in "Explorations" are: "The Eskimo Mask: The Audience as Artist," "E" 10 (Summer 1964); "If Wittgenstein had been an Eskimo"; "We Wed Ourselves to the Mystery"; "Oh, What a Blow That Phantom Gave Me (Don Quixote)," "E" 29 (Christmas 1970); and "Moral Progress and the Media," "E" 30 (Spring 1971). See also Genosko, "The 'Unknown' *Explorations*."

24 Carpenter's highlighting of Lee's contribution to *Explorations*, a number of which were critiqued within the journal itself by Robert Graves, may have been his attempt to assert the significance of the anthropological contributions to the journal, which are in the minority in the anthology *Explorations in Communication*.

25 Lee, "Lineal and Nonlineal Codifications of Reality," 89–97.

26 McLuhan, *The Gutenberg Galaxy*.

27 It is noteworthy that Lee's contributions to *Explorations* were twice rebutted by Robert Graves, including her essay on lineal versus non-lineal modes of communication, as well as her essay on symbolization (both in **E7**). In each instance, Graves's rebuttals follow immediately after Lee's articles. Graves was invited by Carpenter to make these interventions. See the letter from Graves dated 8 January 1957 in the Carpenter Papers.

28 McLuhan, "The Agenbite of Outwit," 43. In the same article, McLuhan writes of "the new electronic media" and "the way in which they return us to the unified fields of the old oral cultures" (43).

29 John Bassett, who funded issues 7 and 8 of *Explorations*, consulted Buckminster Fuller in the 1960s on the potential "revitalization of Toronto," which Fuller's team characterized as a "'second order metropolitan area' that

could distinguish itself with a waterfront university, an enclosed galleria, a crystal pyramid, and three floating residential islands." Quoted by Nevala-Lee, *Inventor of the Future*, 354.

30 Leopold Infeld was a Polish physicist who taught at the University of Toronto from 1939 to 1950. When the atomic bomb was used in WWII, he became a peace activist, which resulted in accusations of communist sympathies. Infeld returned to (communist) Poland in 1950, leading to suspicions that he would betray nuclear secrets to the communists. The University of Toronto refused to grant him a leave of absence and Infeld resigned his position, while Canada's response was to strip him of his citizenship. In 1995, the University of Toronto apologized, and awarded Infeld the title of Professor Emeritus. See "Leopold Infeld," Wikipedia, accessed 13 November 2023, https://en.wikipedia.org/wiki/Leopold_Infeld. Infeld's story helps to contextualize Carpenter's comment that "the 1950s belonged to McCarthy, even in Canada" ("Sea," 4).

31 Carpenter, *They Became What They Beheld*.

32 See Cavell, "Dematerialization and Rematerialization," 83–97.

33 The word is Margaret Mead's from her blurb on the front jacket of *They Became What They Beheld*.

34 The insertion of the letters EP (𝑬𝒑) among the characters would appear to allude to *The Chinese Written Character as a Medium for Poetry* by Fenollosa, edited by Ezra Pound. Pound tended to sign his name with his initials, as on the postcard Carpenter reproduces in "Sea" (237).

35 McLuhan published a book of this title in 1968 with typographical contributions from Harley Parker.

36 These two items were also published in the anthology *Explorations in Communication*, edited by Carpenter and McLuhan.

37 "Sometimes McLuhan called his nonmoral approach 'satire.' He meant that simply putting the spotlight on the features of a situation that most people ignore tends to bring out the latent ridiculousness of the situation" (Marchand, *Marshall McLuhan*, 121).

38 See Hintz, "Dapper Corpse Used to Sell Embalming Fluid in 1903 Advertisement."

39 McLuhan critiqued *Time* in "The Psychopathology of *Time* and *Life*," published by Gershon Legman in *Neurotica* (1949).

40 In this context it is noteworthy that McLuhan had made his name in the world of art criticism in the 1940s. See Cavell, "Re-Mediating the Medium," 80.

41 Quoted by Louis Menand in "Modern Family," 69, a review of Hugh Eakin, *Picasso's War: How Modern Art Came to America*.

42 On Melcarth see Griffey and Reay, "Sexual Portraits," 66–94. Melcarth famously designed the batwing sunglasses of Peggy Guggenheim.

43 See Richard Cavell, "Introduction: The Cultural Production of Canada's Cold War," 3–32.

44 Hoffman, Allen, and Ulrich, *The Little Magazine*, 108.

45 Miller, "Advertising in Poetry," 349.

46 Carpenter also published, under his own name, "The New Languages," 305–15.

47 The article is reprinted in www.torontoist.com from *The Globe and Mail* (15 June 1957). The article in *Torontoist* is by Kevin Plummer.

48 In fact, the experiment analyzing memory retention based on various media was reported by *The New York Times* in March of 1954. Titled "Video Best Teacher, Researchers Find," the story summarized the experiment as demonstrating that "television is a first-class teacher, easily surpassing books and its elder cousin, radio" (quoted by Marchand, *Marshall McLuhan*, 125).

49 MacDonald, "Editor's Note," 52 (note).

50 Carpenter, "Shapers of the Modern Outlook," 9–10. There is a strong sense of identification with Whorf in this article, as well as in Carpenter's comments about Whorf in "Sea," where the reference to Whorf as an "independent scholar" (239) appears to strike a personal note.

51 Jaqueline Tyrwhitt takes up the issue of perspective in "The Moving Eye" (**E4**), arguing that perspectival perception is learned, an idea also present in Jean Piaget's "The Development of Time and Space Concepts in the Child" (**E5**, *118–30*; *113–25*).

52 Helfenstein et al., *Upside Down*. This exhibition catalogue is the revised version of *Upside Down: Les Arctiques*, published by the Musée du quai Branly on the occasion of the exhibition there, 30 September 2008 to 11 January 2009.

53 The reputation of Whorf's theory has gone up and down. J.A. Lucy writes about the "Sapir-Whorf Hypothesis" in the *International Encyclopedia of the Social and Behavioral Sciences* that "Linguistic relativity proposals are sometimes characterized as equivalent to *linguistic determinism* ... the view that all thought is strictly determined by language. Such characterizations of the language–thought linkage bear little resemblance to the proposals of Sapir or Whorf, who spoke in more general terms about language influencing habitual patterns of thought, especially at the conceptual level" (13487). Lucy further notes that Sapir and Whorf "focused on structures of meaning rather than on formal grammatical process such as inflection," and that "Whorf's writings ... form the canonical starting point for all subsequent discussion" (13487).

54 John Paul and John C. Ogilvie confirmed in **E4** the finding that students retained the most information from television ("Mass Media and Retention" **120–3**; *115–18*). An unsigned article in **E7** (**112–16**; *109–13*) reviewing David Riesman's *Constraint and Variety in American Education* (1956) urges that the effects of "movie, TV and LP" (**114**; *111*) be studied both locally and among "totally different cultures" (**114**; *111*). Cognately, an unsigned letter in **E5** notes that, at a recent rally, Billy Graham had made more converts on TV than among those who had participated in person (**63**; *58*).

55 In this regard, the CBC's focus on "high culture" appears curiously like that of Soviet TV, as described in **E6** by V. Sharoyeva (**65–7**; *64–6*). Lister Sinclair's contribution to **E6**, "Time and the Drama" (**68–78**; *67–77*), is a classic example

of the cultural conservatism and pseudo-intellectualism that characterized the CBC while Carpenter was working there.

56 *Explorations* is completely absent from Norris, *The Little Magazine in Canada 1925–80*, and from Irvine, "'Little Magazines' in English Canada," 602–28. As Thacker comments (621), Louis Dudek, a major figure in the promotion of Canadian modernist poetry, was virulently opposed to McLuhan's media theories (as well as to the poetics of the Black Mountain school), which gives a sense of the academic and cultural context into which *Explorations* was born.

57 Not to be confused with the *Black Mountain Review*, which it preceded by six years.

58 The article is prescient. "The steam engine, the atomic bomb, and now the high-speed computing machine are 'commodities' responsible for … spontaneous transformations of society … The computing machines do not merely increase the number of commodities we possess; they transform our life into an entirely different form … Their behavior is analogous to human behavior … The transformation of mechanical energy into electric energy brought about an entirely new problem: that of communication at a distance. Devices allowing communication between men and machines, and between machines, became necessary. It is the problem of communication which ushered us into the XXth century. As long as the communication system had for its purpose to extend the 'voice' of man, a quantitative increase of commodities took place. When, however, communication becomes independent of man's intervention, a transformation of the society can be expected … The next drastic step toward liberation from men consists of the construction of machines capable of learning … It is already necessary now to be acquainted with many fields aside from one's own, to be capable of working intelligently" (n.p.). Born in Russia, Goldowski emigrated to the US and was recruited to the Manhattan Project, but was subsequently denied security clearance owing to her place of birth; she then began her teaching career.

59 "Natasha Goldowski Renner," Wikipedia, accessed 22 November 2023, https://en.wikipedia.org/wiki/Natasha_Goldowski_Renner.

60 See Genosko, "Where the Youth Aren't."

61 The quotations are from Vallye, "The Strategic Universality of *trans/formation* 1950–1952," 28. As Vallye notes, the major question raised by modernism as espoused in this magazine was universality, a question that Carpenter would grapple with when he was editing the Schuster archives.

62 See Darroch and Marchessault's introduction to the reprint of *Explorations* (*E1 vii–viii*).

63 *Explorations* published an article ("Communication Revolution," *E8*) by Gilbert Seldes, editor of *The Dial*, venue for the first publication of "The Waste Land." Seldes was also the first director of television for CBS News. While in that position, he invited Buckminster Fuller to give televised lectures; Fuller understood television as having a considerable pedagogical potential,

including for the teaching of "'ethnology.'" Quoted by Nevala-Lee, *Inventor of the Future*, 169.

64 Many of these are collected in *The Interior Landscape*, edited by McNamara. On McLuhan's "agrarianism," see Jonathan Miller, *McLuhan*.

65 For the Macy discussions see *Cybernetics*, edited by Pias.

66 Brooker, "In the Modernist Grain," 959.

67 See Whitney, *Finks*. Among the most prominent of these magazines and journals were *The Paris Review* and *Encounter*.

68 Hyman was married to the author Shirley Jackson, and it is in her biography that this information appears. See Franklin, *Shirley Jackson*, 310–12.

69 In a 2005 interview, Carpenter remarks that McLuhan and Kelly were planning to write a musical together. See Mywebcowtube, "Edmund Ted Carpenter 2011 – on Marshall McLuhan and Explorations," 1:00:59, 24 June 2016, https://www.youtube.com/watch?v=t6HyFyMjlXA.

70 See Department of Anthropology, University of Toronto, "History of the Department," accessed 16 February 2022, https://www.anthropology .utoronto.ca/about-us/our-department/history-department.

71 Cohen-Cole, "The Creative American," 219–62. Cohen-Cole posits a dynamic in American Cold War culture between the creative individual and the conformist mass.

72 Darwin, *Expression of the Emotions in Man and Animals*. The thesis of the work was that emotional states could be determined by facial expression, a thesis that united the anthropological with the semiotic. The thesis gained notoriety in the 1970s through psychologist Paul Ekman's contention that Darwin's theory was universal. Ekman based his concept of the universality of emotional response in part on films made by Gregory Bateson (married at one time to Margaret Mead) in Bali in the 1930s. Ekman asserted that there were seven basic emotions common to humans: happiness, sadness, anger, contempt, disgust, fear, and surprise. Ekman's theory did not survive empirical research; he was critiqued particularly by anthropologists, including Margaret Mead, who suggested that Ekman had produced "improper anthropology" and that he was wrong to critique Ray Birdwhistell's refutation of the universality of emotions. Nevertheless, Ekman's theories have remained current as the foundation for emotion recognition software that is used (for example) to analyze consumer attitudes towards products. See "Paul Ekman," Wikipedia, accessed 3 December 2023, https://en.wikipedia.org/wiki/ Paul_Ekman.

73 Mead, "Preface" to Darwin, *Expression of the Emotions*, v–vi.

74 Armond R. Towns has argued that McLuhan's media theory is a form of Social Darwinism, an idea Towns bases on McLuhan's use of "tribalism" and "detribalisation" to refer to oral and literate cultures respectively. In this account, detribalization would have a negative implication, in that it would imply that literacy is superior to orality. This, however, was not McLuhan's

position; he lauded orality and critiqued the effects of literacy. Most significantly, Towns leaves "retribalisation" out of his argument; McLuhan's notion
was that electronic media were returning us to the conditions of an oral culture. See *On Black Media Philosophy*, 30–8.

Chapter Two

1 Darroch and Marchessault comment that, "While no one discipline was
privileged above the others, anthropology played a special role in creating a
strong comparative framework from the start ... Indeed, Carpenter's expan-
sive understanding of anthropology was initially the driving force behind the
publication." See their introduction to the reprint of *Explorations* (E1 xvi).
2 Reo Fortune taught at the University of Toronto from 1941 to 1943; he had
been married to Margaret Mead from 1928 to 1936, working with her in New
Guinea from 1931 to 1933. A fictionalized account of the relationships of
Fortune, Mead, and Gregory Bateson (subsequently married to Mead) has
been published as the novel *Euphoria* (2014) by Lily King. I was struck by the
sentence, "You don't realize how language actually interferes with communication until you don't have it, how it gets in the way like an overdominant
sense" (chapter 7).
3 Mead spent the last months of her life living with Carpenter and Adelaide de
Menil at their Long Island estate. See Prins and Bishop, "Edmund Carpenter,"
135.
4 The ascription is given by Michael Darroch and Janine Marchessault in their
annotated reprint of *Explorations* (7, xvi).
5 Carpenter briefly reviewed Bidney's *Theoretical Anthropology*, where he writes
that Bidney ignores "form" in his analysis (480).
6 King, *Gods of the Upper Air*, 2. Carpenter commented that Mead "drew attention to aspects of American culture lacking clearly defined traditions,
e.g., child-rearing, adolescence, male-female roles, and provided readers with
comparative materials, methods, and insights to enable them to develop intelligently their own traditions in the context of American life." See Carpenter,
"Review of Margaret Mead, *People and Places*," 1074–5.
7 Quoted by Salaris, "The Invention of the Programmatic Avant-Garde,"
26, from Boccioni et al., "La pittura futurista: Manifesto tecnico," *Poesia*
(11 April 1910).
8 The movement toward a corporate culture was a particular concern of
McLuhan, who pursues it in his discussion of William H. Whyte's *The
Organization Man* (E8, item 15).
9 See Franklin, *Shirley Jackson*, 338–9.
10 McLuhan was profoundly influenced by the notion of the museum without
walls, applying it to the educational context in his article on the "Classroom
Without Walls" (E8) to suggest that electronic media had shifted the domain
of learning outside the schoolroom and university to the city at large.

11 Grasskamp, *The Book on the Floor*, 3. The title derives from the 1954 photograph of Malraux standing in his living room, surveying hundreds of photographs from his book spread out on the floor.

12 "Jean-Luc Godard specifically paid tribute to Malraux in his *Histoire(s) du cinema*." Grasskamp, *The Book on the Floor*, 130.

13 Morton, "Anthropology of Photography," 1.

14 Gordon, *Marshall McLuhan*, 196, quoting an undated letter from Carpenter to McLuhan in the National Archives of Canada.

15 See Cavell, "Kittler's *Apophrades*: Marshaling McLuhan," 5–32.

16 McLuhan, *Verbi-Voco-Visual Explorations*. In *Design for the Real World: Human Ecology and Social Change*, Papanek claims co-authorship/co-editorship of the book. See the bibliography (326).

17 Jorge Luis Borges, "Mutations" (**E4**, 21; *16*). Borges became known outside Argentina only with the 1961 awarding of the International Publisher's Prize (shared with Samuel Beckett). His appearance in *Explorations* was likely through his translator, Anthony Kerrigan, who translated *Hojoki* in **E3**. Carpenter quotes "Mutations" as an epigraph in Schuster and Carpenter, *Materials for the Study of Social Symbolism*.

18 Clarke, *Victor Papanek*, 91.

19 Papanek's article is peppered with inserts in different fonts which appear to have been added by McLuhan (the editor of **E8**). The inserts tend to take a positive tone toward new technologies and artistic movements whereas Papanek's article is highly critical of technological modernism.

20 In *Nine Chains to the Moon* (1938), Buckminster Fuller described "man" as a "self-balancing, 28-jointed adapter base biped; an electro-chemical reduction-plant, integral with segregated stowages of special energy extracts in storage batteries, for subsequent actuation of thousands of hydraulic and pneumatic pumps, with motors attached ... guided with exquisite precision from a turret in which are located telescopic and microscopic self-registering and recording range finders." As quoted by Nevala-Lee in *Inventor of the Future* 164, from R. Buckminster Fuller, *Nine Chains to the Moon* (Philadelphia: Lippincott Press), 18–19.

21 Hayles, *How We Became Posthuman*, 50.

22 Wiener, *The Human Use of Human Beings*.

23 Pias, "The Age of Cybernetics," in *Cybernetics*, 18–19.

24 "The Loon's Necklace," Wikipedia, accessed 11 May 2022, wikipedia.org/wiki/The_Loon%27s_Necklace.

25 Charles Trick Currelly, first curator of the Royal Ontario Museum, writes about this statue in his memoir *I Brought the Ages Home*: "Our most important Classical acquisition was a little Cretan image in ivory. It shows a young girl beautifully carved in ivory, with gold used for the few draperies. She is holding up her hands, evidently prepared to catch the youth who had taken the charge of the bull on his hands. The youth, turning a somersault, would

have touched the back of the bull with his feet, then sprung to the girl holding out her hands to receive him" (230). The figurine was featured prominently in the museum until 2001, when it was deemed to be a fake. The denominator "Our Lady of [the] Sports" derives from Sir Arthur Evans. See C.L. Cooper, "Biography of the Bull-Leaper: A 'Minoan' Ivory Figurine and Collecting Antiquity," 87. Carpenter comments on Currelly's credulousness in an article on the Beardmore, Ontario "discovery" of Viking artifacts which Currelly bought for the museum and which were displayed as genuine, even though to believe this called for "a naïveté beyond the capacity of ordinary minds" (876). See "Further Evidence on the Beardmore Relics," 875–8. Currelly's discussion of "one of the silliest things that ever came up in the museum's history" (300) is on pages 300–5 of his memoir.

26   "Around 1830 Lamartine pointed to the newspaper as the end of book culture," writes McLuhan in E8, item 14, page 29.

27   As noted by Bringhurst in *The Surface of Meaning*, 63.

28   **E8 n.p.** Reprinted as *Verbi-Voco-Visual Explorations*, edited by McLuhan.

29   Compare Igor Kopytoff: "From a cultural perspective, the production of commodities is also a cultural and cognitive process: commodities must be not only produced materially as things, but also culturally marked as being a certain kind of thing." See "The Cultural Biography of Things: Commoditization as Process," in *The Social Life of Things*, edited by Appadurai, 64.

30   Lapatin, *Chryselephantine Statuary in the Ancient Mediterranean World*.

31   Genosko, "Where the Youth Aren't."

32   See Lauder, "A Clash of Spaces."

33   See *Museum as Process*, edited by Silverman.

34   Fabian, *Time and the Other*. Fabian acknowledges "McLuhan's brilliant insights" (179n12) in the formulation of his thesis. See also Cavell, *McLuhan in Space* (19, 83, 92). Fabian argues that the colonizer substitutes the other in space with the other in time. Carpenter, however, noting that space was culturally construed, argued that the other's space was different from that of the colonizer, or that of the anthropologist.

35   See Bell, "A Bundle of Relations," 241–59.

36   On McLuhan, Carpenter, and Giedion, see Darroch, "Giedion and *Explorations*," 62–87.

37   Jack Jones (1924–2011) was a reporter for the *Los Angeles Times* for many years. See the obituary by Valerie J. Nelson: "Jack Jones Dies at 86; Former Longtime Los Angeles Times Reporter," *Los Angeles Times*, 15 May 2011, https://www.latimes.com/local/obituaries/la-xpm-2011-may-15-la-me-jack-jones-20110515-story.html.

38   The quotation is from Blanchot's *Récit, Au moment voulu*, 166. The citing of Blanchot in 1957 was prescient, as his work was not well known outside of France.

39   Marinetti, "Fondazione e manifesto del Futurismo," 7–14.

40 Kehr, "When Unmanly Men Met Womanly Women."

41 McLuhan, Fiore, and Agel, *The Medium Is the Massage*, 132–6.

42 Carpenter, *Eskimo*.

43 Carpenter, "Eternal Life," *Explorations* 2 (April 1954): 54–60. In 1956, Carpenter published "The Timeless Present in the Mythology of the Aivilik Eskimos" (1–4), where he draws on both T.S. Eliot and James Joyce to contextualize the Aivilik concept of temporal flow, such that past and present are part of a single temporality. Aivilik cosmography excludes the concept of a single beginning point for creation: "The world never came into existence; it has always been, exactly as now ... They regard the past as merely an attribute of the present" (1).

44 Carpenter, "Review of Jean Malaurie," 1096.

45 The radomes (radar domes) built on the DEW line according to specifications associated with Buckminster Fuller's geodesic domes (which would receive an apotheosis at the Montreal World's Fair) were dubbed "igloos." See Nevala-Lee, *Inventor of the Future*, 276.

46 When the radomes were being installed on the DEW line, Buckminster Fuller noted that, whereas the unionized workers contracted to erect the domes took a month to do so, the Inuit did so in fourteen hours. As noted by Nevala-Lee, *Inventor of the Future*, 277.

47 Email to Richard Cavell, 24 July 2022.

48 As noted by Carpenter in "Eternal Life and Self-Definition Among the Aivilik Eskimos," 840.

49 Lee, "Review of *Eskimo* [by] Edmund Carpenter, Frederick Varley and Robert Flaherty," 165–7.

50 Hughes, "Under Four Flags," 3–62.

51 Carpenter writes in his comment (55–6) that he had "done extended fieldwork before, in the tropics" (55), referring to the Japanese POWs whom he supervised in a dig. See Prins and Bishop, "Edmund Carpenter," 112.

52 Carpenter, "Confessions of an Unconventional Anthropologist," 90–7.

53 Carpenter, "Twilight of the University," 1. I am grateful to the Thomas Fisher Rare Book Library at the University of Toronto for making this text available to me.

54 *American Journal of Psychiatry*, "About AJP | The American Journal of Psychiatry," accessed 2 May 2024, https://ajp.psychiatryonline.org/about.

55 Montagu, "Review of Edmund Carpenter, *Eskimo*," 382. Montagu describes the book as "anecdotal rather than systematic," acknowledging that it raises important questions about cognition.

56 From the biographical note to Carpenter, *Honoring Our Elders*, viii.

57 Carpenter, "Review of Marvin K. Opler," 957.

58 Carpenter, "Witch-Fear among the Aivilik Eskimos," 194–9. Carpenter states in "Sea" that he donated his collection of books on witchcraft to St Michael's College (as it then was), but neither the University of St Michael's College

at the University of Toronto nor the Thomas Fisher Rare Book library has a record of such a donation.

59 Prins and Bishop, "Edmund Carpenter," 115. Prins and Bishop have also made a film about Carpenter: *Oh, What a Blow That Phantom Gave Me!* See also http://mediatedcultures.net/phantom/.

60 Carpenter, "Eternal Life and Self-Definition among the Aivilik Eskimos," 840–3.

61 Carpenter, "Alcohol in the Iroquois Dream Quest," 148–51.

62 Carpenter, "Review of J.C. Carothers," 944.

63 McLuhan, letter of 8 November 1960, Carpenter Papers, Box 31.

64 On Carothers and McLuhan, see Philippe Theophanidis, "Marshall McLuhan, John Colin Carothers and Technological Traumas," *Aphelis*, 31 October 2013, aphelis.net/mcluhan-carothers-technological-traumas.

Chapter Three

1 According to Harald Prins, Carpenter arrived at the University of Toronto two years before he completed his doctorate on Iroquoian prehistoric archaeology, defended in 1950. See Prins's obituary for Carpenter in *Anthropology News* 52, no. 9 (2011): 24.

2 Howard, *Margaret Mead*, 267. The context of the quote has to do with a duel [*sic*] fought by Reo Fortune, then married to Mead, with McIlwraith, and Fortune's subsequent firing. As Carpenter remembered it, "It was rumored Fortune got fired for suggesting, in class, that the unique human feature of face-to-face sexual intercourse might have influenced human development. I once asked McIlwraith if this story was true: in a hushed voice, he confided, yes" (267).

3 In this same biographical contribution to *Eskimo*, Carpenter describes himself as having "trained as a mining engineer" who "turned anthropologist." This is not the last time that he would rewrite his biography.

4 Carpenter claimed that "when the University of Toronto found out I was getting a divorce, they asked for my resignation," as quoted by Paul Heyer in his obituary (514). Carpenter was then teaching in St Michael's College, a Roman Catholic college within the University of Toronto.

5 It has returned to life as recently as the second decade of the twenty-first century with Darroch and Marchessault's reissue.

6 Carpenter Papers, letter from Lévi-Strauss to Carpenter, dated 6 June 1961, Box 30.

7 Carpenter and McLuhan, eds., *Explorations in Communication*.

8 Herbert Landar, a linguistic anthropologist who taught at UCLA, reviewed *Explorations in Communications* for *American Anthropologist* (63, no. 4) in 1961 under the rubric "Linguistics," finding the contributions to be unequal in quality and appeal. He likens the contributors to "pilgrims" who are "as subtle and diverse as any set of Chaucerian personae" (874), producing "an

entertaining diversity of opinion, of wide appeal" that "caresses but does not satiate the great expectations spurred by the title of this generally pleasant, if sometimes not properly serious, assemblage" (875).

9 The reference to de Tocqueville (ix) points toward McLuhan, who referenced *Democracy in America* in a number of his publications.

10 Edmund Carpenter, ed., *Anerca*, with drawings by Enooesweetok. Carpenter wrote the introduction to a cognate volume, *I Breathe a New Song: Poems of the Eskimo*, edited by Richard Lewis and illustrated by Oonark (11–23), in which he largely rehearses the material in the *Anerca* volume.

11 Carpenter republished these drawings in an exquisite edition, *Drawings of Enooesweetok of the Sikossilingmint Tribe of Eskimo, Fox Land, Baffin Island* (NY: Rock Foundation, 2001). Each drawing is printed on a separate sheet; Carpenter's commentary is in a separate booklet, and the whole is boxed in an edition of 200 numbered copies that were selling for US$1,500 each in 2023.

12 See "Knud Rasmussen's Fifth Thule Expedition," Visit Greenland, accessed 17 March 2023, https://visitgreenland.com/knud-rasmussens-fifth-thule-expedition/. Rasmussen was surprised to be greeted in one igloo by Italian opera arias played on a gramophone purchased with skins and furs from the Hudson's Bay Company outpost.

13 Carpenter, "The Eskimo Language," 469–70.

14 Lévi-Strauss, *Wild Thought*, 2.

15 Zawadski and Poortenaar, "What Are the Earliest Inuit Prints?"

16 See Zawadski and Poortenaar, "Indelible Ink," 52–4. In the catalogue to *Upside Down*, Carpenter states that a more accurate rendering of Enooesweetok's name would be Noogooshoweetok, meaning "Eternal" (24). Indicative of the strained relationships between Carpenter and those who call themselves "Inuit" is the fact that his republication of the drawings is referenced in this article, but he is not acknowledged as editor.

17 In 1968, Carpenter edited *The Story of Comock the Eskimo as Told to Robert Flaherty*. Carpenter writes, "I heard Robert Flaherty tell Comock's story during the winter of 1949–50, over the BBC. It seemed to me then that this account – of human life reduced to a man, a woman, fire-making stones, and the will to perpetuate life – was ultimately an account of the rebirth of mankind" (8). Carpenter includes in this volume the illustrations of "Enooesweetok" that Flaherty had privately published in 1915.

18 Lantis, "Review of *Anerca*," 924.

19 Carpenter, "Ohnainewk, Eskimo Hunter," 417–26.

20 Ohnainewk died in 1954; Carpenter divorced his first wife in 1955.

21 Carpenter, "Obituary: Robert Cannon (1909–1964)," 453–4.

22 Letters from Lee to Carpenter in the Carpenter papers reveal a degree of tension between the two. She writes at one point, "I know I'm giving up my one chance to teach in an anthropology department that makes sense to me. But there it is. I can't work with you. You even took away from me the right to

know my responsibilities; so how could I carry them out? Anyway, I still love you." Handwritten letter dated "10/21," perhaps 1961, Box 30.

23 Naroll, *Data Quality Control*.

24 Gitelman, *Raw Data Is an Oxymoron*.

25 See Nichols, "Becoming Indigenous Again," 303–20. As Nichols notes, the classic critique of the native informant position was articulated by Gayatri Spivak in *A Critique of Postcolonial Reason: Toward a History of the Vanishing Present* (1999).

26 Sandstrom, "Anthropological Approaches to Information Systems and Behavior," 13.

27 Rappaport, *Pigs for the Ancestors*. The publication coincided with Carpenter's own research in New Guinea. See also Bateson, *Steps to an Ecology of Mind*, especially part two, "Form and Pattern in Anthropology," 70–164, and the essay "From Versailles to Cybernetics," 475–83.

28 Carpenter, "Review of Cornelius Osgood, *Ingalik Mental Culture*," 848.

29 Foucault, *Introduction to Kant's 'Anthropology'*: "It is in the death of man that the death of God is realized" (124).

30 Edmund Snow Carpenter Papers, Box 14, NAA.2017–27.

31 Box 3.

32 Ibid.

33 Ibid.

34 Ibid.

35 Ibid., letter dated Friday, 7 January 1963.

36 Box 31.

37 Ibid.

38 Ibid.

39 Box 14.

40 Prins and Bishop, VAR 119.

41 Carpenter notes that Cannon "loathed narration" ("Obituary," 454).

42 Available for viewing on YouTube: "Georgia Sea Island Singers," https://www.youtube.com/results?app=desktop&search_query=georgia+sea+island+singers. See also the website edmundsnowcarpenter.com for stills from other films.

43 Carpenter and Adelaide de Menil collected a large number of photographs of civil rights protests that became the subject of an exhibition at the Menil Collection titled "The Whole World Was Watching." See "The Whole World Was Watching: Civil Rights-Era Photographs from Edmund Carpenter and Adelaide de Menil," Menil Collection, accessed 1 May 2024, https://www.menil.org/exhibitions/19-the-whole-world-was-watching-civil-rights-era-photographs-from-edmund-carpenter-and-adelaide-de-menil.

44 Peter Stone writes that Mable Hillery (her name is sometimes spelled this way) "was less known than leader, Big John Davis or Bessie Jones, who also had her own performing career." (Bess Lomax Hawes and Bessie Jones write

about Hillery/Hillary in their book *Step It Down* [1972] without resolving the difference in spelling.) "Bess Hawes mentioned that Mable sometimes finished her performance in a 'shout' by inadvertently crossing her legs. 'Shouts,' progenitors of the spiritual (and not simply vocalizations) were performed by singing while stepping in a circular motion, in a religious ritual that trod the line between African dance rites and the European Protestant proscription of dance as a sinful act unfit for church. Participants in the shout frowned on pointing or crossing the feet as 'sinful' – in this way, the movement style retained the traditional flat-footed, close-to-the-ground step style characteristic of African sacred dance." Stone goes on to write, "Music, education, and religion were rarely unyoked in Georgia Sea Island practice. The Newport Folk Festival held a preview concert at New York City's Central Park in the summer of 1965, at the height of the Civil Rights era. Alan Lomax produced and emceed the concert, in order to bring New York audiences closer to the black South and what was happening there through this event. The concert included Mable and the Sea Islanders, among others, who talked about their material." In addition to political activism, Hillary was engaged in educational reform in New York. See Association for Cultural Equity, "Mable Hillery | Association for Cultural Equity," accessed 2 May 2024, http://culturalequity.org/alan-lomax/friends/hillery.

45 Goodwin, Croner, Mankofsky, and Hudson were all filmmakers; Varney was a sound mixer who went on to win Academy Awards for the sound effects on *The Empire Strikes Back* (1980) and *Raiders of the Lost Ark* (1981). Lomax worked with Zora Neale Hurston. See the entries in Wikipedia.

46 Hawes appears in the film made by Prins and Bishop, as do clips from *Georgia Sea Island Singers*.

47 Hawes, *Sing It Pretty*, 72.

48 Published as *Tradition and Creativity in Tribal Art*, edited by Daniel P. Biebuyck.

49 In his bio for this volume, Carpenter refers to his forthcoming book *We Wed Ourselves to the Mystery* (x).

50 See for instance his "Review of *Eskimo-Plastic aus Kanada* by Henry Schaefer-Simmern," 346–8: "Professor Schaefer-Simmern states that modern stone carvings made commercially by Hudson Bay groups are a direct product of Eskimo magico-religious life and constitute an indigenous art, newly discovered but ancient in origin. All I can say of such a thesis is that it is wrong" (346).

51 Carpenter is quoting from Lévi-Strauss's "The Scope of Anthropology," *Current Anthropology* 7, no. 2 (1966): 112–23.

52 Mead, "Visual Anthropology in a Discipline of Words," 3.

53 Anna Grimshaw and Amanda Ravetz note that "Observational cinema ... once hailed as a revolution in ethnographic filmmaking ... quickly fell out of favour. It came to be seen as a form of scientism in which a detached camera served to objectify and dehumanize the human subjects of its gaze" (538).

They seek to reinvigorate the practice with the argument that observational cinema "can be appraised as constitutive of a reflexive praxis – that is, a way of *doing* anthropology that has the potential to fuse creatively the object and medium of inquiry" (552). See "Rethinking Observational Cinema," 538–56.

54   Carpenter, "If Wittgenstein had been an Eskimo," "Explorations," 50–63.

55   Carpenter makes a distinction between "Northwest Coast Indian masks [that] often depict succession or metamorphosis of forms: Wolf suddenly opens, revealing Bear" and "Eskimo masks [that] depict all elements simultaneously" (63).

56   Kepes, ed., *Sign Image Symbol*.

57   Blakinger quotes the term from Sharon Ghamari-Tabrizi, *The Worlds of Herman Kahn: The Intuitive Science of Thermonuclear War* (Cambridge, MA: Harvard University Press, 2005).

58   McLuhan with Nevitt, "The Argument: Causality in the Electric World," 13.

59   Blakinger, *Gyorgy Kepes*, 181, 198.

60   The chapter is largely equivalent to Carpenter's publication *Man and Art in the Arctic* (Browning Montana: Museum of the Plains Indian, 1964), published in conjunction with an exhibition of soapstone carvings and sealskin prints included in a travelling exhibition curated by the Smithsonian Institute in conjunction with the Montana State Centennial, the Arctic material included "to provide an interesting contrast to the modern crafts of the Plains Indians" ("Preface," n.p.). As Claude E. Schaeffer notes in his preface, Carpenter's essay is based on one published in *Current Anthropology* (2, no. 4, 1961). "My acquaintance with the author goes back some twenty years to a joint endeavor involving the excavation of an Adena-like burial mound in northwestern Pennsylvania. During that summer the only phenomenon that presaged a northern area of field work for Doctor Carpenter was, as I recall, an unusually brilliant appearance of the Aurora Borealis. Since then he has made seven trips to the Arctic – three of them to the Aivilik and Iglulik north of Hudson Bay and the others to Greenland, Alaska, Siberia and Outer Mongolia."

Chapter Four

1   Carpenter assessed the manuscript of *War and Peace in the Global Village* for McGraw-Hill (the publisher of *Understanding Media*). His assessment was negative, writing that "publication of this ms., in its present form, might just do nobody any good" (page 1 of 3). Carpenter cited the manuscript's "careless scholarship and sloppy editing"; "the work was produced by McLuhan in a period of seven or eight days, by dictating to a secretary & marking relevant passages to be copied. The ideas were largely ones that had come to him, in reading & conversations with colleagues, while hospitalized before Christmas" (1). The book was published by Bantam. Box 30, dated "1968" in Carpenter's hand.

2   McLuhan, *Verbi-Voco-Visual Explorations* (New York: Something Else Press, 1967). This was the only issue of *Explorations* to be republished. It included

twenty-five items by McLuhan, as well as pieces by V.J. Papanek, J.B. Bessinger, Karl Polanyi, Carol C. Hollis, David Hogg, and Jack Jones. Carpenter is acknowledged as co-editor of the journal but is otherwise absent from the book.

3 McLuhan to Carpenter, letter dated 3 February 1967, Box 31.

4 Fordham was ultimately deemed to be ineligible to host the Schweitzer Chair because Fordham was not a secular university. The university funded the chair, but without the moniker.

5 I am drawing here on Marchand, *Marshall McLuhan*, 194.

6 As Greif notes in *The Age of the Crisis of Man*, 70.

7 Compare the opening of McLuhan and Leonard, "The Future of Sex": "Michael Murphy of California's Esalen recently said 'a young person came up to talk with me, and I couldn't tell if this person was a man or a woman'" (129).

8 Despite this assertion, the notion that McLuhan attached his name to something written by Carpenter persists to the present day, as in the biographical statement accompanying information on the Carpenter archives held by the Smithsonian Institution. In fact, it was Carpenter who attached McLuhan's name to something Carpenter had written in the Los Angeles Free Press.

9 Box 31.

10 Stearn, "Conversations with McLuhan," 50–8. Carpenter's letter to McLuhan is not quoted in this version of the interview. Carpenter confuses this interview with the one given to Eric Norden in *Playboy* ("Sea," 254).

11 Stearn, ed., *McLuhan*.

12 Box 31.

13 Hymes, "Review of *The Gutenberg Galaxy*," 478–9.

14 Mywebcowtube, "Marshall McLuhan 1968 – Lecture by Ted Carpenter – Language as Ritual – Fordham University Tapes #5," 45:00, 13 October 2016, https://www.youtube.com/watch?v=KkKaZwrECyk.

15 Carpenter, "We Wed Ourselves to the Mystery: A Study of Tribal Art," in *Explorations* 1, no. 4 (Summer 1968): 66–74. The issue number appears anomalous because *Explorations* issues published from Summer 1964 to Christmas 1967 were not numbered.

16 Leach, *Lévi-Strauss*, 18, 44.

17 Hawes, *Sing it Pretty*, 72.

18 Kosinski, ed., *Readings on Creativity and Imagination in Literature and Language*. Tellingly, the volume was published to accompany a television series titled *English for Elementary Teachers*. One of the essays is titled "What Shall We Do about Poetry in the Schools?"

19 O'Neill, ed., *Selected Educational Heresies*. The contributors constitute an intellectual who's who, including David Riesman (**E1**), William H. Whyte, Jr, B.F. Skinner, George Orwell, Aldous Huxley, Harold Rosenberg, Erich Fromm, Paul Tillich, Paul Goodman, Norbert Wiener, Susan Sontag, and Margaret Mead.

20 Carpenter, Cornford, Simon, Watts, eds., *Proposals for Art Education*.

21 A large, stand alone, Dan Flavin installation is part of the Menil Collection campus in Houston, at 39 Richmond Hall. See Middleton, *Double Vision*, 649 (hereafter *DV*).

22 McLuhan wrote to Carpenter describing the thesis of *From Cliché to Archetype* on 17 September 1964 and in greater detail on 9 April 1969. Carpenter Papers, Box 31, and McLuhan and Watson, *From Cliché to Archetype*.

23 Carpenter is referring to "Our Enchanted Lives" and "The Party Line" in E4.

24 Intermedia was a major artistic movement of the 1960s that was associated with Dick Higgins, who republished *Explorations* 8 (*Verbi-Voco-Visual*) in 1967. See "Intermedia," Wikipedia, accessed 4 July 2023, https://en.wikipedia.org/wiki/Intermedia.

25 These comments appear in Mead's *Culture and Commitment*.

26 Carpenter, *They Became What They Beheld* (New York: Outerbridge & Dienstfrey, 1970).

27 Davis, *City of Quartz*, 67. Doug Wheeler, who would later collaborate on the *Upside Down* exhibitions, visited the Kienholz exhibition in Los Angeles in 1962, at the Ferus Gallery, founded by Kienholz and Walter Hopps, who would go on to become the first director of the Menil. See Celant, *Wheeler*, 31.

28 McLuhan in the same year published an article, "*Screw* goes to Market," in *Screw: A Sex Review*. Clearly, something was in the air.

29 Carpenter, "Not since Babel," 81–8. Carpenter lists his affiliation as "Communications Arts Department, Fordham University."

30 In a letter to Jack Parr dated 13 October 1969, McLuhan writes, "Carpenter is in Borneo but may be back soon, for all I know. Shall be writing him at once and will mention your interest in a film." This suggests that Carpenter and McLuhan were not regularly in touch at this time. See Toye et al., eds., *Letters of Marshall McLuhan*, 390.

31 Carpenter and Heyman, "They Became What They Beheld," 262–4. The Carpenter/Heyman excerpt appears with pieces by Edward Gordon Craig, Antonin Artaud, Peter Hall, and Jean-Claude van Itallie, among others. The year before, Carpenter and McLuhan had published "Acoustic Space" in the *Canadian Theatre Review* 6 (1975): 46–9.

32 Heyman had accompanied Mead to Bali in 1957 and collaborated with her on *Family* (London: MacMillan, 1965) and on *World Enough: Rethinking the Future* (New York: Little, Brown, 1975). See Genzlinger, "Ken Heyman, Collaborative Photographer."

33 The image is by Joseph Sacco, *Oeil de jeune femme* (1844) and appears on the cover of *La Rime et la raison: Les collections Ménil* (Houston-New York).

34 Raviv Ganchrow, email to Richard Cavell, 24 July 2022.

35 Blake, *Poetry and Prose of William Blake*, *Jerusalem* II, 36, page 477: "All that beheld him [Reuben] fled howling and gnawed their tongues / For pain: they became what they beheld"; "The Seven Nations fled before him: they became what they beheld"; "Hand, Hyle & Coban fled: they became what they beheld."

Chapter Five

1 Carpenter, "Oh, What a Blow That Phantom Gave Me (Don Quixote)," in "Explorations," 90–5.

2 Prins and Bishop, VAR 111.

3 Sir Albert Maori Kiki (1931–1993) was a founder of the Pangu Party, which sought home rule for Papua New Guinea. See "Albert Maori Kiki," Wikipedia, accessed 18 December 2023, https://en.wikipedia.org/wiki/Albert_Maori _Kiki.

4 The work is considered a landmark in its articulation of "what it was like to wake up to the modern realities of New Guinea" (180). See Stella, *Imagining the Other*, quoting Ulli Beier, ed., *Black Writing from New Guinea* (St Lucia: University of Queensland Press, 1973). Moore writes in *New Guinea*, "Development of modern states with sophisticated technologies has led to some quite bizarre cultural mixes. Villagers who remember the first time they saw a European can now make phone-calls to relatives living in other towns or overseas. Motuan women with full facial and upper body tattoos can be seen riding the escalators in Port Moresby shopping centers. Old men wearing *as-tanget* (a leaf-garment) and second-hand coats can be seen at domestic air terminals in the Highlands, sitting next to urban-based public servants on their way to finance meetings, swapping *buai* (betel nut) and chatting in *tok pisin*" (190).

5 Quoted in Prins and Bishop, "Trickster," 229.

6 In fact, Europeans had made contact with Papua New Guinea earlier than this. See Moore, *New Guinea*, especially 42, 103, and 137.

7 Raviv Ganchrow, email to Richard Cavell, 15 September 2022. See also Ganchrow's chapter "Baku's Sirens: Circuits of Industrious Attention" in *The Derailment of the Usual*, 100–12.

8 See Gershon, "Mirrors and Numbers among Others," 85–108, who locates this form of contact much earlier in the use of technologies of identification (such as a mirror) by colonisers. See also Bell, Brown, and Gordon, *Recreating First Contact*.

9 MacDougall, *The Corporeal Image*, 148.

10 As noted by Bishop, "Notes from the Wilderness," 651.

11 Prins, "Visual Media and the Primitivist Perplex," 58–74.

12 From the inside flap of the back jacket. I have been unable to confirm this information.

13 Carpenter, "Media and Moral Progress," in "Explorations," 102.

14 Some of Adelaide de Menil's Papuan photographs are reproduced in *Photographs 1969–73* (Tambaran Gallery, New York), published by the Rock Foundation in 2022 as a centenary tribute to Edmund Carpenter.

15 Gardner, ed., *Human Documents*, 120.

16 Reid and de Menil, *Out of the Silence*. Carpenter corresponded with Reid in the late 1970s and early 1980s with a proposal for a new edition of *Out*

of the Silence, stating "I ... will ask him to make all decisions at every stage of revision & design." Letter to Marjorie Halpin, 28 February 1980, in the Halpin fonds of the Museum of Anthropology Archives, University of British Columbia, file PR 26–22.

17 Weinberger, "Photography and Anthropology (A Contact Sheet)," 16–21. Mead made a similar point in an encyclopedia entry on "Anthropology and the Camera": "Anthropology, which has historically dealt with the behaviour of primitive and exotic peoples in remote parts of the world, has always been highly dependent upon photography." The entry is excerpted in *Public Photographic Spaces*, 451.

18 Skolnick's greatest claim to fame was the design of the Woodstock poster.

19 Bringhurst, ed., *Solitary Raven*, 33n1.

20 Bringhurst provides a detailed account of Reid's production of the manuscript, including the colour of ink he used in successive drafts and a photograph of a manuscript draft in *Solitary Raven*, 17–19. For Carpenter's claim of authorship, see Prins and Bishop, "Trickster," 207–46, especially 223. See also Gerald McMaster, *Iljuwas Bill Reid*, 17.

21 From an email to the author, quoted with permission, dated 19 November 2019.

22 Prins and Bishop, VAR 111.

23 Carpenter, "Notes of an Unconventional Anthropologist," 90–7. The article is said to be "from the forthcoming book, *Oh, What a Blow That Phantom Gave Me: An Anthropologist in the Electronic World*," to be published by Bantam in 1972. The book was in fact published by Holt, Rinehart, and Winston in 1973 (without the subtitle), where this excerpt is acknowledged. *Audience* was published from 1955 to 1973; one of its earlier editors was Ralph Maud, who appears in **E6**. The magazine published a dazzling roster of writers, including several Nobel laureates. Elaborately produced, it ceased publication in 1973 with a seven figure debt. See "*Audience* (magazine)," Wikipedia, accessed 5 January 2024, https://en.wikipedia.org/wiki/Audience_(magazine).

24 Lauren Van Vuuren makes a similar observation about Laurens van der Post's *Lost World of Kalahari* TV series, cautioning that the medium can powerfully alter the message. See "The Many Myths of Laurens van der Post," 47–60.

25 See Patterson, "Prince Modupe," 29–44.

26 For a more positive assessment of post-Houston art, see Swinton, "Who Makes Inuit Art?," 295–302. For a theoretical accounting, see Graburn, "From Aesthetics to Prosthetics and Back," 47–62. The political maneuverings around Inuit sculpture are discussed by Lennox, "Inuit Art and the Quest for Canada's Arctic Sovereignty."

27 Taylor, *Six Journeys*, 75. The pattern discerned by Taylor is that Canadians must go into exile before they are able to discover themselves as Canadians.

28 The quotation, unidentified by Taylor, is from the *Audience* article (96), reprinted in *Oh, What a Blow That Phantom Gave Me!* (New York: Holt, Rinehart, and Winston, 1973), 103–5, with different inflections.

29 Steichen, *The Family of Man*. The exhibition toured internationally for eight years and was seen by millions of viewers. While the exhibition concluded with its one colour photograph – the explosion of a hydrogen bomb – this image was not published in the book. See "*The Family of Man*," Wikipedia, accessed 16 January 2024, https://en.wikipedia.org/wiki/The_Family_of_Man.

30 Sandeen, "The Show You See With Your Heart," 472. Sandeen observes that "a significant part of the Agency's job was to deploy quick bits of information about the United States that would counter Soviet assertions and counteract more general impressions about current events in the United States ... *The Family of Man* furthered careers and helped the agency define its role in the Cold War world, ironic results from an exhibition that fought against Cold War ideologies" (480).

31 Max Horkheimer took a more nuanced view, arguing that the exhibition explored "the identity of human beings in their non-identity," cited by Zamir and Hurm in their introduction to *'The Family of Man' Revisited*, 4.

32 Hilton Kramer, "Exhibiting 'The Family of Man': 'The World's Most Talked About Photographs," first published in *Commentary* 20, no. 5 (1955) and reprinted in Ribalta, *Public Photographic Spaces*, 442.

33 This assessment, however, belies the mode in which the exhibition confronted its viewers, which was not as a book but as an installation. Kerstin Schmidt, in "A Humanism of Relation," in Zamir and Hurm, *'The Family of Man' Revisited* (159–75), argues that "the installation design of the 1955 show in MoMA ... [engaged] the viewer in active, dynamic and relational modes of perception, experience and thought that thwart challenges of monolithic sentimentality" (161). As Schmidt explains, "The exhibition tells the story of 'the family of man,' of humankind, in terms of a linear tale, a 'folktale,' but the tale is a three-dimensional walk-through with a strong emphasis on the integration of the spectator. The spectator is compelled by the story's formal design to actively integrate and participate in that story. *The Family of Man* is a picture sequence modified as an environment" (163). This description resonates with Carpenter's comments on the importance of multiple points of view in understanding Inuit art, and *The Family of Man*'s use of walls made of transparent lucite are cognate with the museal techniques in Carpenter's *Upside Down* exhibitions. In both cases the goal was to produce what Schmidt calls "a multi-directional dialogical structure" (172).

34 Bishop, "Notes from the Wilderness," 650.

35 As noted by Shaul in "With 'the delicacy of a bear,'" 18–40.

36 On *tò metaxú*, see Winthrop-Young, *Kittler and the Media*, 114.

37 Lévi-Strauss, *Tristes Tropiques*, with an introduction and notes by Patrick Wilcken, 325–6.

38 Carpenter reproduces verbatim this section of *Phantom* in "Love Thy Label as Thyself," in *Irving Penn: A Career in Photography*, 54–62.

39 *Phantom* was translated into German as *Sinnes Täuschung: Wie Medien unsere Wahrnehmung verändern* (München: Trickster, 1994) and reviewed in MEDIENwissenschaft 12, no. 2 (1995): 167–8, by Wolfram Buddecke, who concludes that "Konservative Medienkritik ist auch hierzulande nicht mehr sehr populär" (168).

40 Shane Greene's use of this term in a 2017 essay that does not acknowledge Carpenter indicates at once Carpenter's foresight and the extent to which his anthropological practices have been marginalized in the discipline. See Greene's "On Misanthropology: (punk, art, species-hate)," in Bakke and Peterson, *Between Matter and Method*, 35–50.

41 See Price, *Cold War Anthropology*.

42 Geertz, *The Interpretation of Cultures*, 164. Writing about *The Interpretation of Cultures* on its fiftieth anniversary, T.M. Luhrmann states that "anthropology has been in the grip of an intensely self-critical crisis" ever since Geertz's book was published. As an anthropologist, she has learned to repudiate a number of Geertz's strictures, including the one about comparison. "And I am more comfortable about writing imperfect books and papers, because I know that other people will carry on the project and make the answers better." See "Unravelling a Web: *The Interpretation of Cultures* by Clifford Geertz, fifty years on," TLS (8 September 2023): 21.

43 Geertz had accused Carpenter of unethical practices in his filming in Papua New Guinea. See Prins and Bishop, VAR 130.

44 See Carpenter, "Deeply Carved Art of the Northwest Coast," 164.

45 The focus on media in anthropology has become a major area of research. *The Routledge Companion to Media Anthropology*, published in 2022, contains 644 pages, with chapters on "Media Anthropology and the Digital Challenge," "Indigenous Media," "Media Migration," "Media Practices and Their Social Effects," "PhotoMedia as Anthropology," and "Cloudwork," among a myriad of others. See Costa, Lange, Haynes, and Sinanan, *The Routledge Companion to Media Anthropology*.

46 Carpenter, "The Tribal Terror of Self-Awareness," 451–61.

47 Blackburn, *The White Men*; Carpenter's foreword, 6–9.

48 Carpenter, "Review of Jack Goody, ed.," 430–2.

49 Norden, "Playboy Interview," 158.

50 Ohlgren and Berk, eds., *The New Languages: A Rhetorical Approach to the Mass Media and Popular Culture*, 4–12. The chapter is followed by one on McLuhan written by Richard Kostelanetz.

51 *The Limits to Growth: A Report for the Club of Rome's Project on the Predicament of Mankind* (NY: Universe Books, 1972).

52 Willem L. Oltmans, ed., *On Growth* (NY: Capricorn, 1974).

53 Carpenter, "Reality and Television," 42, 44.

54 Carpenter, *Eskimo Realities*.

55 See Loft and Swanson, *Coded Territories*.

56 These three maps show coastlines in Greenland. See Margus, "Inuit Cartography Aka Carving Portable Maps," *EastPole Paddles* (blog), 7 March 2023, https://eastpolepaddles.com/inuit-cartography/. Some scholars believe these maps were storytelling devices rather than maps. See Harmsen, "Greenland's Hand-Sized Wooden Maps."

57 See the special issue of *The Australian Journal of Anthropology* 20 (2009) on "materialisation," particularly the article by Joshua A. Bell and Haidy Geismar, "Materialising Oceania: New Ethnographies of Things in Melanesia and Polynesia" (3–27).

58 Cox, "Review of Edmund Carpenter," 417–19.

59 In "Sea" (236), Carpenter refers to this as a "revised" edition, which, with the first edition, achieved circa 15,000 copies.

60 Ingold, *The Perception of the Environment*. David Howes critiques Ingold's position, and its dismissal of scholars such as Carpenter, in "Sensing Cultures," 173–88. Particularly pertinent is Howes's observation that "the idea of mediation is ... foreign to Ingold."

61 To Lisa Gitelman's questions – "Is the history of media first and foremost the history of technological methods and devices? Or is the history of media better understood as the story of modern ideas of communication? Or is it about modes and habits of perception?" – McLuhan, Ong, and Carpenter would answer yes: sensory cognition and media technologies are interrelated. See *Always Already New*, 1.

62 Olga Belova notes that, "[t]o provide alternatives to vision-centred perspectives, research was undertaken to explore other senses such as hearing," as with Carpenter and McLuhan's essay on acoustic space. Their essay on acoustic space was about the interrelated sensorium, however, not exclusively about hearing. See Belova, "The Event of Seeing," 116–33; 116.

63 Howes likewise cites this passage in *Sensual Relations*, 15.

64 Stoller, *Sensuous Scholarship*, xv.

65 Classen, *Worlds of Sense*, 3.

66 "Symposium on the Sacred in Art," in John Noel Chandler, ed., *artscanada* (April–May 1971), 17.

67 Youngblood was associate editor of the *Los Angeles Free Press*.

68 Carpenter, "Some Notes on the Separate Realities of Eskimo and Indian Art," 281–9.

Chapter Six

1 See Bringhurst, *Solitary Raven*, 33n1.

2 Holm and Reid, *Indian Art of the Northwest Coast*. The book also appeared that same year under the title *Form and Freedom: A Dialogue on Northwest Coast Art*, with the same publisher. Like *Out of the Silence*, this book was designed by Arnold Skolnick. Carpenter's introduction is on pages 9–27. See also McMaster, *Iljuwas Bill Reid*, 18, 86.

3 Helfenstein and Schipsi, *Art and Activism*, 292. Like Carpenter, Pellizzi was then related to the de Menils through marriage. Concurrently at the museum, there was an exhibition of photographs by Adelaide de Menil associated with Bill Reid's *Out of the Silence.*

4 "Personal communication, Claude Lévi-Strauss, November 17, 1974" (257n2). Lévi-Strauss had directed the doctoral dissertation of the anthropologist Francesco Pellizzi, who married Philippa de Menil (daughter of John and Dominique) in 1969. "All of Dominique and John's children ... made their way to Houston for the wedding ... Adelaide, who had become a professional photographer, was also in from New York, although her partner, the esteemed archaeologist [*sic*] Edmund Carpenter, was unable to make the trip because of academic obligations" (Middleton, *DV* 466).

5 Quoted from the catalogue essay by Rushing, "The Impact of Nietzsche," 187.

6 Carpenter, in "Sea" (245), attributes this quality to McLuhan.

7 Middleton, *DV* 416.

8 *DV* 457.

9 John de Menil had died in 1973.

10 Conrad Schlumberger, quoted by Middleton, *DV* 84.

11 *DV* 670–1. Carpenter's and Adelaide de Menil's interest in historical connections between France and the United States also emerges in their support of William Howard Adams's *The Paris Years of Thomas Jefferson* (New Haven: Yale University Press, 1997), which includes photographs by Adelaide de Menil, and *Gouverneur Morris* (New Haven: Yale University Press, 2003), whose publication was supported by Carpenter and de Menil.

12 See Nelson, Sherman, and Hoobler, *Hollywood Arensberg.*

13 As noted on the information cards posted in several galleries of the Menil Collection.

14 Helfenstein and Schipsi, *Art and Activism*. The double-spread photo is on pages 16 and 17. Beginning in 1972, the Carpenters began donating an ongoing collection of "over 2,000 artifacts from American and European popular culture of the nineteenth and twentieth centuries, most depicting black people in demeaning, stereotypical roles. From 1973 to 1999, the Carpenters continue to add significantly to this collection" (290).

15 Originally founded to preserve materials in the Rochester museum, as noted by Sean Mooney in a lecture now posted on the Menil YouTube channel. "Edmund Carpenter and 'Witnesses to a Surrealist Vision': A Look Behind the Curtain," YouTube, 1:08:26, posted by the Menil Collection on 15 December 2022, www.youtube.com/watch?v=m-kXKgRRpN4.

16 See http://www.bigdatabase.com/Big-DB/USFoundation-profiles/ROCK%20 FOUNDATION-060944728 (link now defunct). The president and director of the foundation is stated to be Adelaide de Menil.

17 Carpenter worried that this might look like vanity publishing while admitting it was in a letter to Rodney Needham dated 29 January 1996, Box 31.

18 Carpenter, "Art de la mer de Béring et des Eskimo," 200, my translation. Cited by Hurst, *Arctic Ivory*, 78.

19 Hume, "Heritage Grab: Time Runs Out," *Daily Colonist*, 4 September 1977, 1.

20 Hume, "U.S. Foundation Siphons Finest Native Art," *Daily Colonist*, 7 September 1977, 1.

21 Hume, "Heritage for All, Profits for Some," *Daily Colonist*, 8 September 1977, 2.

22 Carpenter, letter to William N. Taylor, Jr (22 May 1977), Box 31.

23 Letter to Taylor, Box 31.

24 Letter to Taylor, 1 December 1977, Box 31.

25 Carpenter was a classmate of Stephen Gilman, the future Hispanist, and they exchanged several letters about their shared interest in collecting. Carpenter Papers, Box 31.

26 Clifford, *The Predicament of Culture*.

27 Quoted by Prins and Bishop, VAR 132, from an interview with Carpenter conducted by Prins on 12/07.

28 Staal, *Agni*, with the collaboration of C.V. Somayajipad and M. Itti Ravi Nambudiri and with photographs by Adelaide de Menil. Volume 2 with the assistance of Pamela MacFarland.

29 Staal writes that "Disputes arose ... chief among them the Rock Foundation's claim that Asian Humanities Press had misused the grant funds by spending them for ordinary working capital purposes" (xxxii). Legal action was taken, the dispute resolved, and the study was published.

30 Quoted by Brian L. Frye in *Senses of Cinema* 24 (2003) from Gardner and Östör, *Making Forest of Bliss*, 78.

31 Prins and Bishop, VAR 119, 132. Although the authors quote Carpenter to the effect that McLuhan "was not a filmmaker" (117), McLuhan produced *Picnic in Space* while at Fordham, and subsequently a film with Jane Jacobs (1970) that contributed to the halting of an expressway that was planned to run through the middle of Toronto. See Cavell, *McLuhan in Space*, 237–8n85.

32 Moore, "The Limitations of Imagist Documentary," 1–3.

33 Quoted from the back cover of Gardner and Östör's book. The cover also includes lavish praise for the film by Seamus Heaney and Peter Matthiessen.

34 Parry, "Comment on Robert Gardner's *Forest of Bliss*," 4.

35 Östör, "Is that What Forest of Bliss Is All About?," 6.

36 See "Jay Ruby," Wikipedia, accessed 4 March 2023, https://en.wikipedia.org/wiki/Jay_Ruby.

37 Ruby, "The Emperor and His Clothes," 9.

38 As noted by Staal, "Anthropologists against Death," 14.

39 Carpenter, "Assassins and Cannibals or I Got Me a Small Mind and I Means to Use It," 12–13.

40 Carpenter refers to *Robert Flaherty: Photographer / Filmmaker: The Inuit 1910–1922*, ed. Jo-Anne Bernie Danzker (Vancouver: Vancouver Art Gallery,

1980). Carpenter is credited for having provided research information used in the catalogue (7).

41 Jay Ruby, "'The Aggie Will Come First': The Demystification of Robert Flaherty," in Danzker, ed., 71. "Aggie" is the term the Inuit used to refer to Flaherty's camera.

42 This mischaracterizes Ruby's essay, which seeks to separate the Flaherty myth from Flaherty's genuine accomplishments.

43 See, for example, Ronay, "Taxidermy and Romantic Ethnography," 99–126. On the changing fortunes of the film's reception see Grimshaw, "Who Has the Last Laugh?," 421–35.

44 For Jean Rouch, Flaherty invented "participant observation" and "feedback" by showing his film to the Inuit he had filmed. See Rouch, "The Camera and Man," 32.

45 "Alas, for Flaherty" is not included in the catalogue.

46 Carpenter, text of talk on occasion of Jo-Anne Birnie Danzker's exhibition on Flaherty in New York, included with a letter to Marjorie Halpin, in Halpin fonds of the Museum of Anthropology Archives, University of British Columbia, file PR 26-22.

47 Schuster, *Materials for the Study of Social Symbolism.*

48 For Jeoly, see Barnes, "Curiosity, Wonder, and William Dampier's Painted Prince."

49 Carpenter compares McLuhan to Coomaraswamy in "Sea" (247).

50 A Sri Lankan, Coomaraswamy emigrated at the age of two, after the death of his father, with his English mother to England, where he was educated. He subsequently was befriended by Eric Gill and Jacob Epstein. He later emigrated to the United States, where he ended his career. See "Ananda Coomaraswamy," Wikipedia, accessed 2 November 2023, https://en.wikipedia.org/wiki/Ananda_Coomaraswamy, and MacCarthy, *Eric Gill*, who notes that Coomaraswamy had a "profound concern with the erotic" (98).

51 Quinn, *The Only Tradition*, 176.

52 Carpenter also relates his meeting with Schuster in "Decoding the Tribe," *Natural History* 115, no. 4 (2006): 42–7.

53 The essay has been set in print but contains no bibliographical information and is unpaginated. It is housed in Special Collections at the Kelly Library, University of St Michael's College at the University of Toronto. I am grateful to the Kelly Library for making this essay available to me.

54 When the Serpent Mound was threatened by development, Carpenter fought to save it, convinced that a bribe had been paid to a government official to facilitate the bulldozing of the mound. Finding no community support for his efforts, Carpenter eventually contacted the provincial minister of education, asserting his belief that the government was involved in a cover-up, and warning the minister: "Destroy that mound and I'll wipe your fucking ass

across every headline in this province" ("Sea," 252). The mound was saved and is now designated a National Historic Site of Canada.

55 A letter in the Carpenter papers on MIT Press letterhead dated 5 February 1981 states that "four reviews" are enclosed; "they are extremely positive." The letter finds Carpenter's introduction to the volume to be "excellent," and asks for "some theoretical material," concluding that the board will be meeting about the book soon and that the editor "expect[s] no problems." Box 31.

56 Letter to George MacDonald, March ? [*sic*] 1978, Box 30.

57 Carpenter states in "Sea" (238) that Lévi-Strauss was a subscriber to *Explorations*.

58 Carpenter draws on the work of John Cargill, *Notes on the Old Cross at Canna* (1916) and *The Celtic Cross and Greek Proportion* (1930), as well as John Travis, *Miscellanea Musica Celtica* (1968).

59 Siegeltuch, "Random Thoughts on *Angels Fear*," 1–2. The issue was devoted to reviews of Gregory Bateson and Mary Catherine Bateson's *Angels Fear: Towards an Epistemology of the Sacred* (NY: Macmillan, 1987). The first sentence of the quotation made by Carpenter is not in the original.

60 Prins, "Review of *Patterns That Connect*," 841.

61 Letter to Rodney Needham, 29 January 1996, Box 31.

62 Carpenter, "The Megiddo Gaming Boards," 27–50.

63 Carpenter, "Decoding the Tribe," 43.

64 Carpenter, "Review of Laurel Kendall et al.," 771–2. The review is made under the rubric "Visual Anthropology Reviews," curated by Prins.

65 Carpenter writes in "Sea" that in 1949 he had argued in a debate with Northrop Frye "that Frazer & Frobenius, Jung and Campbell, were blinded by racism" (260). He subsequently debated with Frye on the subject of universal symbolism. See *The Diaries of Northrop Frye 1942–1955*, 517–19.

66 Starn, "Introduction," 1.

Chapter Seven

1 De Menil, "Foreword," 7.

2 The curator was Bertrand Davezac. The ascription is noted by museum director Walter Hopps in his introduction to the catalogue (13).

3 Winckelmann, "On the Imitation of the Painting and Sculpture of the Greeks," 61–85.

4 See Eisenstein, "Laocoon," and von Trotha, *Pollak's Arm*.

5 Gell, "Vogel's Net," 37.

6 Haddon, *The Decorative Art of British New Guinea*.

7 Douglas, "The Genuine Article," 20.

8 One chapter in *Chief and Greed* is devoted to repatriation (101–12); it stresses the importance of "recruit[ing] the media" (108) in repatriation claims. Bruchac, in *Savage Kin: Indigenous Informants and American Anthropologists*,

notes that when Carpenter created the Rock Foundation "his explicit goal was to ensure that 'the collection isn't subject to the Repatriation Bill'" (181; the inner quotation is from a letter Carpenter sent to William Fenton in 1991).

9 Saltzstein cites Carpenter's *Eskimo* to this effect in "Misperceiving African and Eskimo Art," 99–107. The article is a response to the "Primitivism" exhibition.

10 Stocking, "Essays on Museums and Material Culture," 6.

11 Goodman, quoting Adelaide de Menil, in "A Central Park Duplex with a Calder in the Trees." For another description of the apartment see Colacello, "The Remains of the Dia."

12 See Nicole Cotroneo, "Historic East Hampton Buildings Gain New Life," *The New York Times*, 18 February 2007; Zak Powers, *Further Lane*, with an afterword by Robert A.M. Stern (who repurposed the buildings for public use) (NY: Quantuck Lane P, 2011); the DVD *Further Lane* by John Melville Bishop, released in 2011 by Media-Generation (ASIN B0059NE7SY); and Grace Glueck, "The De Menil Family: The Medici of Modern Art," *The New York Times*, 18 May 1986, section 6, page 28. The *New Yorker* has described Further Lane as "the best street in Amangasett, the best town in the Hamptons" in a profile of art dealer Larry Gagosian: Keefe, "How Larry Gagosian Reshaped the Art World," 30. Gagosian purchased the townhouse previously owned by Christophe de Menil, where Carpenter saw the Doug Wheeler installation that inspired the layout of the *Upside Down* exhibition. François de Menil redesigned the townhouse for Gagosian, whose Amangasett house had originally been built for François de Menil. See Dan Duray, "Larry Gagosian's House Looks Even Better When It's Not on Fire," *Observer*, 30 June 2011, https://observer.com/2011/06/larry-gagosians-house-looks-even-better-when-its-not-on-fire/; Sarah Cascone, "Why Did Larry Gagosian Sell His Upper East Side Home for $18 Million?," *Artnet*, 14 October 2015, https://news.artnet.com/art-world/larry-gagosian-sells-home-18-million-340288; "Charles Gwathmey's Modernist Masterpieces," *Architectural Digest*, 31 July 2011, https://www.architecturaldigest.com/gallery/charles-gwathmey-residences-retrospective-slideshow.

13 Bissell facilitated the Ford Foundation Grant that funded the Explorations seminar ("Sea," 240). When he was president of the University of Toronto he established McLuhan's Centre for Culture and Technology.

14 I was that graduate student. Carpenter is more sanguine about McLuhan in a video produced in 2011 that can be found on the channel mywebcowtube on YouTube: "Edmund Ted Carpenter 2011 – on Marshall McLuhan and Explorations," 1:00:59, 24 June 2016, https://www.youtube.com/watch?v=t6HyFyMjlXA.

15 Gilberg and Gulløv, eds., *Fifty Years of Arctic Research*.

16 George Swinton, "Who Makes Inuit Art?," 295.

17 Mitenbuler, *Wanderlust*, 198.

18 On the changing fortunes of the film's reception see Grimshaw, "Who Has the Last Laugh?"

19 See "High Arctic relocation," Wikipedia, accessed 3 December 2023, https://en.wikipedia.org/wiki/High_Arctic_relocation.

20 The recent research of Janice Cavell (no relation to the present author) discusses the theories of sovereignty and well-being as motivations for the relocation before proposing a third theory: that the 1949 collapse of the fur trade economy (largely in the control of the Hudson's Bay Company) threatened to put increasing numbers of Inuit on social welfare. Seeking to avoid this prospect, the government sought to use the Inuit of Inukjuak as a test case to see if they could be taught "approved patterns of economic behaviour" (i.e., "personal thrift"), while placing the Inuit outside the HBC's sphere of operations (which had included several relocations of Inuit to do trapping for the company, the exclusive focus on trapping disrupting the cultural economy of the Inuit) and thereby giving the government total control of Inuit income, deemed to be the "crux" of the "northern problem." The problem, in fact, derived from the HBC, which encouraged the Inuit to lavishly spend the profits from their trapping at the HBC stores, where the products were sold at outrageous markups. While the sovereignty issue did not loom large for the Canadian government, it is ironic, given the place of Carpenter's publication, that the greatest threat to Canadian sovereignty in the north was deemed to be from Denmark. It was in fact the Danes who had inspired the Canadian government in their 1953 relocation project by their removal of Inuit from the west coast of Greenland to the uninhabited east coast. See J. Cavell, "'Consolidation and Control of All Eskimo Income.'"

21 Quoting the apology delivered by the Canadian minister of Indian (*sic*) and northern affairs, John Duncan. See CBC, "Inuit Get Federal Apology for Forced Relocation."

22 Harrington, *Padlei Diary, 1950.*

23 The front inside flap of the wrapper has a quotation, in French and English, from a note sent to Carpenter by Henri Cartier-Bresson, who finds the photographs "extremement émouvantes" (Carpenter Papers, Box 30). Cartier-Bresson and his family, had been guests of Carpenter and Adelaide de Menil at their Hampton estate.

24 Elder, "Review of *Padlei Diary*," 659.

25 An unattributed editorial note in the catalogue to *Upside Down* acknowledges that to "the Inuit, 'Eskimo' is perceived as derogatory, and the word is no longer in common use in Canada or Greenland. To the Yup'ik, however, there is no such association, and to some the term 'Eskimo' is preferred, since it includes both the Inuit and Yup'ik peoples, and for them to use the term 'Inuit' to define themselves would be incorrect. As such, 'Eskimo' remains in common use in the United States and Russia ... It is not the intention of this

exhibition to propose solutions to questions of cultural identity that remain political topics" (9).

26 Harper, *Minik the New York Eskimo*. This is a revised and updated version of Harper's *Give Me My Father's Body: The Life of Minik, the New York Eskimo* (1986).

27 Roland W. Force remarks that the "horrors perpetrated by some White researchers toward Native American remains is unbelievable, but tragically true. They did happen. At times, people were so immersed in pursuing their studies that they paid to have Indian burials dug up and brought to them. The retrieval of Indian skulls came to be described as a cottage industry on the frontier. Shockingly, upon occasion, bodies with flesh were boiled to provide clean bones for study" (*Heye and the Mighty*, 194).

28 Frobisher Bay and Newmarket Ontario: Blacklead Books, 1986.

29 Carpenter, "Dead Truth Live Myth," 27–9.

30 On Hrdlička's controversial field practices, especially with reference to the collecting of human skulls, see Morgan, *Sins of the Shovel*.

31 The second edition of Harper's book includes a foreword by the disgraced American actor Kevin Spacey.

32 This is the only reference in Carpenter's published work to his wife, Adelaide de Menil Carpenter.

33 Zumwalt, *Franz Boas*, 312.

34 Gopnik and Fraser, "It's Not Primitive."

35 See Loke, "Aleut Sacred Objects to Be Auctioned."

36 Feest, "Transformations of a Mask," 256.

37 Reif, "Attracted by the Who as Well as the What."

38 He was not supported in this by one of the other contributors to the volume, Frederica de Laguna, who presented a "spirited rebuttal" of Carpenter's essay at the associated conference. See Fitzhugh, "Frederica de Laguna," 231.

39 Carpenter, "Tradition and Continuity in Eskimo Art," 69.

40 Carpenter, "How an Upside-Down Lady Became an Upside-Down Bird," 445.

41 Carpenter, "Imagining the Past," 209–17.

42 Rykwert and Atkin, "Building and Knowing," 1.

43 The Rock Foundation had funded excavations in this area. See Prins's obituary of Carpenter in *Anthropology News* 52, no. 9 (2011): 24.

44 Carpenter Papers, Box 30.

Chapter Eight

1 Menil Collection, www.menil.org/collection/5137-witnesses (link now defunct).

2 See Schneider, "Unfinished Dialogues," 108–35. Schneider argues that Carpenter was among those anthropologists who problematized the distinction between Western and non-Western art, leading thereby to a notion of "symmetrical anthropology" (129, 131).

3 Carpenter, *Witnesses to a Surrealist Vision*, n.p.

4 Morris, "Aligned with Nazca," 26–30.

5 A precedent for "Witnesses" is said to be the 1985 primitivism show as well as the 1984 Paris Menil exhibition, and "I Surrealisti," organized by Arturo Schwartz in 1989. See "Edmund Carpenter and 'Witnesses to a Surrealist Vision': A Look Behind the Curtain," YouTube, 1:08:26, posted by the Menil Collection on 15 December 2022, accessed 2 February 2024, www.youtube .com/watch?v=m-kXKgRRpN4..

6 Menil Collection website, https://www.menil.org/collection/5137-witnesses (link now defunct).

7 As noted in the Menil film, "Edmund Carpenter and 'Witnesses to a Surrealist Vision': A Look Behind the Curtain." The pamphlet states that "the objects in this exhibition were either owned by the Surrealists or are in the spirit of those they collected."

8 See Schneider and Wright, eds., *Anthropology and Art Practice.*

9 Strange, "A Surrealist Vision of the Art Museum," 71, quoting Clifford, *The Predicament of Culture*, 146. See also Conley, "Is Reconciliation Possible?"

10 Smart, "Aesthetics as Vocation." "Off-modern" is a term, coined by Svetlana Boym in her book of that title (London: Bloomsbury, 2017), to refer to non -linear genealogies of the modernist project.

11 Carpenter, "Iroquoian Figurines," 105–13.

12 Force, *The Heye and the Mighty*, 467.

13 Carpenter, "European Motifs in Protohistoric Iroquois Art." The biographical note attached to this article describes Carpenter as "retired."

14 Carpenter, first lecture on Primitive Art, New School, "ESC lecture NewSch 1986 01," www.youtube.com/watch?v=BH3vYaq6HQs.

15 Carpenter, "The Wondrous Head of Roscrea."

16 Chapter 2, note 88 herein.

17 There was a racialized discourse underpinning "Viking" connections to North America, in that this discourse often sought to position white settlers as *preceding* Native peoples. See Puglionesi, *In Whose Ruins*, especially the first part, "Tongues from Tombs" (20–78).

18 I am quoting from the electronic version of this pamphlet, available on the Wikipedia site for Carpenter. The electronic version states that it was published "with minor editorial changes from printed version" (24).

19 Hoag, "Current Cabinet Activities," n.p.

20 Gullbekk, "*Norse Penny.*"

21 Carpenter, "Chief Red Thundercloud (1919–1996)."

22 Carpenter, "Amos H. Gottschall (1854–1938)," 47–50.

23 Carpenter, *Two Essays: Chief and Greed* (North Andover: Persimmon Press, 2005). This is a second edition; I have not been able to locate a first. Carpenter's study of the MAI was preceded by the 1999 publication of Roland W. Force's *The Heye and the Mighty*. Whereas Carpenter was interested in the MAI's de-accessioning "policy" and its implications for the museum, Force's focus was

on the political maneuvering that resulted in the establishment of the NMAI. These manoeuvrings – which grew to include Governor Cuomo, Mayor Ed Koch, and the attorney general of New York – were based on the state of New York's desire to keep the MAI in New York, either as adjunct to the American Museum of Natural History, or in its own space in the former Customs House building in Battery Park, versus the belief that the Native peoples of America should be honoured in a building on the National Mall in Washington, DC.

24 Lonetree, *Decolonizing Museums*, 86.

25 Carpenter had been involved in another deaccessioning debacle in 1999 with reference to Navajo blankets that had been hanging from the rafters in his East Hampton home for twenty-five years. Fearing they were vulnerable to fire, Carpenter and Adelaide de Menil put them up for auction (with an estimated value of US$1.5 million), at which point the Denver Art Museum initiated a lawsuit based on the argument that the blankets had been improperly deaccessioned from the museum's collection. Adelaide de Menil had purchased the blankets from George Terasaki (whose book *Transfigurations* Carpenter would blurb; see the "Conclusion" herein), and Terasaki had confirmed the provenance. But the museum contended that the deaccessioning documents were illegally processed in order to enable the sale of the blankets. "Carpenter contends – quite heatedly – that the couple's purchase of the textiles in 1970 was a legitimate deal ... Any confusion over the sale was an obvious clerical error, Carpenter says ... The museum's lawyers argue that [the deaccessioning document] was not a mistake but an attempt to hide 'a deliberate covert transfer'" of the museum's property. "It's not fair for the museum to rewrite history now, Carpenter says." See Calhoun, "A Blanket Indictment."

26 As Roland Force notes, Carpenter joined the former board in 1973 and his appointment carried over as a trustee of the Museum of the American Indian from 1977 to 1985. See *The Heye and the Mighty*, 466–7.

27 As Carpenter relates in a letter to Marjorie Halpin, an anthropologist associated with the Museum of Anthropology at the University of British Columbia. Letter of 31 October 1978 to Marjorie Halpin, in the Halpin fonds, PR 26-22, Museum of Anthropology Archives. Halpin had reviewed the Wilson Duff / Bill Reid volume in *BC Studies* 37 (1978), and this initiated a correspondence that lasted until 1980.

28 Ferretti, "State Investigates American Indian Museum," 1. The actual number of items in the Heye holdings has never been fully accounted for.

29 Force, *The Heye and the Mighty*, 37.

30 Vine Deloria was a trustee (158), as was N. Scott Momaday (Force, *The Heye and the Mighty*, 466).

31 While Carpenter states that he voted in favour of the move to Texas, Force asserts that Carpenter "was adamantly opposed to a Perot-Texas involvement" (*The Heye and the Mighty*, 254). This suggests that the balloting was done in secret. Carpenter had at a certain point favoured an offer from Eli Lilly

of circa $100 to $129 million to move the MAI to Indianapolis, before shifting his allegiance to the AMNH (Force, 184). Force was opposed to an amalgamation with the AMNH, unless the MAI was given its own building. "I did not believe it appropriate, as we neared the twenty-first century, to have galleries of dinosaurs to the left, bugs to the right, and Indians in between" (194). While some trustees were puzzled by Carpenter's support of an amalgamation with the AMNH, a friend of Carpenter had asserted that Adelaide de Menil was in favour of "get[ting] on with the merger of MAI and AMNH" (Force, 233).

32 Letter to John Mulvaney, 29 April 1989, Box 30.
33 Letter to Mulvaney. The Smithsonian does host academic research, *pace* Carpenter's comment to the contrary. The Carpenter Papers themselves are housed in the National Anthropological Center in Suitland, Maryland, where some of the research for the present volume took place.
34 Lonetree, "Missed Opportunities: Reflections on the NMAI," 642.
35 See also Atalay, "Indigenous Archaeology as Decolonizing Practice," 280–310.
36 See "King Philip's War," Wikipedia, accessed 2 May 2024, en.wikipedia.org/wiki/King_Philip%27s_War.
37 See Bruchac, *Savage Kin*, 136. The Carpenter quotations are from his correspondence with William N. Fenton, who was an anthropologist at the New York State Museum and later at SUNY Albany.
38 Loke, "Sacred and Secular Clash," B3.
39 Keating, "Review of Two Essays," 78–81.
40 Claude Lévi-Strauss, letter to Carpenter dated 7 February 2006, on the stationery of the Laboratoire d'Anthropologie Sociale. Carpenter Papers, National Anthropological Archives. Smithsonian Institution, Box 30.
41 Quoted by McMullen, "Reinventing George Heye," 65.
42 See also Conn, "George Heye in Context," and Zittlau, "George Gustav Heye and the National Museum of the American Indian."
43 See Paul Heyer's obituary (515).
44 Carpenter, "Marshall," *Explorations in Media Ecology*, 179–84. The biographical note attached to this article states that Carpenter has "since 1994 ... been actively engaged with his wife, Adelaide de Menil, in researching two archaeological sites, Zhokhov Island (Mesolithic, 8,000 years old) and Yana River (Paleolithic, 30,000 years old)" (179).
45 Carroll, ed., *Language Thought and Reality*.
46 See Cavell, *McLuhan in Space*, 245n5.
47 See Cavell, *McLuhan in Space*, chapter 8, and Powe, *Marshall McLuhan and Northrop Frye*.
48 Both Herman Northrop Frye and Herbert Marshall McLuhan dropped their H's.

49 Mywebcowtube, "Edmund Ted Carpenter 2011 – on Marshall McLuhan and Explorations," 1:00:59, 24 June 2016, https://www.youtube.com/watch?v=t6HyFyMjlXA.

50 Helfenstein, foreword to *Upside Down*, 10–11. Helfenstein writes as the director of the Menil Collection. This is the revised version of the catalogue originally prepared for the exhibition at the Musée du quai Branly in 2007.

51 Letter to Robert McGhee, 14 January 1993, Box 30.

52 Carpenter, "yup'ik [*sic*] Mask," in *Fondation Beyeler*, 286. Carpenter makes the same point in a glowing review of Ann Fienup-Riordan's *The Living Tradition of Yup'ik Masks* (Seattle, 1996) in *Arctic* 50, no. 1 (1997): 76–7. Riordan, writes Carpenter, "acts as a surrogate tribal elder, recording what otherwise might be lost. For this achievement, I honor her" (76), although he is somewhat critical of her section on surrealism and Yup'ik masks.

53 Bronshtein and Dneprovsky, "Ancient Eskimo Art of Ekven," 123, citing Carpenter's *Man and Art in the Arctic*.

54 Celant, *Doug Wheeler*, 13.

55 Cavell, *McLuhan in Space*, 173. See also 284n16.

56 Carpenter, "Robert Cannon obituary," 454.

57 See Kittler, "Perspective and the Book," 38–53. "'The Life of the Florentine Architect Leone Battista Alberti' as Giorgio Vasari titled his 1570 biography of Alberti ... suggested a parallel between Gutenberg and Alberti ... between the printing press and linear perspective" (42). See also Eriksen, "Vasari and the Kinship of Perspective and Printing," 1–3. With Cannon, Carpenter made a film about Kuskokwim masks that Carpenter associated with surrealist art and its fluid notions of dimensionality. See Prins and Bishop, *VAR* 120.

58 Carpenter, "Silent Music and Invisible Art."

59 Shigeru Ban, an associate of Jean de Gastines, who was the architect of the Musee Branly exhibition, collaborated with Wheeler on the Paris exhibition (224). See Jean de Gastines Architectes, "About," accessed 2 May 2024, https://jdg-architectes.com/en/about/.

60 Meunier, "À propos de l'exposition *Upside Down: Les Arctiques*," 156, my translation here and throughout.

61 Carpenter was unable to attend the opening. By the end of his life, he had lost his ability to speak, as noted by Sean Mooney in a lecture given at the Menil Gallery, "Edmund Carpenter and 'Witnesses to a Surrealist Vision': A Look Behind the Curtain."

62 Prins and McBride, "Arctic Realities and Indigenous Art," 361.

63 Marcia Brennan, "Review of *Upside Down*."

64 Dominique de Menil, quoted by Calvin Tomkins, "The Benefactor," 58. Mme de Menil is describing the exhibition practices of Jermayne MacAgy.

65 Prins and Bishop, "Trickster," 207–45.

Conclusion

1 In his biographical note to *Eskimo*, Carpenter states that he "trained as a mining engineer" before falling into anthropology.

2 Carpenter, "Confessions of an Unconventional Anthropologist," 90–7.

3 Carpenter writes in his biographical statement for *Transfigurations: North Pacific Coast Art* that he "has taught anthropology for forty years at the Universities of Toronto, California, and Harvard" (n.p.). In this same note, Carpenter states that he is at work on a book about Eskimo maps "that will include four hundred original drawings all made before 1900 and some as early as the 18th century." The book highlights artifacts from the collection of George Terasaki, whom Carpenter knew for forty years. See Brown, *Transfigurations*. According to Roland Force in *The Heye and the Mighty*, Terasaki was involved in "exchanges" with the MAI under Dockstader (33).

4 From the biographical note at the end of *Eskimo*.

5 Carpenter, "Confessions," 90–7.

6 Carpenter, "We Wed Ourselves to the Mystery," 66–74. These comments ally Carpenter with auto-ethnography, to a certain extent, although auto-ethnography as Carpenter pursued it always moved in the direction of disciplinary critique. See the discussions in Roth, *Auto/Biography and Auto/Ethnography*.

7 Carpenter quoting Berlin in "Arctic Witnesses," Gilberg and Gulløv, eds., *Fifty Years of Arctic Research*, 307.

8 Carpenter, "Letter to Harald Prins, 2.9.01."

9 Carpenter, "Response to Charles Campbell Hughes." Compare this statement to Carpenter's comment that "ethnologists who identify completely with tribesmen, who 'pass over' (some have) stop writing" ("Sea," 257).

10 Resnais, Marker, and Cloquet, *Les statues meurent aussi*.

11 Haselberger, "Method of Studying Ethnological Art," 341–84. The journal invited forty-nine scholars to comment on Haselberger's article, and Carpenter's comments are at 361–3. Haselberger was an Africanist whose principal work is *Kunstethnologie: Grundbegriffe, Methoden, Darstellung*.

12 The reference is to Schaeffer-Simmern, *Eskimo Plastik aus Kanada*, reviewed negatively by Carpenter in Carpenter, "Review of Henry Scharffer-Simmern, *Eskimo Plastik aus Kanada*," 346–8.

13 See the biographical note accompanying the fonds description in the National Anthropological Archives, Smithsonian Institution, accessed 2 May 2024, collections.si.edu/search/detail/ead_collection:sova-naa-2017-27.

14 Howard, *Margaret Mead*, 414.

15 Quoted by Prins and Bishop, "Edmund Carpenter," 135, from Bunny McBride's interview with Carpenter published in her 1980 Columbia University master's thesis.

16 Lee, "Letter to Carpenter 11/24/6."

17 Particularly Prins and Bishop, "Edmund Carpenter: Explorations in Media and Anthropology," 110–40.

18 Prins and Bishop, "Edmund Carpenter: Explorations in Media and Anthropology," 131.
19 Prins, "Visual or Virtual Anthropology?," 279–94.
20 Howes, "Polysensoriality," 435–50, cf. 440.
21 Takaragawa et al., "Bad Habitus," 517.
22 Edwards, "Objects of Affect," 224. Note also Campt, *Listening to Images*, who begins her introduction with a "'throat-clearing gesture'" that she describes as creating "an analytic space" (3).
23 Howes, "Polysensoriality," 435–50.
24 See also Pink, *The Future of Visual Anthropology*: "Howes complains that [the] emphasis on text also subdued the anthropological interest in the senses that had emerged during the mid- to late twentieth century (developed variously by Lévi-Strauss, McLuhan, Ong, Carpenter, Hall, and Mead and Métraux)." A major implication of the focus on the senses is that "it inspired new forms of representing anthropologists' own and other people's experiences," thereby helping "to bring reflexivity to the fore in anthropology" and thus emphasizing "how ethnographers might learn from their own sensory experiences in fieldwork," which begins to turn anthropology upside down. Pink, 13.
25 The problematics of sensory anthropology are articulated by Takaragawa et al., "Bad Habitus": "Are multimodal methods in sensory anthropology claiming to narrow the gap between documentation and lived experience?" (520). This would be to suggest that such modalities are unmediated.
26 Mitchell and Hansen, "Introduction," viii–ix.
27 See the essay on memes at Iresearchnet, under "Anthropology," accessed 2 May 2024, https://anthropology.iresearchnet.com/memes/, and Iloh, "Do It for the Culture."
28 Cobb, "Connecting the Ancient Afro-Eurasian World," 329–42; Liu, "Intertwined Maritime Silk Road and Austronesian Routes," 384–400.
29 See Clarence-Smith, Pomeranz, and Vries, "Editorial," 1–2.
30 Singh, "Ghengis the Good."
31 See the comments of Mark Siegeltuch, who was a student when Carpenter was lecturing at the New School: "Lectures," Edmund Snow Carpenter website, accessed 2 May 2024, edmundsnowcarpenter.com/2016/11/15/lectures/.
32 Ginsburg, "Rethinking the Digital Age," 302. A classic example of strategic traditionalism is Zacharias Kunuk's film *Atanarjuat* (2001). See also Coleman, "Ethnographic Approaches to Digital Media," 487–505, who writes about "how cultural identities, representations, and imaginaries, such as those hinged to youth, diaspora, nation, and [I]ndigeneity, are remade, subverted, communicated, and circulated through individual and collective engagement with digital technologies" (488).
33 Loft, "Introduction: Decolonizing the Web," in Loft and Swanson, eds., *Coded Territories*, xvi.

34 Jackson 2Bears, "My Post-Indian Technological Autobiography," in Loft and Swanson, eds., *Coded Territories*, 17.

35 Loft, "Mediacosmology," in Loft and Swanson, eds., *Coded Territories*, 170–86, quoting Deloria, *God Is Red*, 62.

36 Prins and Bishop, "Edmund Carpenter," 136.

37 From the back cover of Feld, *Sound and Sentiment.*

38 Schafer, *The Tuning of the World*, 157–8.

39 Prins and Bishop, *VAR*, 136.

40 From an interview Carpenter gave on the occasion of the 1999 opening of the surrealist gallery at the Menil Collection. See Rock Foundation, Inc., "Edmund Carpenter Talk 1, ISSS Conference 2021," 11 January 2022, https://www.youtube.com/watch?v=JEyV-zmYBXo.

41 The museumification of ethnographic artifacts is highly fraught. While Andrea Wulf is able to write a 474-page book on Alexander von Humboldt, *The Invention of Nature: Alexander Humboldt's New World*, the word "museum" does not appear in the index, an omission that is rectified in Penny's *In Humboldt's Shadow.* Penny writes of the "tensions between voices that emphasize the cosmopolitan visions epitomized in Alexander von Humboldt's writings, which inspired ... the largest collecting museums in the world, and those voices that wish to underscore the roles (whether inadvertent or intentional) such scientists and institutions played in the crimes of the nineteenth and twentieth centuries, particularly the legacies of colonial and Nazi violence" (12). Penny concludes, "Working relations ... are the future of German ethnological museums, and the best relations require openness to cultural difference as well as a keen understanding of the history of the collections. Through a combination of contemporary technology – new modes of communication, exhibition, and reproduction – new information, brought to the museums by indigenous participants, and a new generation of curators and directors, who are more willing to work with these indigenous groups and less insistent about guarding and hiding their collections and histories, the museums, perhaps for the first time, have the potential to achieve a good part of the Humboldtian goals that drove their creation" (194). Götz Aly, in examining the specific case of the Luf boat, now given pride of place in the Humboldt Forum in Berlin, writes that the appropriation of "these ethnographic treasures ... dealt an irrevocably fatal blow to the societies and cultures that had produced such impressive examples of artisanship and art" (146). See Aly, *The Magnificent Boat.* Johnson, in "Loot under the Lindens," writes that, for generations, museums such as the Humboldt Forum "have misrepresented their true nature. Their premise is that their holdings are encyclopedic and collected for the public good, explaining cultures and peoples in the detached voice of art history or social science. The reality is that large swaths of their collections were randomly acquired by hoarders, looters, and donors. This

raises fundamental questions about the stories they tell, not to mention the provenance of their holdings." In response, museums have adopted an "explain and retain" practice: "It's a performance of white fragility. What should we do? Oh my'" (quoting Dan Hicks, an Oxford archaeologist and proponent of repatriation). Many of these critics agree broadly with Carpenter's contention that museums changed for the worse when they shifted from research to entertainment.

42 Silverman, "Museum as Process," in Silverman, ed., *Museum as Process*, 3.

43 Prins and Bishop, "Edmund Carpenter," 117.

44 Starn, "Introduction," in Starn, ed., *Writing Culture and the Life of Anthropology*, 22.

45 I met James Clifford in 1988 at a semiotics conference, and the venue is significant. Clifford's critique, as acute as it was, ultimately devolved on verities of Saussurean linguistic theory and referential arbitrariness that failed to take into account the mediatic *a priori*.

46 "There is a conception of ethnology not fulfilled by the discovery and assembly of facts alone. It involves something which moves and touches the reader." Carpenter, "Frank Speck," 81.

47 Greif, *The Age of the Crisis of Man*.

48 See Kittler, *Literature, Media, Information Systems*, edited by John Johnston, 133.

Bibliography

Works by Edmund [Snow] Carpenter

"Alcohol in the Iroquois Dream Quest." *American Journal of Psychiatry* 116, no. 2 (1959): 148–151.

"Amos H. Gottschall (1854–1938)." *European Review of Native American Studies* 17, no. 2 (2003): 47–50.

Anerca. Toronto: Dent, 1959.

"Arctic Witnesses." In *Fifty Years of Arctic Research*, edited by R. Gilberg and H.C. Gulløv, 303–10. Copenhagen: National Museum of Denmark, 1997.

"Art de la mer de Béring et des Eskimo." In *La Rime et la raison: Les collections Ménil (Houston- New York)*, 200. Paris: Éditions de la Réunion des musées nationaux, 1984.

"Assassins and Cannibals or I Got Me a Small Mind and I Means to Use It." *Society for Visual Anthropology Newsletter* 5, no. 1 (1989): 12–13.

"Biographical note." In *Honoring Our Elders: A History of Eastern Arctic Archaeology*, viii. Washington, DC: Smithsonian Institution, 2002.

"Chief Red Thundercloud (1919–1996)." *European Review of Native American Studies* 17, no. 2 (2003): 51–4.

"Confessions of an Unconventional Anthropolgist." *Audience* 2, no. 6 (1972): 90–7.

"Dead Truth Live Myth." *Native American Studies* 11, no. 2 (1997): 27–9.

"Decoding the Tribe." *Natural History* 115, no. 4 (2006): 42–7.

"Deeply Carved Art of the Northwest Coast." In *The Menil Collection*, 164–7. New York: Abrams, 1987.

Drawings of Enooesweetok of the Sikossilingmint Tribe of Eskimo, Fox Land, Baffin Island. New York: Rock Foundation, 2001.

Eskimo. Toronto: University of Toronto Press, 1959.

"The Eskimo Language." *Etc.: A Review of General Semantics* 25, no. 4 (1968): 467–73.

Eskimo Realities. New York: Holt, Rinehart, and Winston, 1973.

"Eternal Life and Self-Definition among the Aivilik Eskimos." *American Journal of Psychiatry* 110, no. 11 (1954): 840–3.

"European Motifs in Protohistoric Iroquois Art." In *Anthropology, History, and American Indians: Essays in Honor of William Curtis Sturtevant*, 255–62. Smithsonian Washington: Smithsonian Institution Press, 2002.

"Five Sites of the Intermediate Period." *American Antiquity* 15, no. 4 (1950): 298–314.

"Foreword." In *The White Men: The First Response of Aboriginal Peoples to the White Men*, by Julia Blackburn, 6–9. London: Orbis, 1979.

"Foreword." In *Transfigurations: North Pacific Coast Art: George Terasaki, Collector*, by Steven Clay Brown. Seattle: Marquand Books, 2006.

"Four Hopewellian Tumuli in Western New York." *Journal of the Washington Academy of Sciences* 40, no. 7 (1950): 209–16.

"Frank Speck: Quiet Listener." In *The Life and Times of Frank G. Speck, 1881–1950*, edited by Roy Blankenship, 78–84. Philadelphia: University of Pennsylvania Press, 1991.

"Further Evidence on the Beardmore Relics." *American Anthropologist* 59, no. 5 (1957): 875–8.

"How an Upside-Down Lady Became an Upside-Down Bird." In *Man Does Not Go Naked: Textilien und Handwerk aus afrikanischen und anderen Ländern*, edited by Beate Engelbrecht and Bernhard Gardi, 443–61. Basel: Ethnologisches Seminar de Universität und Museum für Völkerkunder, 1989.

"If Wittgenstein had been an Eskimo." "Explorations." *The Varsity Graduate* 12, no. 3 (April 1966): 50–63.

"Imagining the Past." In *Structure and Meaning in Human Settlements*, edited by Tony Atkin and Joseph Rykwert, 209–17. Philadelphia: University of Pennsylvania Museum of Archaeology and Anthropology, 2005.

"Introduction." In *Indian Art of the Northwest Coast: A Dialogue on Craftsmanship and Aesthetics*, by Bill Holm and Bill Reid, 9–27. Houston: Institute for the Arts, Rice University, 1975.

"Introduction." In *I Breathe a New Song: Poems of the Eskimo*, edited by Richard Lewis, illustrations by Oonark, 11–23. New York: Simon and Schuster, 1971.

"Iroquoian Figurines." *American Antiquity* 8, no. 1 (1942): 105–13.

"Lecture on Primitive Art, New School, 27 January 1986," YouTube, 1:02:21, posted by Sean Mooney on 29 October 2021, "ESC lecture NewSch 1986 01," accessed 2 February 2024. www.youtube.com/watch?v=BH3vYaq6HQs.

"Letter to Marjorie Halpin, 28 February 1980." Halpin Fonds, Museum of Anthropology Archives. University of British Columbia. File PR 26-22.

"Letter to William N. Taylor, Jr (22 May 1977)." Carpenter Papers. Smithsonian Institution. Box 31.

"Letter to John Mulvaney, 29 April 1989." Carpenter Papers. National Anthropological Archives. Smithsonian Institution. Box 30.

"Letter to Harald Prins, 2.9.01." Carpenter Papers. National Anthropological Archives. Smithsonian Institution. Box 30.

"Letter to Robert McGhee, 14 January 1993." Carpenter Papers. National Anthropological Archives. Smithsonian Institution. Box 30.

"Letter to George MacDonald, March ? [*sic*] 1978." Carpenter Papers. National Anthropological Archives. Smithsonian Institution. Box 30.

"Letter to Rodney Needham, 29 January 1996." Carpenter Papers. National Anthropological Archives. Smithsonian Institution. Box 31.

"Love Thy Label as Thyself." In *Irving Penn: A Career in Photography*, edited by Colin Westerbeck, 54–62. Boston: The Art Institute of Chicago, 1997.

Man and Art in the Arctic. Browning Montana: Museum of the Plains Indian, 1964.

"Marshall." *Explorations in Media Ecology* 5, no. 3 (2006): 179–84.

"The Megiddo Gaming Boards." In *Art as Means of Communication in Pre-Literate Societies*, edited by Dan Eban et al., 27–50. Jerusalem: The Israel Museum, 1990.

"The New Languages." *Cross Currents* 7, no. 4 (1957): 305–15.

"The New Languages." In *Readings on Creativity and Imagination in Literature and Language*, edited by Leonard V. Kosinski, 132–40. Champaign: National Council of Teachers of English, 1968.

"The New Languages." In *Selected Educational Heresies: Some Unorthodox Views Concerning the Nature and Purposes of Contemporary Education*, edited by William F. O'Neill, 223–45. Glenview: Scott, Foresman and Company, 1969.

"The New Languages." In *The New Languages: A Rhetorical Approach to the Mass Media and Popular Culture*, edited by Thomas H. Ohlgren and Lynn M. Berk, 4–12. Englewood Cliffs: Prentice-Hall, 1977.

"Not Since Babel." *Los Angeles Free Press* 5, no. 192 (22–28 March 1968): 7, 9.

"Not Since Babel." *ETC* 27, no. 1 (1970): 81–8.

"Obituary: Robert Cannon (1909–1964)." *American Anthropologist* 67, no. 2 (1965): 453–4.

"Ohnainewk, Eskimo Hunter." In *In the Company of Man: Twenty Portraits by Anthropologists*, edited by Joseph B. Casagrande, 417–26. New York: Harper and Brothers, 1960.

"On Designing Public Buildings for Play." *Los Angeles Free Press.* 31 May 1968, 26.

[On Robert Flaherty]. Text of talk on Jo-Anne Birnie Danzker's exhibition on Flaherty in New York. Included with a letter to Marjorie Halpin. Halpin Fonds. Museum of Anthropology Archives. University of British Columbia. File PR 26-22.

"Reality and Television: An Interview with Dr. Edmund Carpenter." *Television Quarterly* 10, no. 1 (1972): 42–6.

"Recently Acquired Manuscripts Relating to the Archaeology of Pennsylvania." *Proceedings of the American Philosophical Society* 93, no. 2 (1949): 166–8.

"Remembering *Explorations.*" *Canadian Notes and Queries* 46 (1992): 3–14.

"Response to Charles Campbell Hughes, 'Under Four Flags: Recent Culture Change Among the Eskimos.'" *Current Anthropology* 6, no. 1 (1965): 3–62.

"Response to Herta Haselberger, 'Method of Studying Ethnological Art.'" *Current Anthropology* 2, no. 4 (1961): 361–3.

"Review of Cornelius Osgood, *Ingalik Mental Culture.*" *American Anthropologist* 63, no. 4 (1961): 848.

"Review of Henry Schaeffer-Simmern, *Eskimo Plastik aus Kanada.*" *American Anthropologist* 62, no. 2 (1960): 346–8.

"Review of David Bidney, *Theoretical Anthropology*." *American Journal of Psychiatry* 111, no. 6 (1954): 480.

"Review of Jack Goody, ed., *Literacy in Traditional Societies*." *American Anthropologist* 72, no. 2 (1970): 430–2.

"Review of Margaret Mead, *People and Places*." *American Anthropologist* 62, no. 6 (1960): 1074–5.

"Review of Jean Malaurie, *The Last Kings of Thule*, trans. Gwendolen Freeman." *American Anthropologist* 59, no. 6 (1957): 1096.

"Review of J.C. Carothers, *The African Mind in Health and Disease: A Study in Ethnopsychiatry*." *American Journal of Psychiatry* 110, no. 12 (1954): 944.

"Review of Marvin K. Opler, *Culture, Psychiatry and Human Values: The Methods and Values of a Social Psychiatry*." *American Journal of Psychiatry* 114, no. 10 (1958): 957.

"Review of Ann Fienup-Riordan, *The Living Tradition of Yup'ik Masks*." *Arctic* 50, no. 1 (1997): 76–7.

"Review of Laurel Kendall et al., *Drawing Shadows to Stone: The Photography of the Jesup North Pacific Expedition, 1897–1902*." *American Anthropologist* 100, no. 3 (1998): 771–2.

Serpent on the Hill. Privately printed.

"The Tribal Terror of Self-Awareness." In *Principles of Visual Anthropology*, edited by Paul Hockings, 451–61. The Hague: Mouton, 1975.

"Shapers of the Modern Outlook: Benjamin Lee Whorf." *Canadian Forum* (April 1953): 9–10.

"Silent Music and Invisible Art." *Natural History* 87, no. 5 (1978): 90–9.

"Some Notes on the Separate Realities of Eskimo and Indian Art." In *The Far North: 2000 Years of American Eskimo and Indian Art*, 281–9. Washington: National Gallery of Art, 1973.

The Story of Comock the Eskimo as Told to Robert Flaherty. New York: Simon & Schuster, 1968.

"That Not-So-Silent Sea." Appendix to *The Virtual Marshall McLuhan*, by Donald F. Theall, 236–61. Kingston: McGill-Queen's University Press, 2001.

"They Became What They Beheld." *Los Angeles Free Press*, April–August 1969.

They Became What They Beheld. New York: Outerbridge & Dienstfrey / Ballantine, 1970.

"The Timeless Present in the Mythology of the Aivilik Eskimos." *Anthropologica* 3 (1956): 1–4.

"Tradition and Continuity in Eskimo Art." In *Honoring Our Elders: A History of Eastern Arctic Archaeology*, edited by William W. Fitzhugh, Stephen Loring, and Daniel Odess, 69–77. Washington, DC: Smithsonian Institution, 2002.

"Tumuli in Southwestern Pennsylvania." *American Antiquity* 16, no. 4 (1951): 329–46.

"Twilight of the University." Unpublished typescript (six pages).

Two Essays: Chief and Greed. North Andover: Persimmon Press, 2005.

"An Unusual Pottery Jar from East Milton." *Bulletin of the Massachusetts Archaeological Society* 4, no. 3 (1943): 38.

"We Wed Ourselves to the Mystery: A Study of Tribal Art." "Explorations." *The Varsity Graduate* 1, no. 4 (Summer 1968): 66–74.

"Witch-Fear Among the Aivilik Eskimos." *American Journal of Psychiatry* 110, no. 3 (1953): 194–9.

Witnesses to a Surrealist Vision. [Pamphlet]. Houston: Menil Collection, 2020.

"The Wondrous Head of Roscrea: A Personal Account." *Curator* 38, no. 1 (1995): 38–48.

"yup'ik [*sic*] Mask." In *Fondation Beyeler*, 286. Munich: Prestel Verlag, 1997.

Carpenter, Edmund Snow, Christopher Cornford, Sidney Simon, and Robert Watts, eds. *Proposals for Art Education.* New York: Carnegie Corporation, 1970.

Carpenter, Edmund Snow, and Royal B. Hassrick. "Rappahannock Games and Amusements." *Primitive Man* 1, no. 1, 2 (1944): 29–39.

Carpenter, Edmund Snow, and Ken Heyman. "They Became What They Beheld." In *The Director in a Changing Theatre: Essays on Theory and Practice, with New Plays for Performance*, edited by J. Robert Wills, 262–4. Palo Alto: Mayfield Publishing, 1976.

Carpenter, Edmund Snow, and Marshall McLuhan. "Acoustic Space." *Canadian Theatre Review* 6 (1975): 46–9.

– eds. *Explorations in Communication.* Boston: Beacon Press, 1960.

Carpenter, Edmund Snow, and Carl Schuster. *Materials for the Study of Social Symbolism in Ancient and Tribal Art: A Record of Tradition and Continuity, Based on the Researches and Writings of Carl Schuster, Edited and Written by Edmund Carpenter, assisted by Lorraine Spiess.* 12 vols. NY: Rock Foundation, 1986–88.

Works by Other Authors

2Bears, Jackson. "My Post-Indian Technological Autobiography." In *Coded Territories: Tracing Indigenous Pathways in New Media Art*, edited by Steve Loft and Kerry Swanson, 12–29. Calgary: University of Calgary Press, 2014.

Aly, Götz. *The Magnificent Boat: The Colonial Theft of a South Seas Cultural Treasure.* Cambridge Massachusetts: Harvard University Press, 2023.

Atalay, Sonya. "Indigenous Archaeology as Decolonizing Practice." *The American Indian Quarterly* 30, no. 3, 4 (2006): 280–310.

Barnes, Geraldine. "Curiosity, Wonder, and William Dampier's Painted Prince." *Journal for Early Modern Cultural Studies* 6.1 (2006): 31–50.

Bateson, Gregory. *Steps to an Ecology of Mind: Critical Essays in Anthropology, Psychiatry, Evolution, and Epistemology.* 2nd ed. London: Jason Aronson, 1987.

Bell, Joshua A. "A Bundle of Relations: Collections, Collecting, and Communities." *Annual Review of Anthropology* 46 (2017): 241–59.

Bell, Joshua A., and Haidy Geismar. "Materialising Oceania: New Ethnographies of Things in Melanesia and Polynesia." *The Australian Journal of Anthropology* 20 (2009): 3–27.

Bell, Joshua, Alison K. Brown, and Robert J. Gordon, eds. *Recreating First Contact: Expeditions, Anthropology, and Popular Culture.* Washington, DC: Smithsonian Institution Scholarly Press, 2013.

Belova, Olga. "The Event of Seeing: A Phenomenological Perspective on Visual Sense-Making." In *Museum Objects: Experiencing the Properties of Things,* edited by Sandra H. Dudley, 116–33. London: Taylor & Francis, 2011.

Biebuyck, Daniel P., ed. *Tradition and Creativity in Tribal Art.* Berkeley: University of California Press, 1969.

Bishop, John Melville. "Notes from the Wilderness." *American Anthropologist* 116, no. 3 (2014): 651.

Blake, William. *Poetry and Prose of William Blake.* Edited by Geoffrey Keynes. London: Nonesuch, 1961.

Blakinger, John R. *Gyorgy Kepes: Undreaming the Bauhaus.* Cambridge: Massachusetts Institute of Technology Press, 2019.

Blanchot, Maurice. *Au moment voulu.* 1951. Rpt. Paris: Gallimard, 1979.

Brennan, Marcia. "Review of *Upside Down: Arctic Realities.*" *CAA.reviews,* 4 January 2012. http://dx.doi.org/10.3202/caa.reviews.2012.2.

Bringhurst, Robert, ed. *Solitary Raven: The Essential Writings of Bill Reid.* 2000. 2nd ed. Vancouver: Douglas and McIntyre, 2009.

– *The Surface of Meaning: Books and Book Design in Canada.* Vancouver: Canadian Centre for Studies in Publishing Press, 2008.

Bronshtein, Mikhail and Kirill Dneprovsky. "Ancient Eskimo Art of Ekven." In Helfenstein et al., *Upside Down,* 118–59.

Brooker, Peter. "In the Modernist Grain." In *The Oxford Critical and Cultural History of Modernist Magazines* 2, 959. New York: Oxford, 2009.

Brown, Steven Clay. *Transfigurations: North Pacific Coast Art: George Terasaki, Collector.* Foreword by Edmund Carpenter. Photographs by George Terasaki. Seattle: Marquand Books, 2006.

Bruchac, Margaret. *Savage Kin: Indigenous Informants and American Anthropologists.* Tucson: University of Arizona Press, 2018.

Buddecke, Wolfram. "Review of Edmund Carpenter, *Sinnes Täuschung: Wie Medien unsere Wahrnehmung verändern.*" MEDIENwissenschaft 12, no. 2 (1995): 167–8.

Buxton, William J. "The Ford Foundation and Communication Studies: The University of Toronto Program (1953–1955)." *Rockefeller Archive Center* (June 2018). rockarch.issuelab.org/resource/the-ford-foundation-and-communication-studies-the-university-of-toronto-program-1953-1955.html.

Calhoun, Patricia. "A Blanket Indictment." *Westword,* 3 June 1999. www.westword.com/news/a-blanket-indictment-5059953.

Campt, Tina M. *Listening to Images.* Durham: Duke University Press, 2017.

Carroll, John B., ed. *Language Thought and Reality: Selected Writings of Benjamin Lee Whorf.* Cambridge: Massachusetts Institute of Technology Press, 1956.

Cavell, Janice. "'Consolidation and Control of All Eskimo Income': The Motive for the 1953 High Arctic Relocation." *Journal of Canadian Studies* 55, no. 1 (2021): 118–51.

Cavell, Richard. "Dematerialization and Rematerialization: Mediatic Flipflop and the Anthropocene." *Berlin Journal of Critical Theory* 3, no. 1 (2019): 83–97.

– "Introduction: The Cultural Production of Canada's Cold War." In *Love, Hate, and Fear in Canada's Cold War*, edited by Cavell, 3–32. Toronto: University of Toronto Press, 2004.

– "Kittler's *Apophrades*: Marshaling McLuhan." *Berlin Journal of Critical Theory* 6, no. 1 (2022): 5–32.

– *McLuhan in Space: A Cultural Geography.* Toronto: University of Toronto Press, 2002.

– "Re-Mediating the Medium." In *Remediating McLuhan*, 79–87. Amsterdam: Amsterdam University Press, 2016.

– "Specters of McLuhan: Derrida, Media, and Materiality." In *Transforming McLuhan*, edited by Paul Grosswiler, 135–61. New York: Peter Lang, 2010.

CBC (Canadian Broadcasting Corporation). "Inuit Get Federal Apology for Forced Relocation," 19 August 2010. https://www.cbc.ca/news/canada/north/ inuit-get-federal-apology-for-forced-relocation-1.897468.

Celant, Germano. *Doug Wheeler.* New York: David Zwirner, 2019.

Chandler, John Noel, ed. "Symposium on the Sacred in Art." *artscanada* (April–May 1971): 17–25.

Clarence-Smith, William Gervase, Kenneth Pomeranz, and Peer Vries. "Editorial." *Journal of Global History* 1 (2006): 1–2.

Clarke, Alison J. *Victor Papanek: Designer for the Real World.* Cambridge: Massachusetts Institute of Technology Press, 2021.

Classen, Constance. *Worlds of Sense: Exploring the Senses in History and Across Cultures.* London: Routledge, 1993.

Clifford, James. *The Predicament of Culture: Twentieth-Century Ethnography, Literature, and Art.* Cambridge: Harvard University Press, 1986.

Cobb, Matthew Adam. "Connecting the Ancient Afro-Eurasian World." In "Travellers, Traders, and Diaspora in Antiquity: Networks and Nodes across the Indian Ocean and Eurasian World," Special Issue, *Journal of Global History* 18, no. 3 (2023): 329–42.

Cohen-Cole, Jamie. "The Creative American: Cold War Salons, Social Science, and the Cure for Modern Society." *Isis* 100, no. 2 (2009): 219–62.

Colacello, Bob. "The Remains of the Dia." *Vanity Fair*, September 1996. archive. vanityfair.com/article/1996/9/remains-of-the-dia.

Coleman, E. Gabriella. "Ethnographic Approaches to Digital Media." *Annual Review of Anthropology* 39 (2010): 487–505.

Conley, Katharine. "Is Reconciliation Possible? Non-Western Objects at the Menil Collection and the Quai Branly Museum." *South Central Review* 27, no. 3 (2010): 34–53.

Conn, Steven. "George Heye in Context." *Journal of American History* 97, no. 2 (2010): 483–4.

Cooper, C.L. "Biography of the Bull-Leaper: A 'Minoan' Ivory Figurine and Collecting Antiquity." In *New Approaches to Ancient Material Culture in the Greek and Roman World*, edited by Cooper, 79–100. Leiden: Brill, 2021.

Costa, Elisabetta, Patricia G. Lange, Nell Haynes, and Jolynna Sinanan, eds. *The Routledge Companion to Media Anthropology*. London: Routledge, 2022.

Cox, Bruce. "Review of Edmund Carpenter, *Eskimo Realities*; Richard Nelson's *Hunters of the Northern Forest: Design for Survival Among the Alaskan Kutchin*; and Joseph Senungetuk's *Give or Take a Century: An Eskimo Chronicle*." *American Anthropologist* 76, no. 2 (1974): 417–19.

Currelly, Charles Trick. *I Brought the Ages Home*. Toronto: Ryerson, 1956.

Darroch, Michael. "Giedion and *Explorations*: Confluences of Space and Media in Toronto School Theorisation." In *Media Transatlantic: Developments in Media and Communication Studies*, edited by Norm Friesen, 62–87. Basel: Springer, 2016.

Darroch, Michael, and Janine Marchessault, eds. *Explorations: Studies in Culture and Communication*. 8 vols. Eugene: Wipf and Stock, 2016.

– "Introduction." In Darroch and Marchessault, *Explorations* 1, v–xxv.

Darwin, Charles. *Expression of the Emotions in Man and Animals*. Preface by Margaret Mead. New York: Philosophical Library, 1955.

Datta, Amaresh. *Encyclopaedia of Indian Literature: A-Devo*. Sahitya Akademi, 1987.

Davis, Mike. *City of Quartz*. New York: Verso, 1990.

Deloria, Vine. *God Is Red: A Native View of Religion*. 1973; rpt. New York: Putnam, 2003.

De Menil, Adelaide. *Photographs 1969-73*. New York: The Rock Foundation, 2022.

Derrida, Jacques. "Signature Even Context." In *Limited Inc.*, 1–23. Evanston: Northwestern University Press, 1988.

Douglas, Mary. "The Genuine Article." In *The Socialness of Things*, edited by S.H. Riggins, 9–22. Berlin: de Gruyter, 1994.

Edwards, Elizabeth. "Objects of Affect: Photography beyond the Image." *Annual Review of Anthropology* 41 (2012): 221–34.

Eisenstein, Sergei. "Laocoon." In *Selected Works 2: Towards a Theory of Montage*, edited by Michael Glenny and Richard Taylor, translated by Michael Glenny, 114–54. London: British Film Institute, 1991.

Elder, Sarah. "Review of *Padlei Diary*." *American Anthropologist* 104, no. 2 (2002): 657–9.

Eriksen, Roy. "Vasari and the Kinship of Perspective and Printing." *Notes in the History of Art* 17, no. 2 (1981): 1–3.

"Explorations." Internet Archive. https://archive.org/details/varsitygraduate.

Fabian, Johannes. *Time and the Other: How Anthropology Makes its Object.* New York: Columbia University Press, 1983.

Feest, Christian F. "Transformations of a Mask: Confidential Intelligence from the Lifeway of Things." *Baessler-Archiv,* New Series, vol. 46 (1998): 255–93.

Feld, Steven. *Sound and Sentiment: Birds, Weeping, Poetics, and Song in Kaluli Expression.* 1982; 3rd ed. Durham: Duke University Press, 2012.

Fenollosa, Ernest. *The Chinese Written Character as a Medium for Poetry,* edited by Ezra Pound. London: Stanley Nott, 1936.

Ferrara, Silvia. *The Greatest Invention: A History of the World in Nine Mysterious Scripts.* Translated by Todd Portnowitz. New York: Farrar, Straus, and Giroux, 2022.

Ferretti, Fred. "State Investigates American Indian Museum." *The New York Times,* 3 October 1974, 1.

Fitzhugh, William W. "Frederica de Laguna: The Last Arctic Universalist and Bridge to the Future." In *Early Inuit Studies: Themes and Transitions, 1850s–1980s,* edited by Igor Krupnik, 219–41. Washington, DC: Smithsonian Institution, 2016.

Floridi, Luciano. *Information: A Very Short Introduction.* New York: Oxford, 2010.

Force, Roland. *The Heye and the Mighty: Politics and the Museum of the American Indian.* Honolulu: Mechas Press, 1999.

Foucault, Michel. *Introduction to Kant's "Anthropology,"* edited by Roberto Nigro. Translated by Nigro and Kate Briggs. Los Angeles: Semiotext(e), 2008.

Franklin, Ruth. *Shirley Jackson: A Rather Haunted Life.* New York: Liverwright, 2016.

Frye, Northrop. *The Diaries of Northrop Frye 1942–1955,* edited by Robert Denham. Toronto University of Toronto Press, 2001.

Fulford, Robert. "'All Ignorance Is Motivated': Re-Examining the Seedbed of McLuhanism." *Canadian Notes and Queries* 45 (1991): 3–8.

Ganchrow, Raviv. "Baku's Sirens: Circuits of Industrious Attention." In *The Derailment of the Usual,* edited by Eline Kersten, 100–12. Paris: Hématomes Éditions, 2023.

Gardner, Robert, ed. *Human Documents: Eight Photographers.* Cambridge, Massachusetts: Harvard University Press, 2009.

Gardner, Robert, and Ákos Östör. *Making Forest of Bliss: Intention, Circumstance and Chance in Non-Fiction Film.* Cambridge, Massachusetts: Harvard Film Archive, 2002.

Geertz, Clifford. *The Interpretation of Cultures.* 1973. Rpt. New York: Basic Books, 2000.

Gell, Alfred. "Vogel's Net: Traps as Artworks and Artworks as Traps." *Journal of Material Culture* 1, no. 1 (1996): 15–39.

Genosko, Gary. "The 'Unknown' *Explorations.*" *Amodern* 1 (2013). Unpaginated.

– "Where the Youth Aren't." *Amodern* 5 (Dec. 2015). Unpaginated. amodern.net/article/where-the-youth-arent/.

Genzlinger, Neil. "Ken Heyman, Collaborative Photographer with a Keen Eye, Dies at 89." *The New York Times*, 19 December 2019, A28.

Gershon, Ilana. "Mirrors and Numbers among Others: Technologies of Identification in Papua New Guinea." *Paideuma* 54 (2008): 85–108.

Gilberg, R. and H.C. Gulløv, eds. *Fifty Years of Arctic Research*. Copenhagen: National Museum of Denmark, 1997.

Ginsburg, Faye. "Rethinking the Digital Age." In *Global Indigenous Media: Cultures, Poetics and Politics*, edited by Pamela Wilson and Michelle Stewart, 289–302. Durham, NC: Duke University Press, 2008.

Gitelman, Lisa. *Always Already New: Media, History, and the Data of Culture*. Cambridge, Massachusetts: Massachusetts Institute of Technology Press, 2006.

– *Raw Data is an Oxymoron*. Cambridge: Massachusetts Institute of Technology Press, 2013.

Goldowski, Natasha. "High Speed Computing Machines." *The Black Mountain College Review* 1, no. 1 (1951): Unpaginated.

Goodman, Wendy. "A Central Park Duplex with a Calder in the Trees." *New York Magazine*, 18 April 2016.

Gopnik, Blake and Graham Fraser. "It's Not Primitive, It's Not Very Old. Is It Even Art? Chirac's Interest Raises Questions among Critics, Anthropologists." *The Globe and Mail*, 3 September 1999, 1, 3.

Gordon, W. Terrence. *Marshall McLuhan: Escape into Understanding*. Toronto: Stoddart, 1997.

Graburn, Nelson H. "From Aesthetics to Prosthetics and Back: Materials, Performance and Consumers in Canadian Inuit Sculptural Arts; or, Alfred Gell in the Canadian Arctic." In *Les cultures à l'oeuvre: rencontres en art*, edited by Michèle Coquet et al., 47–62. Paris: Biro Editeur, 2005.

Grasskamp, Walter. *The Book on the Floor: André Malraux and the Imaginary Museum*. Translated by Fiona Elliott. Los Angeles: Getty Research Institute, 2016.

Greene, Shane. "On Misanthropology: (punk, art, species-hate)." In *Between Matter and Method: Encounters in Anthropology and Art*, edited by Gretchen Bakke and Marina Peterson, 35–50. London: Routledge, 2017.

Greif, Mark. *The Age of the Crisis of Man: Thought and Fiction in America, 1933–1973*. Princeton: Princeton University Press, 2015.

Griffey, Erin and Barry Reay. "Sexual Portraits: Edward Melcarth and Homoeroticism in Modern American Art." *History Workshop Journal* 73, no. 1 (2012): 66–94.

Grimes, William. "Edmund Carpenter, Archaeologist and Anthropologist, Dies at 88." *The New York Times*, 7 July 2011.

Grimshaw, Anna. "Who Has the Last Laugh? *Nanook of the North* and Some New Thoughts on an Old Classic." *Visual Anthropology* 27, no. 5 (2014): 421–35.

Grimshaw, Anna and Amanda Ravetz. "Rethinking Observational Cinema." *Journal of the Royal Anthropological Institute* 15 (2009): 538–56.

Gullbekk, Svein. "Norse Penny." *Journal of the North Atlantic* 33 (2017): 1–8.

Haddon, A.C. *The Decorative Art of British New Guinea: A Study in Papuan Ethnography*. 1894. Rpt. New York: AMS Press, 1977.

Hafsteinsson, Sigurjón Baldur. "Review of Harald Prins and John Bishop, *Oh, What a Blow that Phantom Gave Me!*" *Visual Anthropology Review* 22, no. 2 (2006): 77–8.

Harmsen, Hans. "Greenland's Hand-Sized Wooden Maps Were Used for Storytelling, Not Navigation." *Atlas Obscura*, 2 May 2018. www.atlasobscura.com/articles/greenland-wooden-maps-ammassalik.

Harper, Kenn. *Minik the New York Eskimo*. Hanover: Steerforth Press, 2017.

Harrington, Richard. *Padlei Diary, 1950*, edited by Edmund Carpenter. New York: Rock Foundation, 2000.

Haselberger, Herta. *Kunstethnologie: Grundbegriffe, Methoden, Darstellung*. München / Wien: Schroll, 1969.

– "Method of Studying Ethnological Art." *Current Anthropology* 2, no. 4 (1961): 341–84.

Hawes, Bess Lomax. *Sing It Pretty: A Memoir*. Urbana: University of Illinois Press, 2008.

Hayles, N. Katherine. *How We Became Posthuman: Virtual Bodies in Cybernetics, Literature, and Informatics*. Chicago: University of Chicago Press, 1999.

Helfenstein, Josef. "Foreword." In Helfenstein et al., *Upside Down*, 10–11.

Helfenstein, Josef, and Laureen Schipsi, eds. *Art and Activism: Projects of John and Dominique de Menil*. Houston: Menil Foundation, 2010.

Helfenstein, Josef, et al. *Upside Down: Arctic Realities*. Houston: Menil Foundation, 2011.

Heyer, Paul. "In Memoriam Edmund Snow Carpenter." *Canadian Journal of Communication* 36, no. 3 (2011): 513–15.

Higgins, Hannah and Douglas Kahn. *Mainframe Experimentalism: Early Computing and the Foundations of the Digital Arts*. California: University of California Press, 2013.

Hintz, Charlie. "Dapper Corpse Used to Sell Embalming Fluid in 1903 Advertisement." *Cult of Weird*, 2 March 2020. https://www.cultofweird.com/curiosities/vintage-embalming-fluid-ad/.

Hoag, Robert Wilson. "Current Cabinet Activities." *ANS Magazine* 4, no. 1 (2005).

Hoffman, Frederick J., Charles Allen, and Carolyn F. Ulrich, eds. *The Little Magazine: A History and a Bibliography*. Princeton: Princeton University Press, 1947.

Holm, Bill, and Bill Reid. *Indian Art of the Northwest Coast: A Dialogue on Craftsmanship and Aesthetics*. Houston: Institute for the Arts, Rice University, 1975.

Howard, Jane. *Margaret Mead: A Life.* New York: Simon and Schuster, 1984.

Howes, David. "Polysensoriality." In *A Companion to the Anthropology of the Body and Embodiment*, edited by Frances E. Mascia-Lees, 435–50. Oxford: Blackwell, 2011.

– "Sensing Cultures: Cinema, Ethnography, and the Senses." In *Beyond Text? Critical Practices and Sensory Anthropology*, edited by Rupert Cox et al., 173–88. Manchester: Manchester University Press, 2016.

– *Sensual Relations: Engaging the Senses in Culture and Social Theory.* Ann Arbor: University of Michigan Press, 2003.

Hughes, Charles Campbell. "Under Four Flags: Recent Culture Change among the Eskimos." *Current Anthropology* 6, no. 1 (1965): 3–62.

Hume, Stephen. "Heritage for All, Profits for Some." *Daily Colonist*, 8 September 1977, 2.

– "Heritage Grab: Time Runs Out." *Daily Colonist*, 4 September 1977, 1.

– "U.S. Foundation Siphons Finest Native Art." *Daily Colonist*, 7 September 1977, 1.

Hurst, Norman. *Arctic Ivory: Two Thousand Years of Alaskan Eskimo Art and Artifacts.* Cambridge, Massachusetts: Hurst Gallery, 1998.

Hymes, Dell. "Review of *The Gutenberg Galaxy*." *American Anthropologist* 65, no. 2 (1963): 478–9.

Iloh, Constance. "Do It for the Culture: The Case for Memes in Qualitative Research." *International Journal of Qualitative Methods,* July 2021, 20. https://doi.org/10.1177/16094069211025896.

Ingold, Tim. *The Perception of the Environment: Essays on Livelihood, Dwelling, and Skill.* London: Routledge, 2000.

Irvine, Dean. "'Little Magazines' in English Canada." In *The Oxford Critical and Cultural History of Modernist Magazines 2: North America 1894–1960*, edited by Peter Brooker and Andrew Thacker, 602–28. Oxford: Oxford University Press, 2012.

Johnson, Ian. "Loot Under the Lindens." *New York Review*, 25 May 2023.

Johnson, Norris Brock. "Anthropology and the Humanities: A Reconsideration." *Anthropology and Humanism Quarterly* 14, no. 3 (1989): 82–9.

Keating, Neil B. "Review of Two Essays: Chief and Greed," *Museum Anthropology* 32, no. 1 (2009): 78–81.

Keefe, Patrick Radden. "How Larry Gagosian Reshaped the Art World." *New Yorker*, 31 July 2023, 30–49.

Kehr, Dave. "When Unmanly Men Met Womanly Women." *The New York Times*, 20 August 2006.

Kepes, Gyorgy, ed. *Sign Image Symbol.* New York: George Braziller, 1966.

King, Charles. *Gods of the Upper Air: How a Circle of Renegade Anthropologists Reinvented Race, Sex, and Gender in the Twentieth Century.* New York: Doubleday, 2019.

King, Lily. *Euphoria.* Toronto: HarperCollins, 2014.

Kittler, Friedrich. *Literature, Media, Information Systems*. Edited by John
    Johnston. Amsterdam: Overseas Publishers Association, 1997.
– "Perspective and the Book." *Grey Room* 5 (2001): 38–53.
Kopytoff, Igor. "The Cultural Biography of Things: Commoditization as Process."
    In *The Social Life of Things: Commodities in Cultural Perspective*, edited by
    Arjun Appadurai, 64–91. Cambridge: Cambridge University Press, 1986.
Kramer, Hilton. "Exhibiting 'The Family of Man': The World's Most Talked
    About Photographs." In Ribalta, *Public Photographic Spaces*, 437–44.
Kuper, Adam. *The Museum of Other People*. London: Profile Books, 2023.
La Barre, Weston. "Review of Frank Speck, Royal B. Hassrick, and Edmund
    Carpenter, *Rappahannock Herbals*." *American Anthropologist* 45, no. 3 (1943): 66.
Landar, Herbert. "Review of Carpenter and McLuhan, *Explorations in
    Communications*." *American Anthropologist* 63, no. 4:874.
Lantis, Margaret. "Review of *Anerca*." *American Anthropologist* 62, no. 5 (1960):
    924.
Lapatin, Kenneth. *Chryselephantine Statuary in the Ancient Mediterranean
    World*. Oxford: Oxford University Press, 2001.
Lauder, Adam. "A Clash of Spaces." *Amodern* 5 (Dec. 2015).
Leach, Edmund. *Lévi-Strauss*. London: Fontana, 1970.
Lee, Dorothy. "Letter to Edmund Carpenter 11/24/61." Carpenter Papers. National
    Anthropological Archives. Smithsonian Institution. Box 30.
– "Lineal and Nonlineal Codifications of Reality." *Psychosomatic Medicine* 12
    (1950): 89–97.
– "Review of *Eskimo* [by] Edmund Carpenter, Frederick Varley and Robert
    Flaherty." *American Anthropologist* 62, no. 1 (1960): 165–7.
Lennox, Patrick. "Inuit Art and the Quest for Canada's Arctic Sovereignty."
    Calgary Papers in Military and Strategic Studies no. 5 (2012) [ISBN 978-1-55238-
    593-7].
Lévi-Strauss, Claude. *Tristes Tropiques*. Translated by John Weightman and
    Doreen Weightman. Introduction and notes by Patrick Wilcken. New York:
    Penguin, 1973. Intro. 2012.
– *Wild Thought*. Translated by Jeffrey Mehlman and John Leavitt. Chicago:
    University of Chicago Press, 2021.
Liu, Jiun-Yu. "Intertwined Maritime Silk Road and Austronesian Routes: a
    Taiwanese Archaeological Perspective." In "Travellers, Traders, and Diaspora
    in Antiquity: Networks and Nodes across the Indian Ocean and Eurasian
    World," Special Issue, *Journal of Global History* 18, no. 3 (2023): 384–400.
Loft, Steven. "Mediacosmology." In *Coded Territories: Tracing Indigenous
    Pathways in New Media Art*, edited by Steven Loft and Kerry Swanson, 170–86.
    Calgary: University of Calgary Press, 2014.
Loft, Steven, and Kerry Swanson, eds. *Coded Territories: Tracing Indigenous
    Pathways in New Media*. Calgary: University of Calgary Press, 2014.

Loke, Margaret. "Aleut Sacred Objects to Be Auctioned at Sotheby's Despite Protests by the Tribe." *The New York Times*, 30 November 1998, section E, 5.

Lonetree, Amy. *Decolonizing Museums: Representing Native America in National and Tribal Museums.* Chapel Hill: University of North Carolina Press, 2012.

– "Missed Opportunities: Reflections on the NMAI." *The American Indian Quarterly* 30, no. 3, 4 (2006): 632–45.

Lucy, J.A. "Sapir-Whorf Hypothesis." In *International Encyclopedia of the Social and Behavioral Sciences*, 13486–13490. Amsterdam: Elsevier, 2001.

MacCarthy, Fiona. *Eric Gill.* London: Faber and Faber, 1989.

MacDonald, Lachlan. "Editor's Note." *Chicago Review* 10, no. 1 (1956): 46–51.

MacDougall, David. *The Corporeal Image: Film, Ethnography, and the Senses.* Princeton: Princeton University Press, 2005.

Marchand, Philip. *Marshall McLuhan: The Medium and the Messenger.* Toronto: Random House, 1989.

Marinetti, Filippo Tommaso. "Fondazione e manifesto del Futurismo." In *Teoria e invenzione futurista*, edited by Luciano De Maria, 7–14. Milano: Mondadori I Meridiani, 1983.

Mattelart, Armand. *The Information Society: An Introduction.* SAGE Publications Limited, 2003.

McLuhan, Marshall. "The Agenbite of Outwit." *Location Magazine* 1, no. 1 (1963): 41–4.

– *The Gutenberg Galaxy: The Making of Typographic Man.* Toronto University of Toronto Press, 1962.

– *The Interior Landscape: The Literary Criticism of Marshall McLuhan 1943/1962.* Edited by Eugene McNamara. New York: McGraw-Hill, 1969.

– "Letter to Jack Parr October 13, 1969." In *Letters of Marshall McLuhan*, edited by William Toye et al., 390. Toronto: Oxford University Press, 1987.

– "The Psychopathology of *Time* and *Life*." In *The Scene Before You: A New Approach to American Culture*, edited by Chandler Brossard, 147–60. New York: Rinehart, 1955.

– "*Screw* Goes to Market." *Screw: A Sex Review* 1, no. 2 (21 December 1968).

– *Verbi-Voco-Visual Explorations.* New York: Something Else Press, 1967.

McLuhan, Marshall, with Quentin Fiore and Jerome Agel. *The Medium Is the Massage.* New York: Random House, 1967.

McLuhan, Marshall, and George B. Leonard. "The Future of Sex." In *On the Nature of Media: Essays in Understanding Media*, edited by Richard Cavell, 125–42. Berkeley: Gingko Press, 2016.

McLuhan, Marshall, with Barrington Nevitt. "The Argument: Causality in the Electric World." *Technology and Culture* 14, no. 1 (1973): 1–18.

McLuhan, Marshall, and Wilfred Watson. *From Cliché to Archetype.* New York: Viking, 1970.

McMaster, Gerald. *Iljuwas Bill Reid: Life and Work.* Toronto: Art Canada Institute, 2020.

McMullen, Anne. "Reinventing George Heye: Nationalizing the Museum of the American Indian and its Collections." In *Contesting Knowledge: Museums and Indigenous Perspectives*, edited by Susan Sleeper-Smith, 65–105. Lincoln: University of Nebraska Press, 2009.

Mead, Margaret. "Anthropology and the Camera" [excerpt]. In Ribalta, *Public Photographic Spaces*, 451–5.

– *Culture and Commitment: A Study of the Generation Gap.* New York: Doubleday, 1970.

– "Visual Anthropology in a Discipline of Words." In *Principles of Visual Anthropology*, edited by Paul Hockings, 3–10. The Hague: Mouton, 1975.

Mekas, Jonas. *Movie Journal: The Rise of the New American Cinema, 1959–1971.* Columbia: Columbia University Press, 2016.

Menand, Louis. "Modern Family." *New Yorker*, 4 July 2022, 68–71.

Menil, Dominique de. "Foreword." In *The Menil Collection: A Selection from the Paleolithic to the Modern Era*, 7–8. New York: Harry N. Abrams, 1987.

Meunier, Yannick. "À propos de l'exposition *Upside Down: Les Arctiques.*" Études Inuit Studies 32, no. 1 (2008): 155–61.

Middleton, William. *Double Vision: The Unerring Eye of Art World Avatars Dominique and John de Menil.* New York: Knopf, 2018.

Mignolo, Walter D. *The Darker Side of the Renaissance: Literacy, Territoriality, and Colonization.* Ann Arbor: University of Michigan Press, 1995.

Miller, Jonathan. *McLuhan.* London: Fontana, 1971.

Miller, Lewis H. "Advertising in Poetry: A Reading of E.E. Cummings' 'Poem, or Beauty Hurts Mr. Vinal.'" *Word and Image* 2, no. 1 (1986): 349–62.

Mitchell, W.J.T., and Mark B.N. Hansen. "Introduction." In *Critical Terms for Media Studies*, edited by Mitchell and Hansen, vii–xxii. Chicago: University of Chicago Press, 2010.

Mitenbuler, Reid. *Wanderlust: An Eccentric Explorer, an Epic Journey, a Lost Age.* Boston: Mariner, 2023.

Montagu, Ashley. "Review of Edmund Carpenter, *Eskimo.*" *American Journal of Psychiatry* 117, no. 4 (1960): 382.

Moore, Alexander. "The Limitations of Imagist Documentary: A Review of Robert Gardner's *Forest of Bliss.*" *Society for Visual Anthropology Newsletter* 4, no. 2 (1989): 1–3.

Moore, Clive. *New Guinea: Crossing Boundaries and History.* Honolulu: University of Hawai'i Press, 2003.

Morgan, Rachel. *Sins of the Shovel: Looting, Murder, and the Roots of American Archaeology.* Chicago: University of Chicago Press, 2023.

Morris, Robert. "Aligned with Nazca." *Artforum* 1, no. 2 (1975): 26–30.

Morton, Christopher. "Anthropology of Photography." In *The International Encyclopedia of Anthropology*, edited by Hilary Callan, 1–14. London: Wiley, 2018.

Naroll, Raoul. *Data Quality Control – A New Research Technique: Prolegomena to a Cross-Cultural Study of Culture Stress*. New York: Free Press of Glencoe, 1962.

Nelson, Mark, William H. Sherman, and Ellen Hoobler. *Hollywood Arensberg: Avant-Garde Collecting in Midcentury L.A.* Los Angeles: Getty, 2020.

Nevala-Lee, Alex. *Inventor of the Future: The Visionary Life of Buckminster Fuller*. New York: Dey Street, 2022.

Nichols, Lizzy. "Becoming Indigenous Again: The Native Informant and Settler Logic in Richard Powers's *Overstory*." *Environmental Humanities* 14, no. 2 (2022): 303–20.

Norden, Eric. "Playboy Interview: Marshall McLuhan: A Candid Conversation with the High Priest of Popcult and Metaphysician of Media." *Playboy* 16, no. 3 (March 1969): 53–74, 158.

Norris, Ken. *The Little Magazine in Canada 1925–80: Its Role in the Development of Modernism and Post-Modernism in Canada*. Toronto: ECW Press, 1984.

Östör, Ákos. "Is That What Forest of Bliss Is All About? A Response." *Society for Visual Anthropology Newsletter* 5, no. 1 (1989): 4–8.

Papanek, Victor. *Design for the Real World: Human Ecology and Social Change*. New York: Pantheon, 1971.

Parry, Jonathan P. "Comment on Robert Gardner's *Forest of Bliss*." *Society for Visual Anthropology Newsletter* 4, no. 2 (1989): 4–7.

Patterson, Karin. "Prince Modupe: An African in Early Hollywood." *Black Music Research Journal* 31, no. 1 (2011): 29–44.

Penny, H. Glenn. *In Humboldt's Shadow: A Tragic History of German Ethnology*. Princeton: Princeton University Press, 2021.

Pias, Claus, ed. *Cybernetics: The Macy Conferences 1946–1953 – The Complete Transactions*. Berlin: Diaphanes, 2016.

Pink, Sarah. *The Future of Visual Anthropology: Engaging the Senses*. London: Routledge, 2006.

Powe, Bruce W. *Marshall McLuhan and Northrop Frye: Apocalypse and Alchemy*. Toronto: University of Toronto Press, 2014.

Price, David H. *Cold War Anthropology: The CIA, the Pentagon, and the Growth of Dual Use Anthropology*. Durham: Duke University Press, 2016.

Prins, Harald. "Obituary: Edmund Snow Carpenter." *Anthropology News* 52, no. 9 (2011): 24.

– "Review of *Patterns That Connect*." *American Anthropologist* 100, no. 3 (1998): 841.

– "Visual Media and the Primitivist Perplex." In *Media Worlds: Anthropology on New Terrain*, edited by Faye D. Ginsburg, Lila Abu-Lughod, and Brian Larkin, 58–74. Berkeley: University of California Press, 2002.

– "Visual or Virtual Anthropology? In the Wilderness of a Troubled Genre." *Reviews in Anthropology* 26 (1997): 279–94.

Prins, Harald, and John Bishop. "Edmund Carpenter: Explorations in Media and Anthropology." *Visual Anthropology Review* 17, no. 2 (2001): 110–40.

- "Edmund Carpenter: A Trickster's Explorations of Culture and Media." In *Memories of the Origins of Ethnographic Film*, edited by Beate Engelbrecht, 207–45. Frankfurt: Peter Lang, 2007.

- *Oh, What a Blow That Phantom Gave Me!* DVD. MediaGeneration. http://media-generation.com/DVD%20PAGES/OWB/OWB.htm. With related texts, photographs, and notes: http://mediatedcultures.net/phantom/.

Prins, Harald, and Bunnie McBride. "Arctic Realities and Indigenous Art." *American Anthropologist* 114, no. 2 (2012): 359–70.

Puglionesi, Alicia. *In Whose Ruins: Power, Possession, and the Landscapes of American Empire*. New York: Scribner, 2022.

Quinn, William W., Jr. *The Only Tradition*. Albany: State University of New York Press, 1997.

Rappaport, Roy. *Pigs for the Ancestors: Ritual in the Ecology of a New Guinea People*. New Haven: Yale University Press, 1968.

Reid, Bill, and Adelaide de Menil. *Out of the Silence*. Fort Worth: Amon Carter Museum, 1971.

Reif, Rita. "Attracted by the Who as Well as the What." *The New York Times*, 1 June 1997, section 2, 35.

Resnais, Alain, Chris Marker, and Ghislain Cloquet. *Les statues meurent aussi*. Film. 1953.

Ribalta, Jorge, ed. *Public Photographic Spaces: Exhibitions of Propaganda, from 'Pressa' to 'The Family of Man,' 1928–55*. Barcelona: Museu d'Art Contemporani de Barcelona, 2009.

Ronay, Fatimah Tobing. "Taxidermy and Romantic Ethnography: Robert Flaherty's *Nanook of the North*." In *The Third Eye: Race, Cinema, and Ethnographic Spectacle*, 99–126. Durham: Duke University Press, 1996.

Roth, Wolf-Michael, ed. *Auto/Biography and Auto/Ethnography: Praxis of Research Method*. Leiden: Brill, 2005.

Rouch, Jean. "The Camera and Man." In *Cine-Ethnography*. Minneapolis: University of Minnesota Press, 2003, 29–46.

Rushing, W. Jackson. "The Impact of Nietzsche and Northwest Coast Indian Art on Barnett Newman's Idea of Redemption in the Abstract Sublime." *Art Journal* 47, no. 3 (1988): 187–95.

Ruby, Jay. "The Emperor and His Clothes." *Society for Visual Anthropology Newsletter* 5, no. 1 (1989): 9–11.

Rykwert, Joseph, and Tony Atkin. "Building and Knowing." edited by Tony Atkin and Joseph Rykwert, 1–12. Philadelphia: University of Pennsylvania Museum of Archaeology and Anthropology, 2005.

Salaris, Claudia. "The Invention of the Programmatic Avant-Garde." In *Italian Futurism 1909–1944: Reconstructing the Universe*, edited by Vivien Green, 22–49. New York: Guggenhein Museum, 2014.

Saltzstein, Peter A. "Misperceiving African and Eskimo Art." *The Journal of Aesthetic Education* 32, no. 2 (1998): 99–107.

Sandeen, Eric. "The Show You See With Your Heart: 'The Family of Man' on Tour in the Cold War World." In Ribalta, *Public Photographic Spaces*, 471–86.

Sandstrom, Pamela Effrein. "Anthropological Approaches to Information Systems and Behavior." *Bulletin of the American Society for Information Science and Technology* 30, no. 3 (2004): 12–16.

Schaeffer-Simmern, Henry. *Eskimo Plastik aus Kanada*. Kassel: Friedrich Lometsch Verlag, 1958.

Schafer, R. Murray. *The Tuning of the World*. New York: Knopf, 1977.

Schmidt, Kerstin. "A Humanism of Relation." In Zamir and Hurm, *'The Family of Man' Revisited*, 159–75.

Schneider, Arnd. "Unfinished Dialogues: Notes Toward an Alternative History of Art and Anthropology." In *Made to Be Seen: Perspectives on the History of Visual Anthropology*, edited by Marcus Banks and Jay Ruby, 108–35. Chicago: University of Chicago Press, 2011.

Schneider, Arnd, and Christopher Wright, eds. *Anthropology and Art Practice*. London: Routledge, 2013.

Schuster, Carl, and Edmund Carpenter. *Materials for the Study of Social Symbolism in Ancient and Tribal Art: A Record of Tradition and Continuity, Based on the Researches and Writings of Carl Schuster, Edited and Written by Edmund Carpenter, assisted by Lorraine Spiess*. 12 vols. NY: Rock Foundation, 1986–88.

Serres, Michel. *Le Tiers-Instruit*. Paris: Editions François Bourin, 1991.

Shaul, Dylan. "With 'the delicacy of a bear': Lévi-Strauss, Derrida, and the Logic of Anthropology." *Distinktion* 18, no. 1 (2017): 18–40.

Shoskes, Ellen. *Jaqueline Tyrwhitt: A Transnational Life in Urban Planning and Design*. London: Routledge, 2013.

Siegeltuch, Mark. "Random Thoughts on *Angels Fear*." *Continuing the Conversation: A Newsletter of Ideas in Cybernetics* 10 (1987): 1–2.

Silverman, Raymond A. "Museum as Process." In *Museum as Process: Translating Local and Global Knowledges*, edited by Silverman, 1–18. London: Routledge, 2014.

Singh, Manvir. "Ghengis the Good." *The New Yorker* (1 and 8 January 2024).

Smart, Pamela G. "Aesthetics as Vocation." In Helfenstein and Schipsi, *Art and Activism*, 20–39.

Smith, Owen F. *Fluxus: The History of an Attitude*. San Diego: San Diego State University Press, 1998.

Speck, Frank. "Reflections on the Past and Present of the Massachusetts Indian." *Bulletin of the Massachusetts Archaeological Society* 4, no. 3 (1943): 33–8.

Speck, Frank, Royal B. Hassrick, and Edmund S. Carpenter. *Rappahannock Taking Devices: Traps, Hunting and Fishing* (Joint Publications: Museum of the University of Pennsylvania and the Philadelphia Anthropological Society). Philadelphia: University Museum, 1946.

Spiess, Lorraine. "Edmund Carpenter." In Helfenstein et al., *Upside Down: Arctic Realities*, 228–9.

Staal, Frits. *Agni: The Vedic Ritual of the Fire Altar.* With the collaboration of C.V. Somayajipad and M. Itti Ravi Nambudiri. Vol. 2 with the assistance of Pamela MacFarland. Photographs by Adelaide de Menil. 2 vols. Berkeley: Asian Humanities Press, 1983.

– "Anthropologists against Death." *Society for Visual Anthropology Newsletter* 5, no. 1 (1989): 14, 19.

Starn, Orin. "Introduction." In *Writing Culture and the Life of Anthropology*, edited by Starn, 1–24. Durham: Duke University Press, 2015.

Stearn, Gerald Emmanuel. "Conversations with McLuhan." *Encounter* 28, no. 6 (1967): 50–8.

– ed. *McLuhan: Hot and Cool: A Critical Symposium.* New York: Dial Press, 1967.

Steichen, Edward. *The Family of Man.* New York: Museum of Modern Art, 1955.

Stella, Regis Tove. *Imagining the Other: The Representation of the Papa New Guinean Subject.* Honolulu: University of Hawai'i Press, 2007.

Stocking, George W., Jr. "Essays on Museums and Material Culture." In *Objects and Others: Essays on Museums and Material Culture*, edited by George W. Stocking Jr, 3–14. Madison: University of Wisconsin Press, 1988.

Stoller, Paul. *Sensuous Scholarship.* Philadelphia: University of Pennsylvania Press, 1997.

Strange, Kristen Laura. "A Surrealist Vision of the Art Museum: Conventions of Display in the 'Witnesses' Room at the Menil Collection." Master's thesis. University of Arizona, 2014.

Swinton, George. "Who Makes Inuit Art? Confessions of a Para-Anthropologist." In *Fifty Years of Arctic Research*, edited by R. Gilberg and H.C. Gulløv, 295–302. Copenhagen: National Museum of Denmark, 1997.

Takaragawa, Stephanie, Trudi Lynn Smith, Kate Hennessy, Patricia Alvarez Astacio, Jenny Chio, Coleman Nye, and Shalini Shankar. "Bad Habitus: Anthropology in the Age of the Multimodal." *American Anthropologist* 121, no. 2 (2019): 517–24.

Taylor, Charles. *Six Journeys: A Canadian Pattern.* Toronto: Anansi, 1977.

Tomkins, Calvin. "The Benefactor." *New Yorker*, 8 June 1998, 52–67.

Towns, Armond R. *On Black Media Philosophy.* Berkeley: University of California Press, 2022.

Trotha, Hans von. *Pollak's Arm.* Translated by Elisabeth Lauffer. New York: New Vessel Press, 2022.

Vallye, Anna. "The Strategic Universality of *trans/formation* 1950–1952." *Grey Room* 35 (2009): 28–57.

Van Vuuren, Lauren. "The Many Myths of Laurens van der Post: Van der Post and Bushmen in the Television Series *Lost World of Kalahari* (1958)." *South African Historical Journal* 48 (2003): 47–60.

Walker Art Center, Eric Crosby, Liz Glass, Natilee Harren, Mason Leaver-Yap, Michael Maizels, Tina Rivers Ryan, Abigail Sebaly, Maja Wismer, and Nicole L. Woods. *Art Expanded, 1958–1978.* Minneapolis: Walker Art Center, 2015.

Weinberger, Eliot. "Photography and Anthropology (A Contact Sheet)." In Gardner, *Human Documents*, 16–21.

Whitney, Joel. *Finks: How the CIA Tricked the World's Best Writers.* New York: OR Books, 2016.

Wiener, Norbert. *The Human Use of Human Beings.* New York: Houghton Mifflin, 1950.

Williams, Hywell. *Cassell's Chronology of World History.* London: Weidenfeld and Nicolson, 2005.

Winckelmann, Johann Joachim. "On the Imitation of the Painting and Sculpture of the Greeks." In *Winckelmann: Writings on Art*, edited by David Irwin, 61–85. London: Phaidon, 1972.

Winthrop-Young, Geoffrey. *Kittler and the Media.* London: Polity, 2011.

Wulf, Andrea. *The Invention of Nature: Alexander Humboldt's New World.* New York: Knopf, 2015.

Zamir, Shamoon and Gerd Hurm. "Introduction." In *'The Family of Man' Revisited*, edited by Shamoon Zamir and Gerd Hurm, 1–21. London: Routledge, 2018.

Zawadski, Krista Ulujuk and Jo Poortenaar. "Indelible Ink: The Enduring Images of Nungusuituq." *Inuit Art Quarterly* 32, no. 3 (2019): 52–4.

– "What Are the Earliest Inuit Prints? The Enduring Images of Nungusuituq." *Inuit Art Quarterly*, 24 June 2022. https://www.inuitartfoundation.org/iaq-online/what-are-the-earliest-inuit-prints.

Zittlau, Andrea. "George Gustav Heye and the National Museum of the American Indian – Collecting the Collector." *Current Objectives of Postgraduate American Studies* 8 (2007). https://copas.uni-regensburg.de/article/view/100/124.

Zumwalt, Rosemary Lévy. *Franz Boas: The Emergence of the Anthropologist.* Lincoln: University of Nebraska Press, 2019.

Index